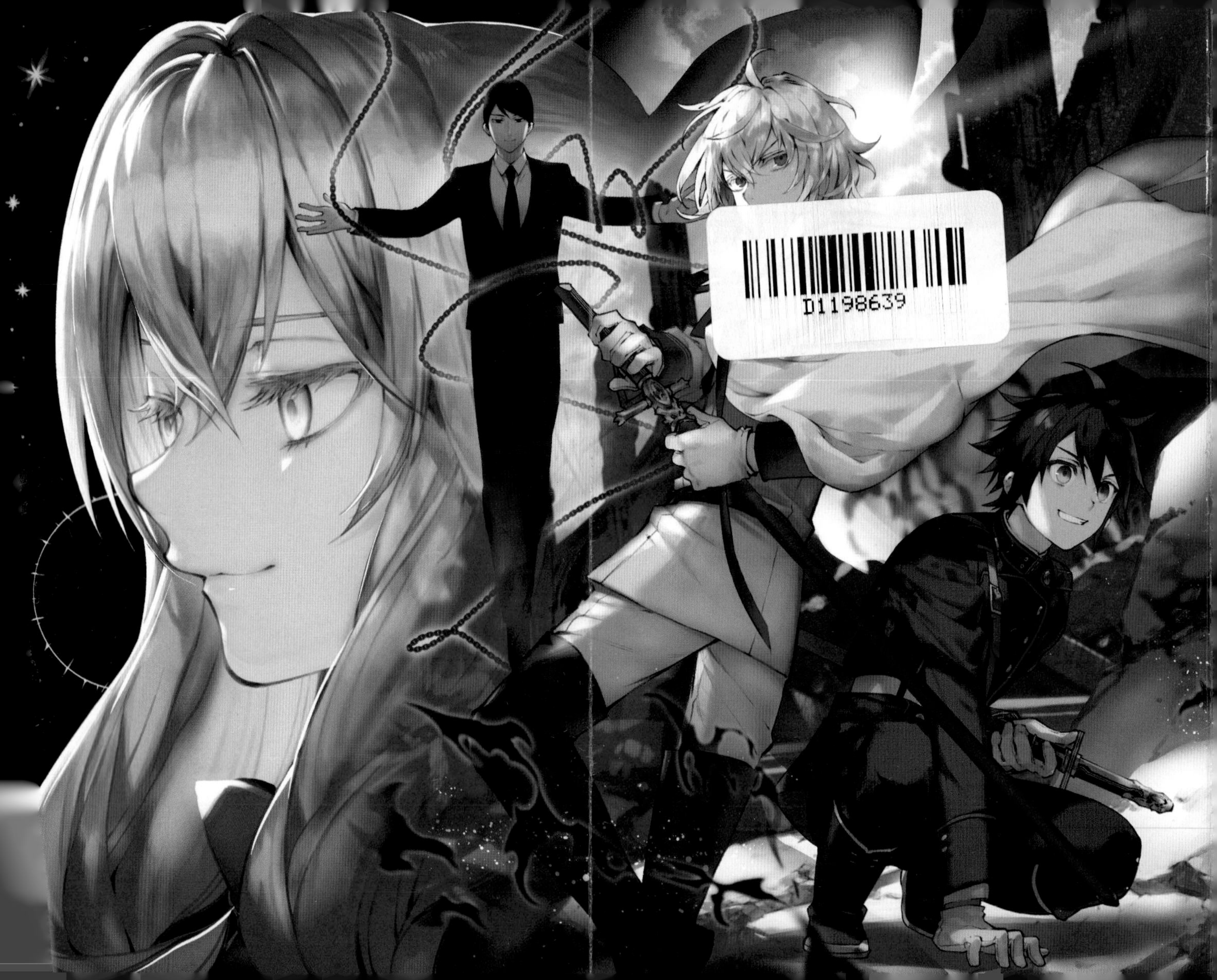

Seraph of the End

—VAMPIRE REIGN—

20

STORY BY **Takaya Kagami**
ART BY **Yamato Yamamoto**
STORYBOARDS BY **Daisuke Furuya**

CHARACTERS

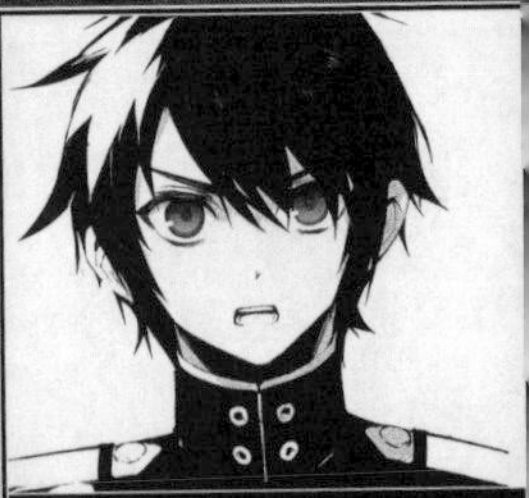

YUICHIRO HYAKUYA

A boy who escaped from the vampire capital, he has both great kindness and a great desire for revenge. Lone wolf. His Cursed Gear is Asuramaru, a katana.

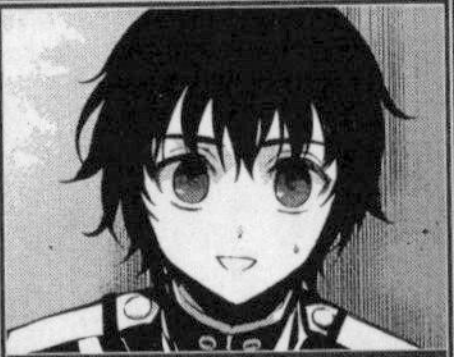

YOICHI SAOTOME

Yuichiro's friend. His sister was killed by a vampire. His Cursed Gear is Gekkouin, a bow.

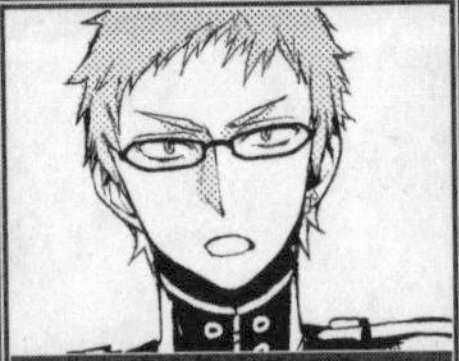

SHIHO KIMIZUKI

Yuichiro's friend. Smart but abrasive. His Cursed Gear is Kiseki-o, twin blades.

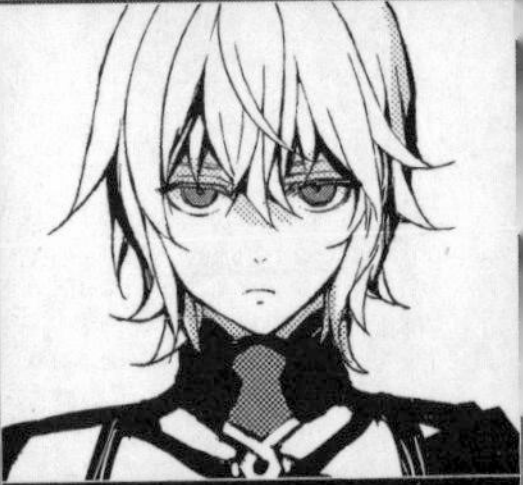

MIKAELA HYAKUYA

Yuichiro's best friend. He was supposedly killed but has come back to life as a vampire. Currently working with Shinoa Squad.

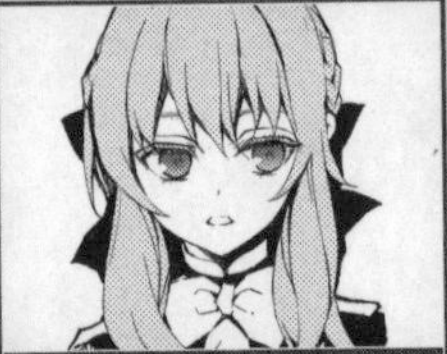

SHINOA HIRAGI

Guren's subordinate and Yuichiro's surveillance officer. Member of the illustrious Hiragi family. Her Cursed Gear is Shikama Doji, a scythe.

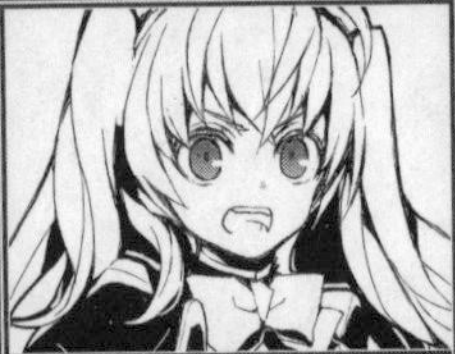

MITSUBA SANGU

An elite soldier who has been part of the Moon Demon Company since age 13. Bossy. Her Cursed Gear is Tenjiryu, a giant axe.

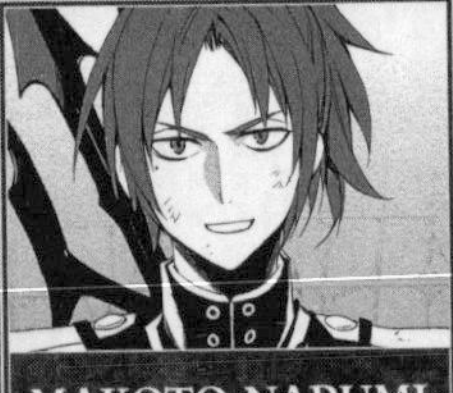

MAKOTO NARUMI

Former leader of Narumi Squad. After his entire squad died during the battle of Nagoya, he deserted the Demon Army with Shinoa Squad.

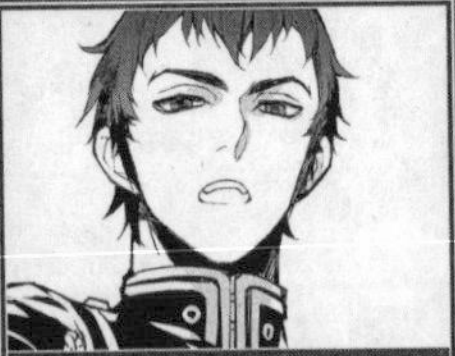

KURETO HIRAGI

A Lieutenant General in the Demon Army. Heir apparent to the Hiragi family, he is cold, cruel and ruthless.

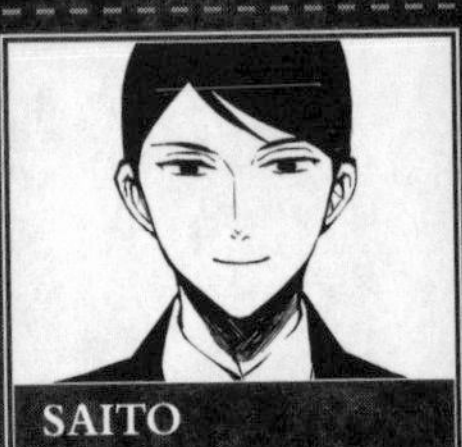

SAITO

A mysterious man somehow connected with the Hyakuya Sect. He was once a Second Progenitor vampire.

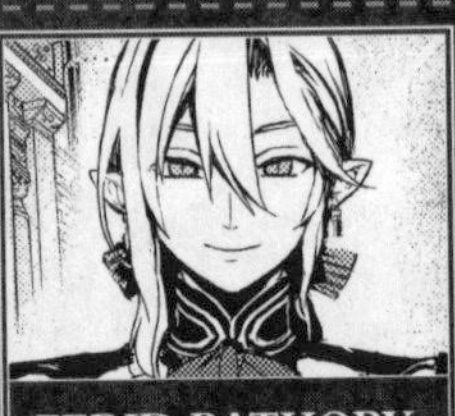

FERID BATHORY

A Seventh Progenitor vampire, he killed Mikaela.

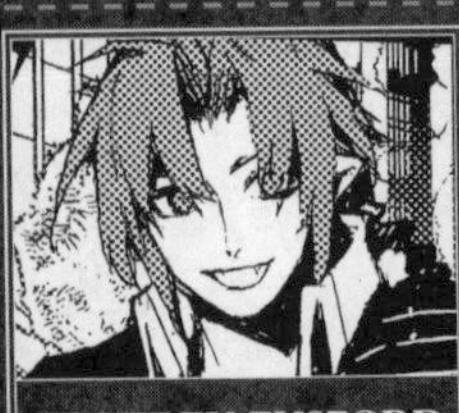

CROWLEY EUSFORD

A Thirteenth Progenitor vampire. Part of Ferid's faction.

KRUL TEPES
Third Progenitor and Queen of the Vampires. She is currently being held prisoner by Urd Geales.

MAHIRU HIRAGI
Shinoa's older sister. Most believe her dead, but she currently inhabits Guren's sword.

GUREN ICHINOSE
Lt. Colonel of the Moon Demon Company. He recruited Yuichiro into the Demon Army. During the battle in Nagoya, he began acting strangely... His Cursed Gear is Mahiru-no-yo, a katana.

SHIKAMA DOJI
The being that inhabits Shinoa's scythe. He's actually the long-missing First Progenitor of the vampires.

ASURAMARU
The demon that possesses Yuichiro's sword. A long time ago, he was a human boy named Ashera.

SHINYA HIRAGI
A Major General and adoptee into the Hiragi Family. He was Mahiru Hiragi's fiancé.

STORY

A mysterious virus decimates the human population, and vampires claim dominion over the world. Yuichiro and his adopted family of orphans are kept as vampire fodder in an underground city until the day Mikaela, Yuichiro's best friend, plots an ill-fated escape for the orphans. Only Yuichiro survives and reaches the surface.

Four years later, Yuichiro enters into the Moon Demon Company, a Vampire Extermination Unit in the Japanese Imperial Demon Army, to enact his revenge. There he gains Asuramaru, a demon-possessed weapon capable of killing vampires, and a squad of trusted friends—Shinoa, Yoichi, Kimizuki and Mitsuba.

In his battles against the vampires, Yuichiro discovers that not only is Mikaela alive, but he also has been turned into a vampire. After misunderstandings and near-misses, Yuichiro and Mikaela finally rejoin each other in Nagoya.

After the chaos and confusion of the Seraph of the End experiment and Guren's betrayal in Nagoya, Shinoa Squad deserts the Demon Army and accompanies Ferid to Osaka. There, they clash with the vampire nobility and defeat an angel that went on a rampage.

They aren't there long before Shinoa's body is taken over by Shikama Doji, a godlike being who is the First Vampire. To add to the mess, the Hyakuya Sect, led by Saito, attacks the Demon Army's Shibuya base and takes Yuichiro hostage.

Facing their greatest threat ever, Mahiru tells Guren that it's time to betray everyone, just as they had planned...?!

Seraph of the End
—VAMPIRE REIGN—

20

CONTENTS

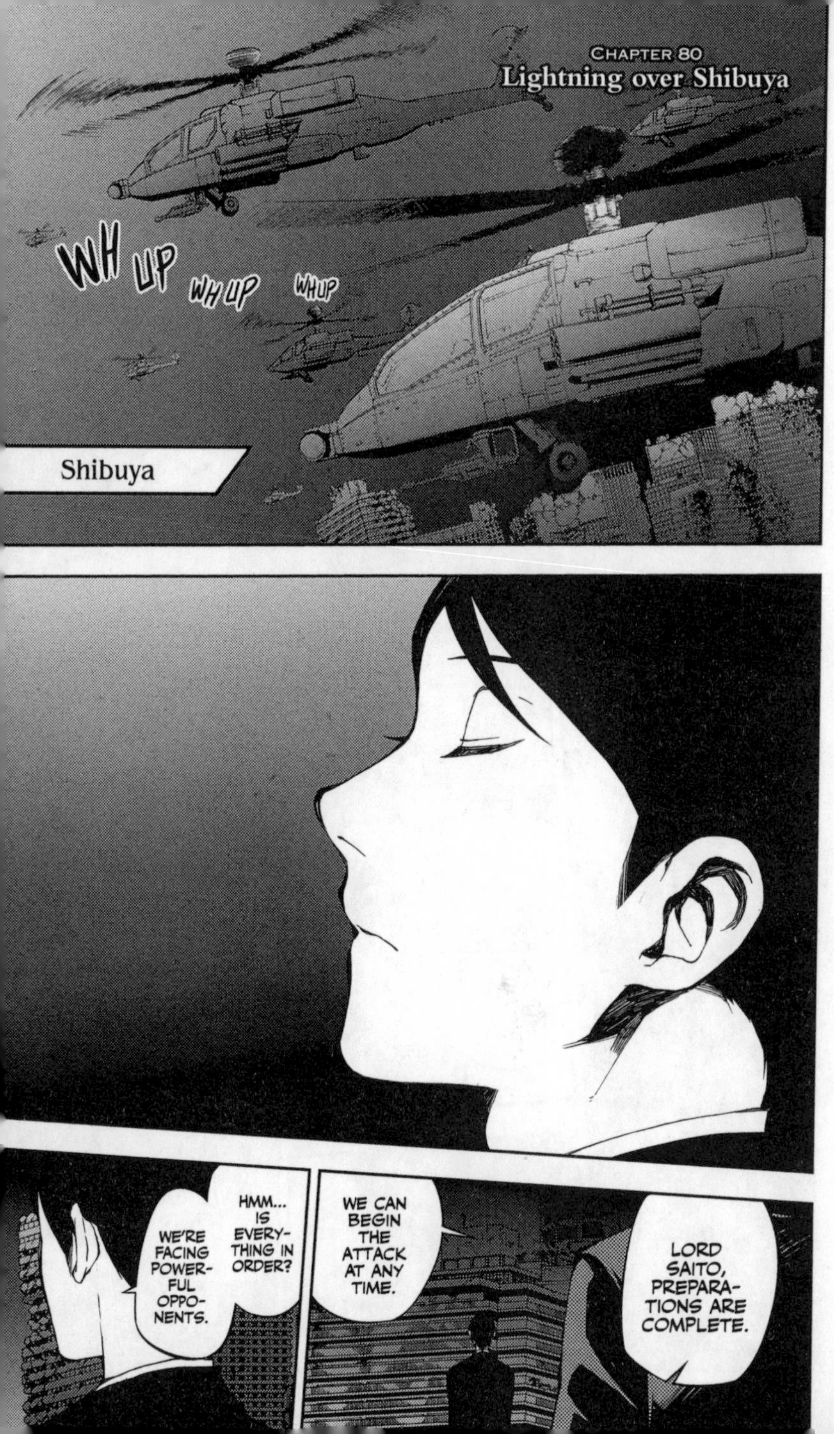
CHAPTER 80
Lightning over Shibuya
WH UP WH UP WHUP
Shibuya
LORD SAITO, PREPARATIONS ARE COMPLETE.
WE CAN BEGIN THE ATTACK AT ANY TIME.
HMM... IS EVERYTHING IN ORDER?
WE'RE FACING POWERFUL OPPONENTS.

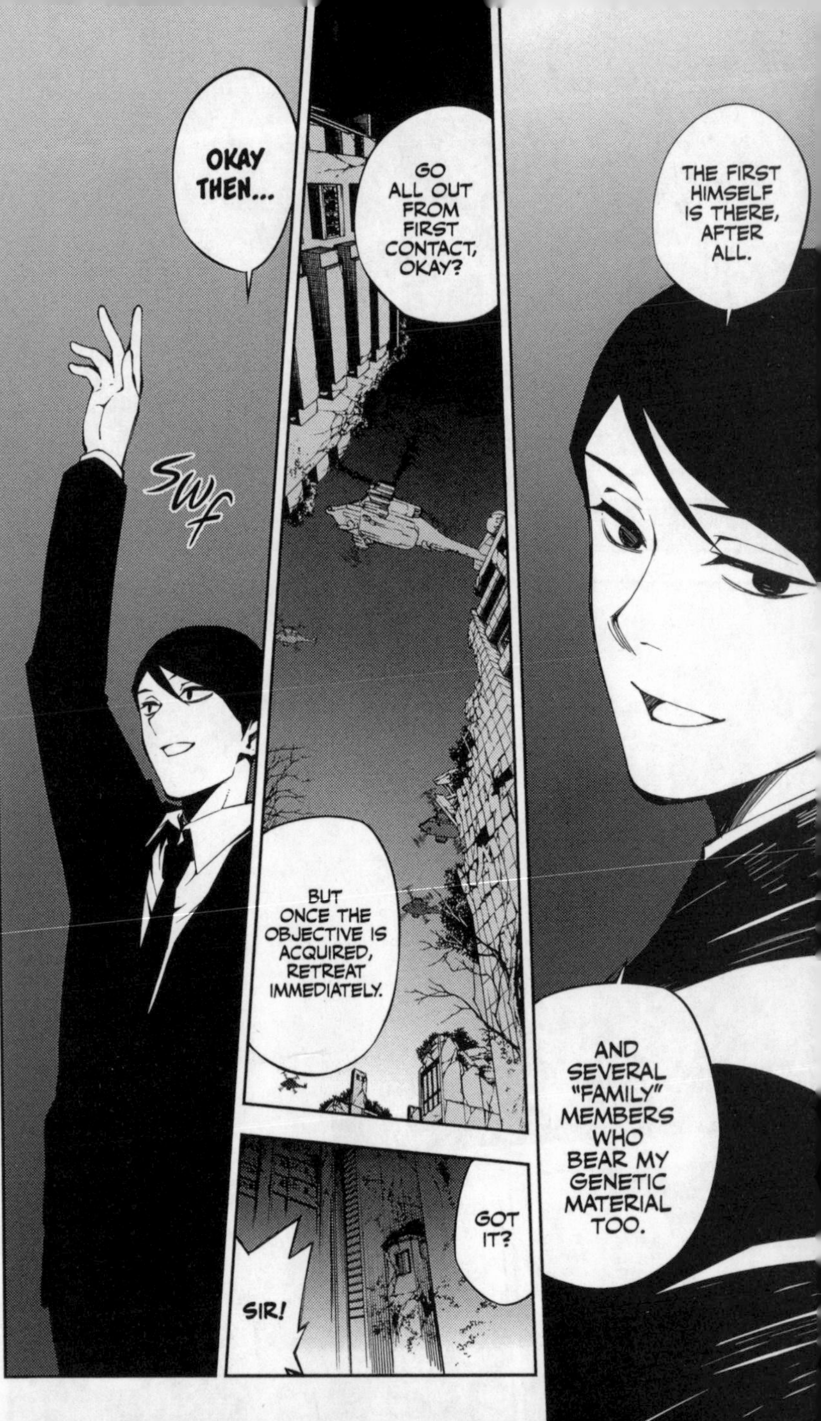
THE FIRST HIMSELF IS THERE, AFTER ALL.
AND SEVERAL "FAMILY" MEMBERS WHO BEAR MY GENETIC MATERIAL TOO.
GO ALL OUT FROM FIRST CONTACT, OKAY?
BUT ONCE THE OBJECTIVE IS ACQUIRED, RETREAT IMMEDIATELY.
GOT IT?
SIR!
OKAY THEN...
SWF

CHAPTER 80
Lightning over Shibuya

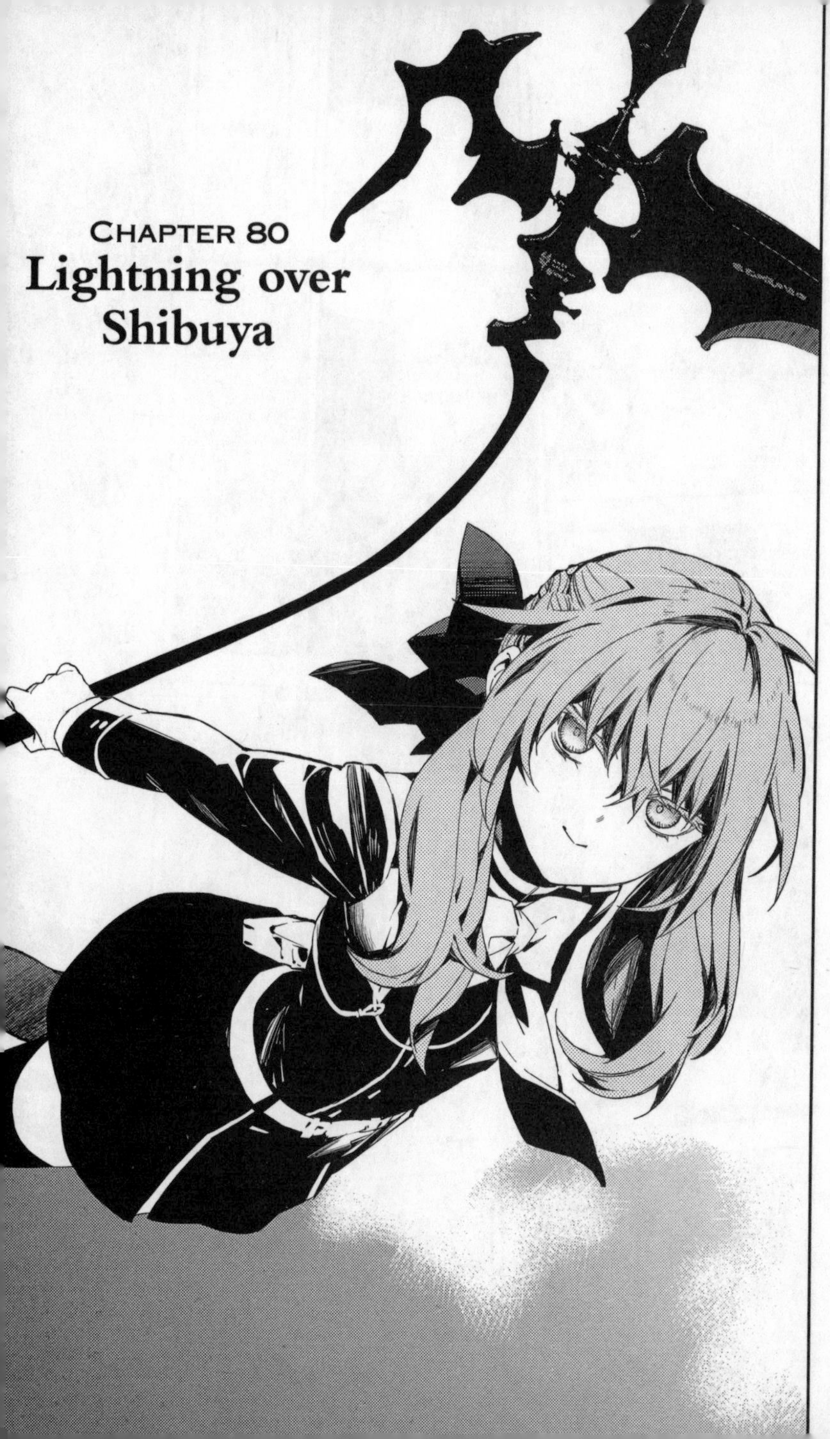

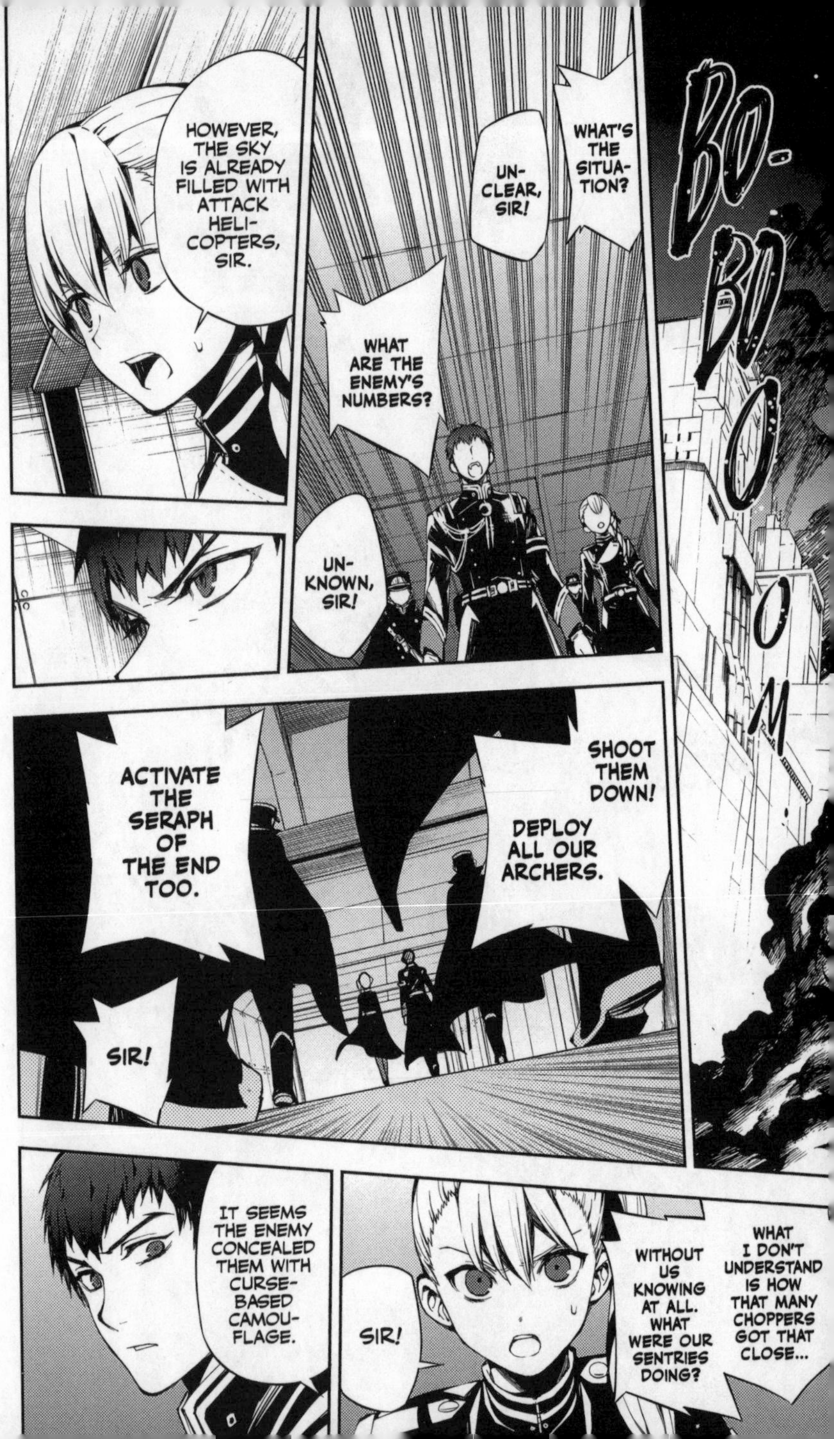
BO-BO-OOOM
WHAT'S THE SITUATION?
UNCLEAR, SIR!
WHAT ARE THE ENEMY'S NUMBERS?
UNKNOWN, SIR!
HOWEVER, THE SKY IS ALREADY FILLED WITH ATTACK HELICOPTERS, SIR.
SHOOT THEM DOWN!
DEPLOY ALL OUR ARCHERS.
ACTIVATE THE SERAPH OF THE END TOO.
SIR!
WHAT I DON'T UNDERSTAND IS HOW THAT MANY CHOPPERS GOT THAT CLOSE...
WITHOUT US KNOWING AT ALL. WHAT WERE OUR SENTRIES DOING?
SIR!
IT SEEMS THE ENEMY CONCEALED THEM WITH CURSE-BASED CAMOUFLAGE.

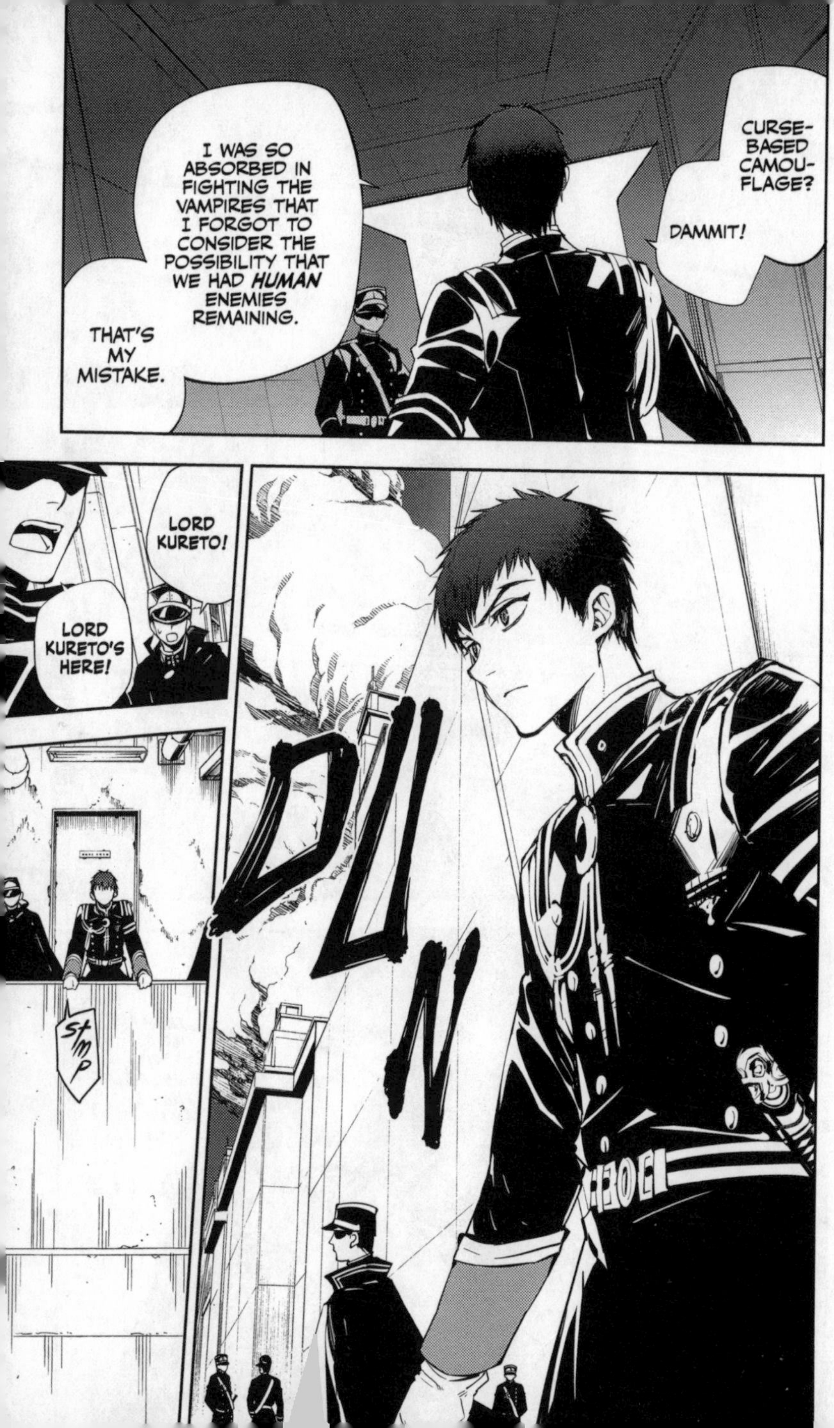
CURSE-BASED CAMOUFLAGE?
DAMMIT!
I WAS SO ABSORBED IN FIGHTING THE VAMPIRES THAT I FORGOT TO CONSIDER THE POSSIBILITY THAT WE HAD *HUMAN* ENEMIES REMAINING.
THAT'S MY MISTAKE.
DUN
LORD KURETO!
LORD KURETO'S HERE!
stmp

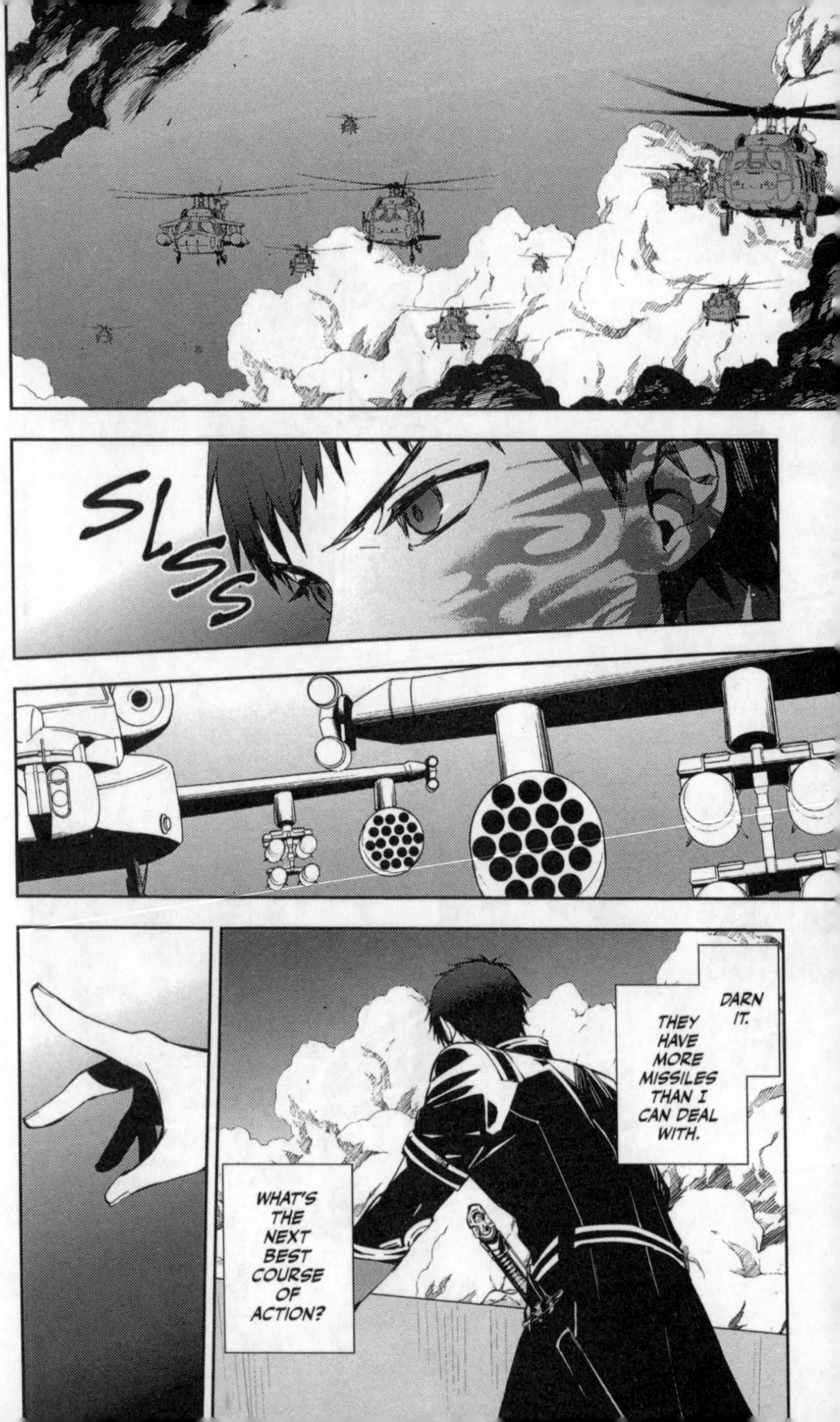
SLSSS
DARN IT.
THEY HAVE MORE MISSILES THAN I CAN DEAL WITH.
WHAT'S THE NEXT BEST COURSE OF ACTION?

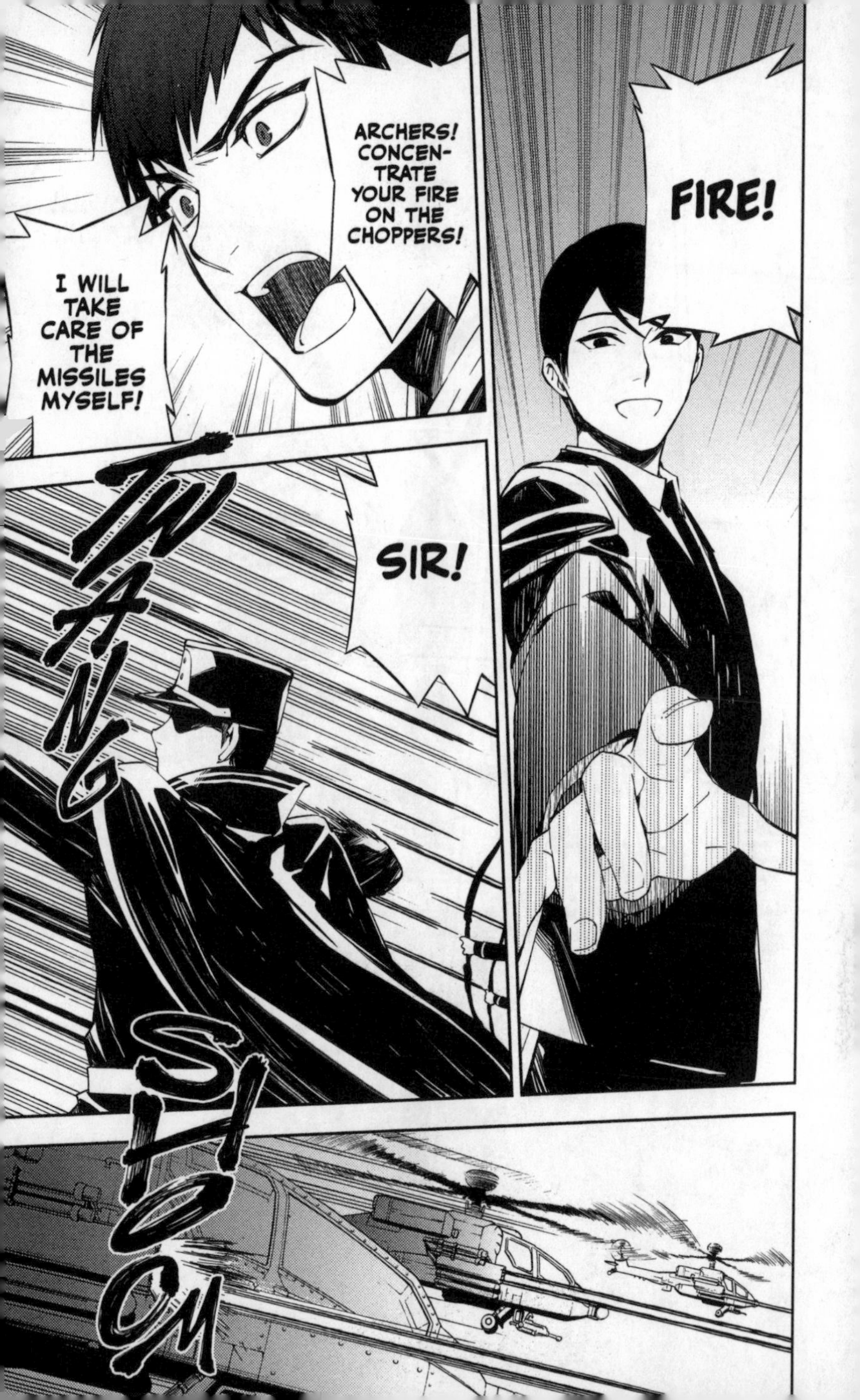
FIRE!
ARCHERS! CONCEN-TRATE YOUR FIRE ON THE CHOPPERS!
I WILL TAKE CARE OF THE MISSILES MYSELF!
SIR!
THWANG
SHOOM

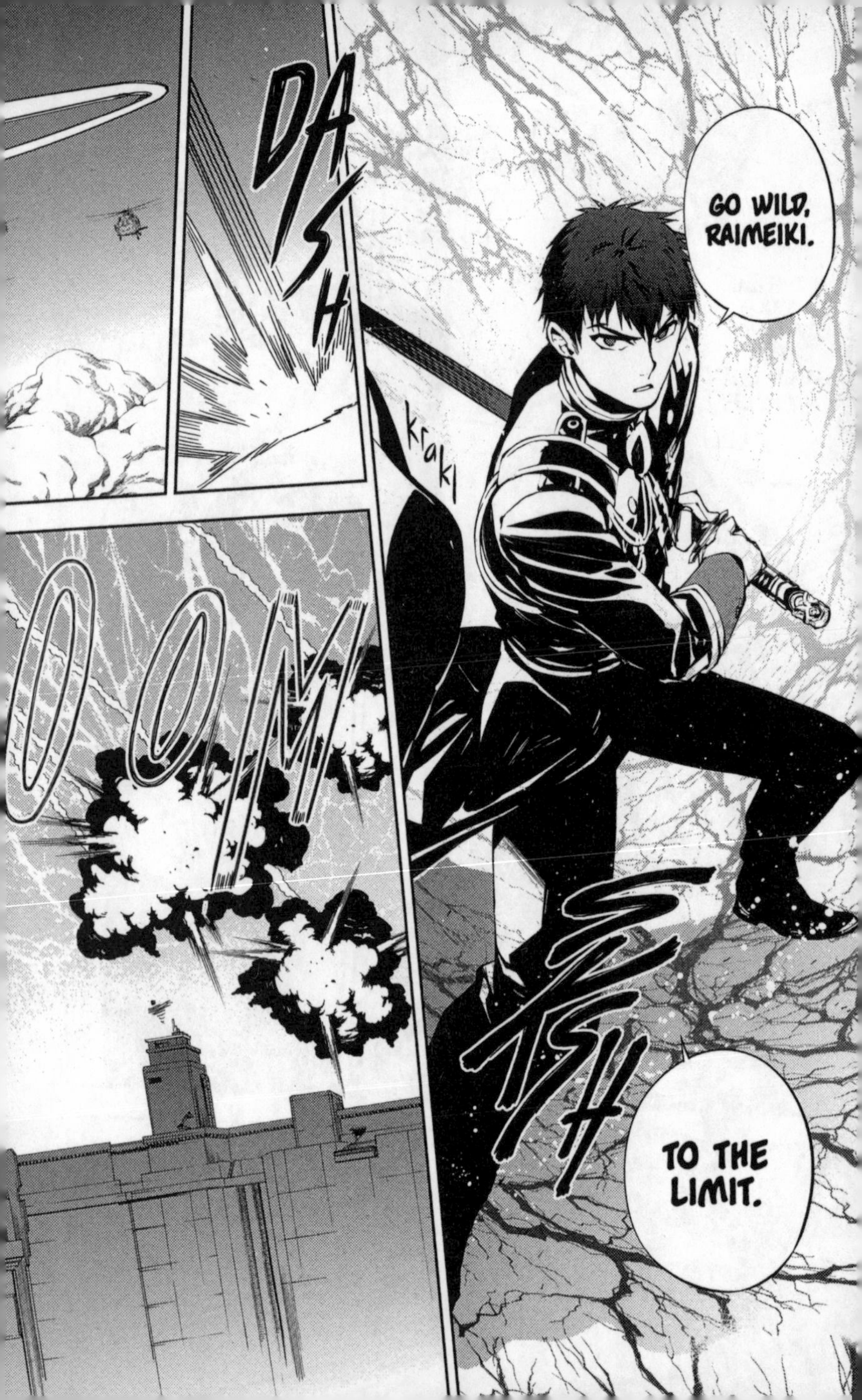
GO WILD, RAIMEIKI.
TO THE LIMIT.
DASH
OOM

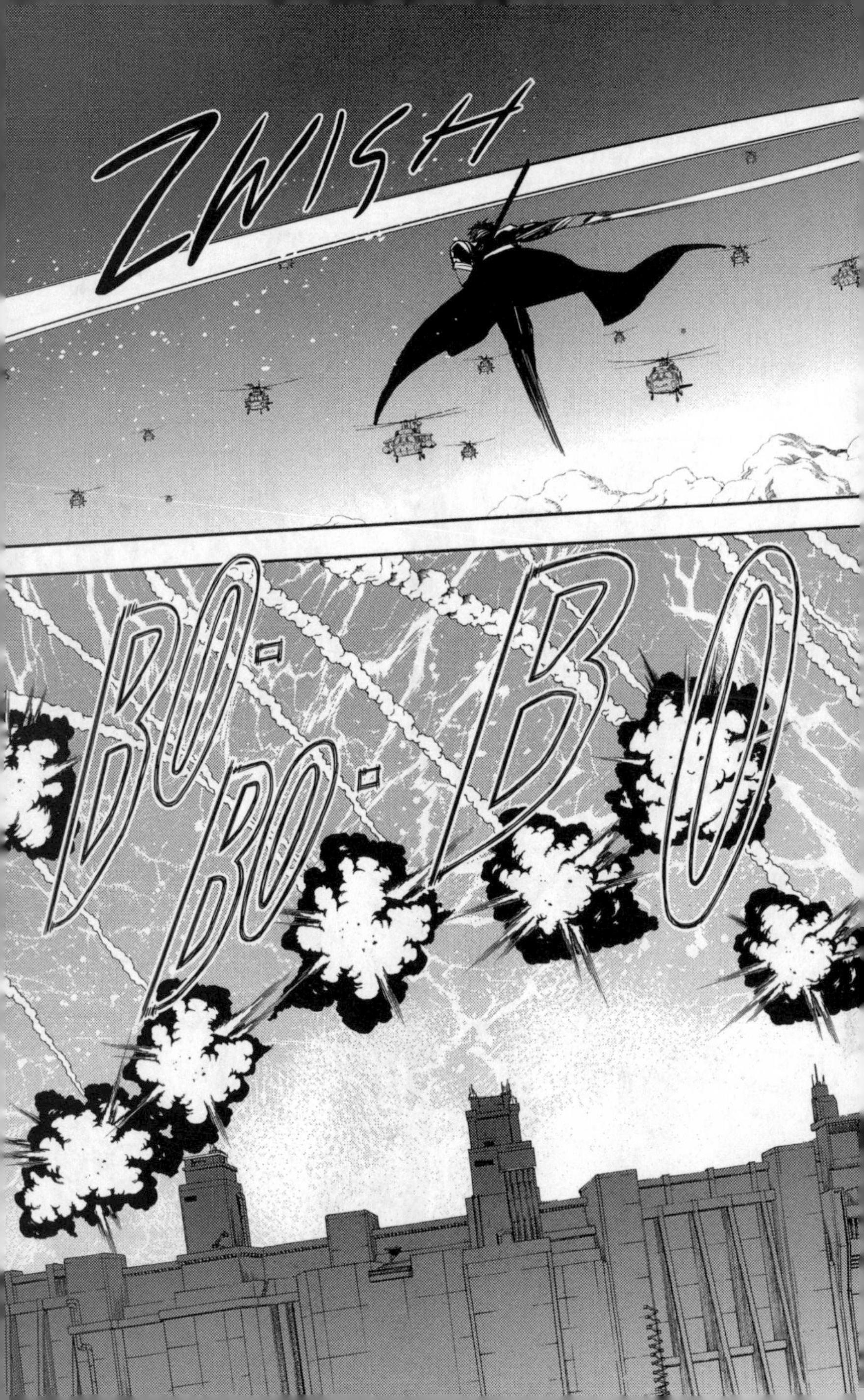
ZWISH
BO-BO-BO

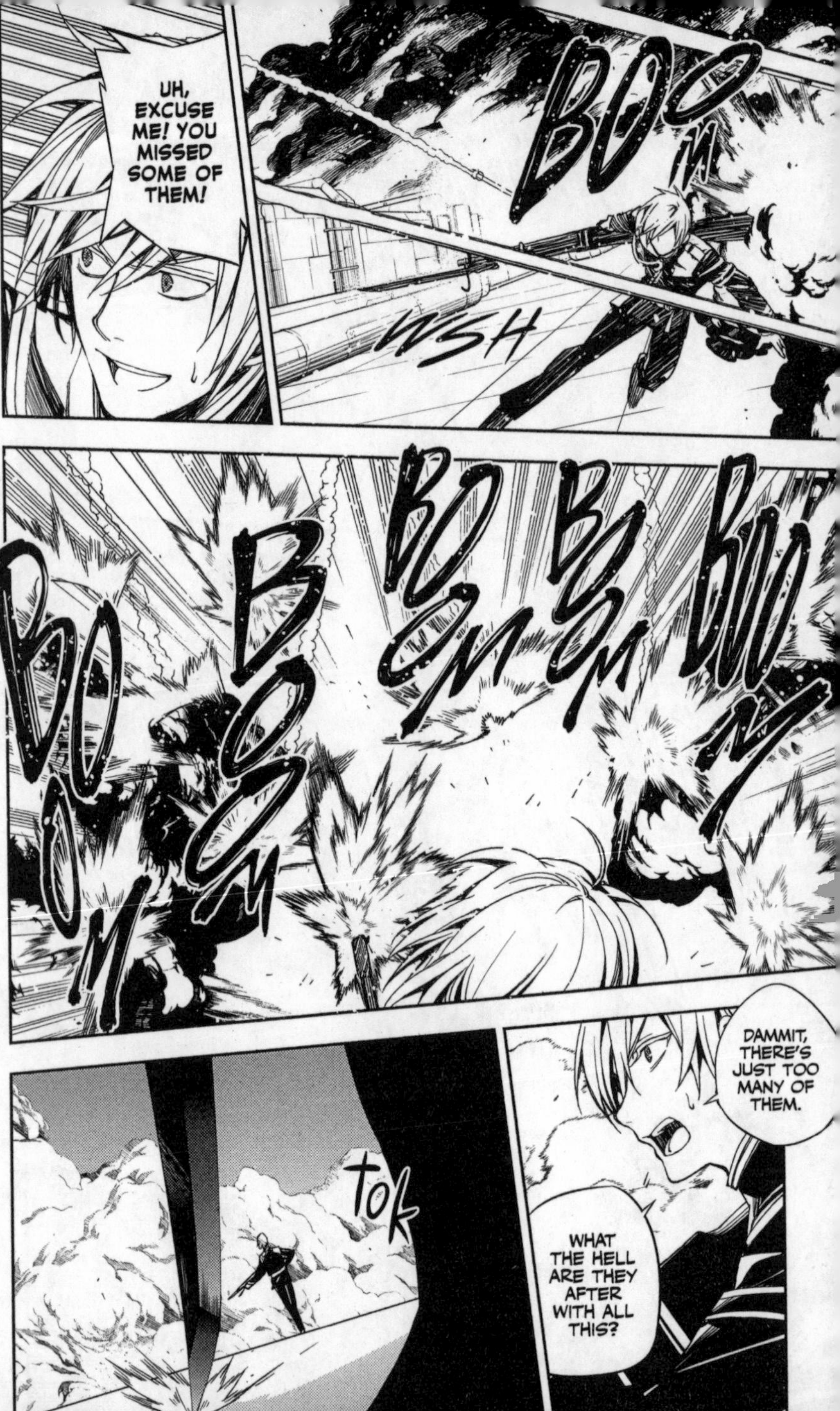
BOOM
WSH
UH, EXCUSE ME! YOU MISSED SOME OF THEM!
BOOM
BOOM
BOOM
BOOM
BOOM
DAMMIT, THERE'S JUST TOO MANY OF THEM.
WHAT THE HELL ARE THEY AFTER WITH ALL THIS?
TOK

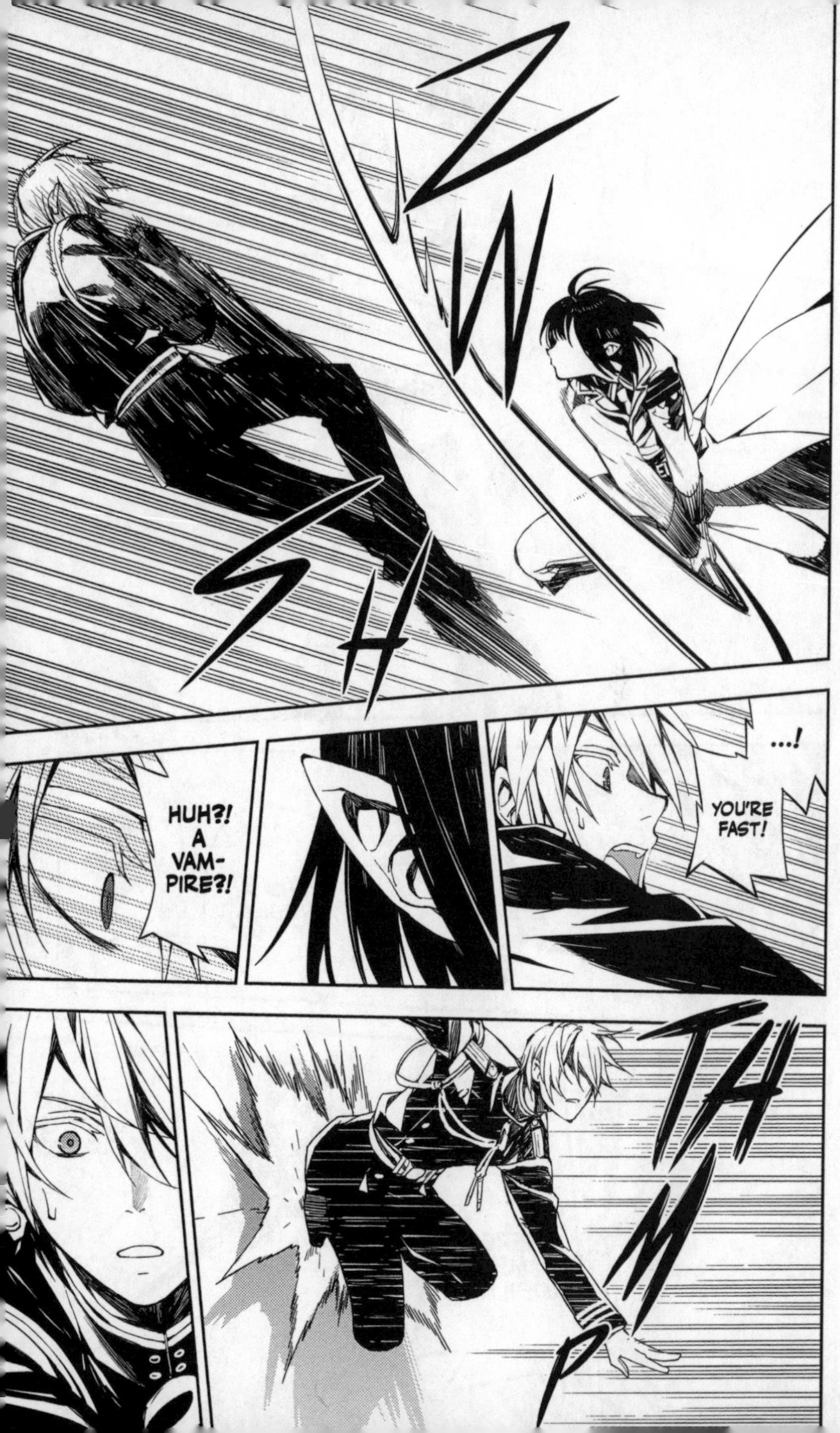
ZWSH
...!
YOU'RE FAST!
HUH?! A VAM-PIRE?!
THMP

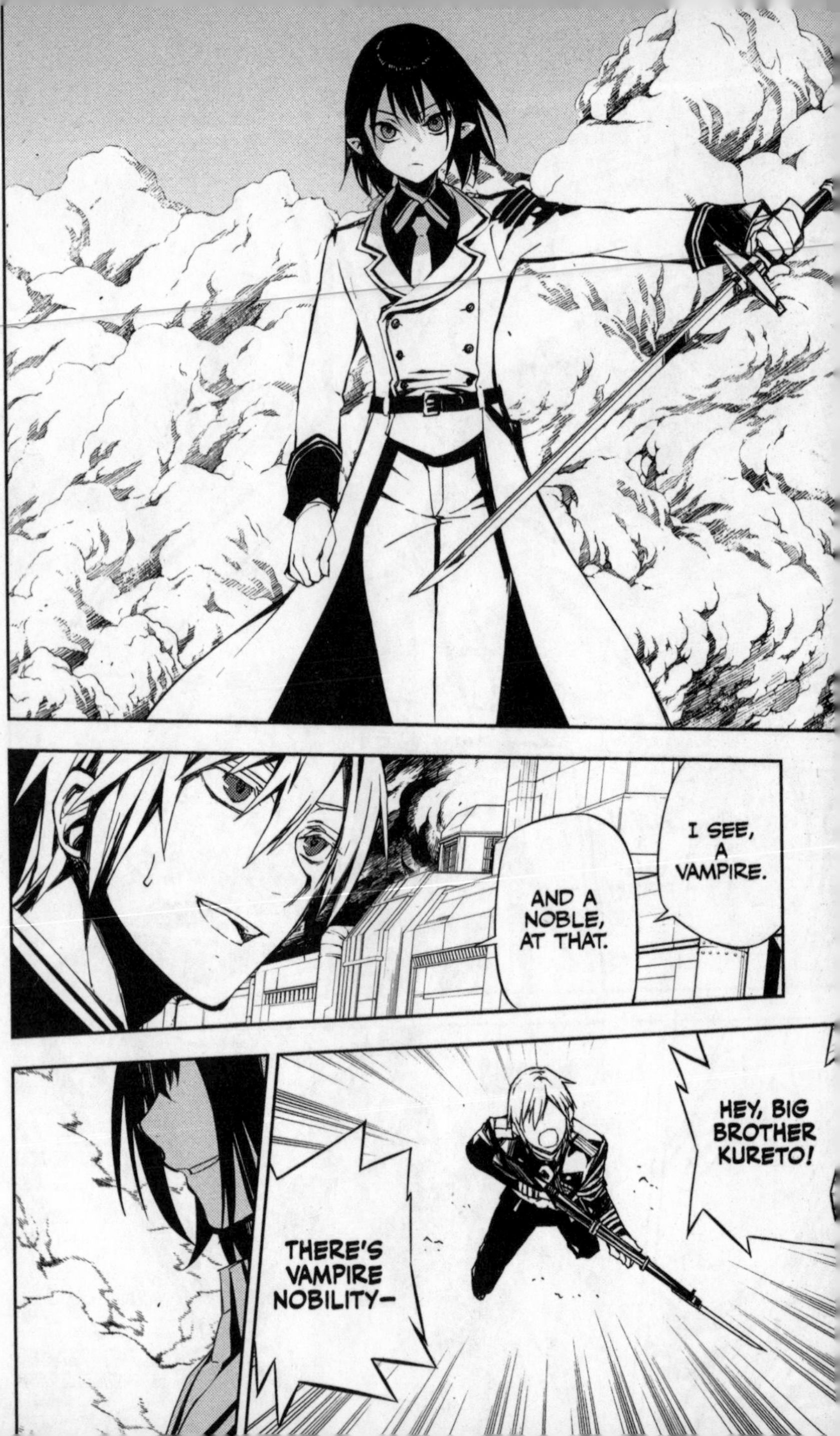
I SEE, A VAMPIRE.
AND A NOBLE, AT THAT.
HEY, BIG BROTHER KURETO!
THERE'S VAMPIRE NOBILITY—

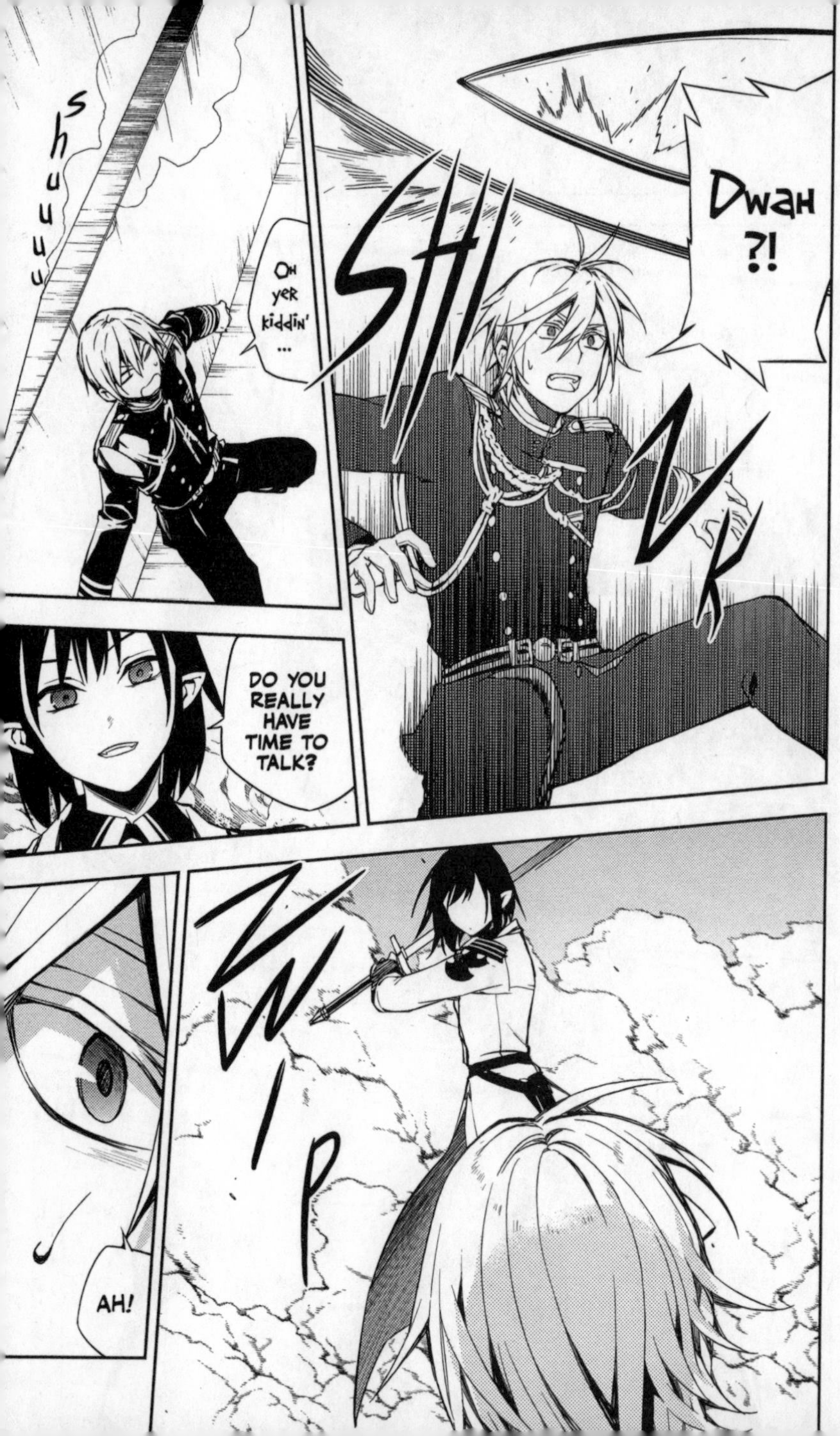

Dwah ?!
SHINK
shuuuuu
Oh yer kiddin' ...
DO YOU REALLY HAVE TIME TO TALK?
ZWIP
AH!

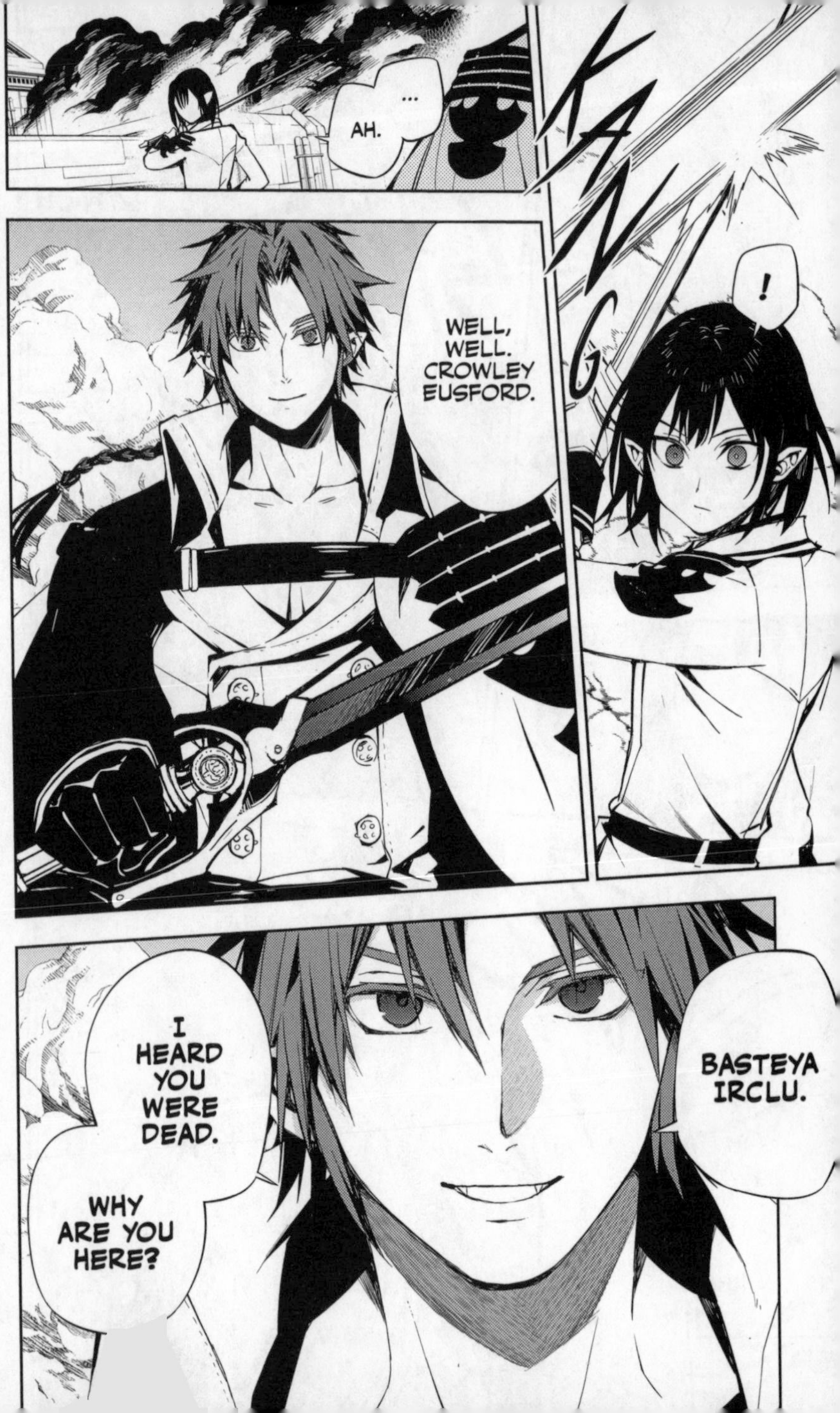
KANG
!
...
AH.
WELL, WELL. CROWLEY EUSFORD.
BASTEYA IRCLU.
I HEARD YOU WERE DEAD.
WHY ARE YOU HERE?

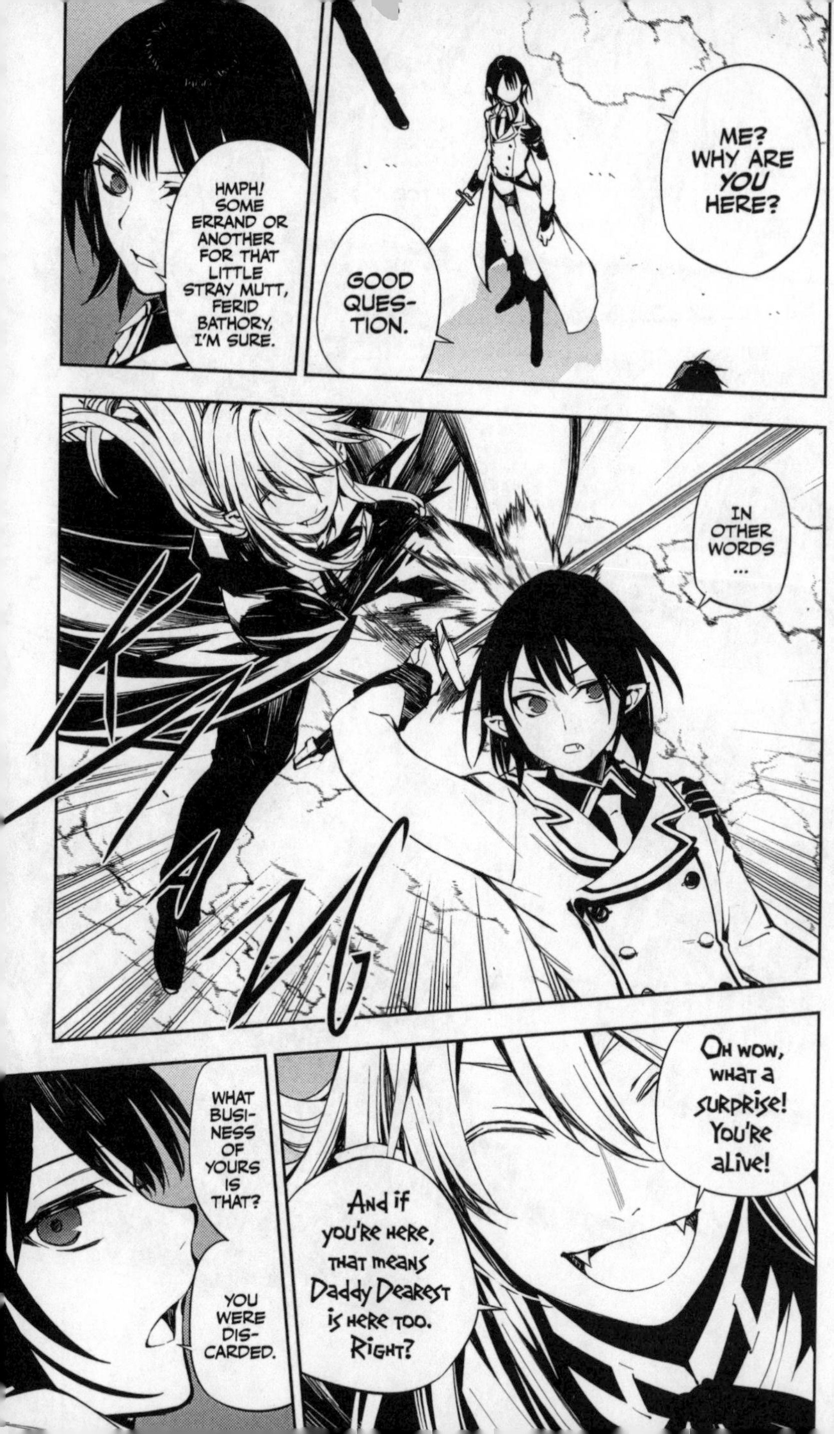
ME? WHY ARE *YOU* HERE?
GOOD QUES-TION.
HMPH! SOME ERRAND OR ANOTHER FOR THAT LITTLE STRAY MUTT, FERID BATHORY, I'M SURE.
IN OTHER WORDS ...
KANG
Oh wow, what a surprise! You're alive!
And if you're here, that means Daddy Dearest is here too. Right?
WHAT BUSI-NESS OF YOURS IS THAT?
YOU WERE DIS-CARDED.

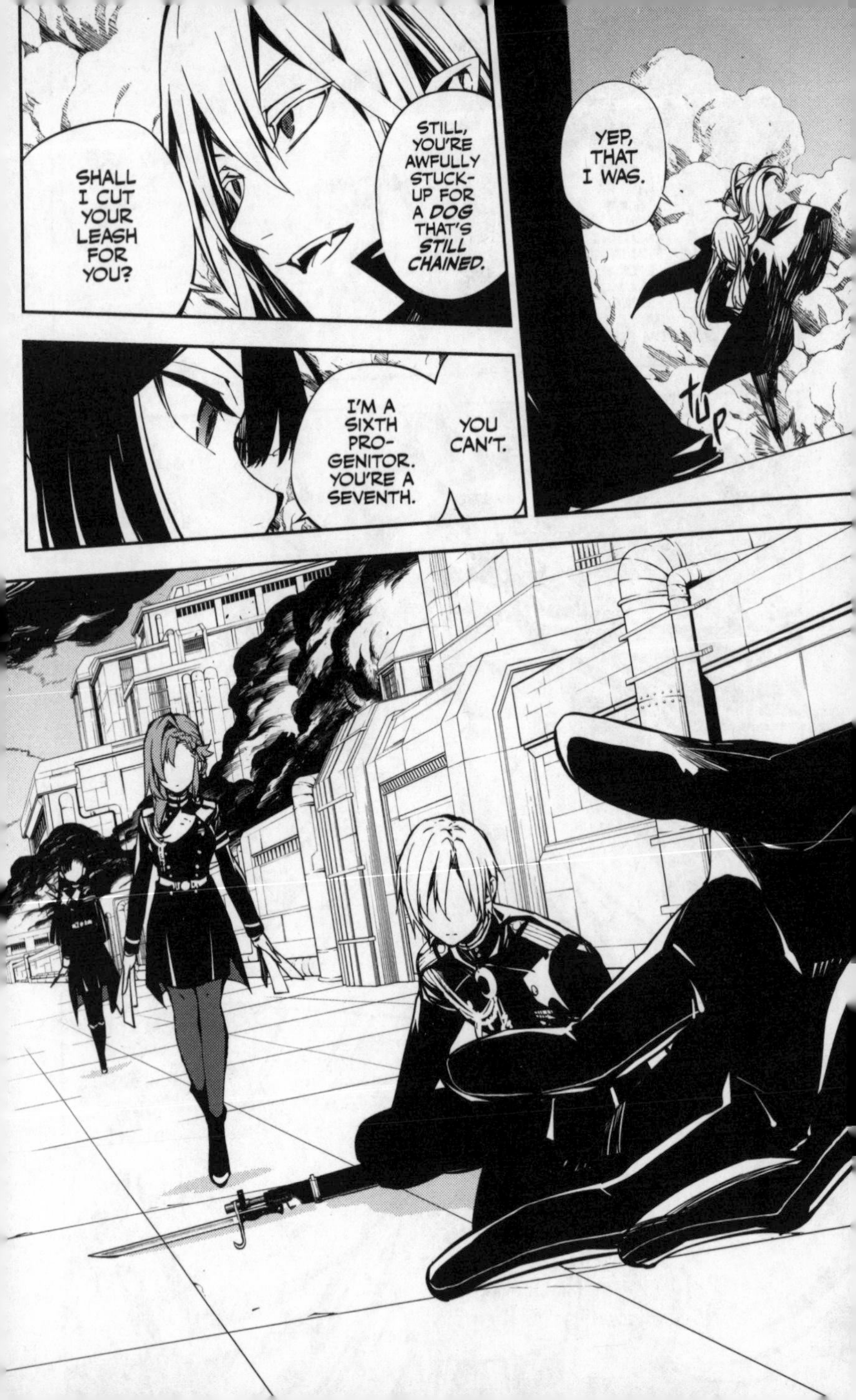
YEP, THAT I WAS.
TUP
STILL, YOU'RE AWFULLY STUCK-UP FOR A *DOG* THAT'S *STILL CHAINED.*
SHALL I CUT YOUR LEASH FOR YOU?
YOU CAN'T.
I'M A SIXTH PRO-GENITOR. YOU'RE A SEVENTH.

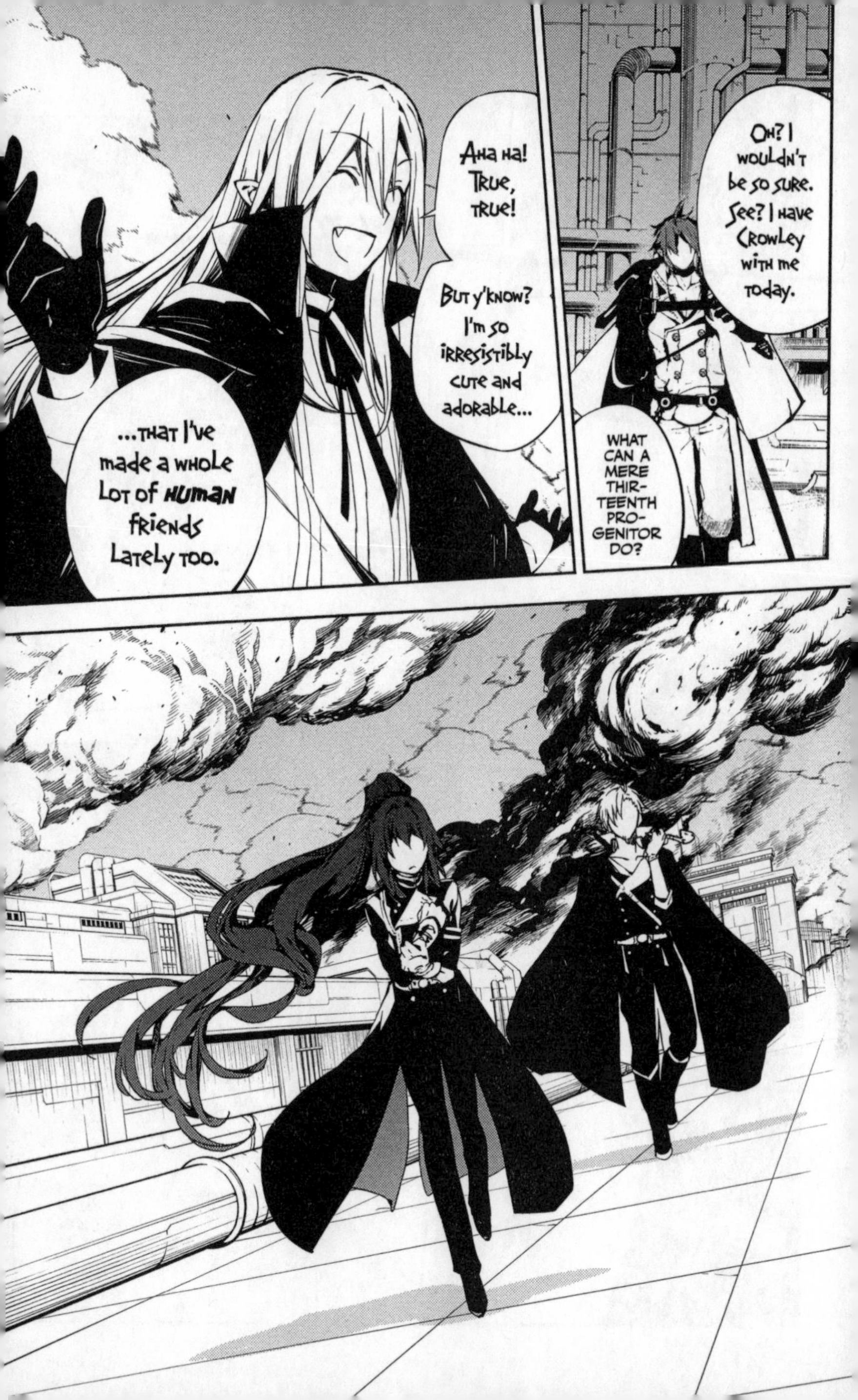
Oh? I wouldn't be so sure. See? I have Crowley with me today.
WHAT CAN A MERE THIRTEENTH PROGENITOR DO?
Aha ha! True, true!
But y'know? I'm so irresistibly cute and adorable...
...that I've made a whole lot of **HUMAN** friends lately too.

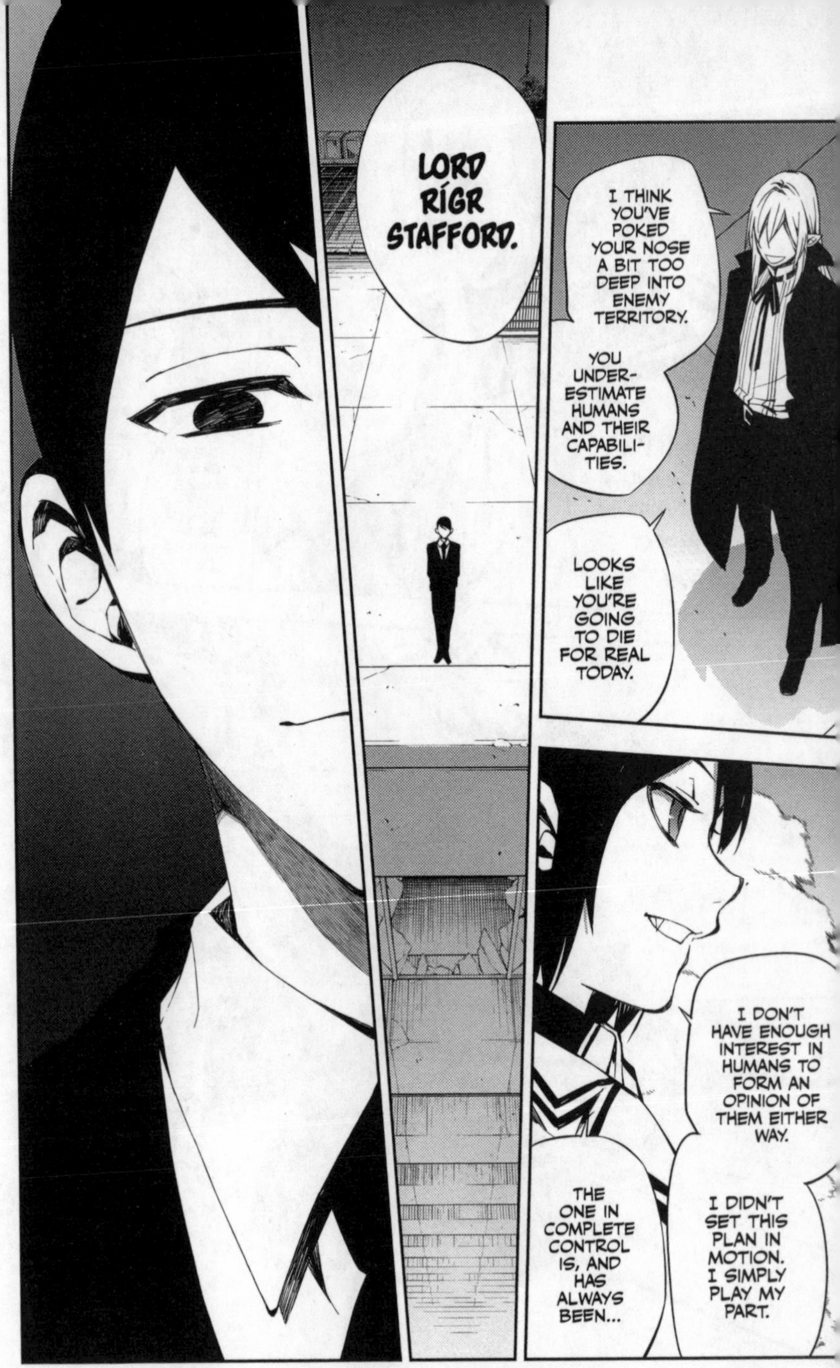
I THINK YOU'VE POKED YOUR NOSE A BIT TOO DEEP INTO ENEMY TERRITORY.
YOU UNDER-ESTIMATE HUMANS AND THEIR CAPABILI-TIES.
LOOKS LIKE YOU'RE GOING TO DIE FOR REAL TODAY.
I DON'T HAVE ENOUGH INTEREST IN HUMANS TO FORM AN OPINION OF THEM EITHER WAY.
I DIDN'T SET THIS PLAN IN MOTION. I SIMPLY PLAY MY PART.
THE ONE IN COMPLETE CONTROL IS, AND HAS ALWAYS BEEN...
LORD RÍGR STAFFORD.

JIGENSO.
SLICE IT OPEN.
ZZSHH
OHO?
A HUMAN?!
THAT'S CURSED GEAR!
BYAKKO-MARU!
BLAM

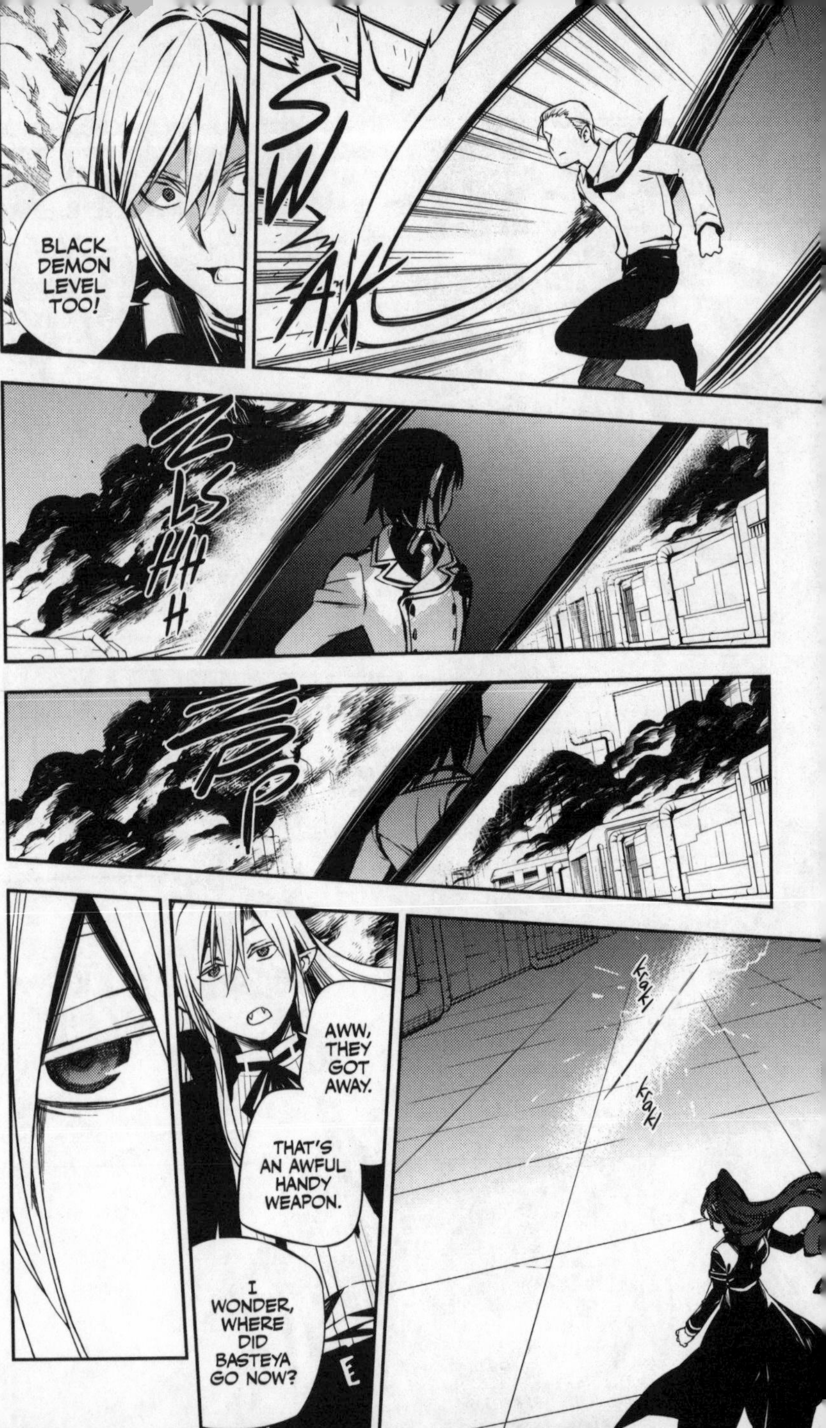
SWAK
BLACK DEMON LEVEL TOO!
krakl
krakl
AWW, THEY GOT AWAY.
THAT'S AN AWFUL HANDY WEAPON.
I WONDER, WHERE DID BASTEYA GO NOW?

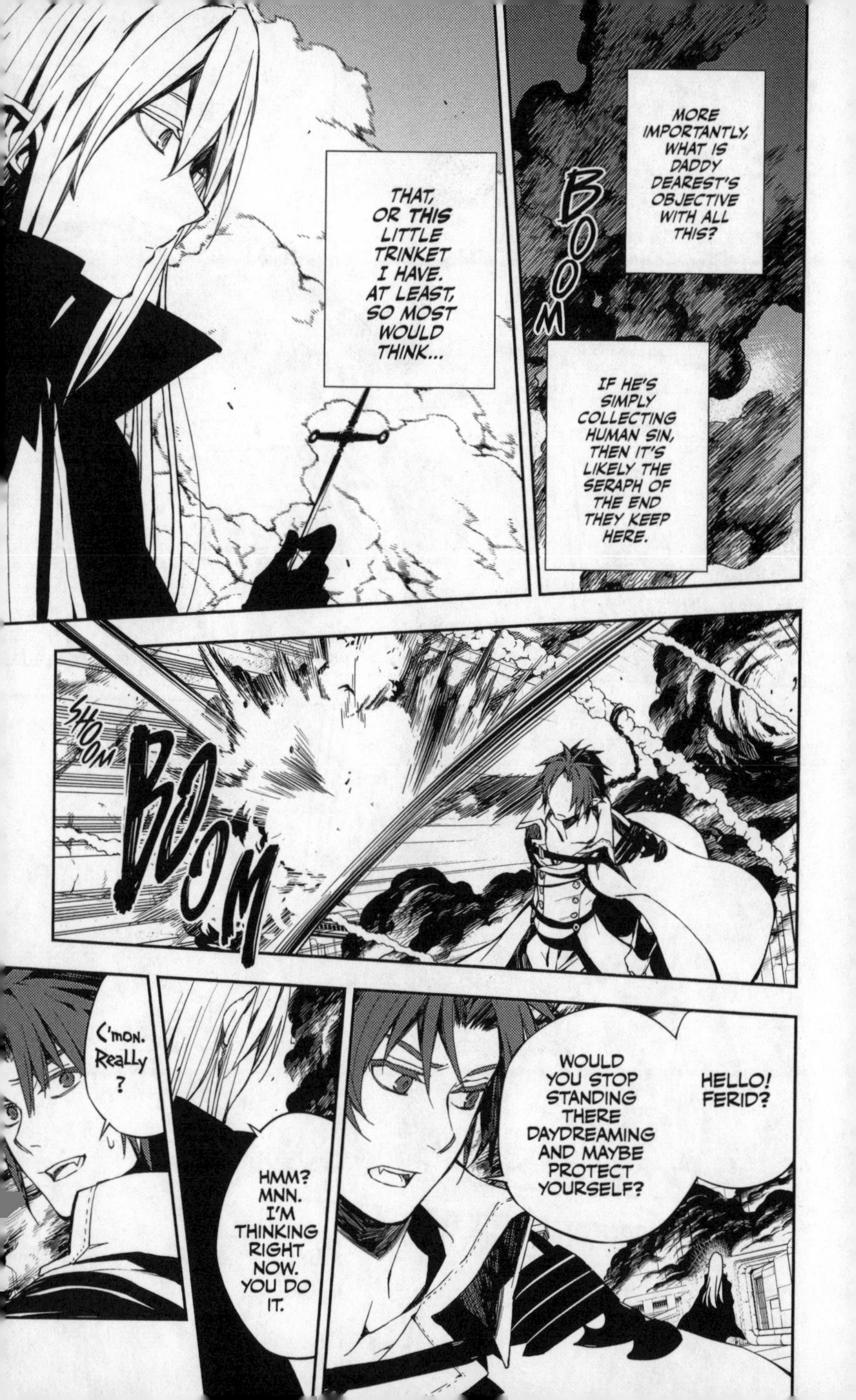
MORE IMPORTANTLY, WHAT IS DADDY DEAREST'S OBJECTIVE WITH ALL THIS?
BOOOM
IF HE'S SIMPLY COLLECTING HUMAN SIN, THEN IT'S LIKELY THE SERAPH OF THE END THEY KEEP HERE.
THAT, OR THIS LITTLE TRINKET I HAVE. AT LEAST, SO MOST WOULD THINK...
SHOOM
BOOM
HELLO! FERID?
WOULD YOU STOP STANDING THERE DAYDREAMING AND MAYBE PROTECT YOURSELF?
HMM? MNN. I'M THINKING RIGHT NOW. YOU DO IT.
C'mon. Really?

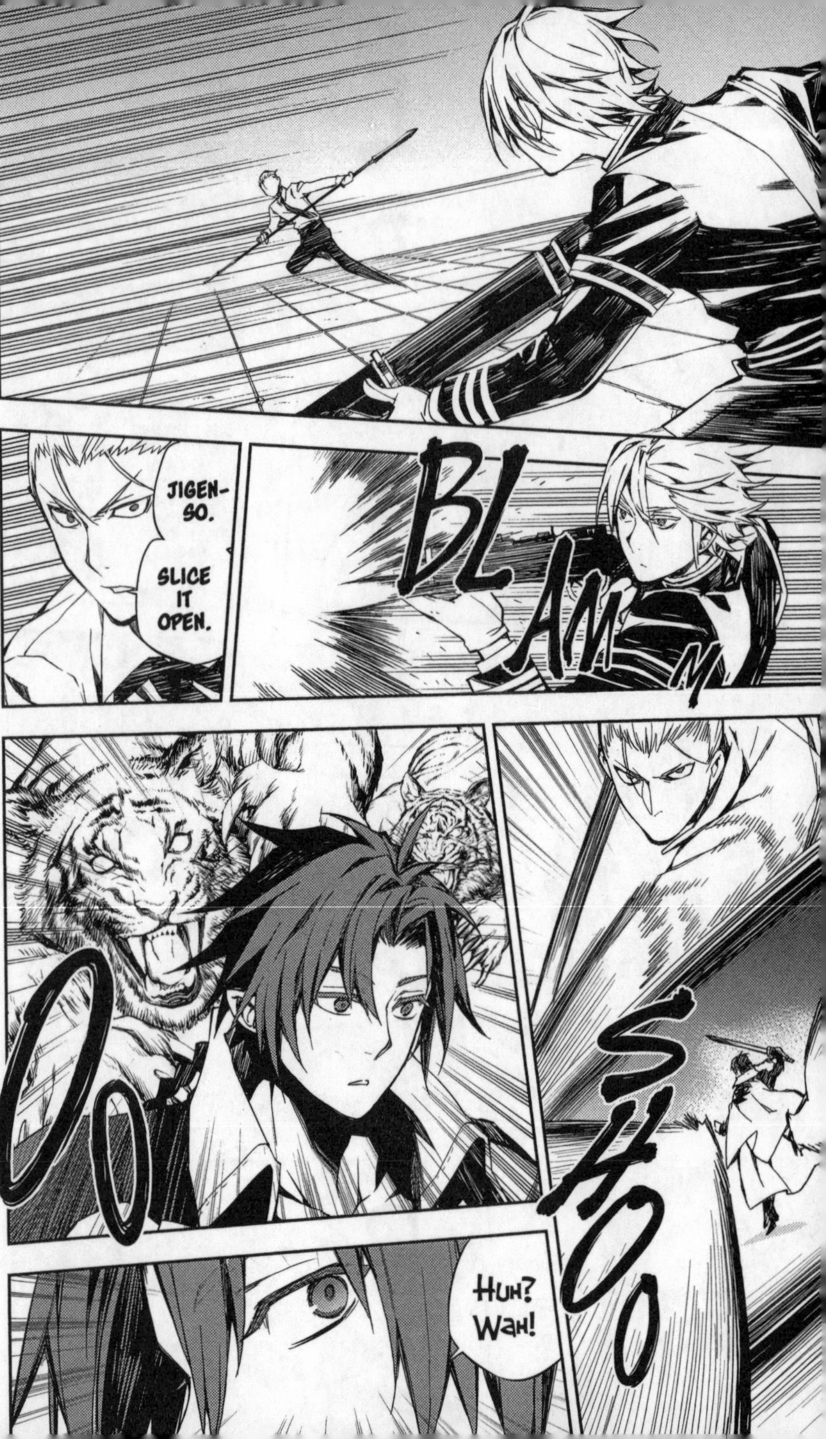
BLAMM
JIGEN-SO.
SLICE IT OPEN.
SHOO
OO
HUH? WAH!

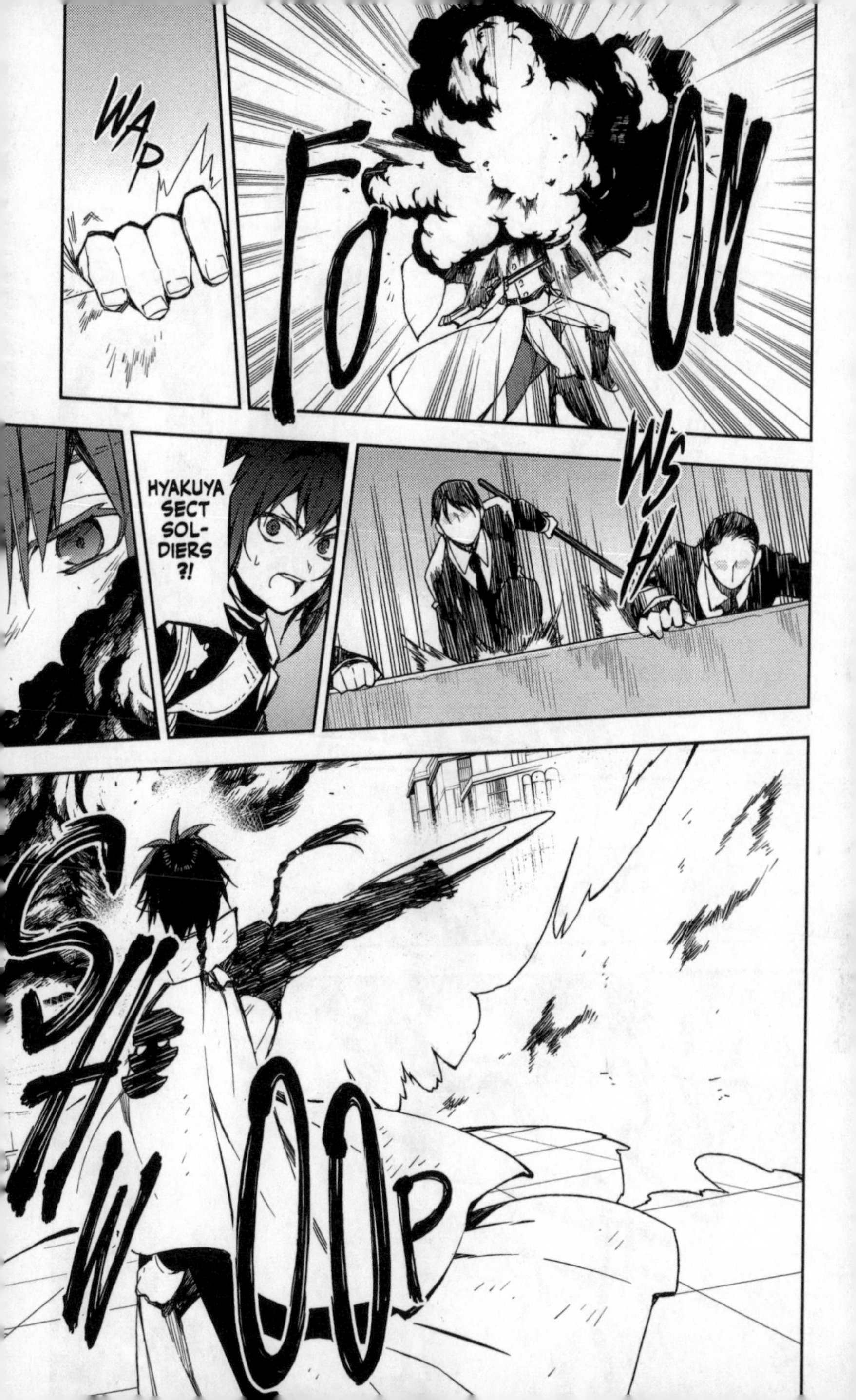
FOOM
WAP
WSH
HYAKUYA SECT SOL-DIERS ?!
SHWOOP

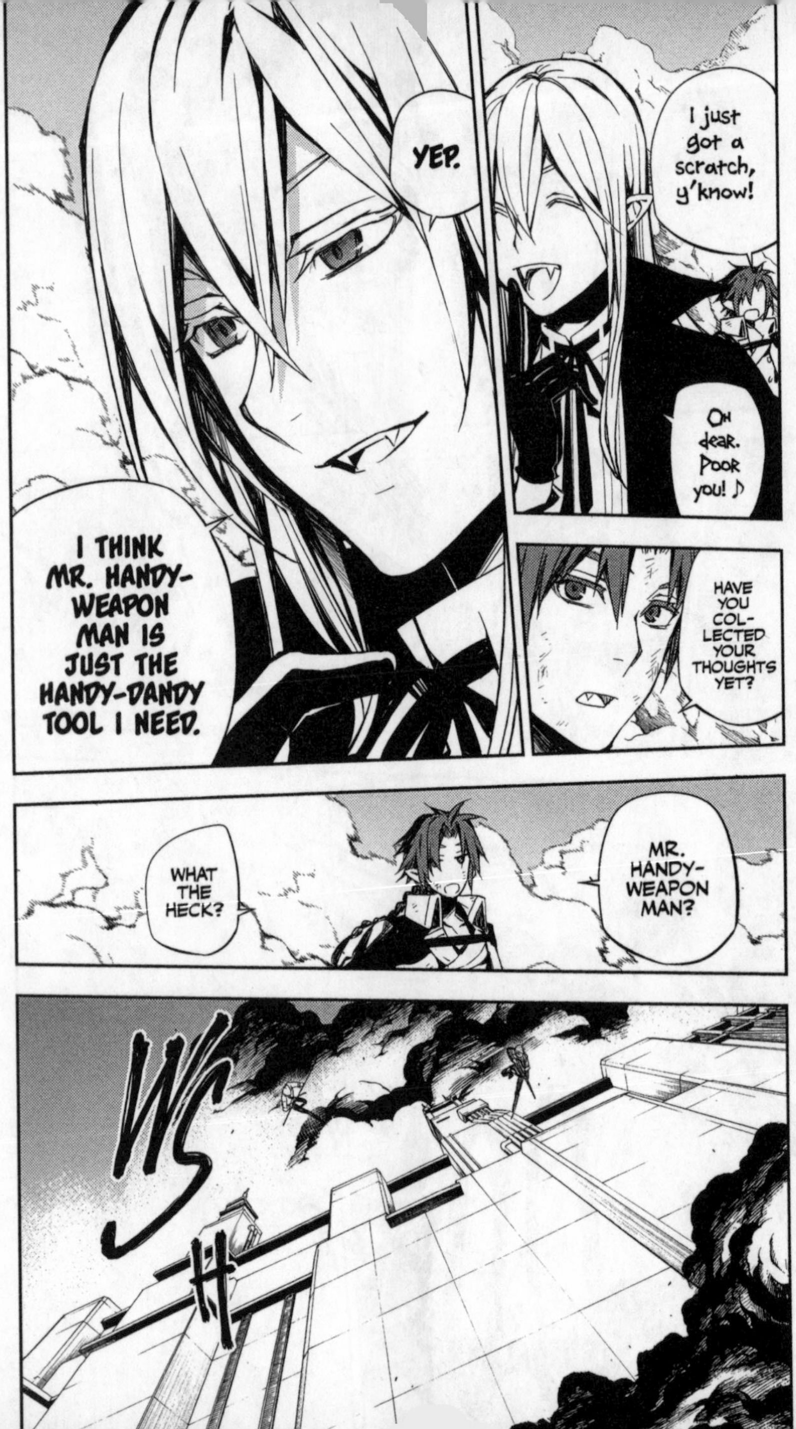

I just got a scratch, y'know!
Oh dear. Poor you! ♪
HAVE YOU COL-LECTED YOUR THOUGHTS YET?
YEP.
I THINK MR. HANDY-WEAPON MAN IS JUST THE HANDY-DANDY TOOL I NEED.
MR. HANDY-WEAPON MAN?
WHAT THE HECK?
WSH

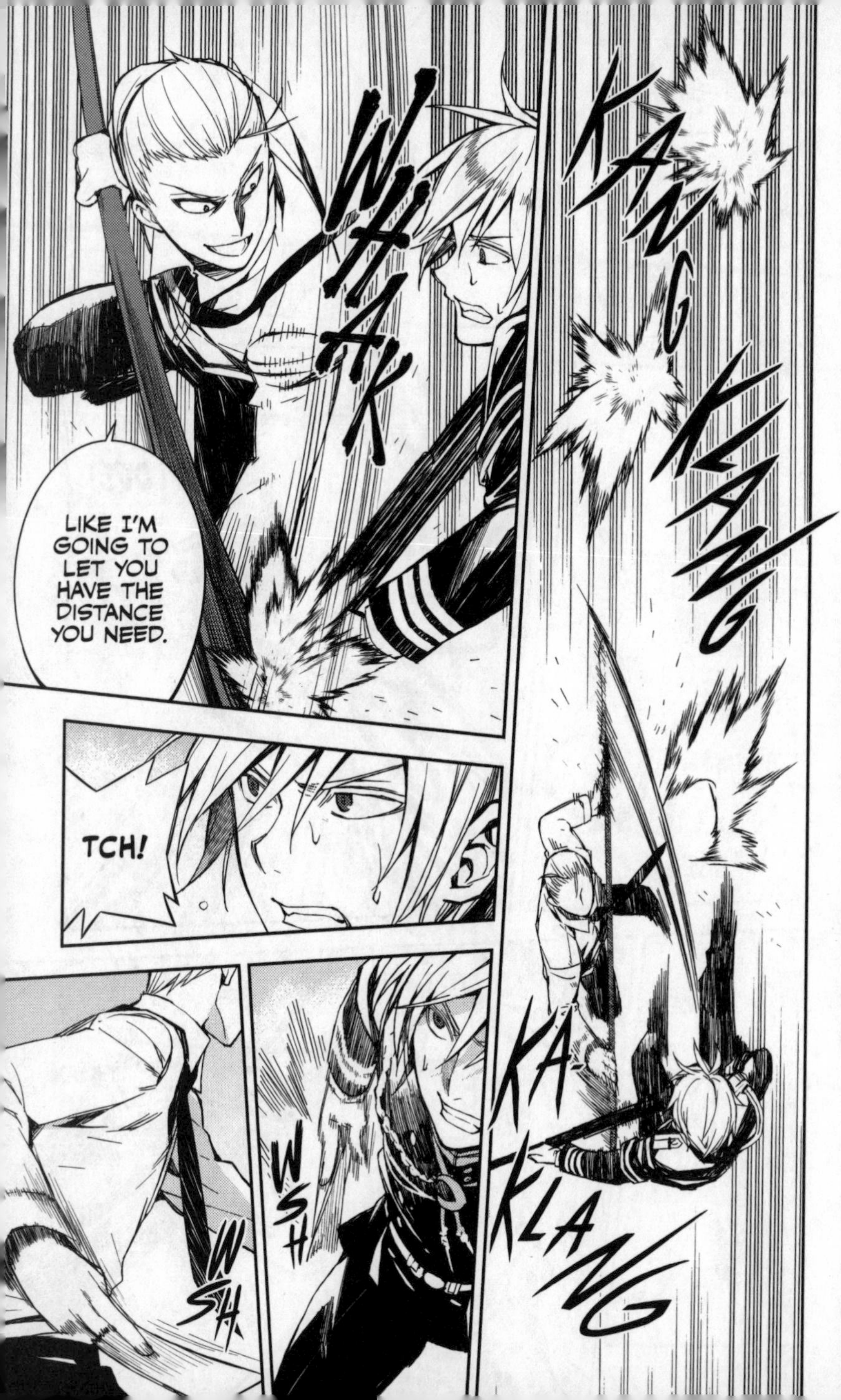
KANG
KLANG
KA-KLANG
WHAK
LIKE I'M GOING TO LET YOU HAVE THE DISTANCE YOU NEED.
TCH!
WSH
WSH

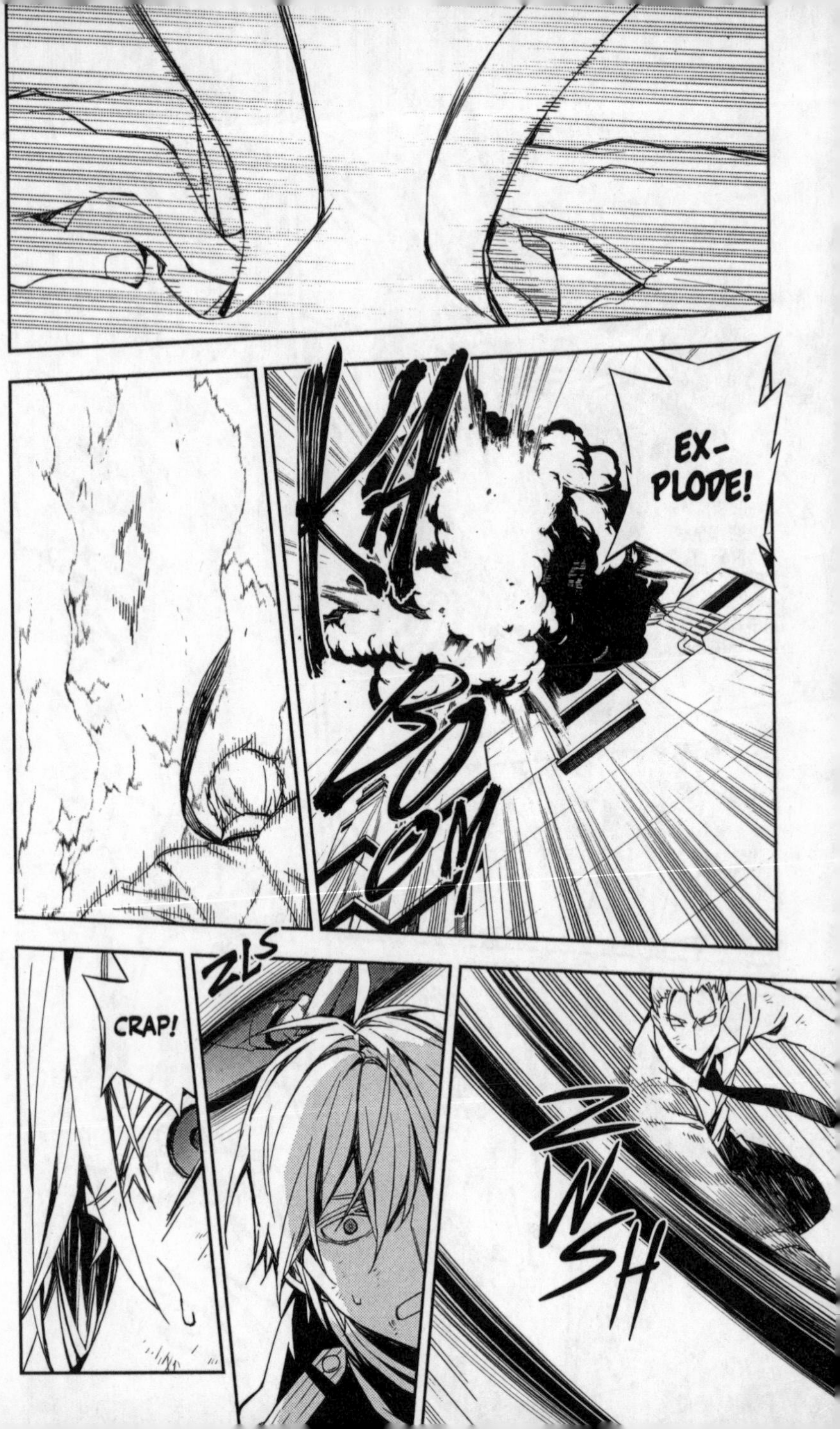
EX-
PLODE!
KABOOM
ZWSH
ZLS
CRAP!

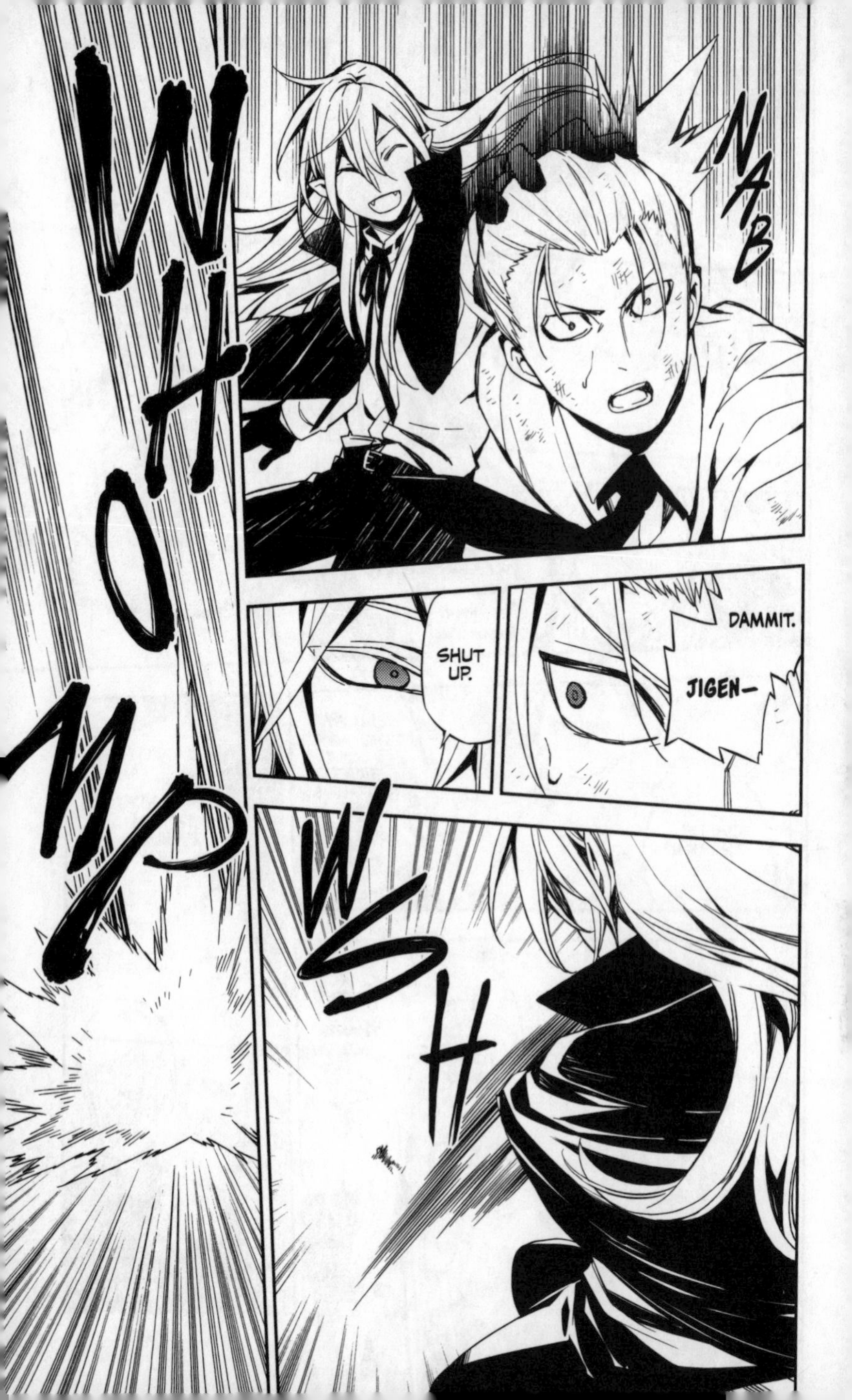
NAB
DAMMIT.
JIGEN—
SHUT UP.
WSH
WHOMP

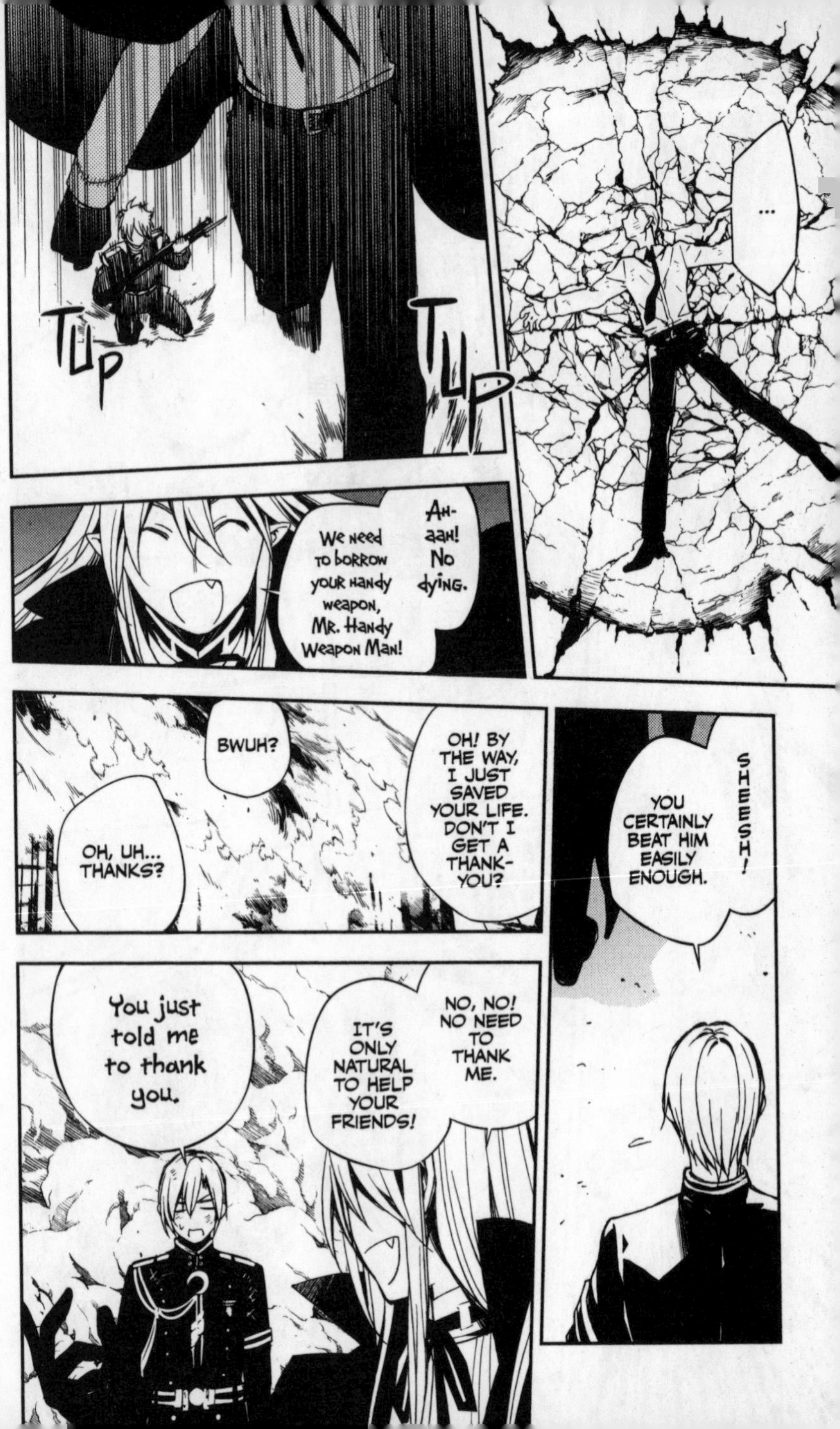
...
TUP
TUP
Ah-aah! No dying.
We need to borrow your handy weapon, Mr. Handy Weapon Man!
SHEESH!
YOU CERTAINLY BEAT HIM EASILY ENOUGH.
OH! BY THE WAY, I JUST SAVED YOUR LIFE. DON'T I GET A THANK-YOU?
BWUH?
OH, UH... THANKS?
NO, NO! NO NEED TO THANK ME.
IT'S ONLY NATURAL TO HELP YOUR FRIENDS!
You just told me to thank you.

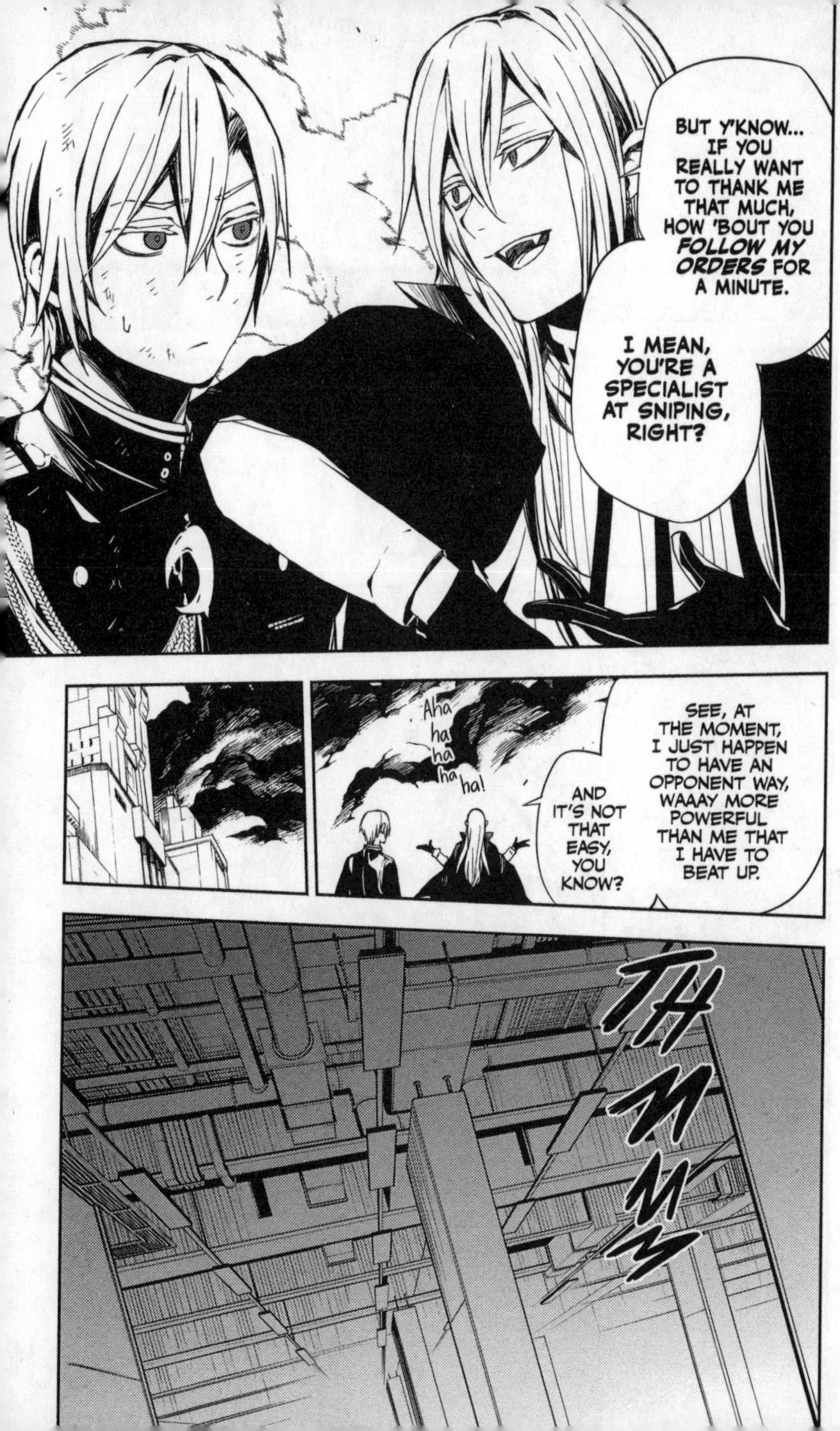
BUT Y'KNOW... IF YOU REALLY WANT TO THANK ME THAT MUCH, HOW 'BOUT YOU ***FOLLOW MY ORDERS*** FOR A MINUTE.
I MEAN, YOU'RE A SPECIALIST AT SNIPING, RIGHT?
SEE, AT THE MOMENT, I JUST HAPPEN TO HAVE AN OPPONENT WAY, WAAAY MORE POWERFUL THAN ME THAT I HAVE TO BEAT UP.
AND IT'S NOT THAT EASY, YOU KNOW?
Aha ha ha ha ha!
THMMMM

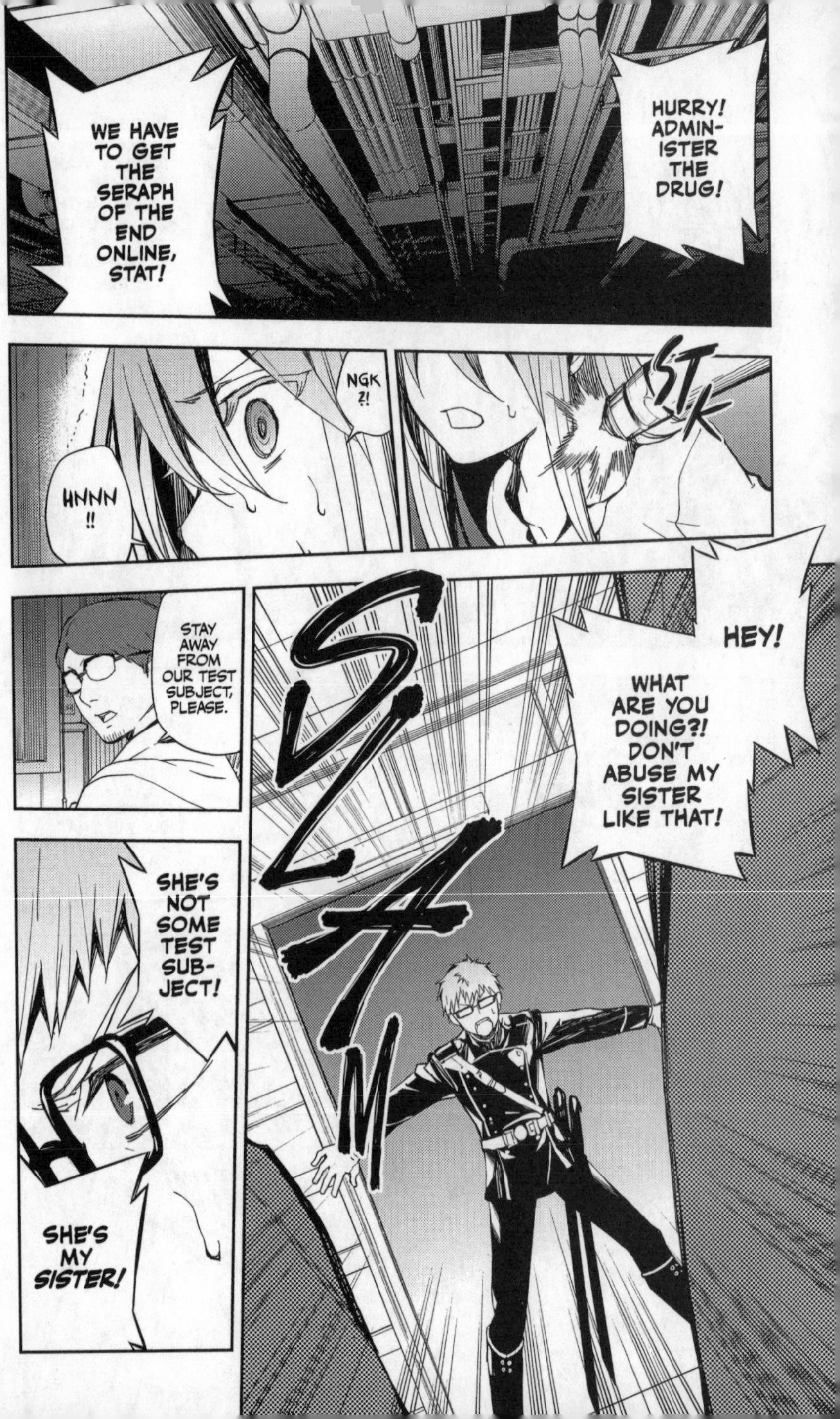
HURRY! ADMINISTER THE DRUG!
WE HAVE TO GET THE SERAPH OF THE END ONLINE, STAT!
STK
NGK?!
HNNN!!
HEY!
WHAT ARE YOU DOING?! DON'T ABUSE MY SISTER LIKE THAT!
SLAM
STAY AWAY FROM OUR TEST SUBJECT, PLEASE.
SHE'S NOT SOME TEST SUBJECT!
SHE'S MY SISTER!

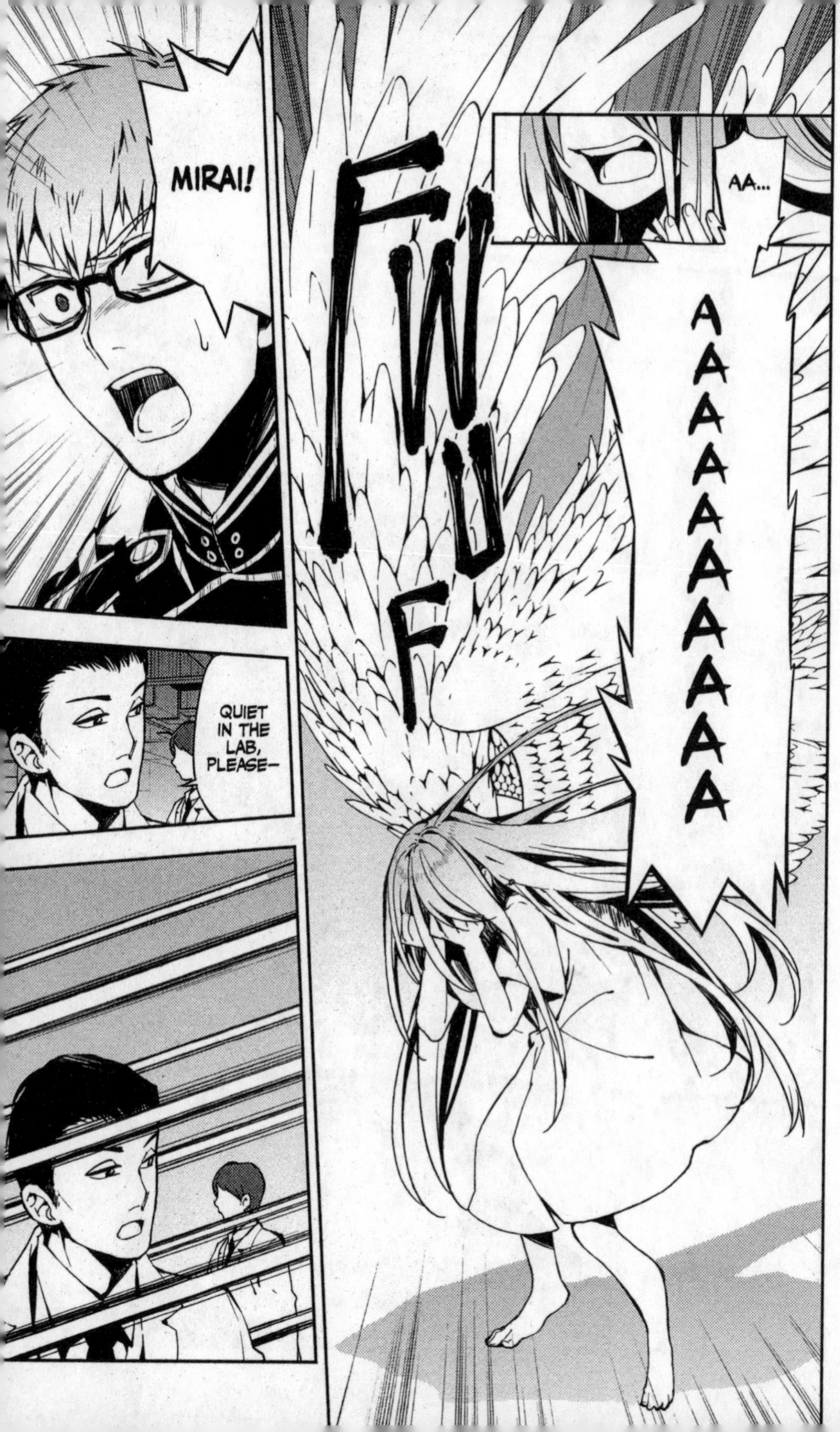
AA...
AAAAAAAAAA
FWUF
MIRAI!
QUIET IN THE LAB, PLEASE—

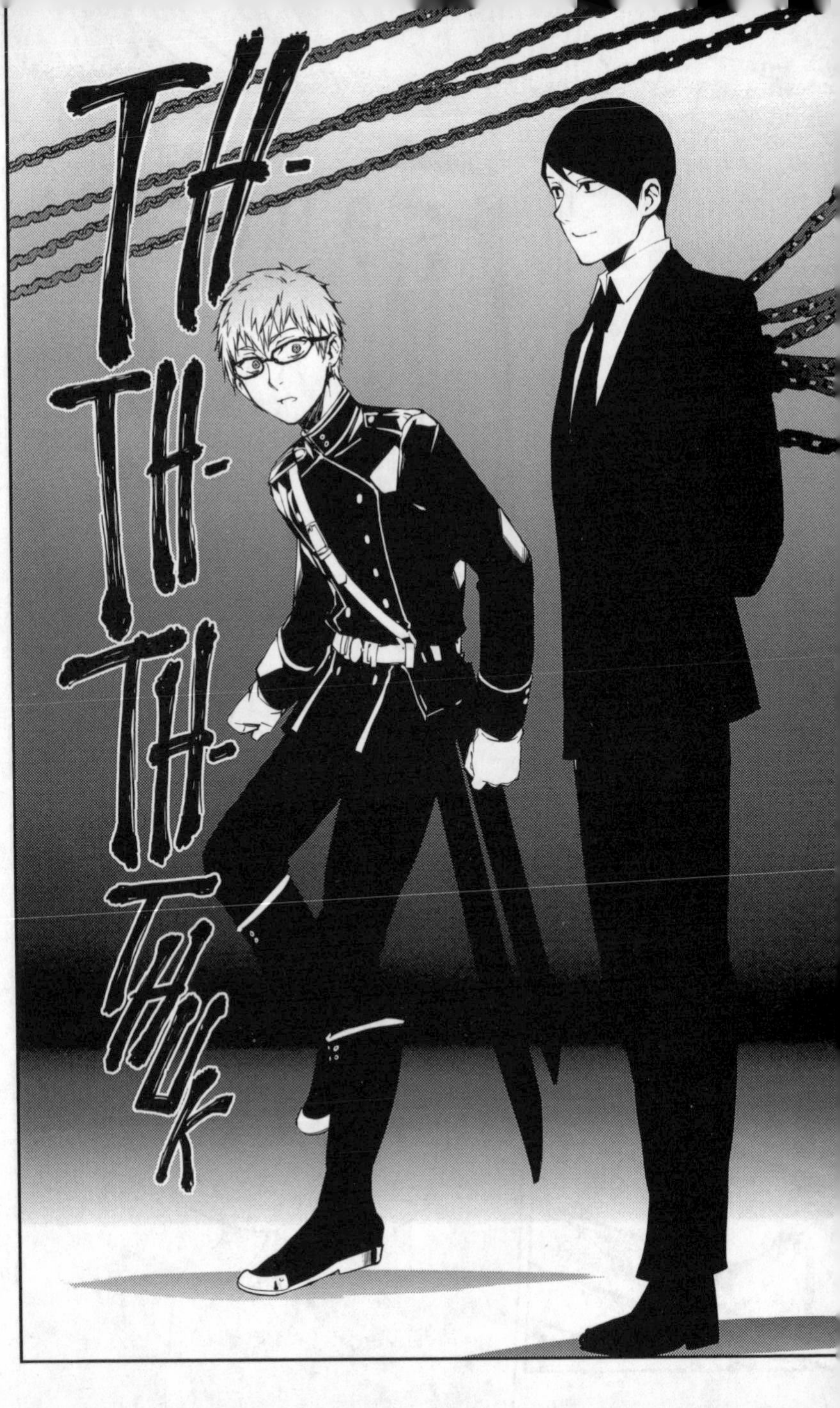
TH-TH-TH-THUNK

OHO! IT'S YOUR SISTER, HM?

I GUESS I'LL HAVE TO TREAT *IT* WITH CARE.

WHO ARE YOU?!

WHA ...?

HMM ...

I'M AFRAID I DON'T HAVE THE TIME TO SPEAK WITH YOU NOW.

BESIDES, WHAT DO I MATTER TO YOU, ANYWAY?

ARE YOU SURE YOU SHOULDN'T GO TO YOUR SISTER?

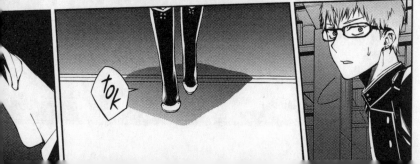

XOK

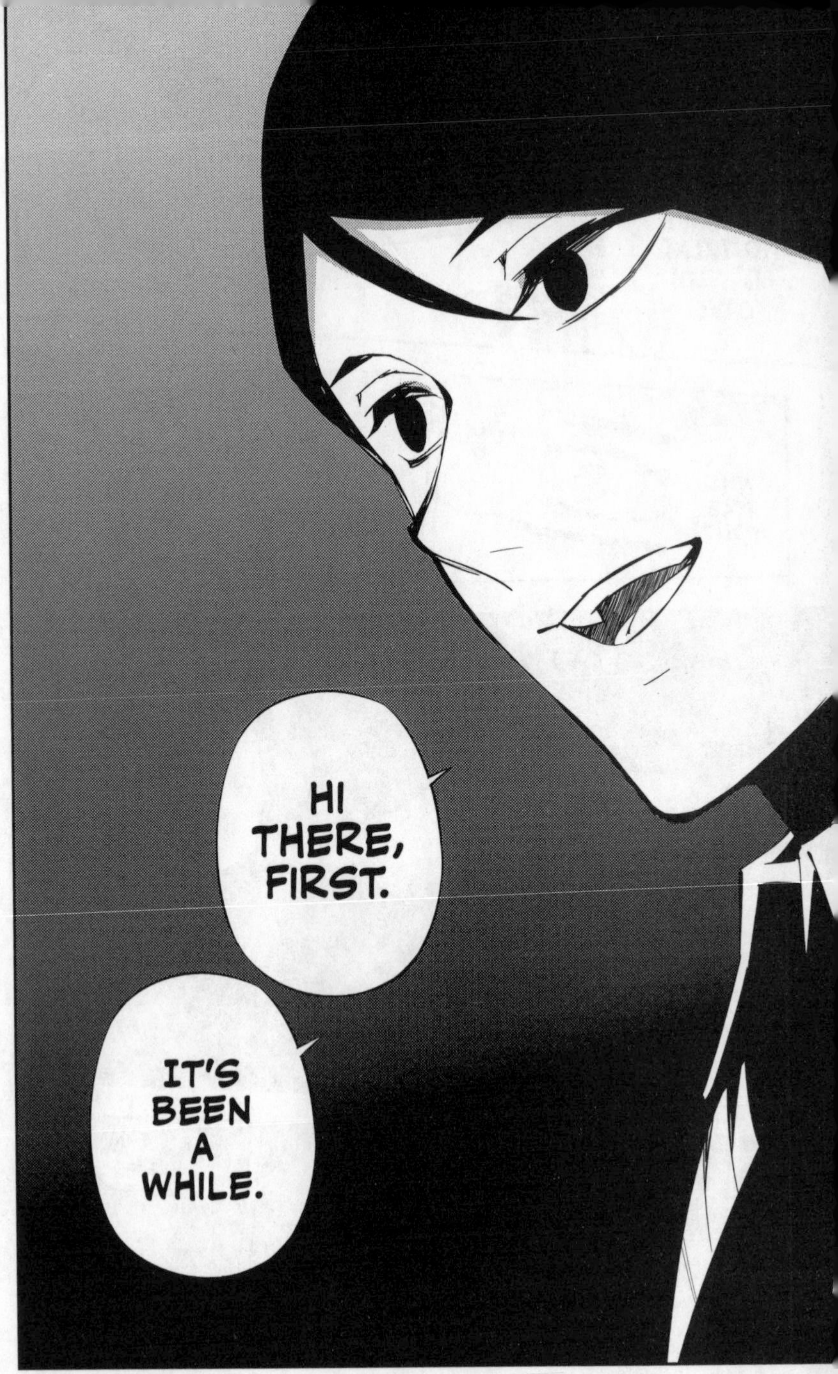
HI THERE, FIRST.
IT'S BEEN A WHILE.

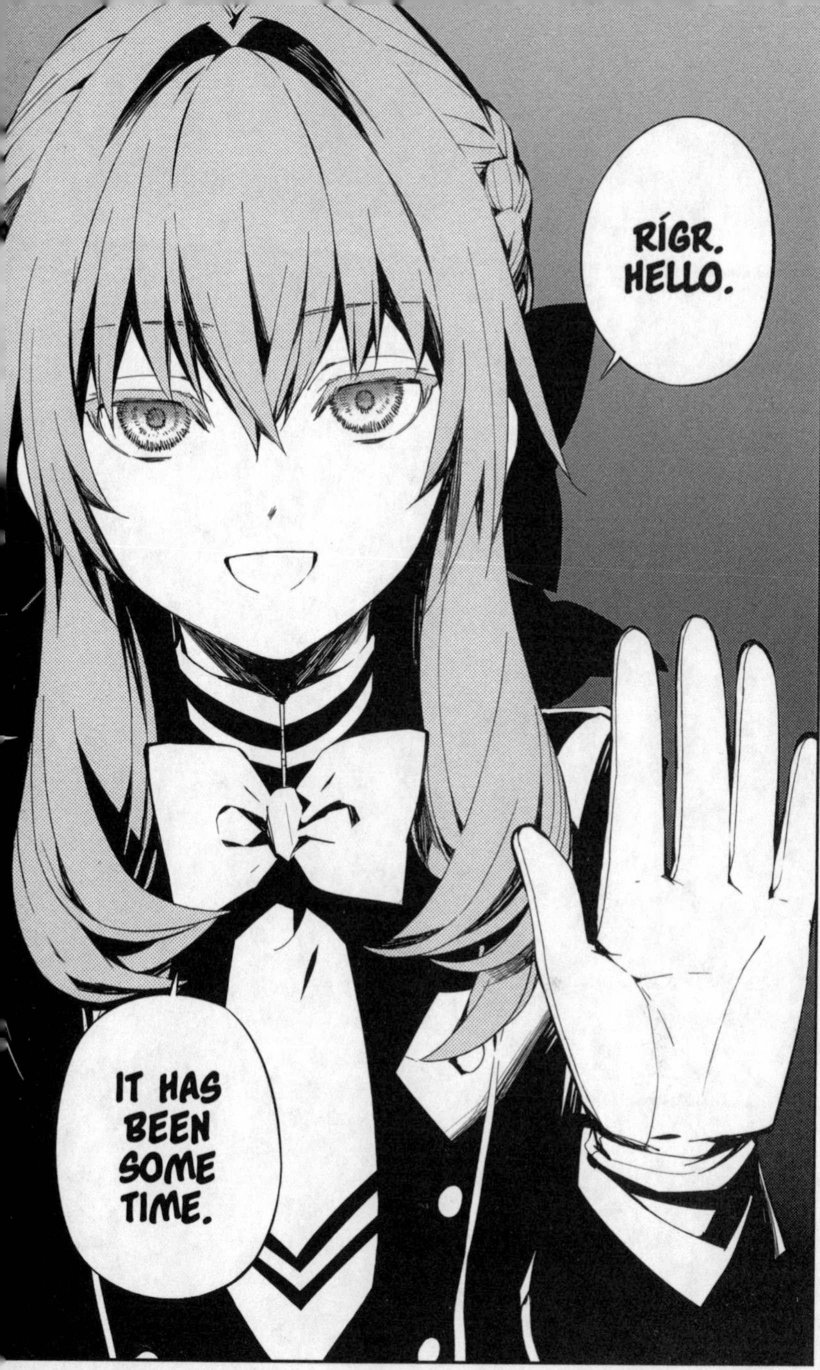
RÍGR. HELLO.
IT HAS BEEN SOME TIME.

Seraph of the End

VAMPIRE REIGN

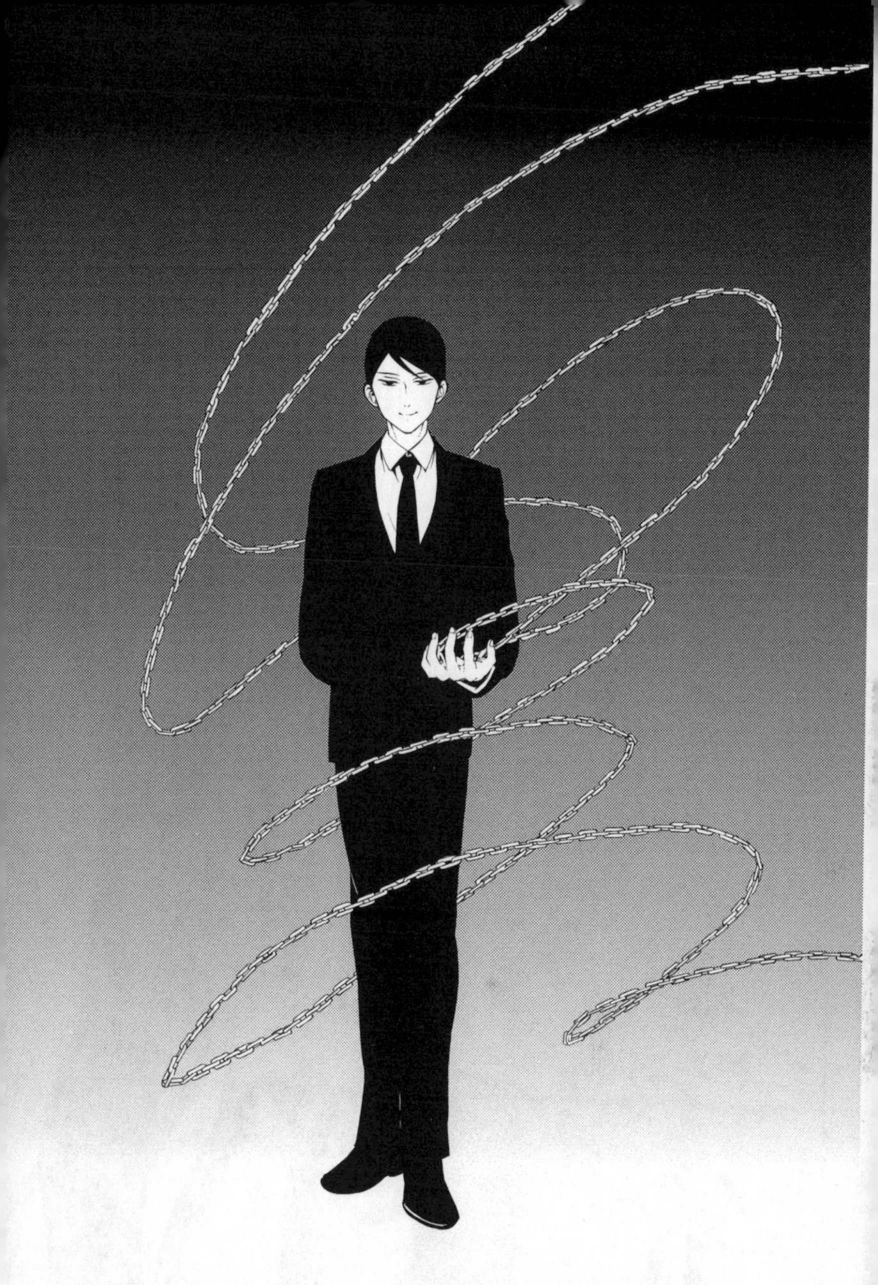

CHAPTER 81 Fallen Wings

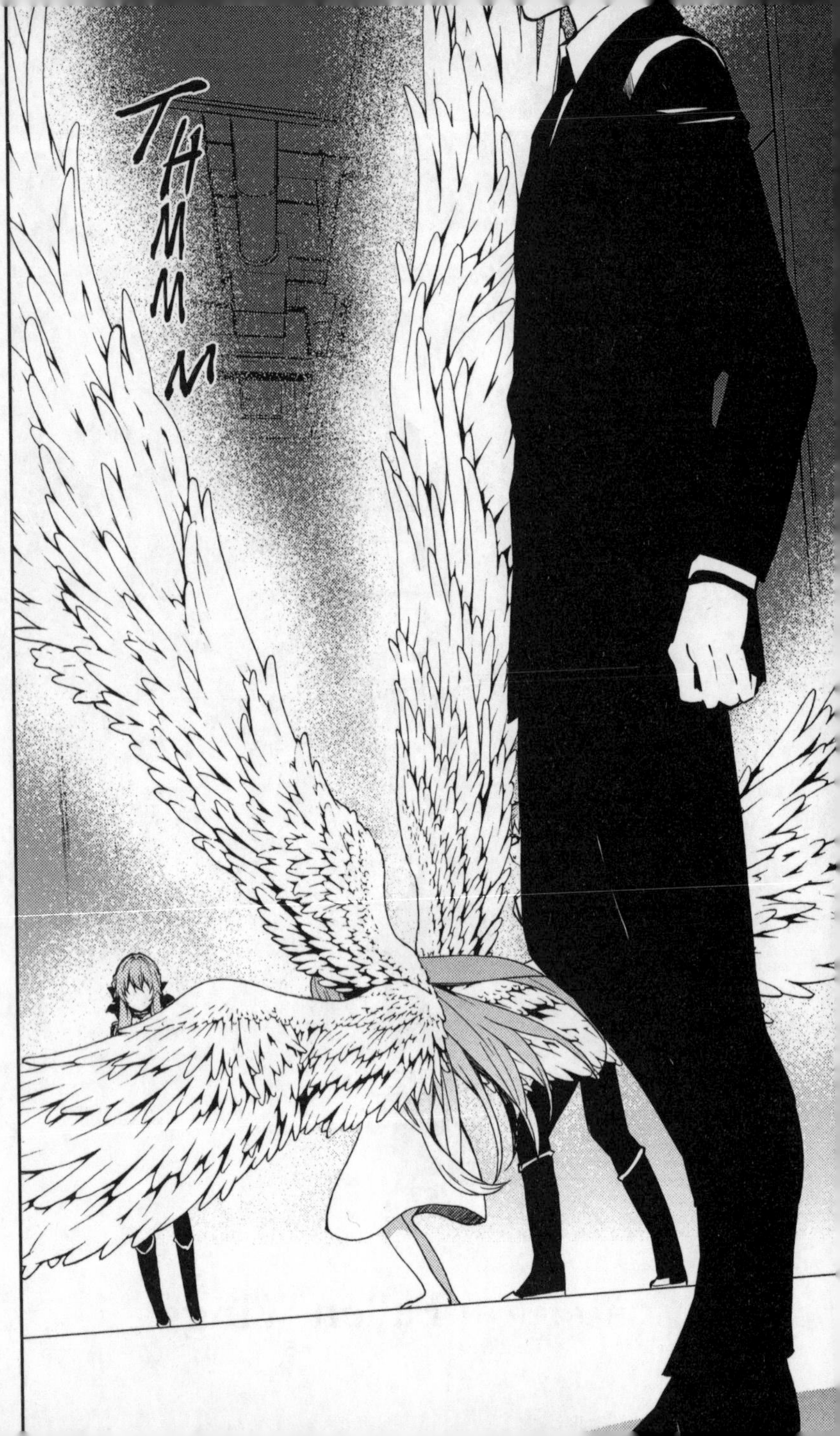
THMMM

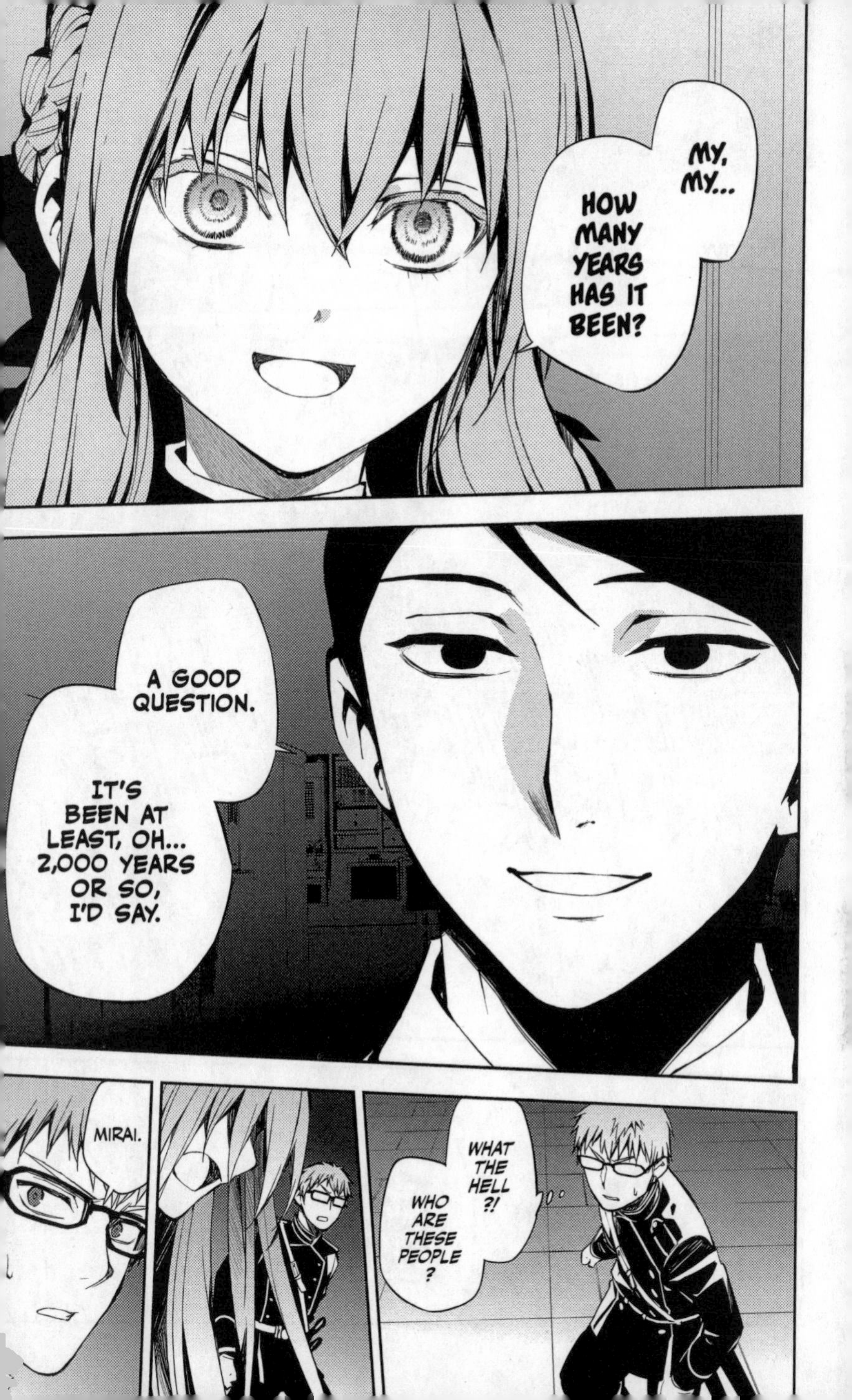
MY, MY...
HOW MANY YEARS HAS IT BEEN?
A GOOD QUESTION.
IT'S BEEN AT LEAST, OH... 2,000 YEARS OR SO, I'D SAY.
WHAT THE HELL?!
WHO ARE THESE PEOPLE?
MIRAI.

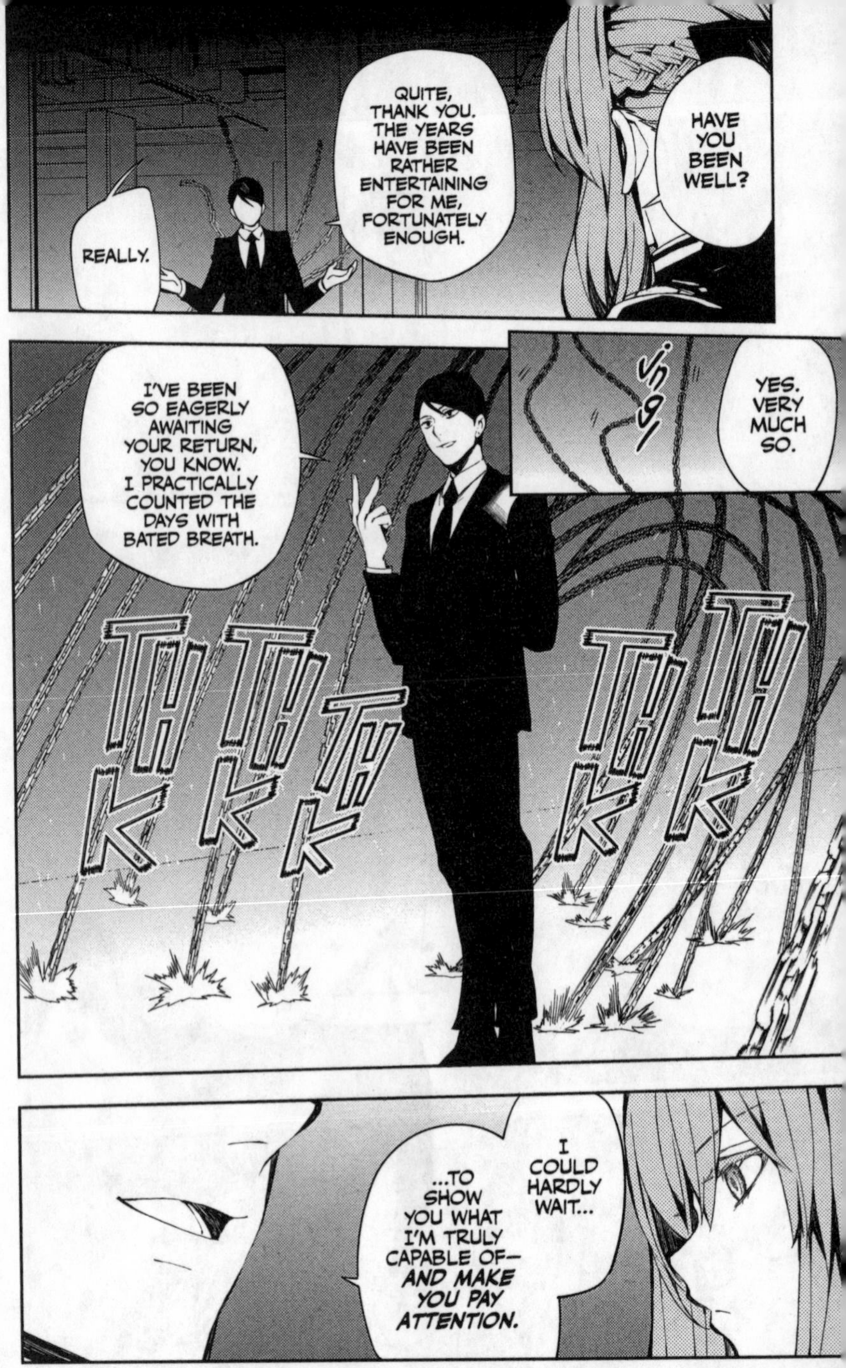
HAVE YOU BEEN WELL?
QUITE, THANK YOU. THE YEARS HAVE BEEN RATHER ENTERTAINING FOR ME, FORTUNATELY ENOUGH.
REALLY.
YES. VERY MUCH SO.
I'VE BEEN SO EAGERLY AWAITING YOUR RETURN, YOU KNOW. I PRACTICALLY COUNTED THE DAYS WITH BATED BREATH.
THK
THK
THK
THK
THK
I COULD HARDLY WAIT...
...TO SHOW YOU WHAT I'M TRULY CAPABLE OF—*AND MAKE YOU PAY ATTENTION.*

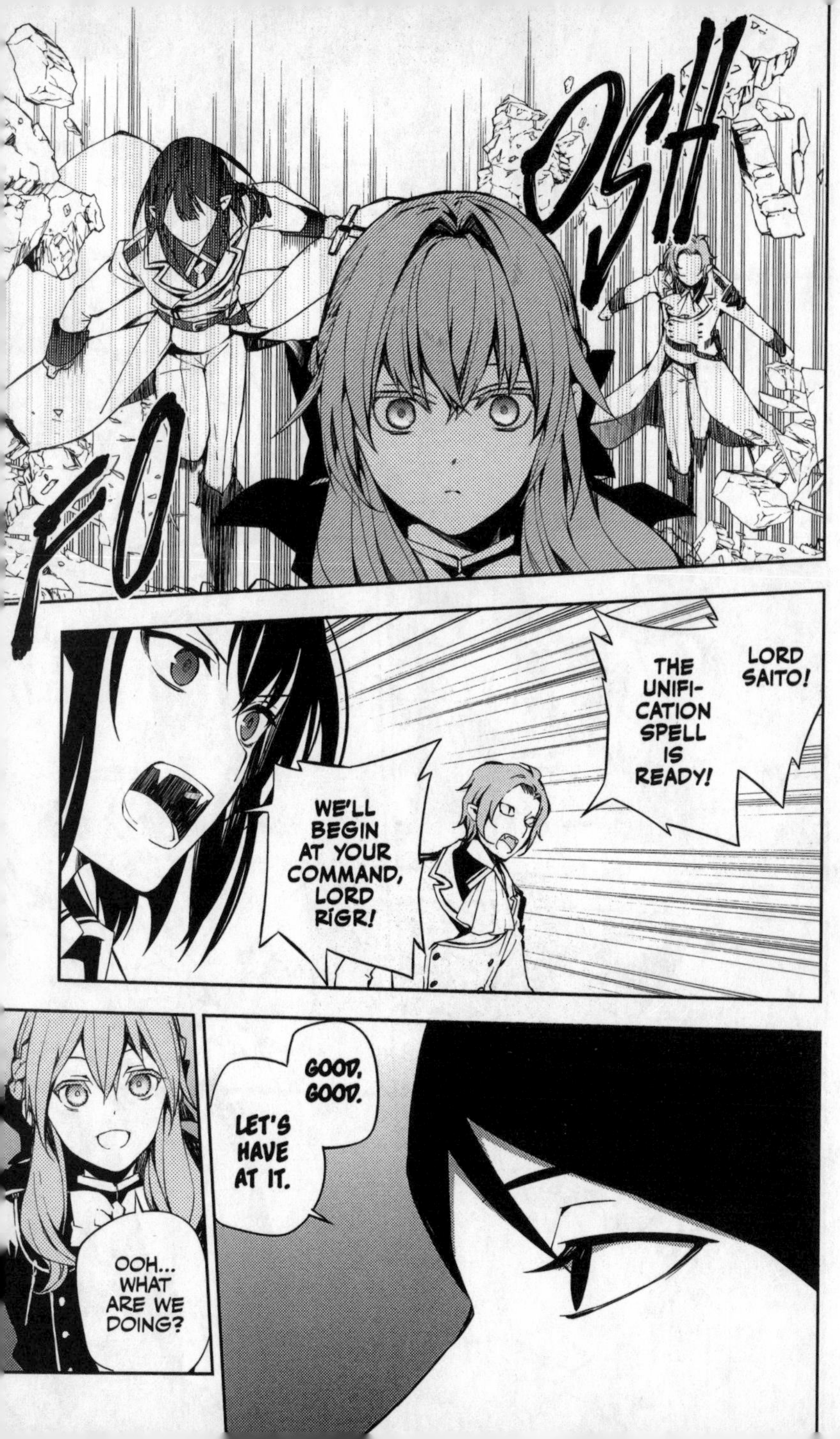
FOOSH
LORD SAITO!
THE UNIFICATION SPELL IS READY!
WE'LL BEGIN AT YOUR COMMAND, LORD RIGR!
GOOD, GOOD.
LET'S HAVE AT IT.
OOH... WHAT ARE WE DOING?

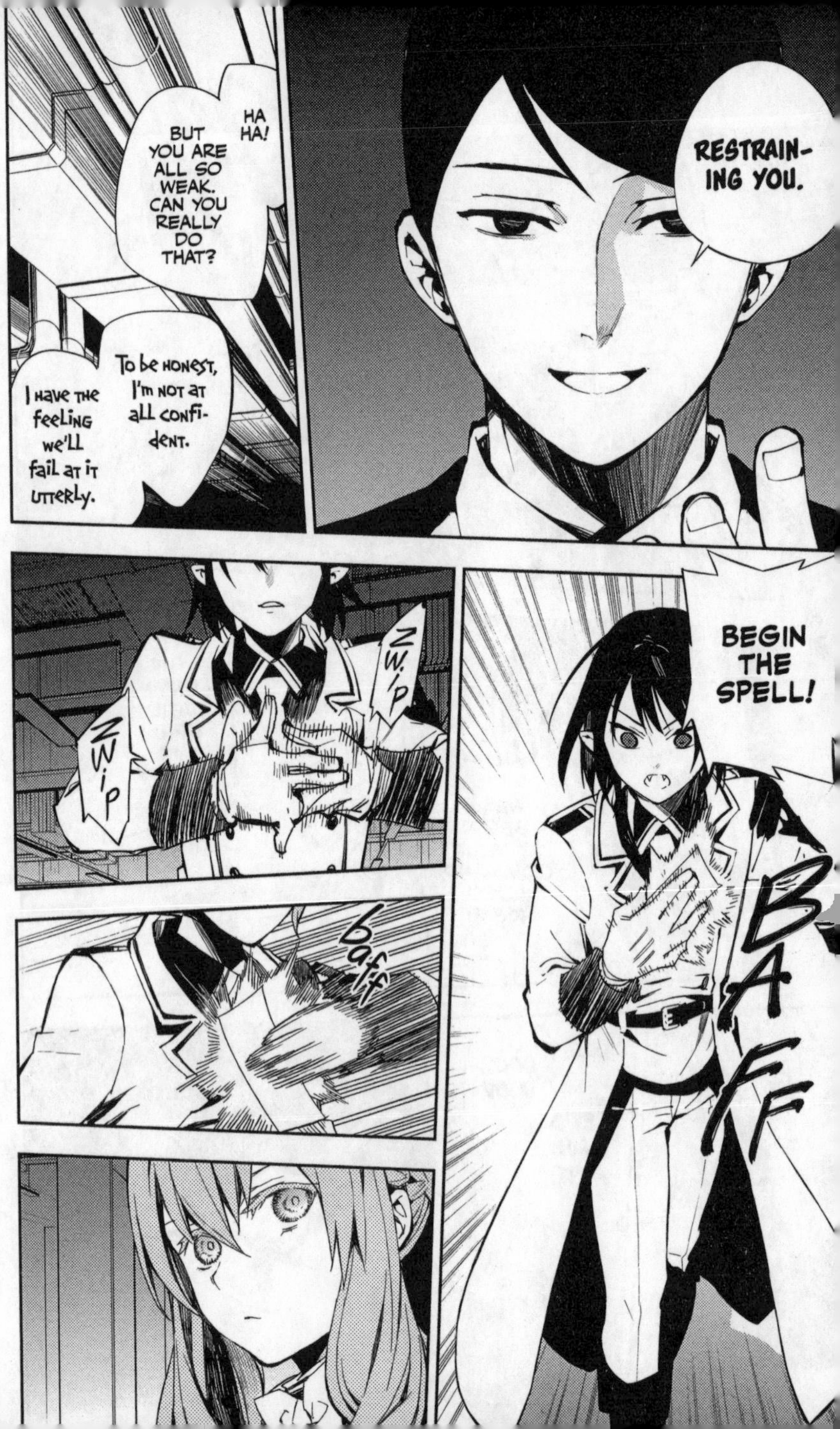
RESTRAIN-ING YOU.
HA HA! BUT YOU ARE ALL SO WEAK. CAN YOU REALLY DO THAT?
To be honest, I'm not at all confi-dent.
I have the feeling we'll fail at it utterly.
BEGIN THE SPELL!
BAFF
ZWIP
ZWIP
baff

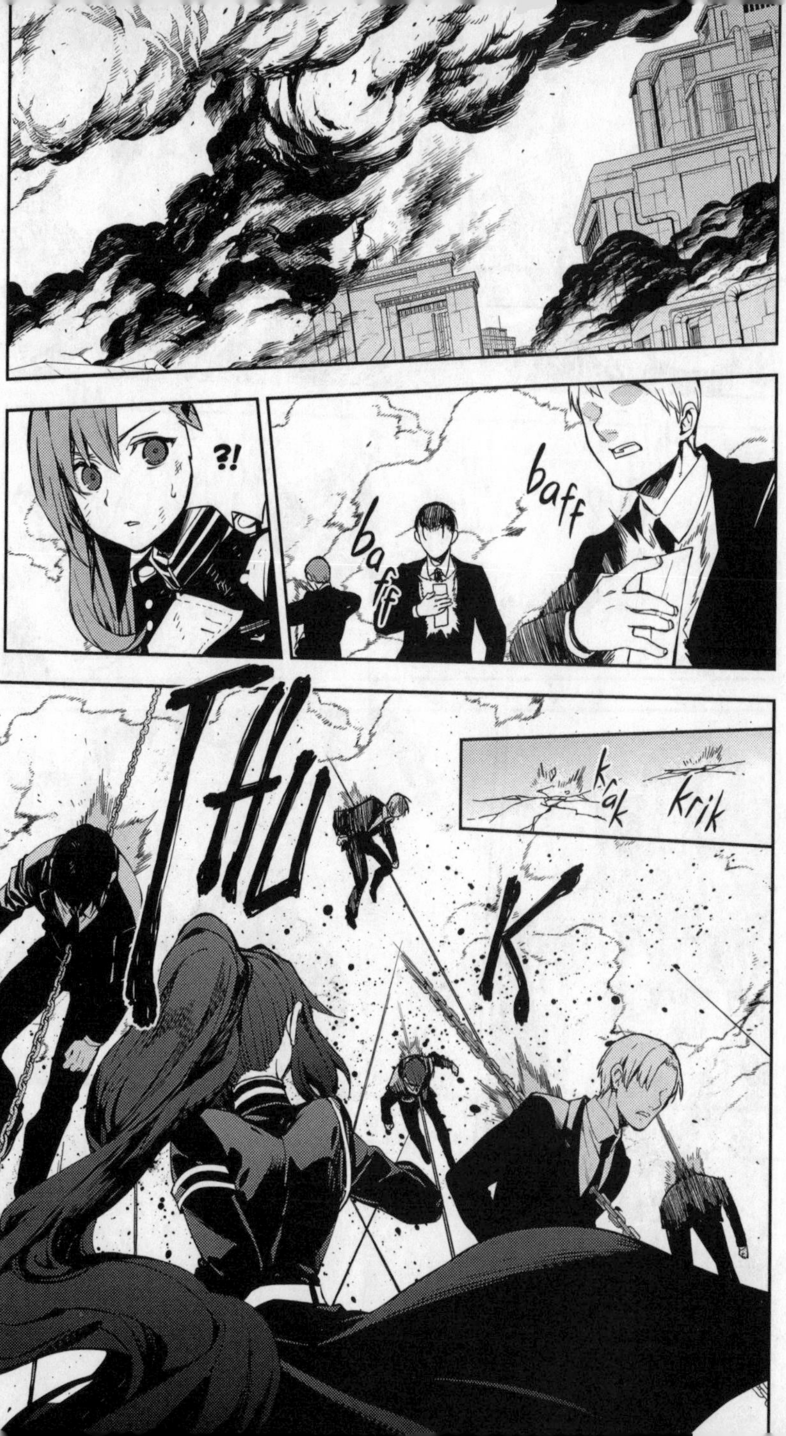
baff
baff
?!
krik
krak
THUK

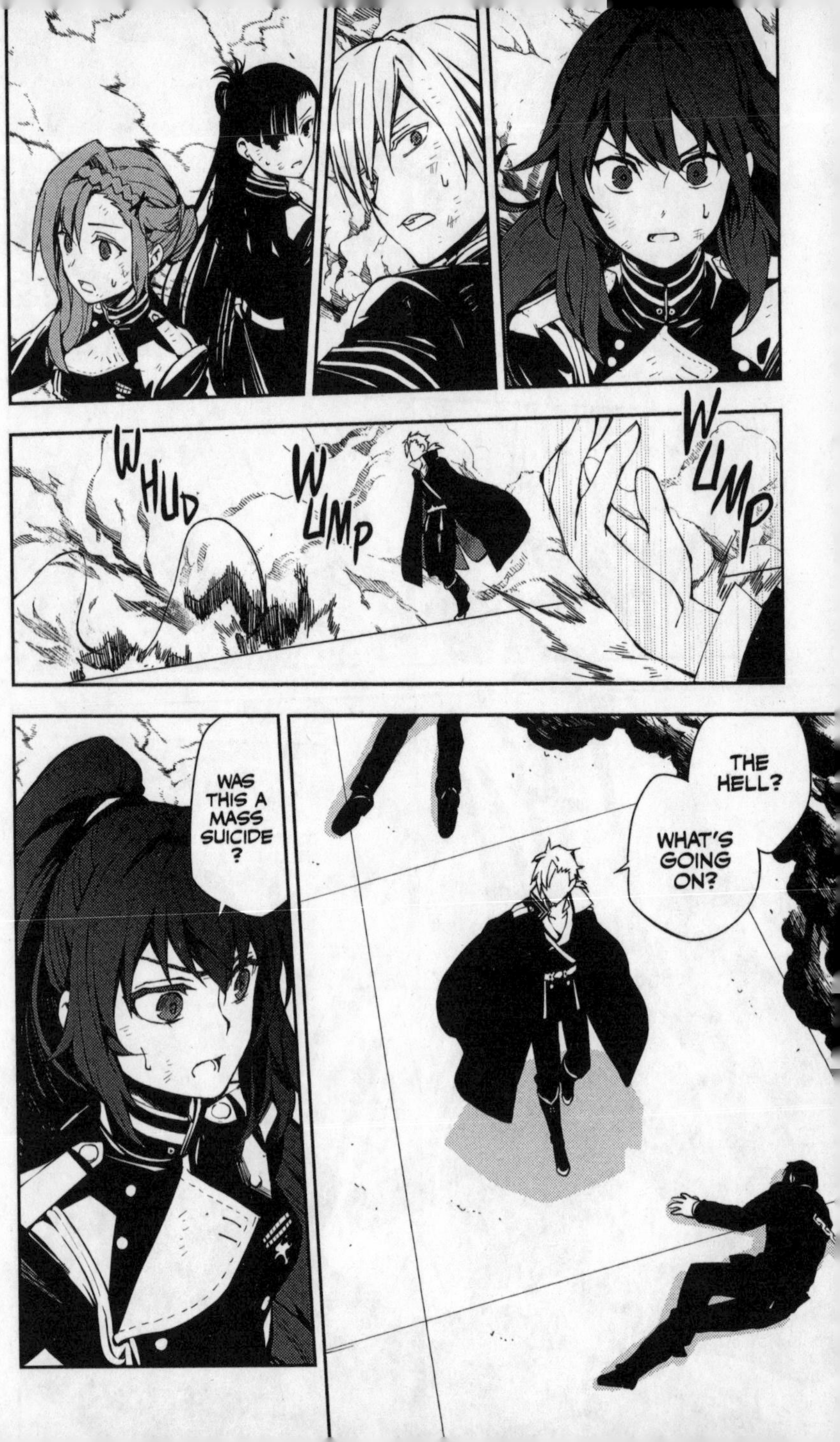
WUMP
WUMP
WHUD
THE HELL?
WHAT'S GOING ON?
WAS THIS A MASS SUICIDE?

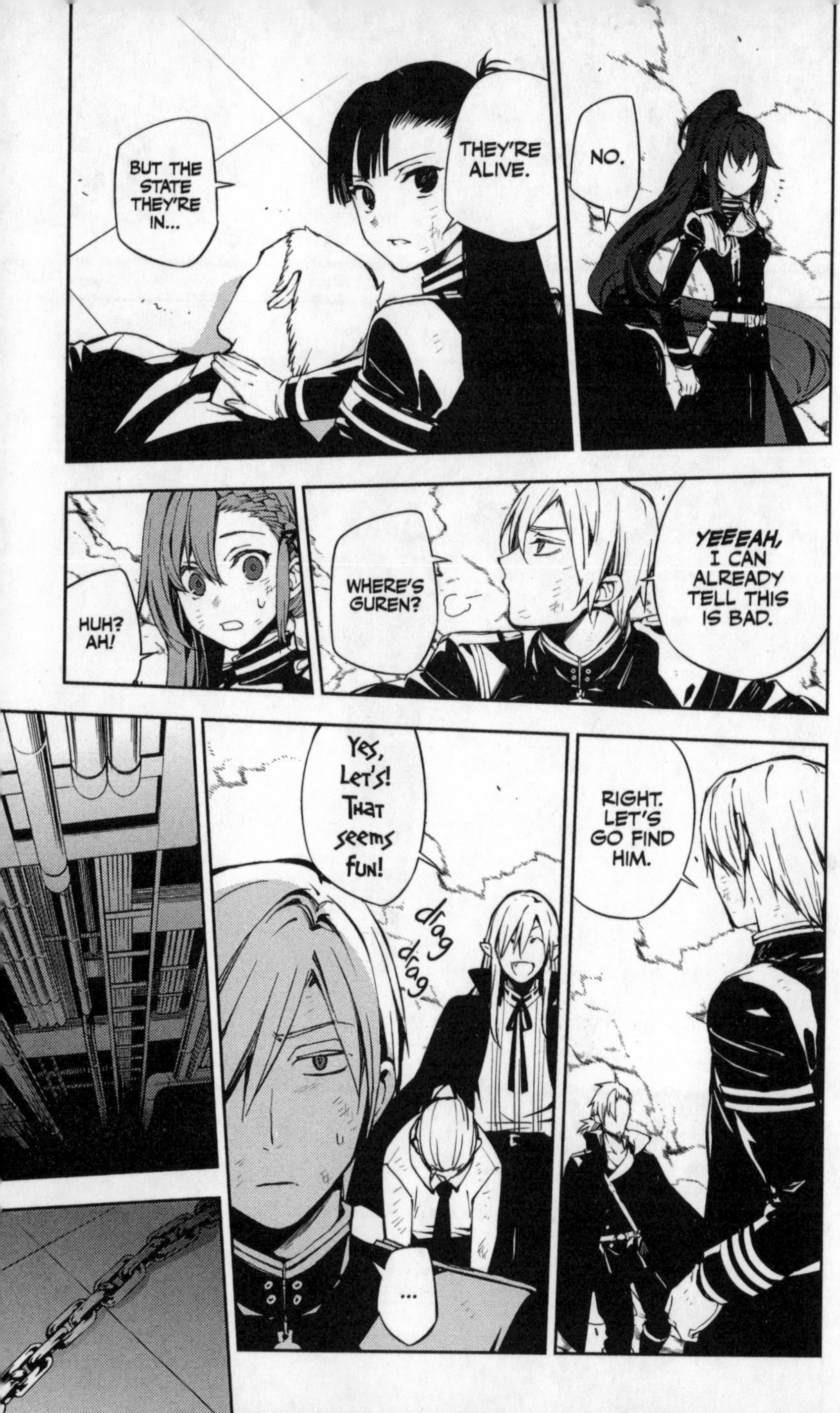
NO.
THEY'RE ALIVE.
BUT THE STATE THEY'RE IN...
YEEEAH, I CAN ALREADY TELL THIS IS BAD.
WHERE'S GUREN?
HUH? AH!
RIGHT. LET'S GO FIND HIM.
Yes, Let's! That seems fun!
drag drag
...

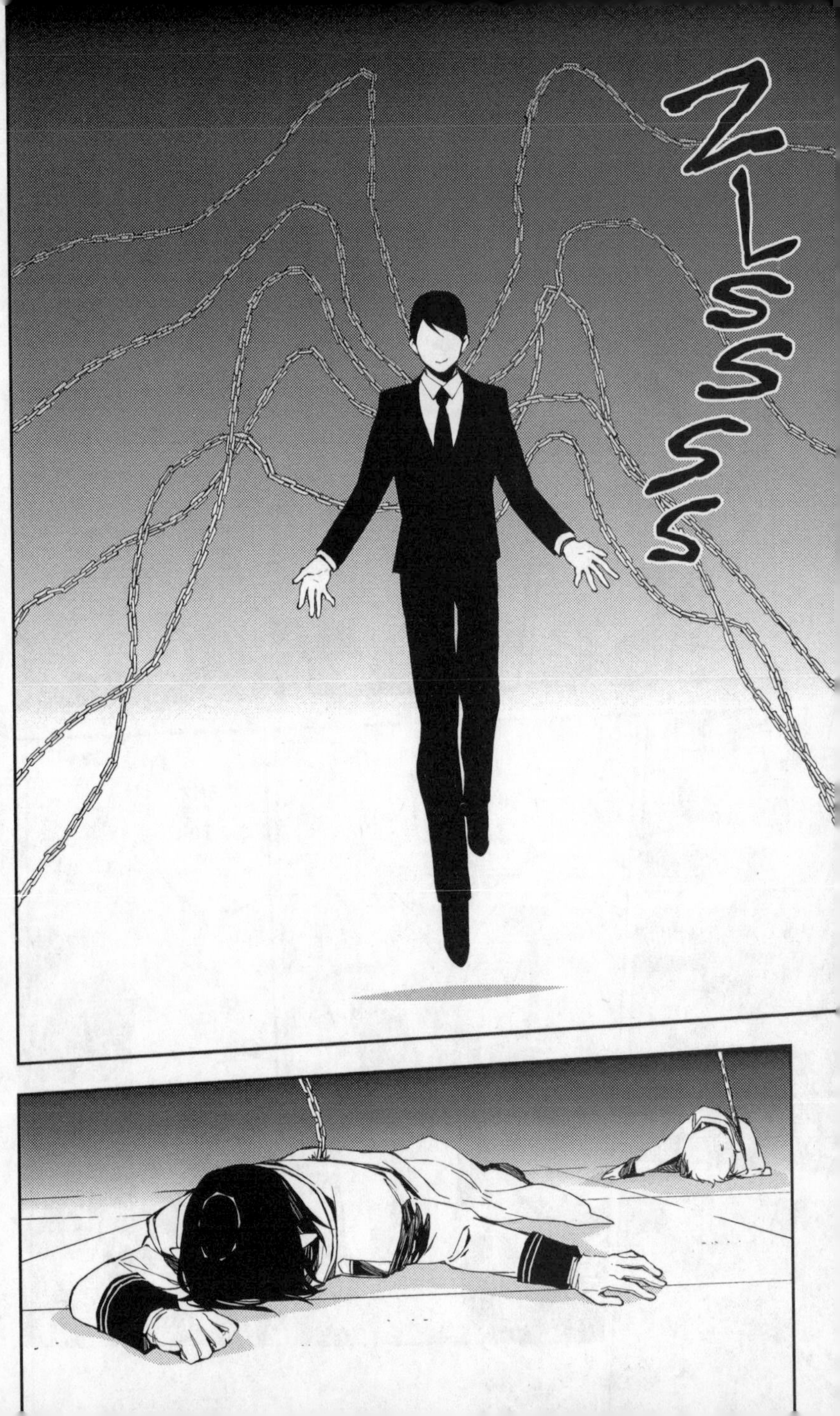
ZLSSSS

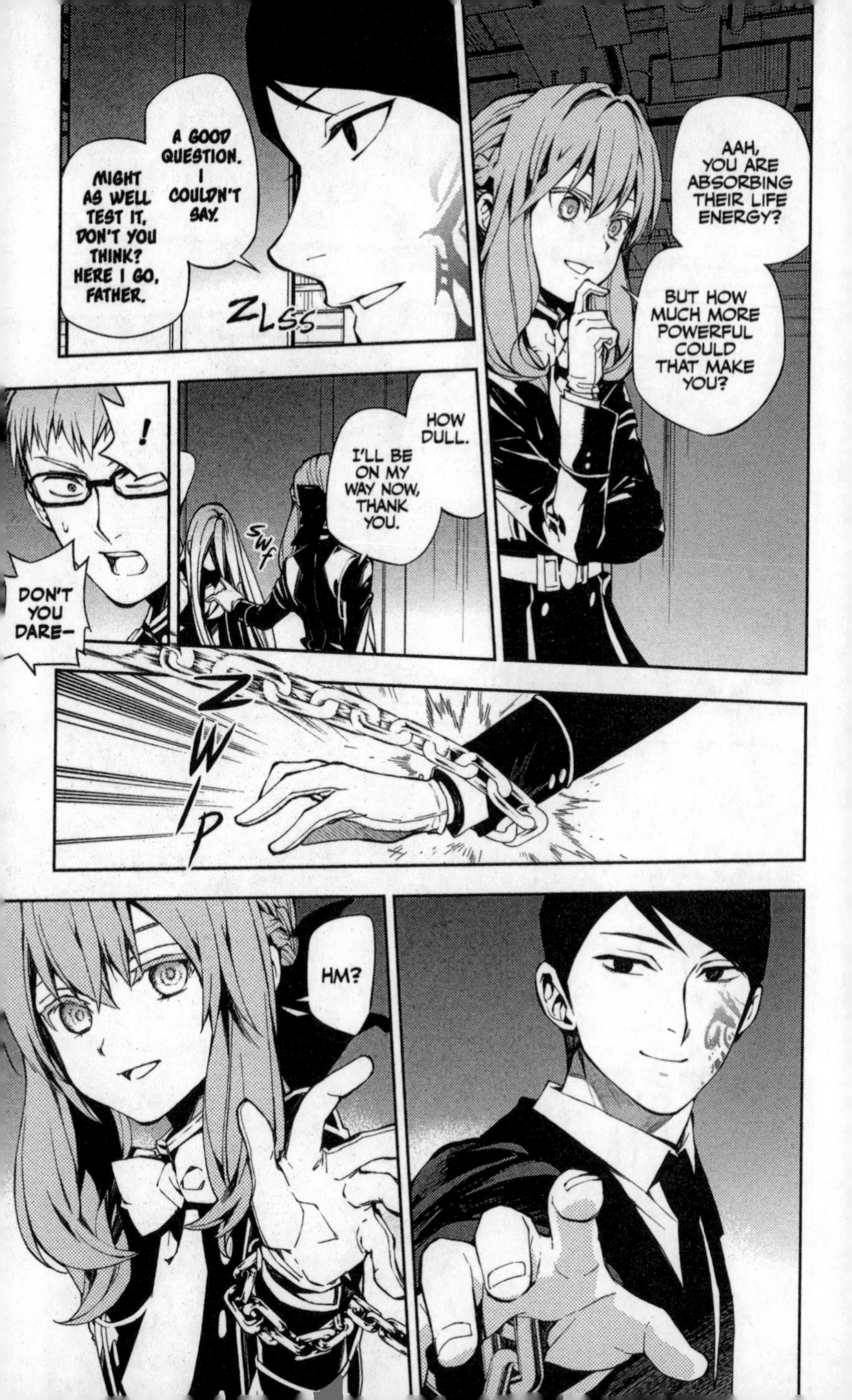
AAH, YOU ARE ABSORBING THEIR LIFE ENERGY?
BUT HOW MUCH MORE POWERFUL COULD THAT MAKE YOU?
A GOOD QUESTION. I COULDN'T SAY.
MIGHT AS WELL TEST IT, DON'T YOU THINK? HERE I GO, FATHER.
ZLSS
HOW DULL.
I'LL BE ON MY WAY NOW, THANK YOU.
SWF
!
DON'T YOU DARE–
ZWIP
HM?

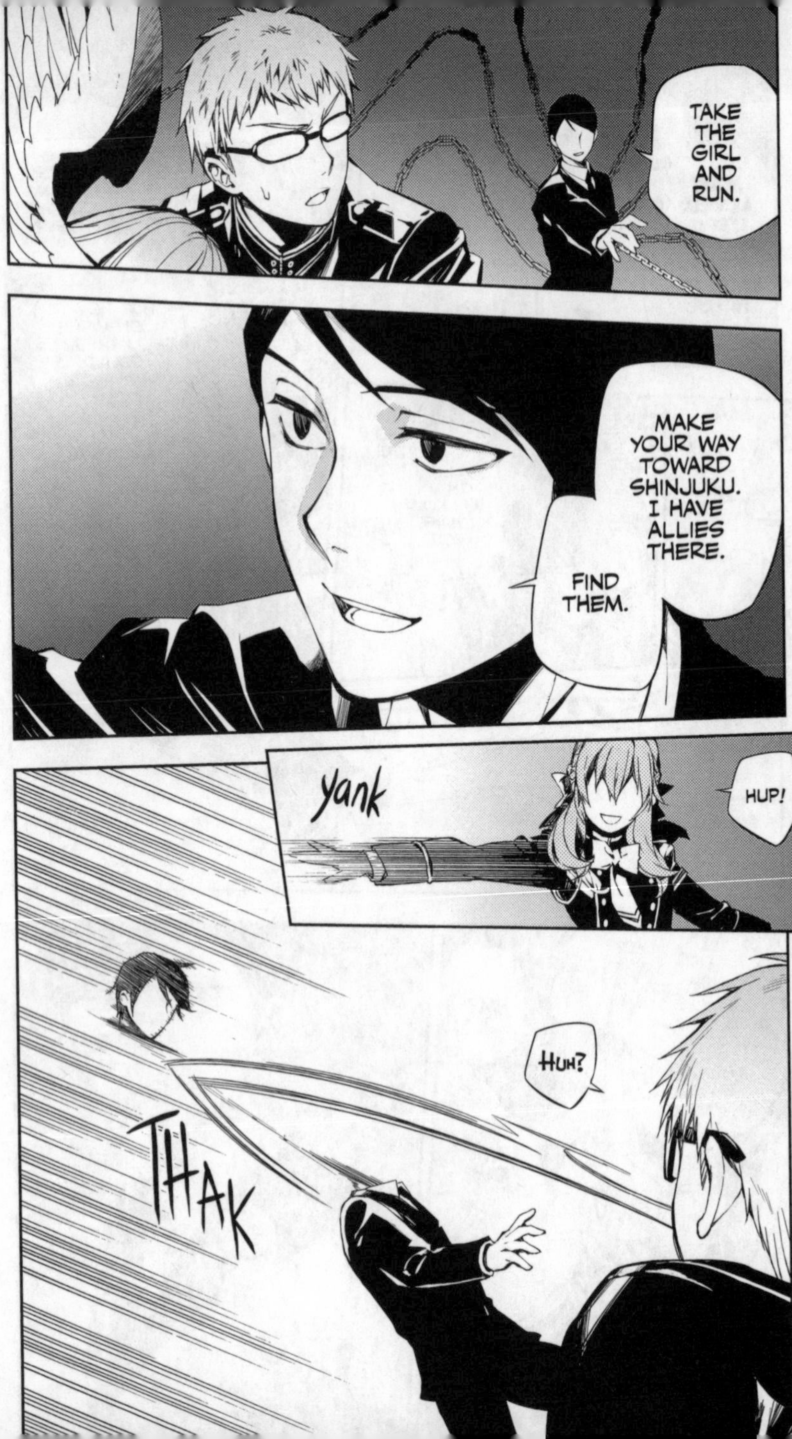
TAKE THE GIRL AND RUN.
MAKE YOUR WAY TOWARD SHINJUKU. I HAVE ALLIES THERE.
FIND THEM.
HUP!
yank
HUH?
THAK

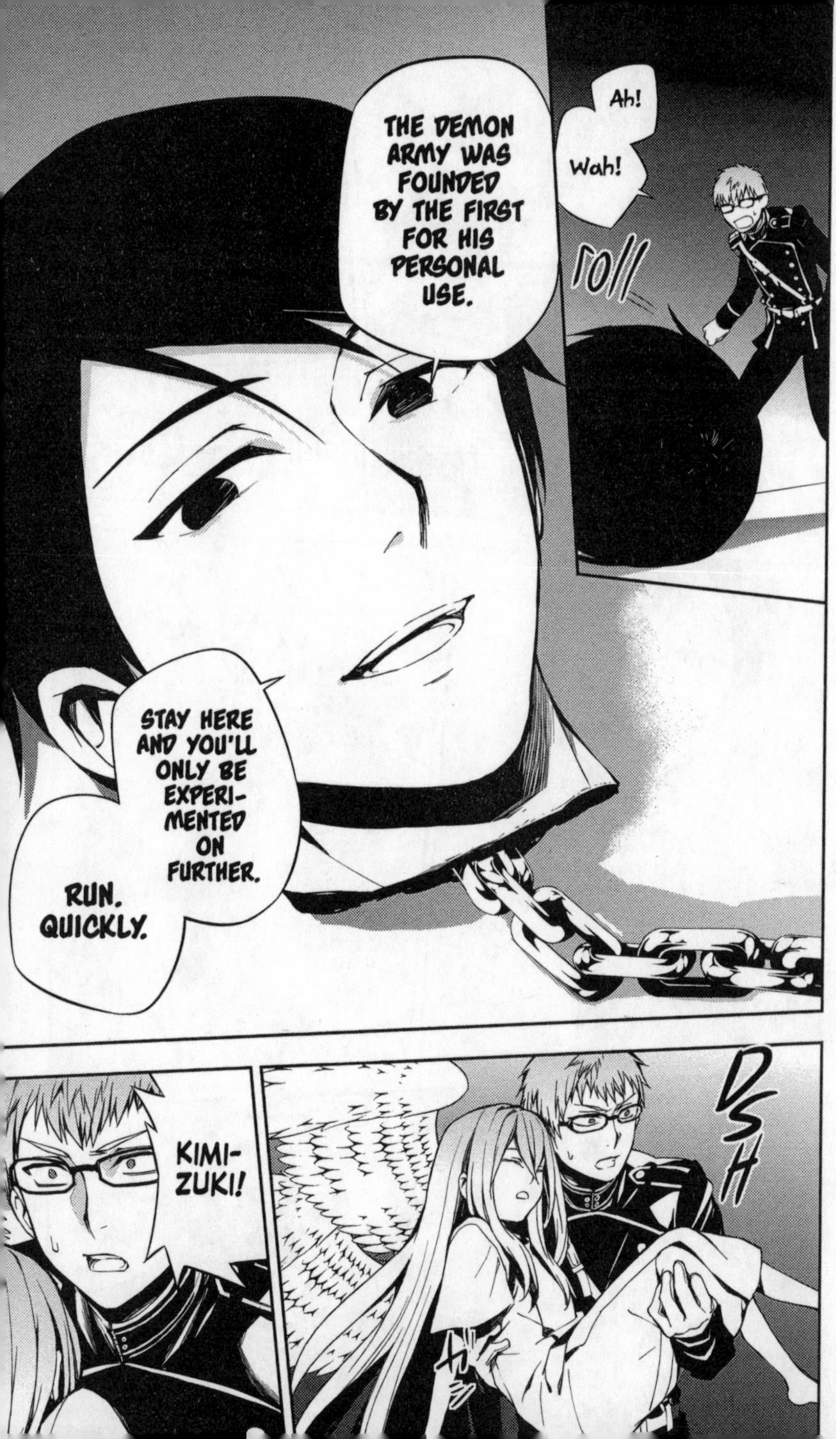
Ah!
Wah!
roll
THE DEMON ARMY WAS FOUNDED BY THE FIRST FOR HIS PERSONAL USE.
STAY HERE AND YOU'LL ONLY BE EXPERI-MENTED ON FURTHER.
RUN. QUICKLY.
DSH
KIMI-ZUKI!

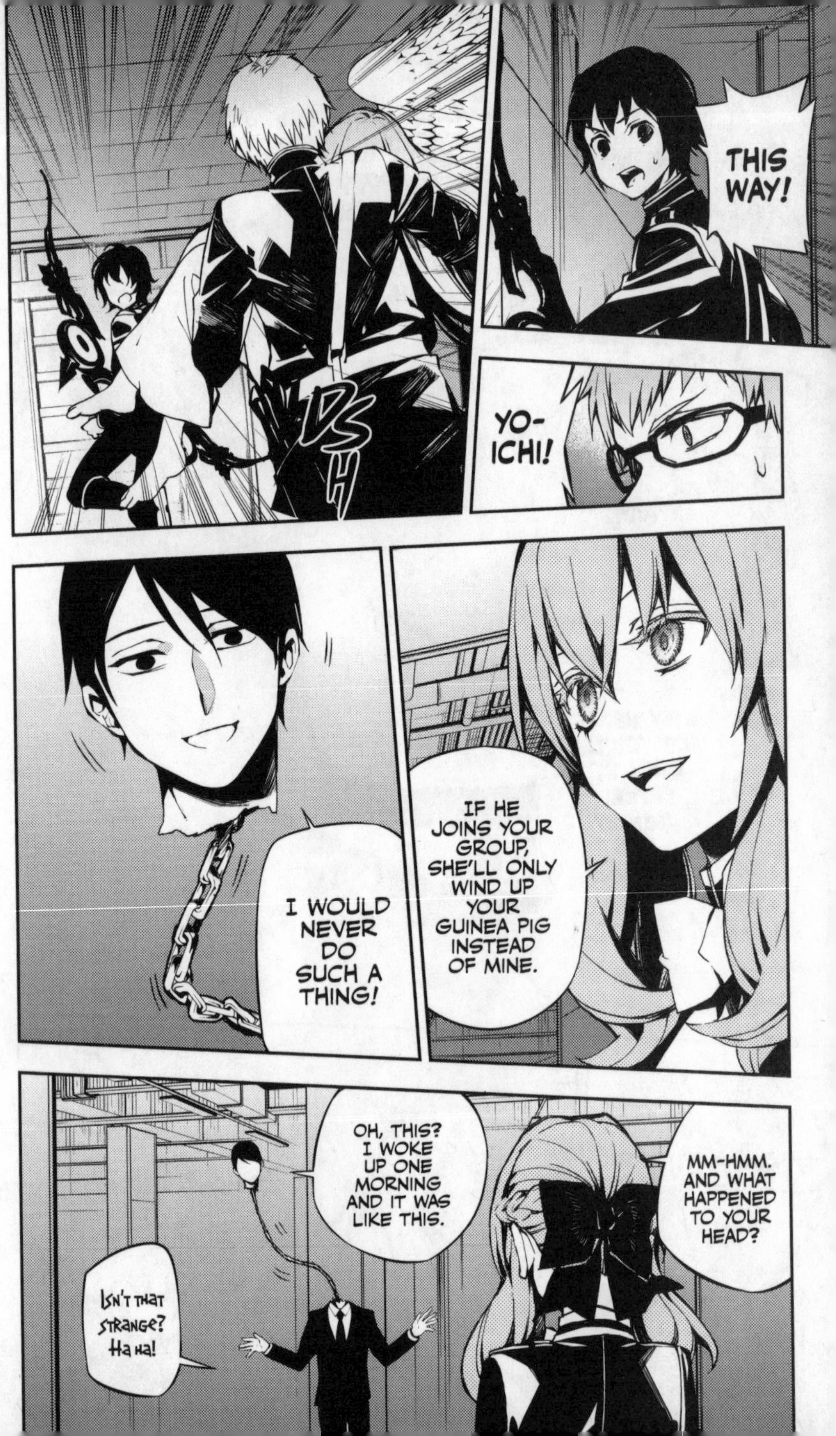
THIS WAY!
YO-ICHI!
DSH
IF HE JOINS YOUR GROUP, SHE'LL ONLY WIND UP YOUR GUINEA PIG INSTEAD OF MINE.
I WOULD NEVER DO SUCH A THING!
MM-HMM. AND WHAT HAPPENED TO YOUR HEAD?
OH, THIS? I WOKE UP ONE MORNING AND IT WAS LIKE THIS.
ISN'T THAT STRANGE? HA HA!

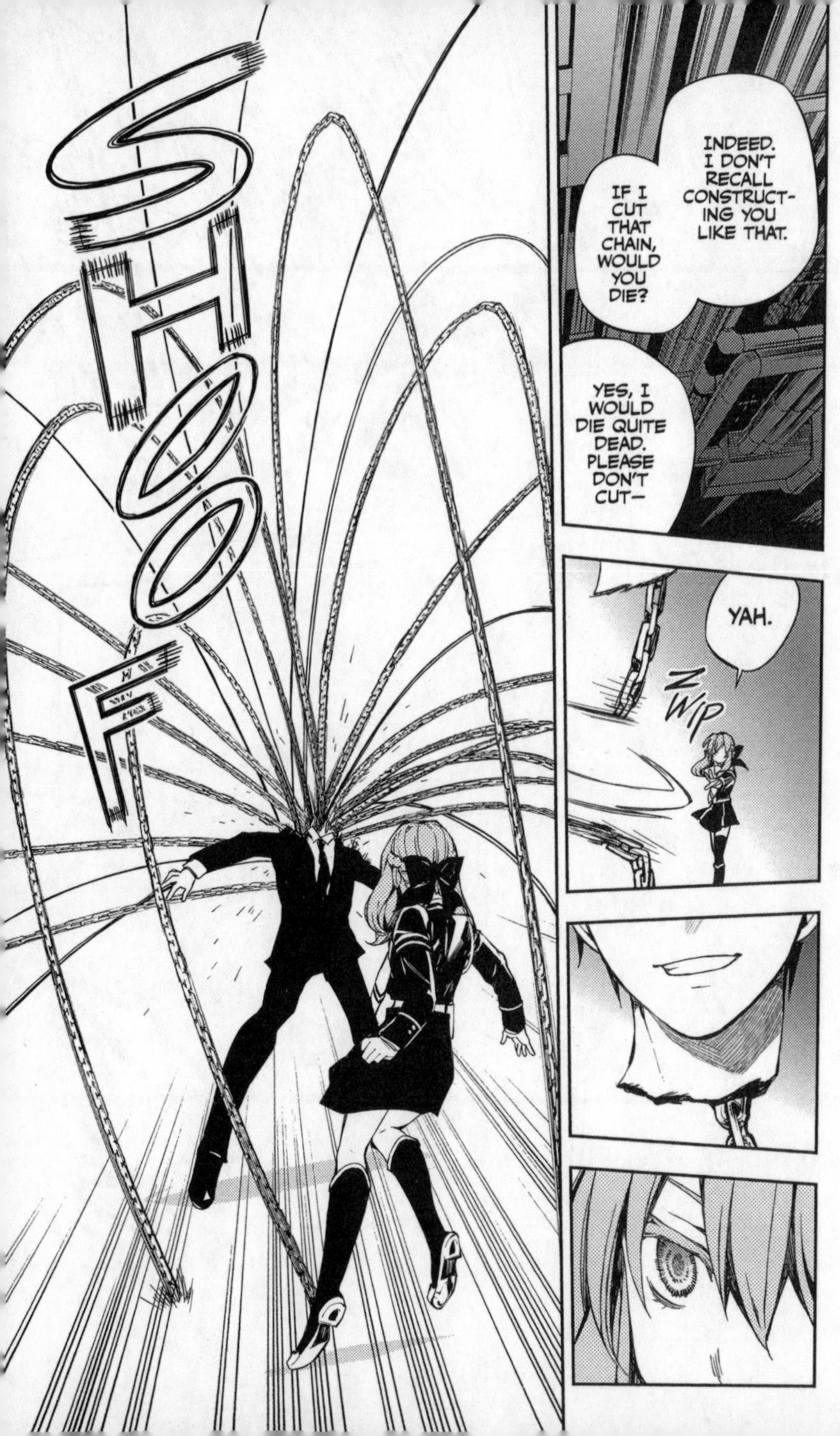
INDEED. I DON'T RECALL CONSTRUCT-ING YOU LIKE THAT.
IF I CUT THAT CHAIN, WOULD YOU DIE?
YES, I WOULD DIE QUITE DEAD. PLEASE DON'T CUT—
YAH.
ZWIP
SHOOF

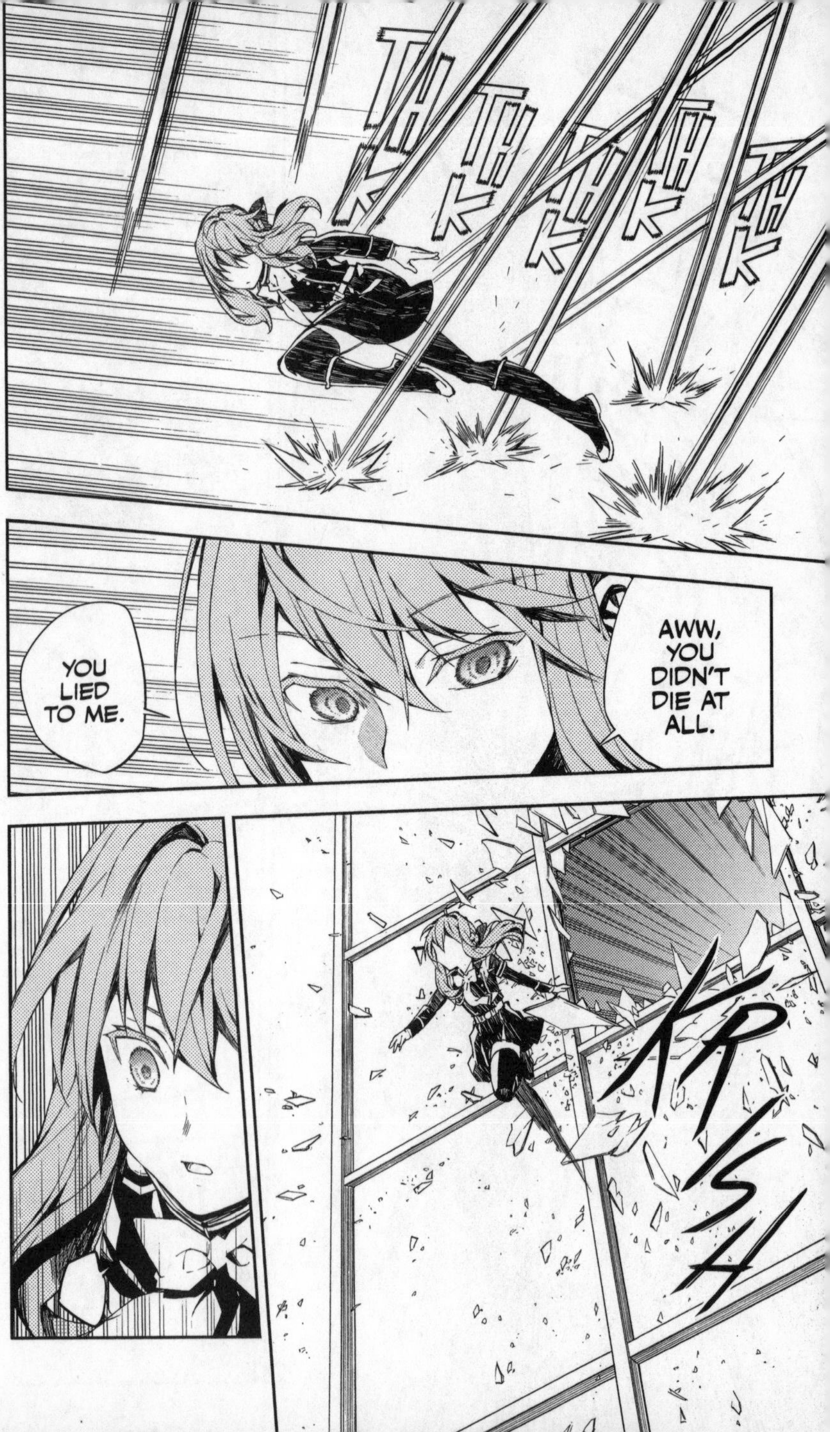
THK
THK
THK
THK
THK
AWW, YOU DIDN'T DIE AT ALL.
YOU LIED TO ME.
KRISH

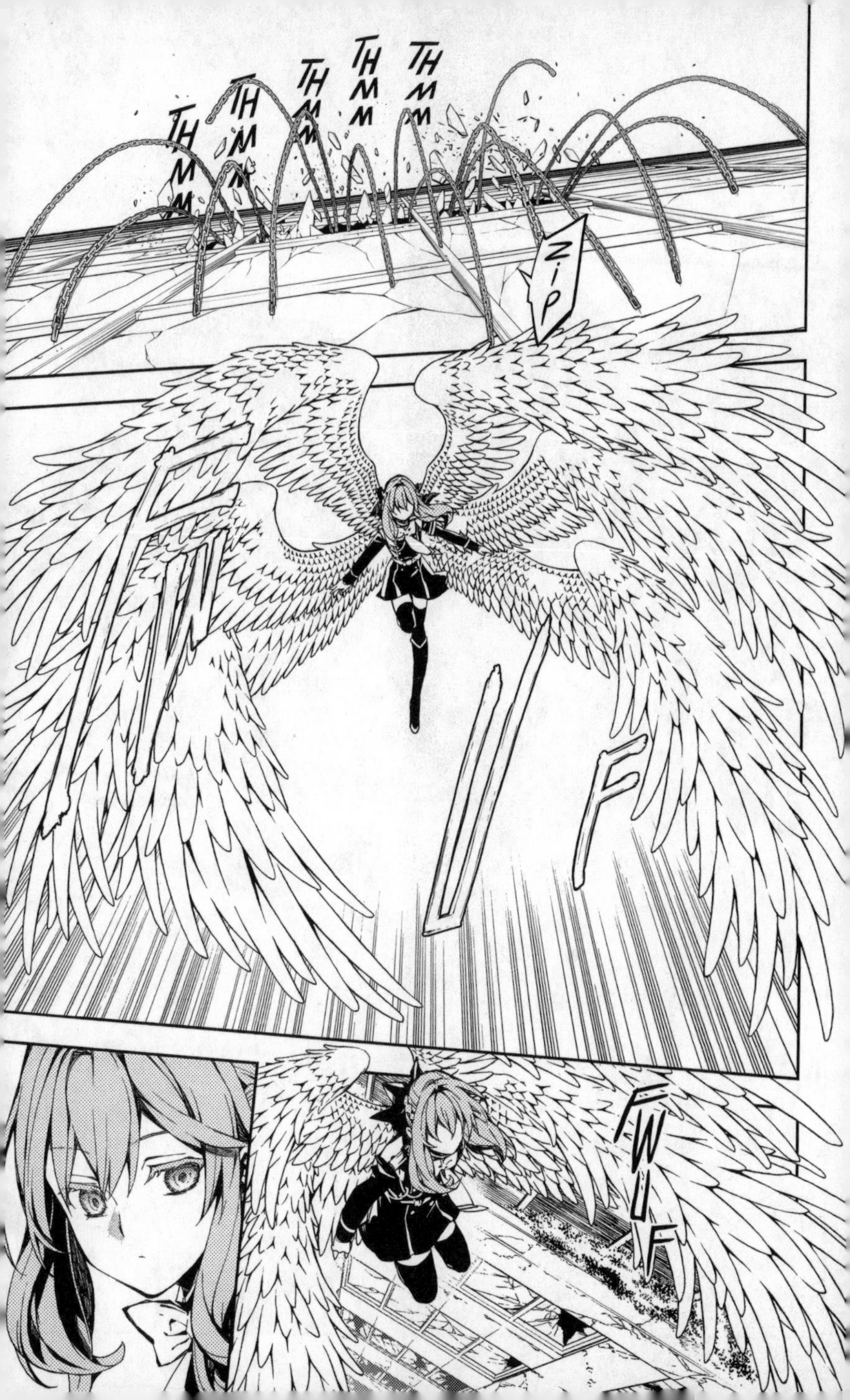
THMM
THMM
THMM
THMM
THMM
ZIP
FWUF

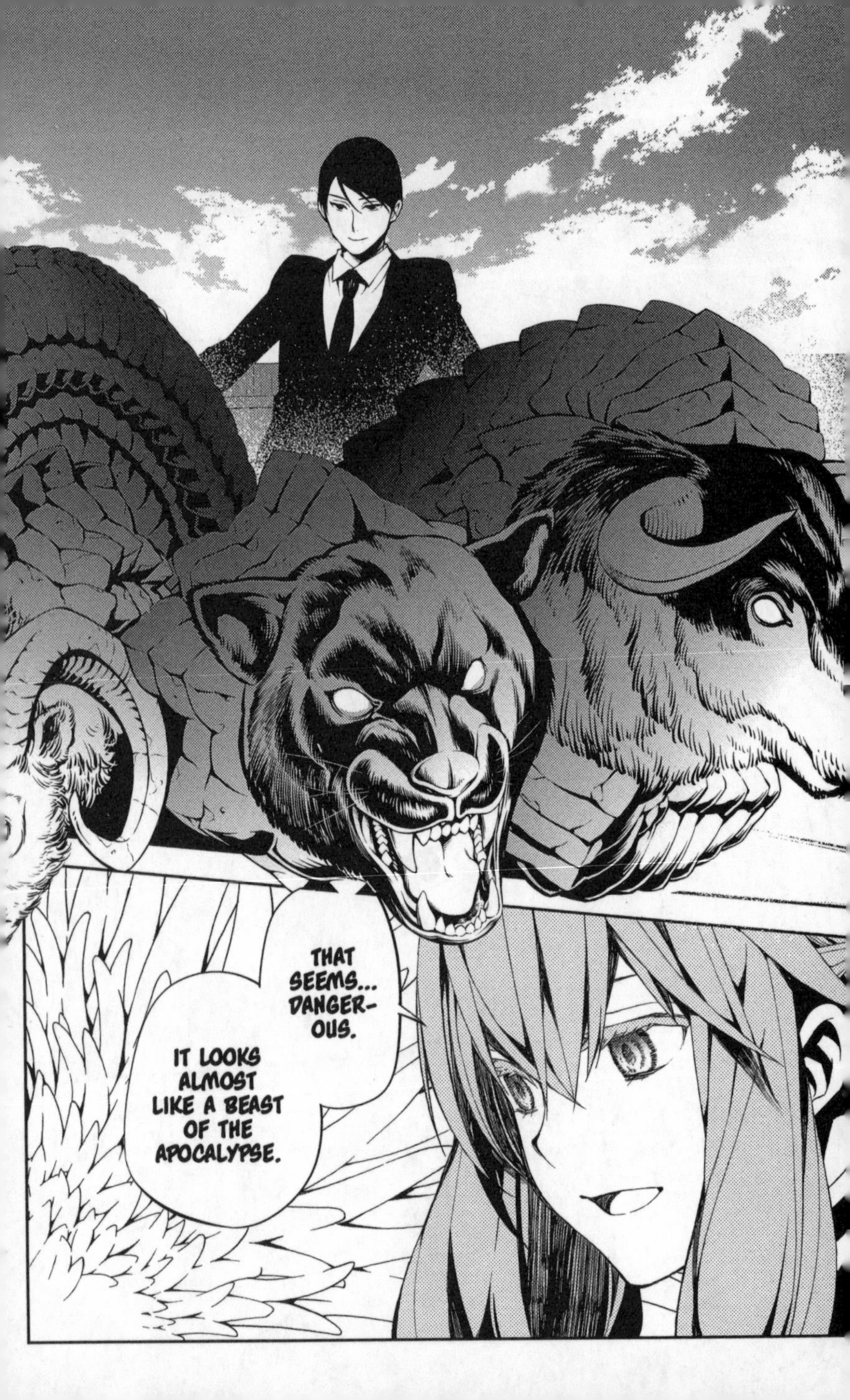
THAT SEEMS... DANGER-OUS.
IT LOOKS ALMOST LIKE A BEAST OF THE APOCALYPSE.

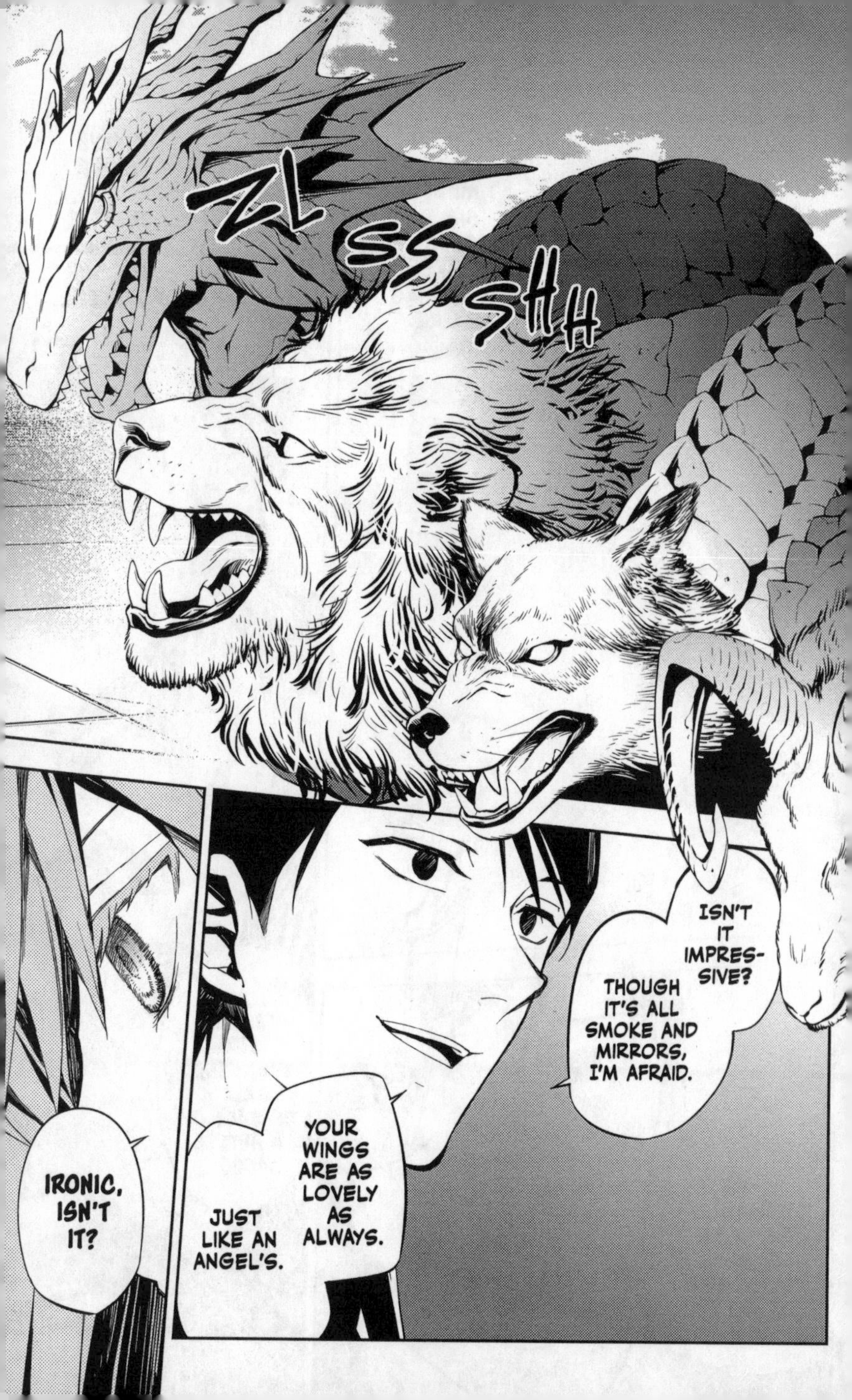
ZLSSSHH
ISN'T IT IMPRESSIVE?
THOUGH IT'S ALL SMOKE AND MIRRORS, I'M AFRAID.
YOUR WINGS ARE AS LOVELY AS ALWAYS.
JUST LIKE AN ANGEL'S.
IRONIC, ISN'T IT?

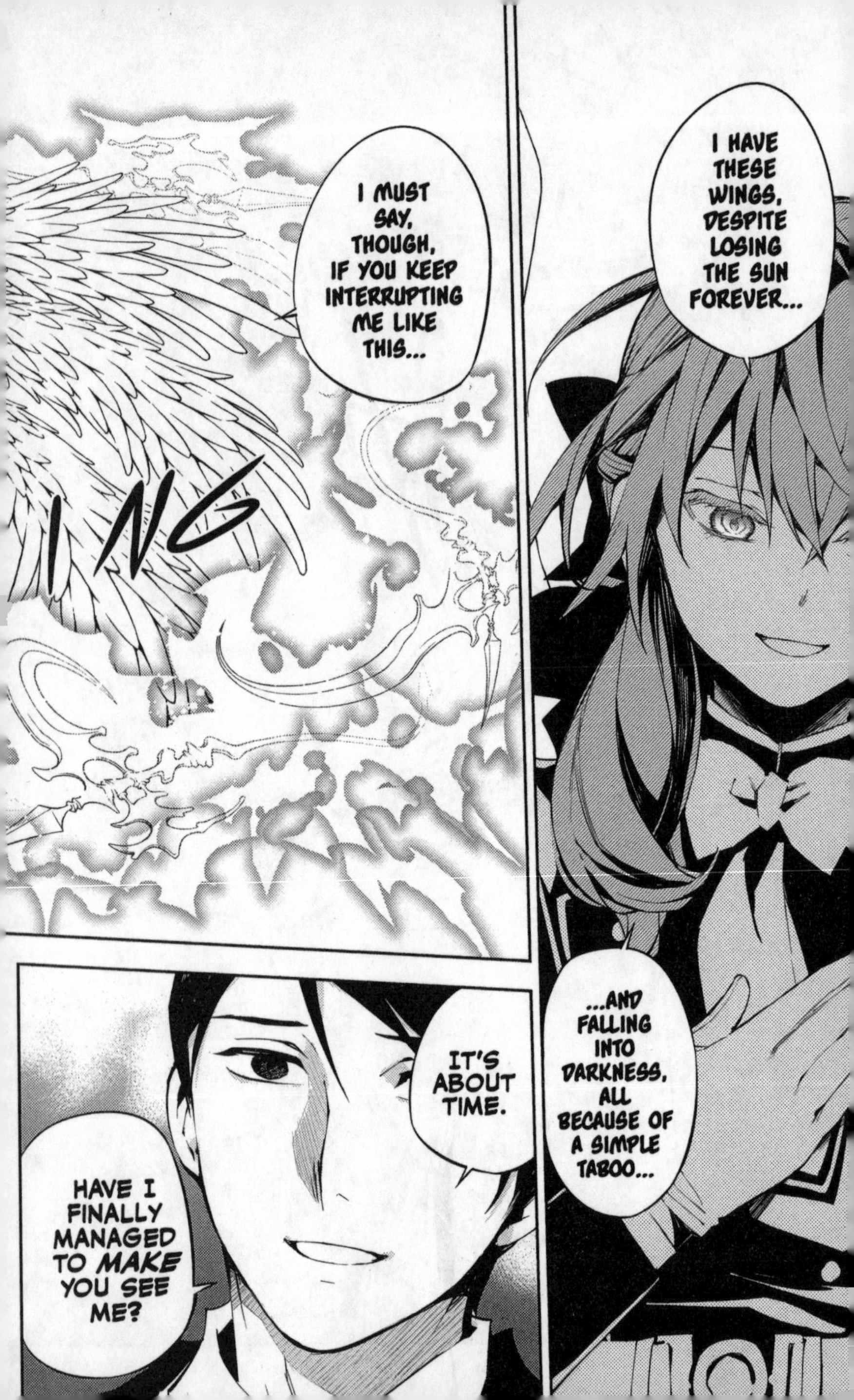
I HAVE THESE WINGS, DESPITE LOSING THE SUN FOREVER...
...AND FALLING INTO DARKNESS, ALL BECAUSE OF A SIMPLE TABOO...
I MUST SAY, THOUGH, IF YOU KEEP INTERRUPTING ME LIKE THIS...
ING
IT'S ABOUT TIME.
HAVE I FINALLY MANAGED TO *MAKE* YOU SEE ME?

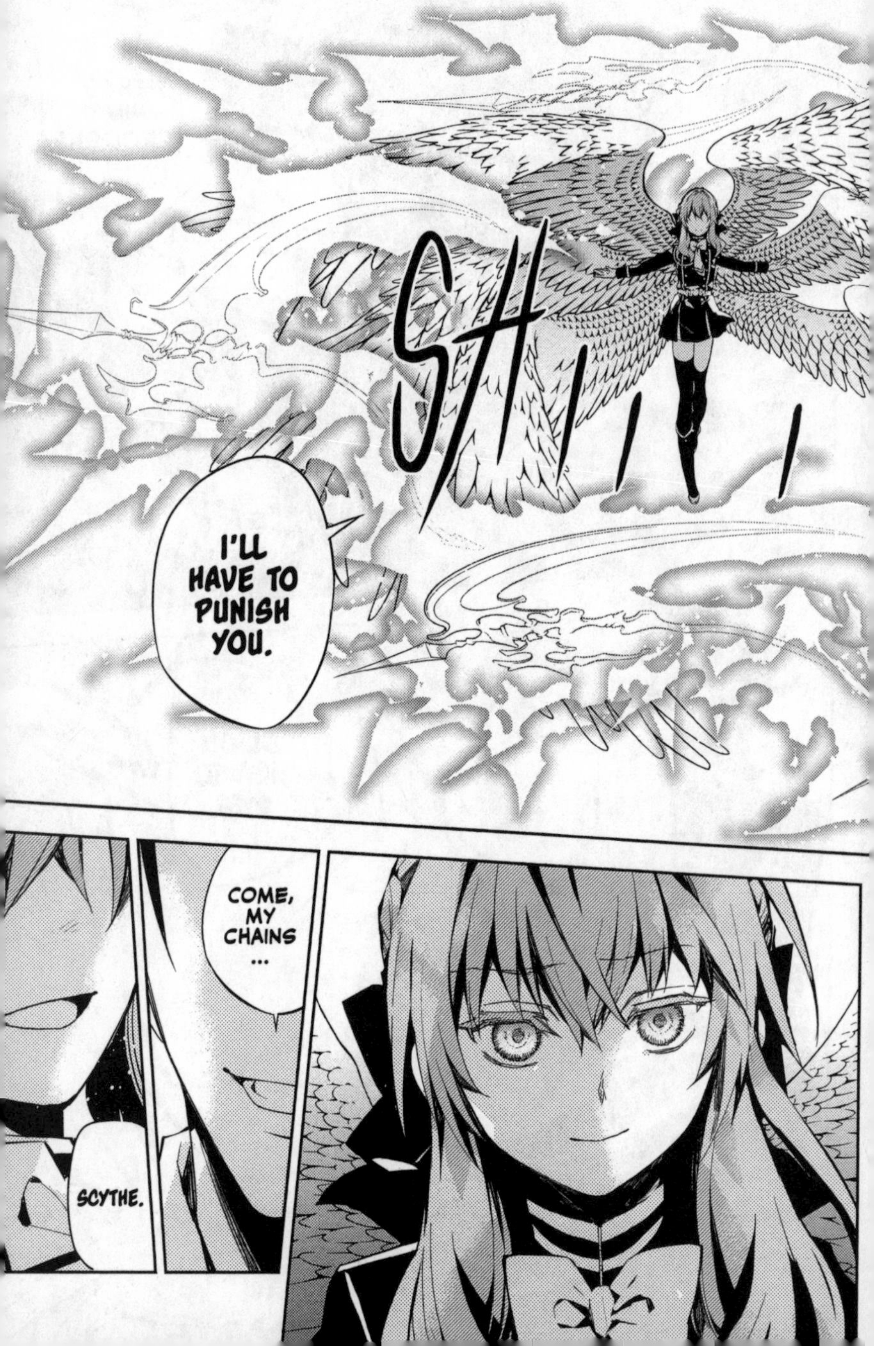
SH
I'LL HAVE TO PUNISH YOU.
COME, MY CHAINS ...
SCYTHE.

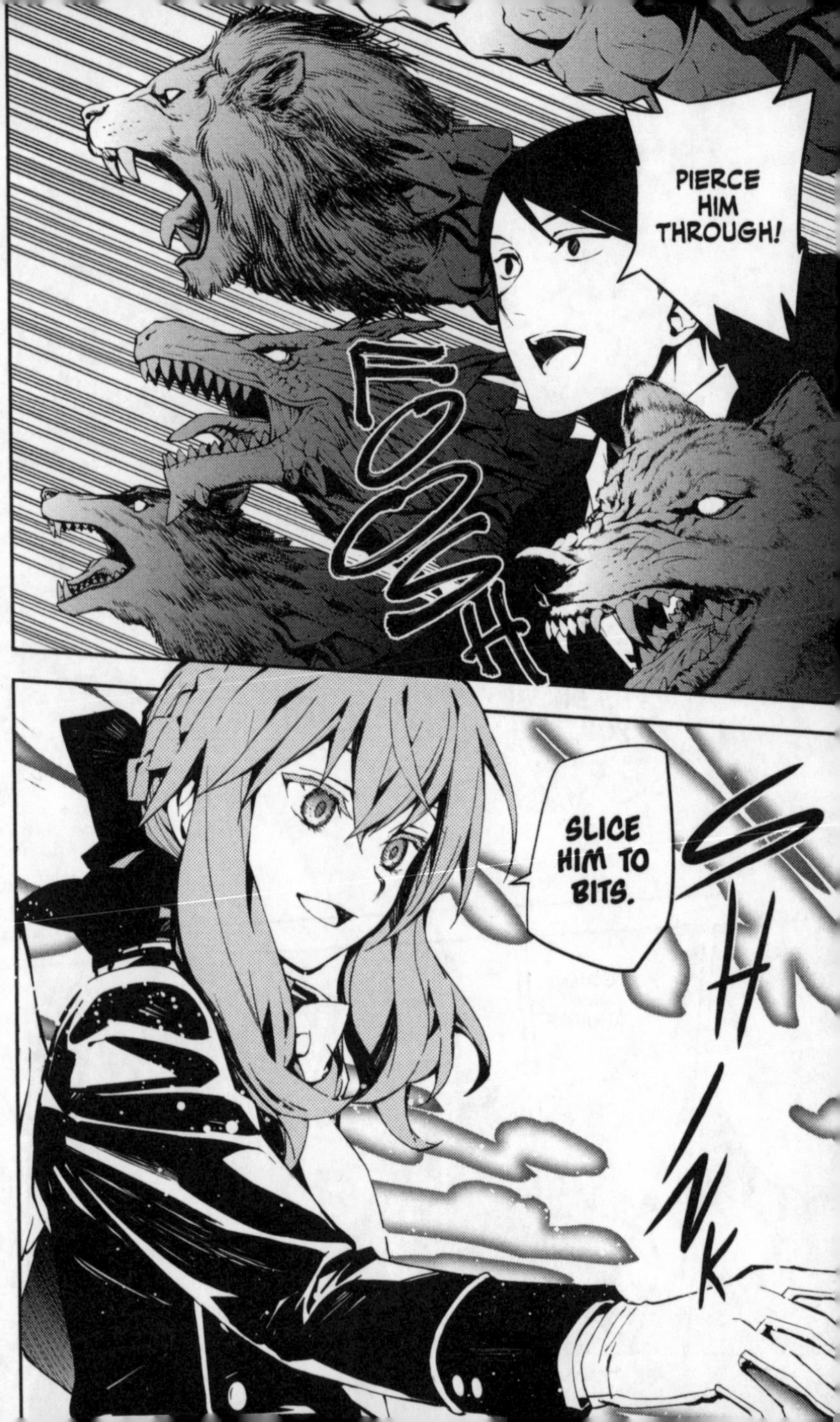
PIERCE HIM THROUGH!
FOOSH
SLICE HIM TO BITS.
SHINK

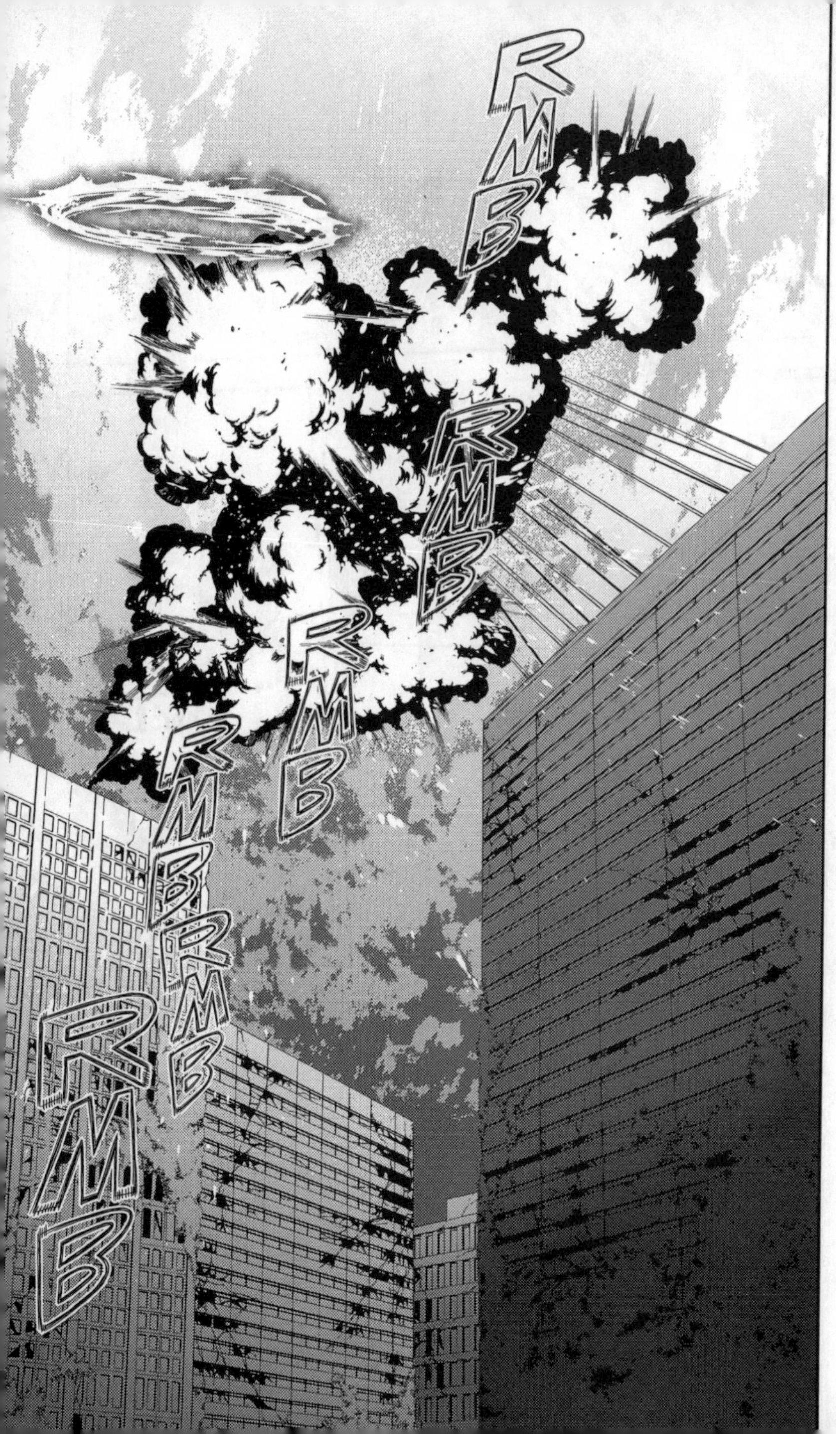
RMMB
RMMB
RMMB
RMMB
RMMB
RMMB

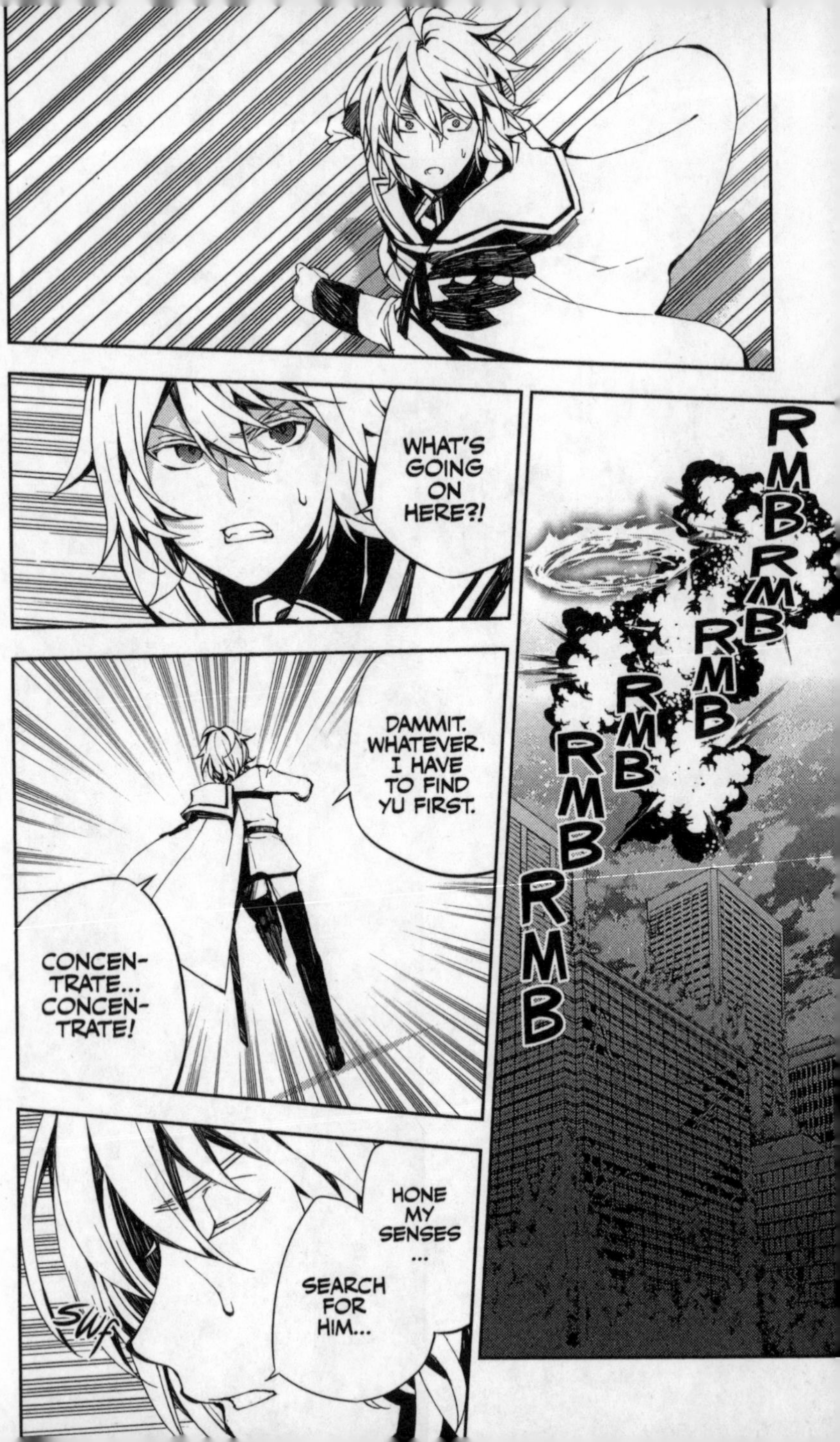
RMBRMB
RMB
RMB
RMBRMB
WHAT'S GOING ON HERE?!
DAMMIT. WHATEVER. I HAVE TO FIND YU FIRST.
CONCEN-TRATE... CONCEN-TRATE!
HONE MY SENSES ...
SEARCH FOR HIM...
SWF

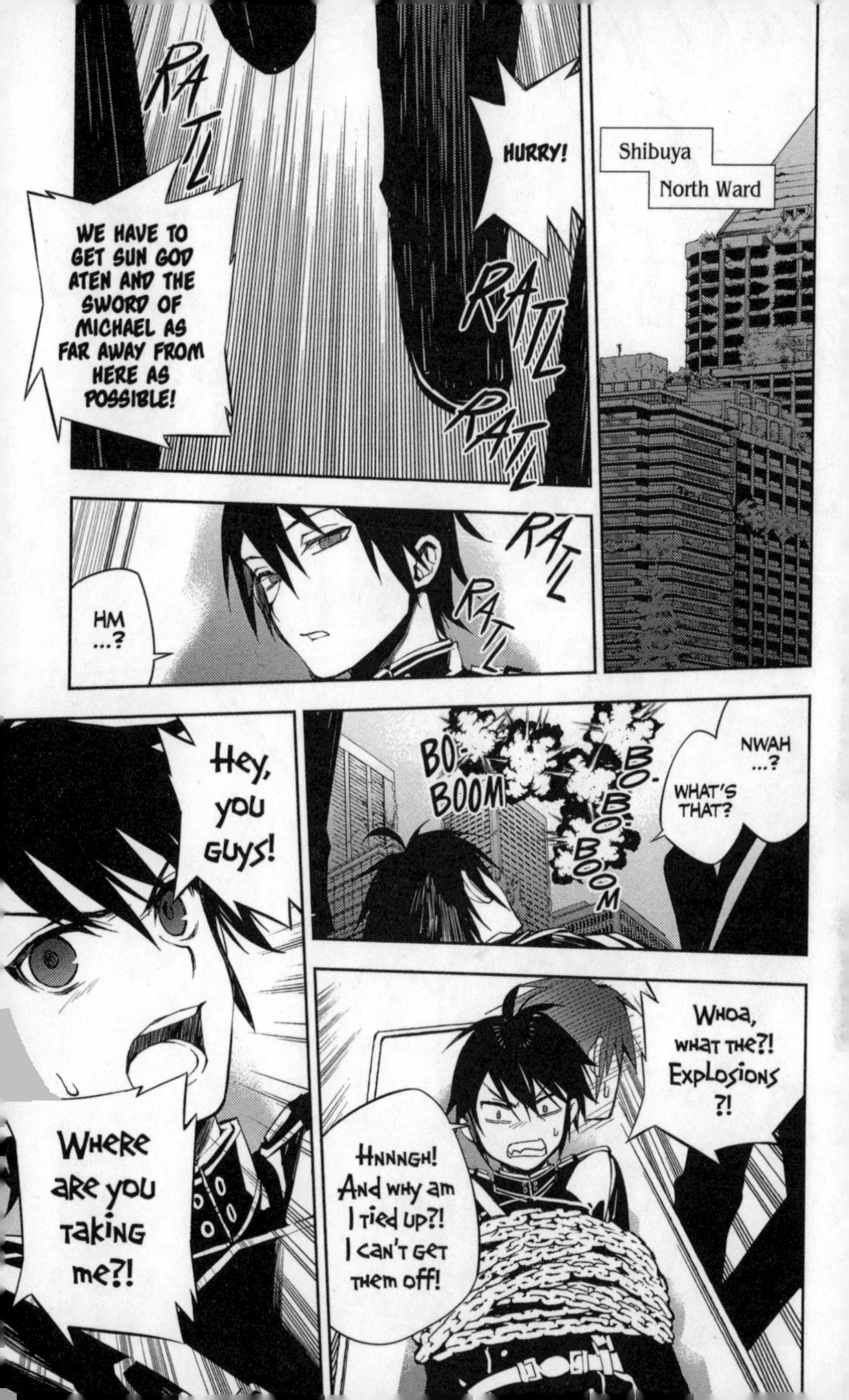

Shibuya
North Ward
HURRY!
RATTL
RATTL
RATTL
WE HAVE TO GET SUN GOD ATEN AND THE SWORD OF MICHAEL AS FAR AWAY FROM HERE AS POSSIBLE!
RATTL
RATTL
HM ...?
NWAH ...?
WHAT'S THAT?
BO-BOOM
BO-BO-BO-BOOM
Whoa, what the?! Explosions?!
Hnnngh! And why am I tied up?! I can't get them off!
Hey, you guys!
Where are you taking me?!

blink

AHA! FOUND HIM!

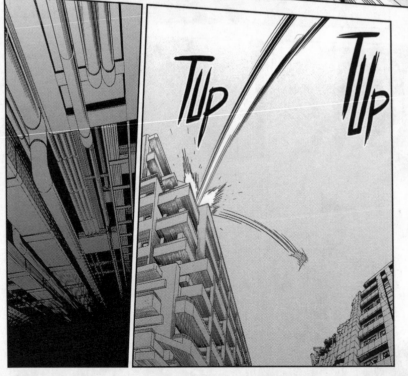

TUP

TUP

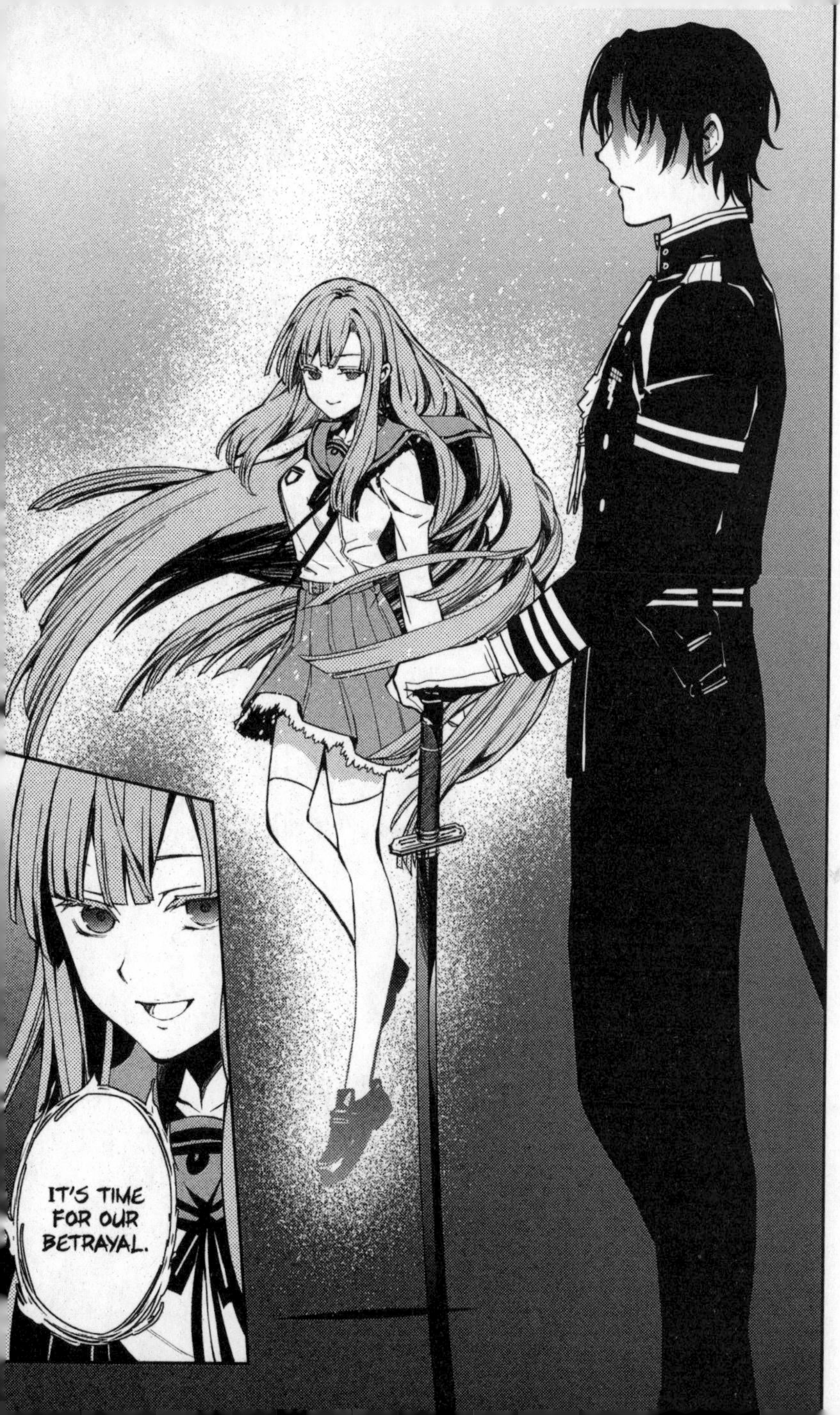
IT'S TIME FOR OUR BETRAYAL.

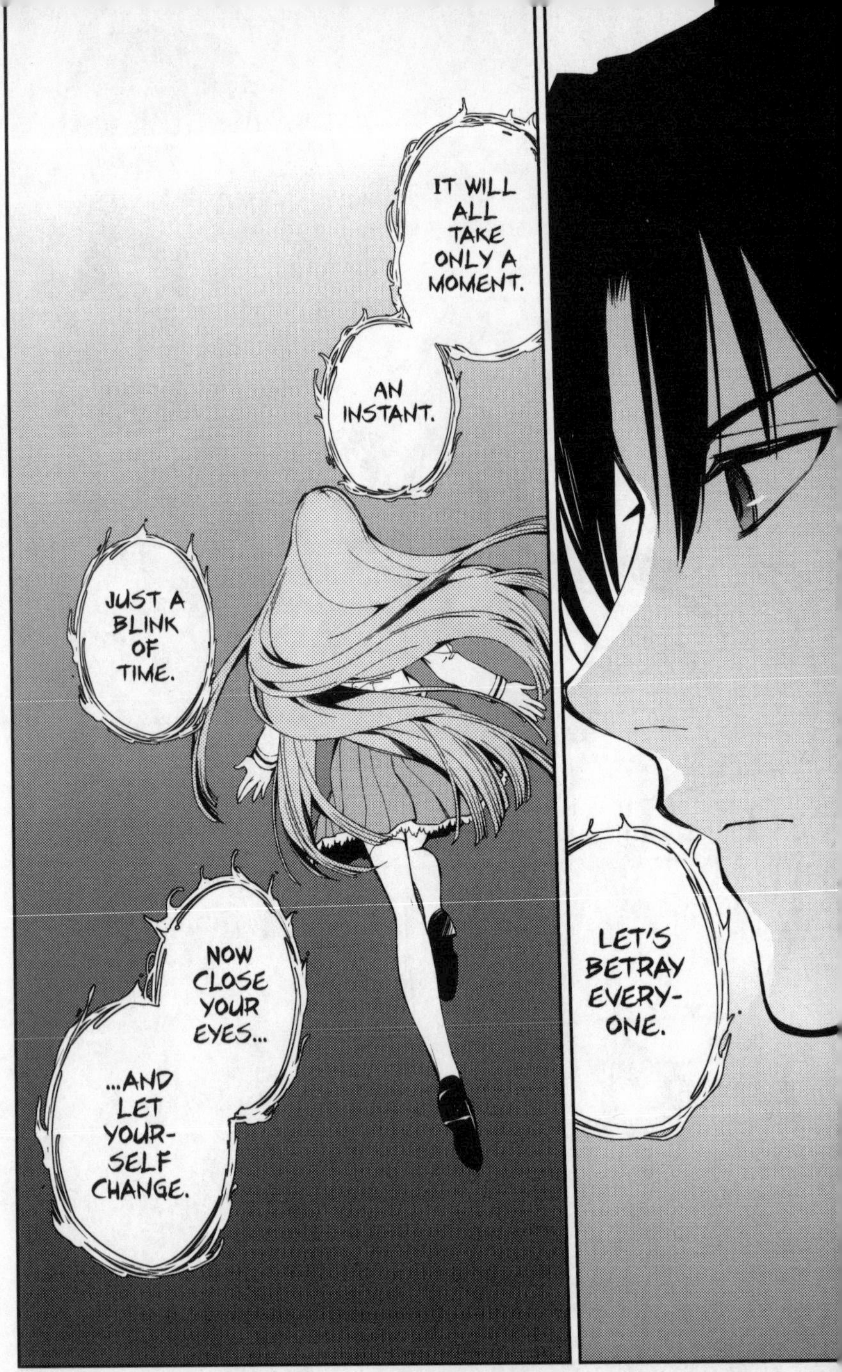
LET'S BETRAY EVERY-ONE.
IT WILL ALL TAKE ONLY A MOMENT.
AN INSTANT.
JUST A BLINK OF TIME.
NOW CLOSE YOUR EYES...
...AND LET YOUR-SELF CHANGE.

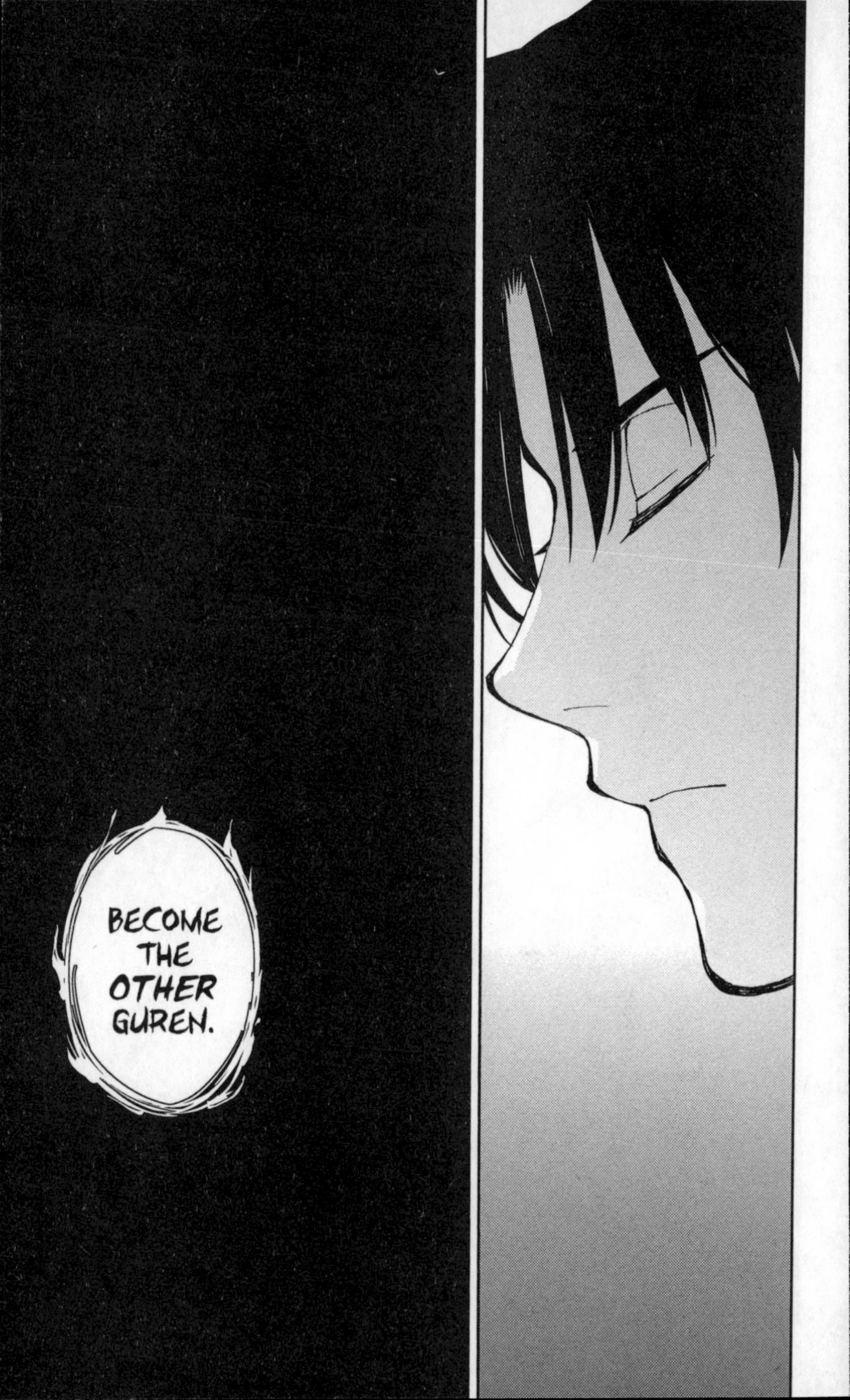
BECOME THE OTHER GUREN.

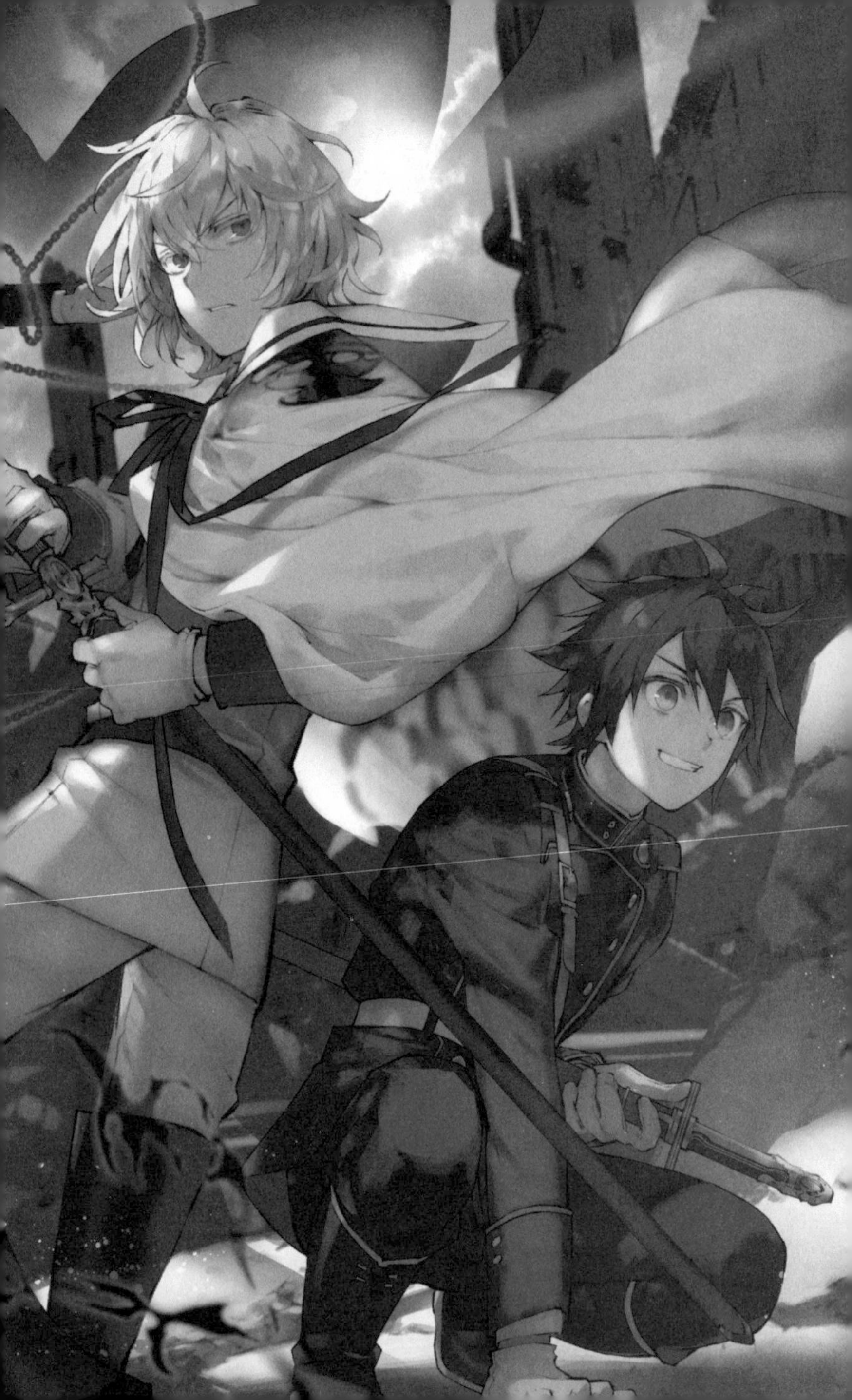

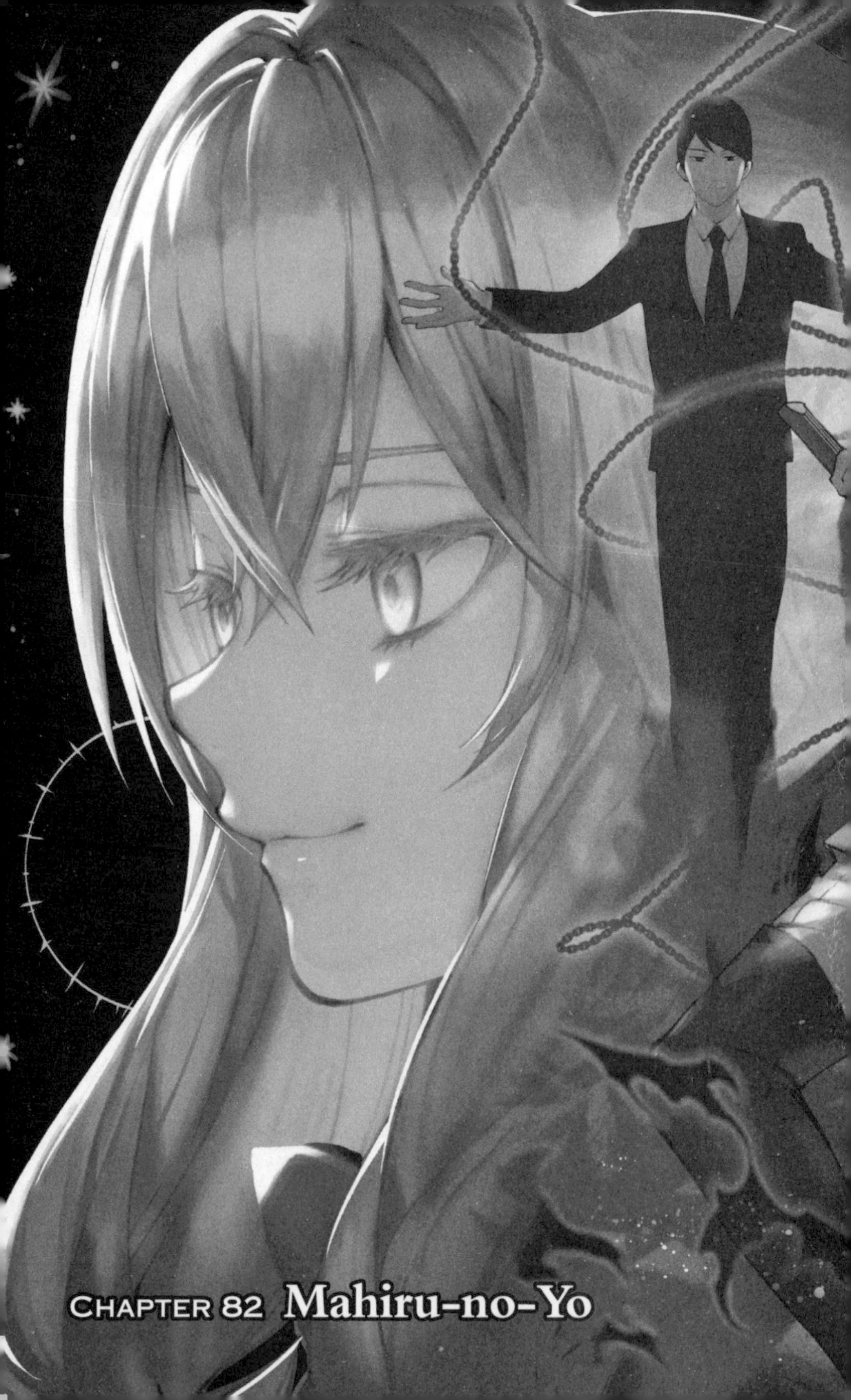
CHAPTER 82 Mahiru-no-Yo

Seraph of the End
VAMPIRE REIGN

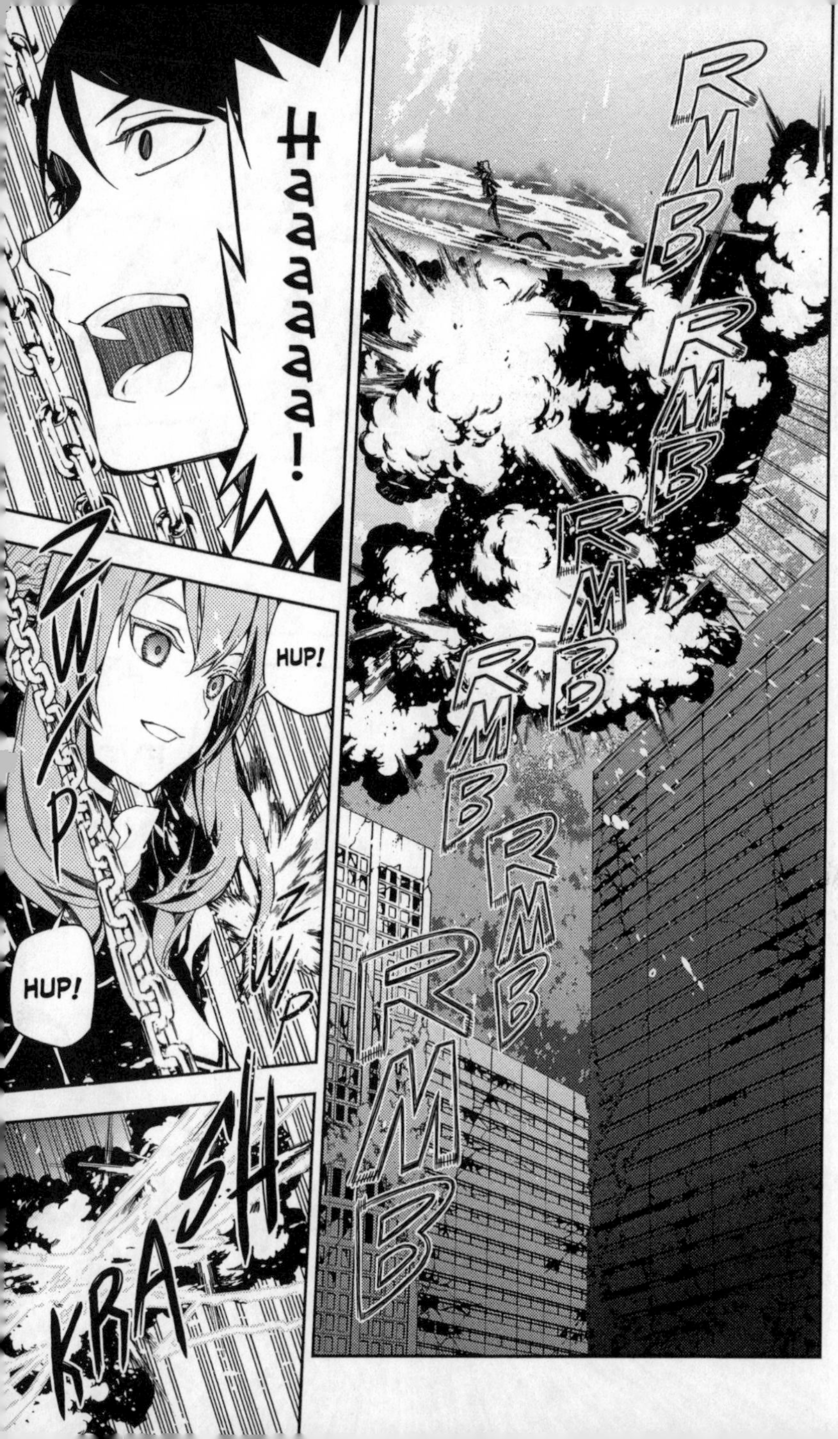
RMMB
RMMB
RMMB
RMMB
RMMB
RMMB
Haaaaaaa!
HUP!
ZWIP
ZWIP
HUP!
KRASH

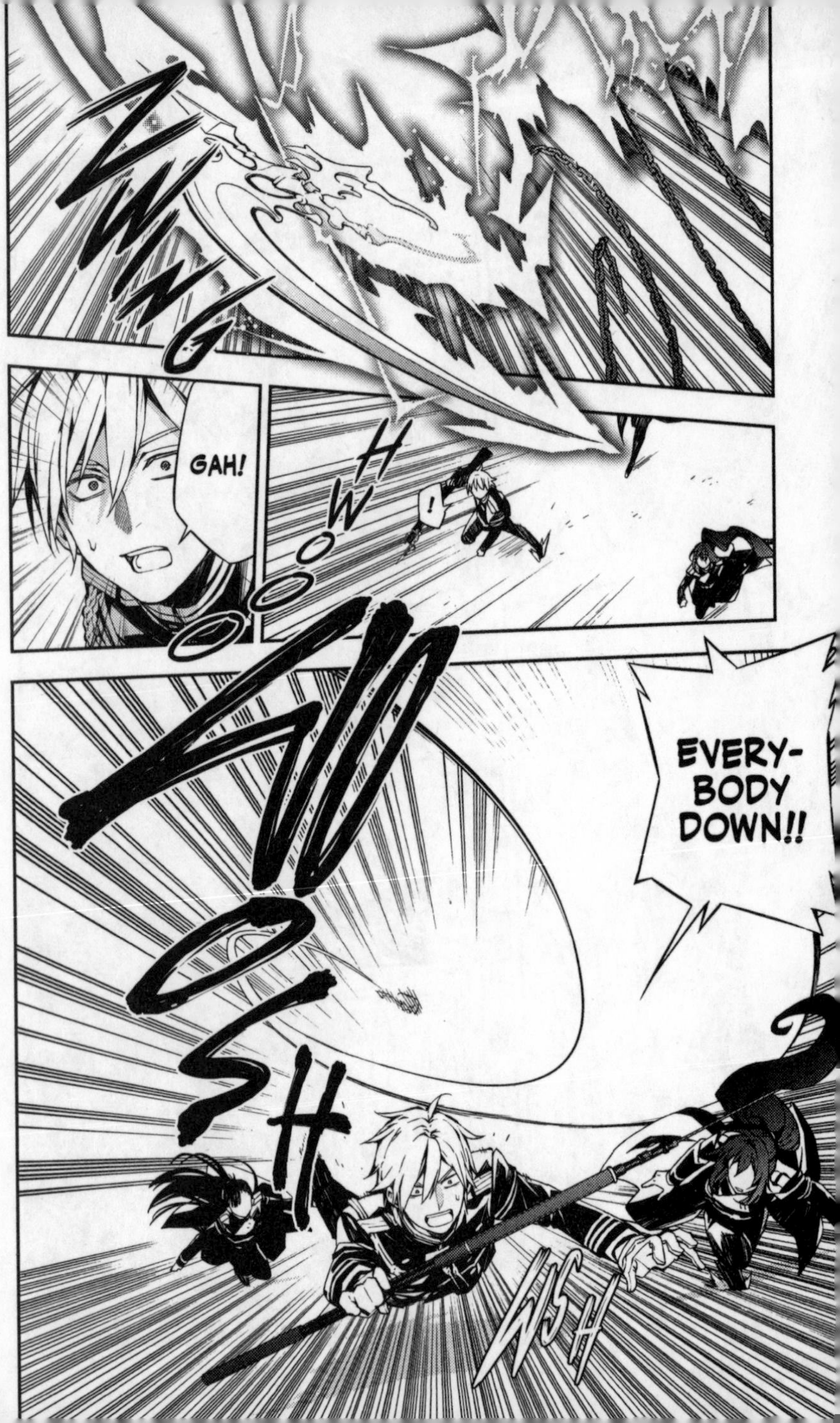
HWOOOO
!
GAH!
EVERY-
BODY
DOWN!!
WOOSH
WSH

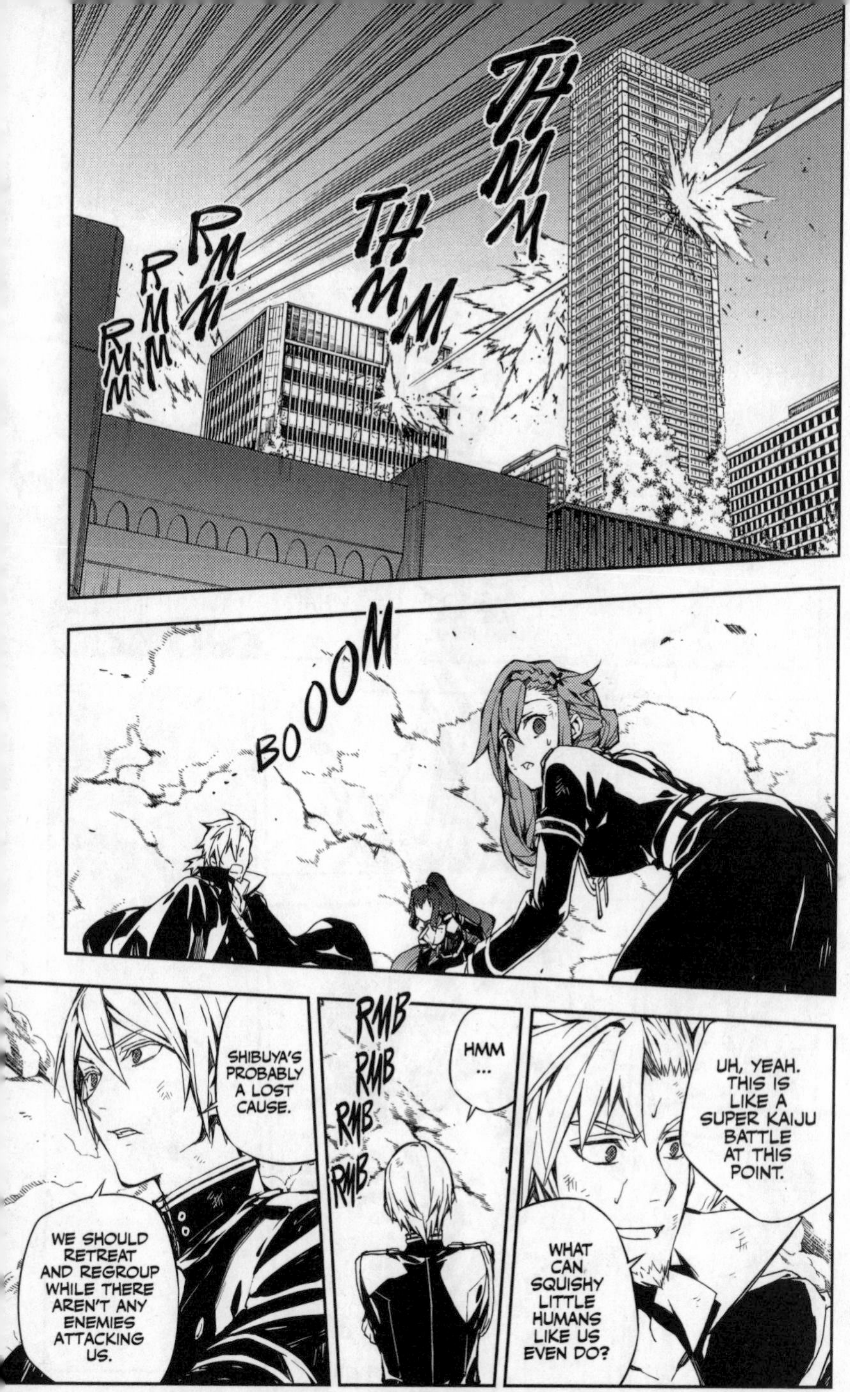
THMM
THMM
RMM
RMM
RMM
BOOOM
UH, YEAH. THIS IS LIKE A SUPER KAIJU BATTLE AT THIS POINT.
WHAT CAN SQUISHY LITTLE HUMANS LIKE US EVEN DO?
HMM ...
RMB RMB RMB RMB
SHIBUYA'S PROBABLY A LOST CAUSE.
WE SHOULD RETREAT AND REGROUP WHILE THERE AREN'T ANY ENEMIES ATTACKING US.

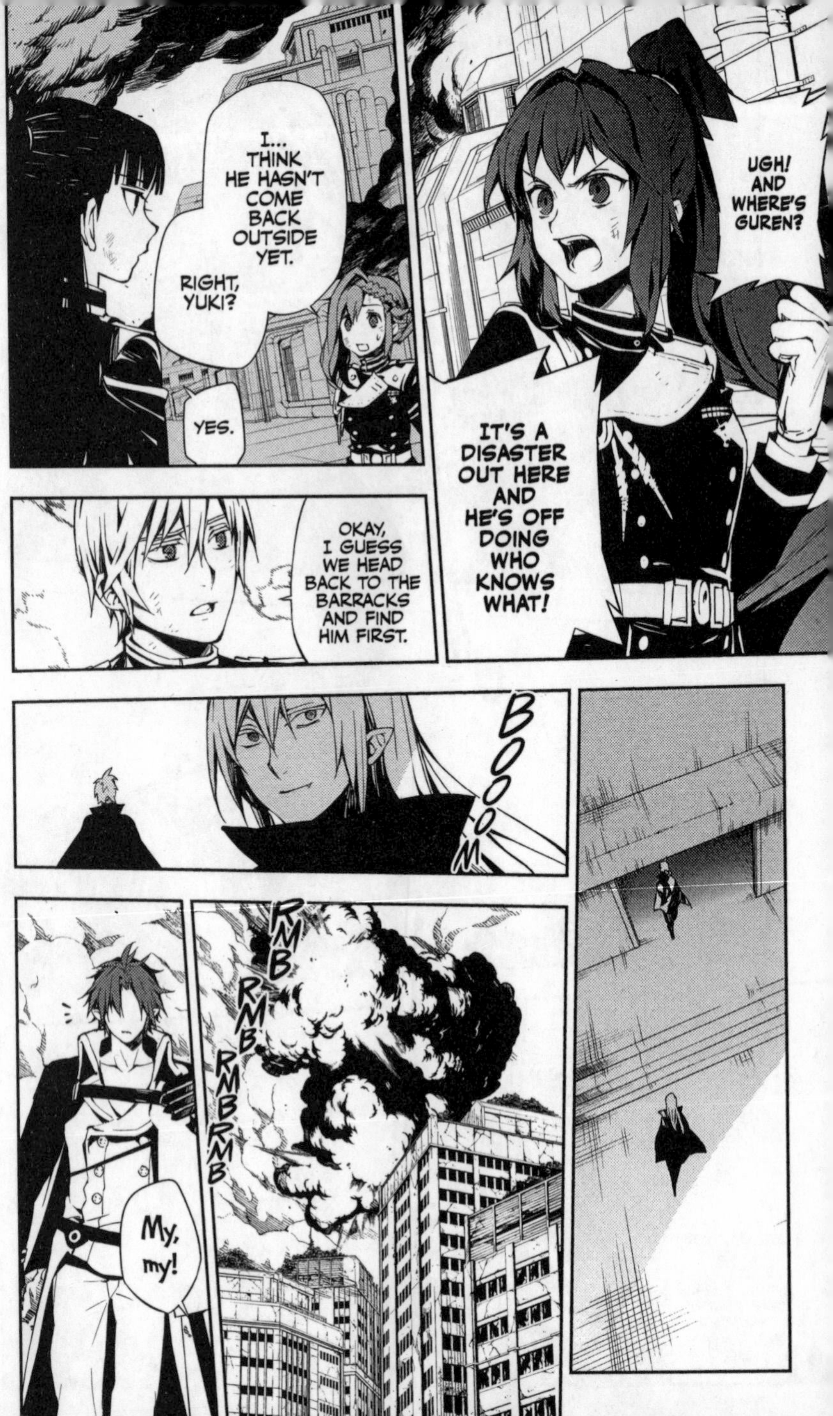
UGH! AND WHERE'S GUREN?
IT'S A DISASTER OUT HERE AND HE'S OFF DOING WHO KNOWS WHAT!
I... THINK HE HASN'T COME BACK OUTSIDE YET.
RIGHT, YUKI?
YES.
OKAY, I GUESS WE HEAD BACK TO THE BARRACKS AND FIND HIM FIRST.
BOOOOOM
RMB RMB RMBRMB
My, my!

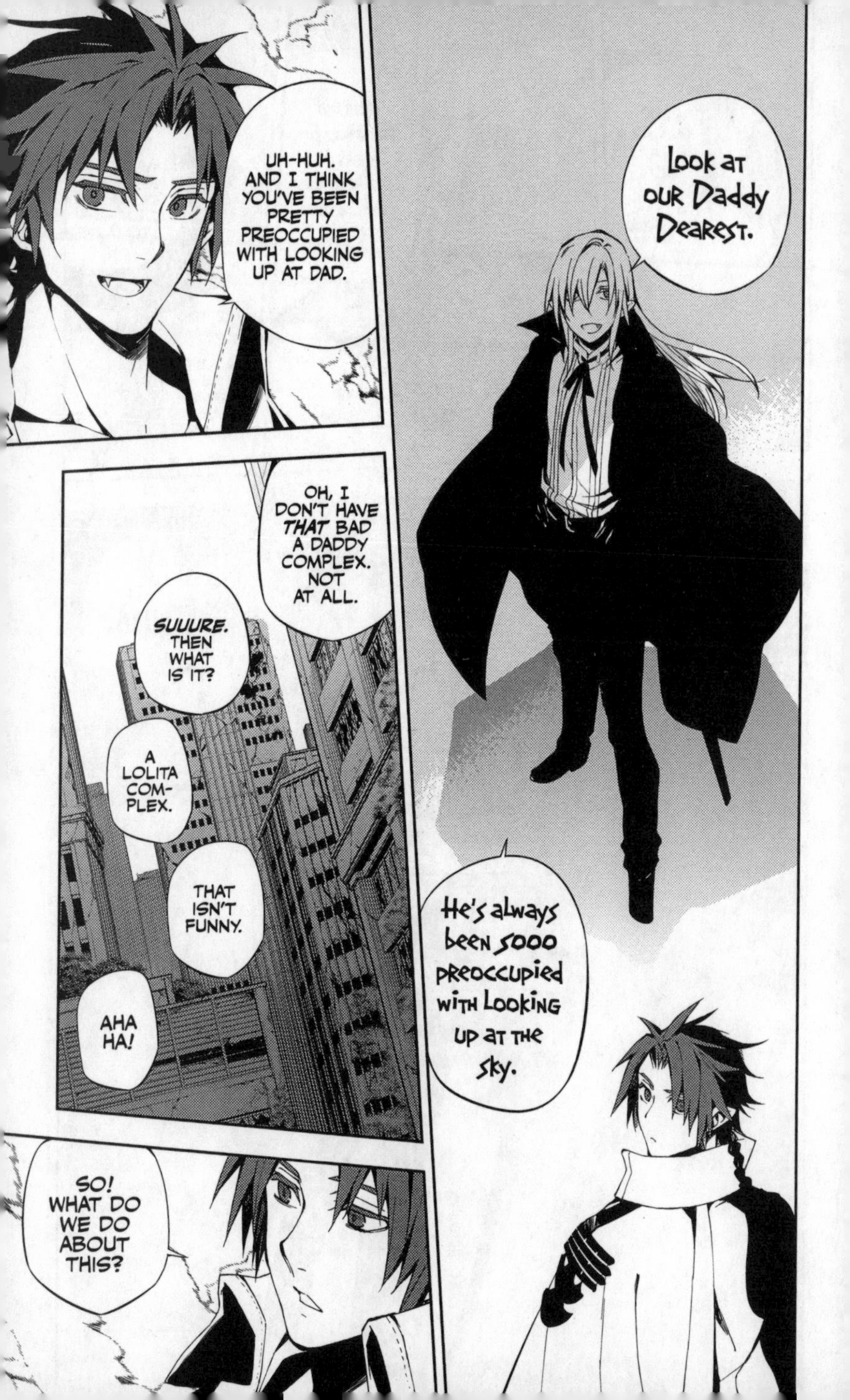
Look at our Daddy Dearest.
He's always been sooo preoccupied with looking up at the sky.
UH-HUH. AND I THINK YOU'VE BEEN PRETTY PREOCCUPIED WITH LOOKING UP AT DAD.
OH, I DON'T HAVE THAT BAD A DADDY COMPLEX. NOT AT ALL.
SUUURE. THEN WHAT IS IT?
A LOLITA COMPLEX.
THAT ISN'T FUNNY.
AHA HA!
SO! WHAT DO WE DO ABOUT THIS?

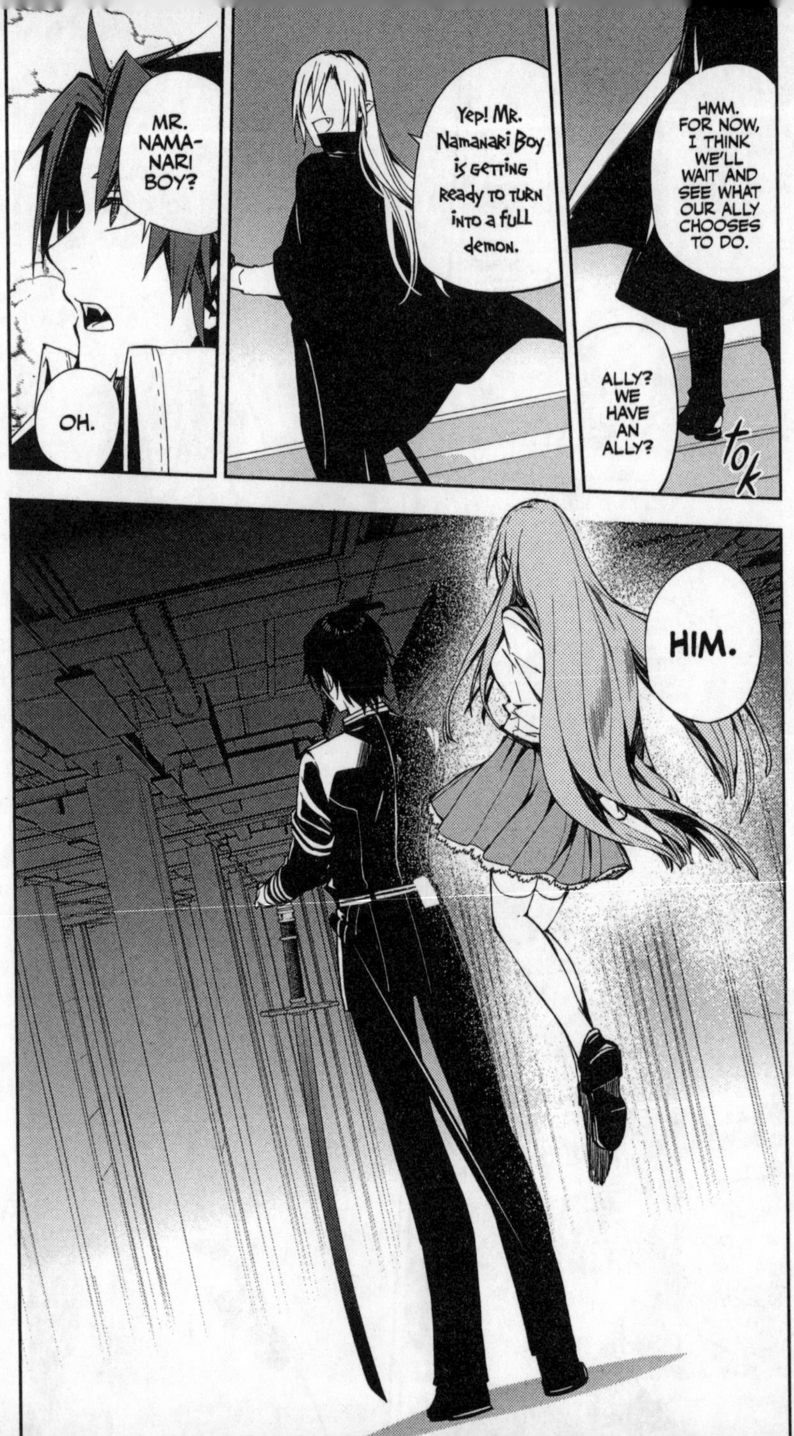
HMM. FOR NOW, I THINK WE'LL WAIT AND SEE WHAT OUR ALLY CHOOSES TO DO.
ALLY? WE HAVE AN ALLY?
tok
Yep! Mr. Namanari Boy is getting ready to turn into a full demon.
MR. NAMA-NARI BOY?
OH.
HIM.

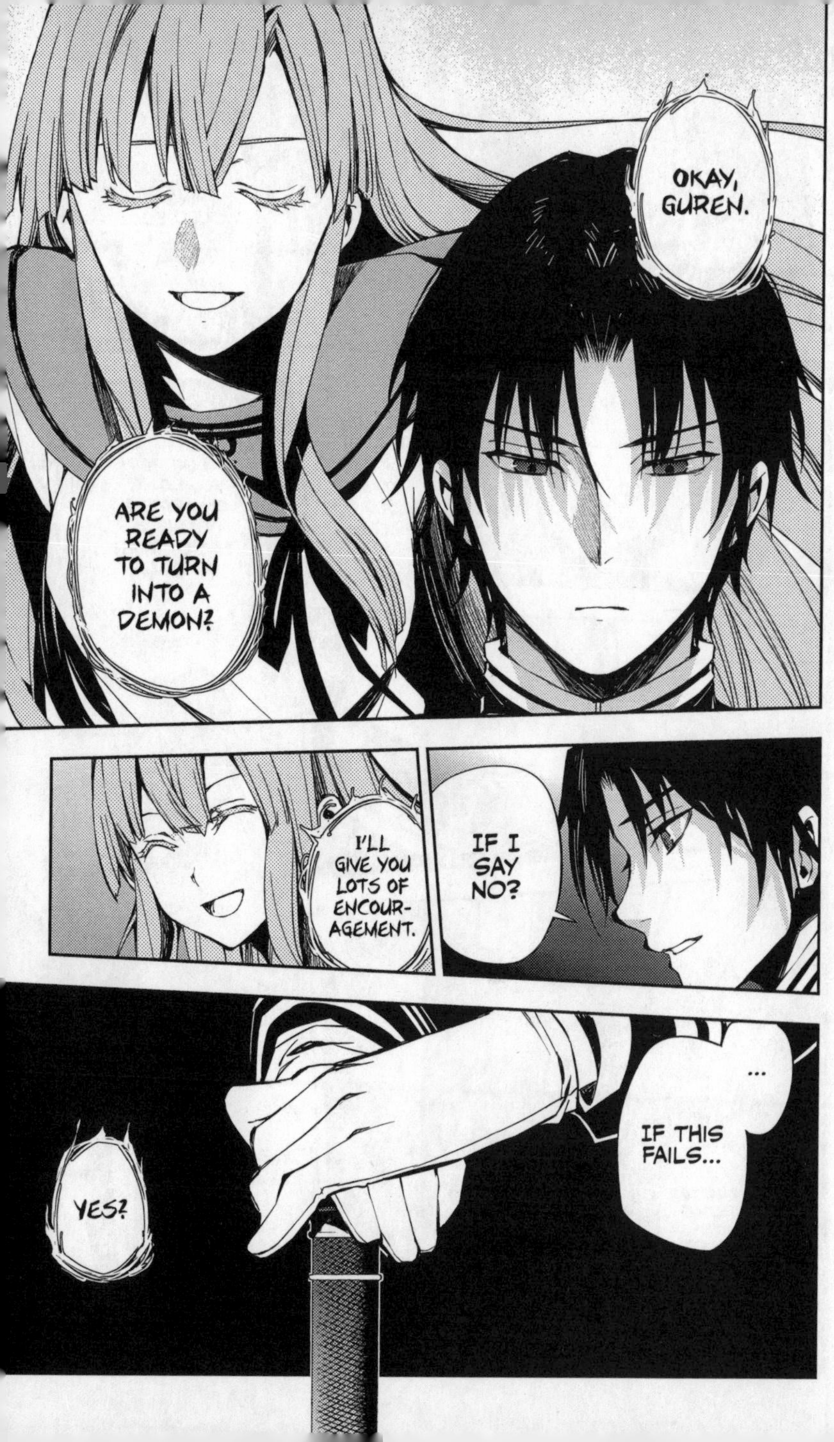
OKAY, GUREN.
ARE YOU READY TO TURN INTO A DEMON?
IF I SAY NO?
I'LL GIVE YOU LOTS OF ENCOUR-AGEMENT.
...
IF THIS FAILS...
YES?

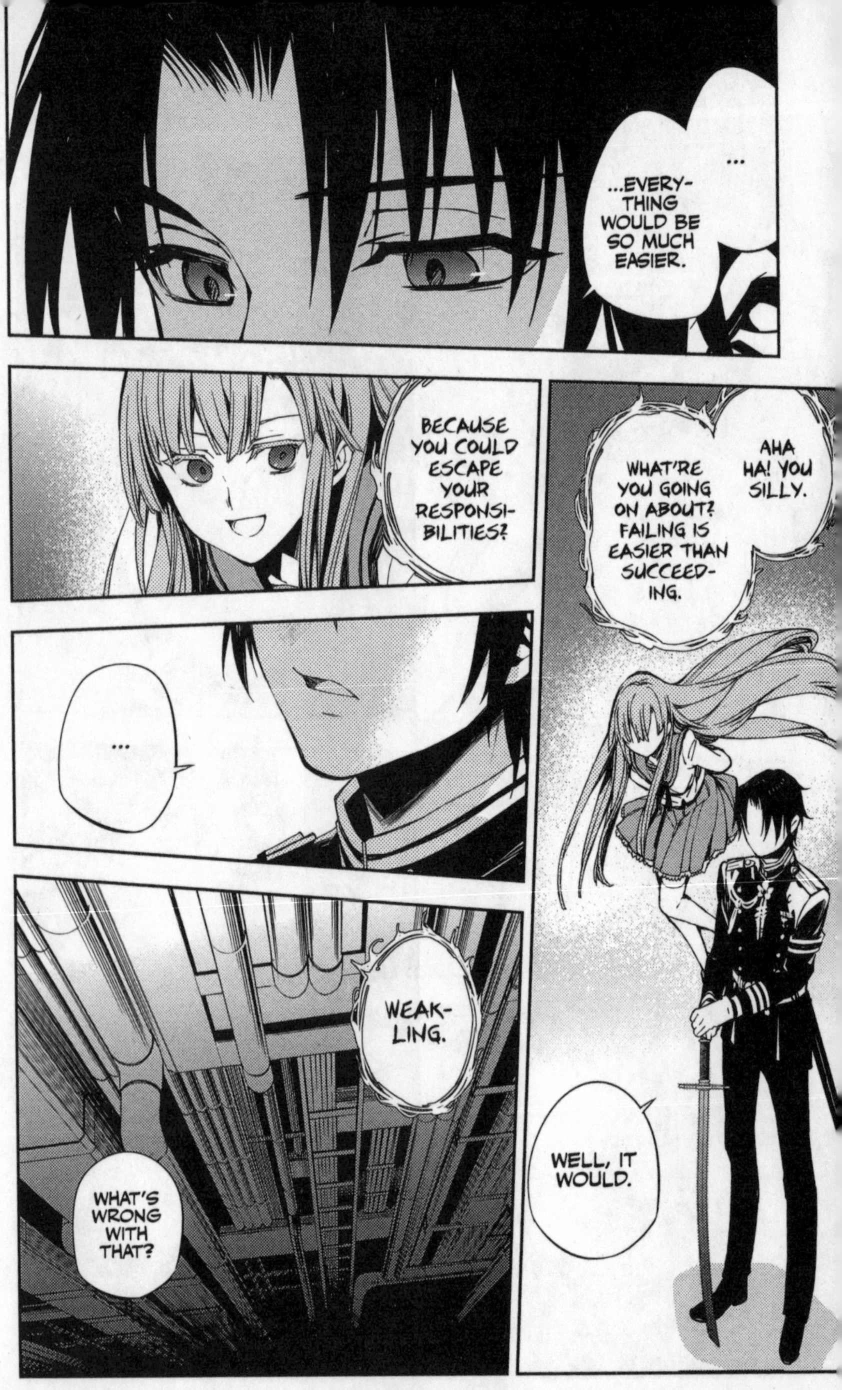
...
...EVERYTHING WOULD BE SO MUCH EASIER.
AHA HA! YOU SILLY.
WHAT'RE YOU GOING ON ABOUT? FAILING IS EASIER THAN SUCCEEDING.
WELL, IT WOULD.
BECAUSE YOU COULD ESCAPE YOUR RESPONSIBILITIES?
...
WEAKLING.
WHAT'S WRONG WITH THAT?

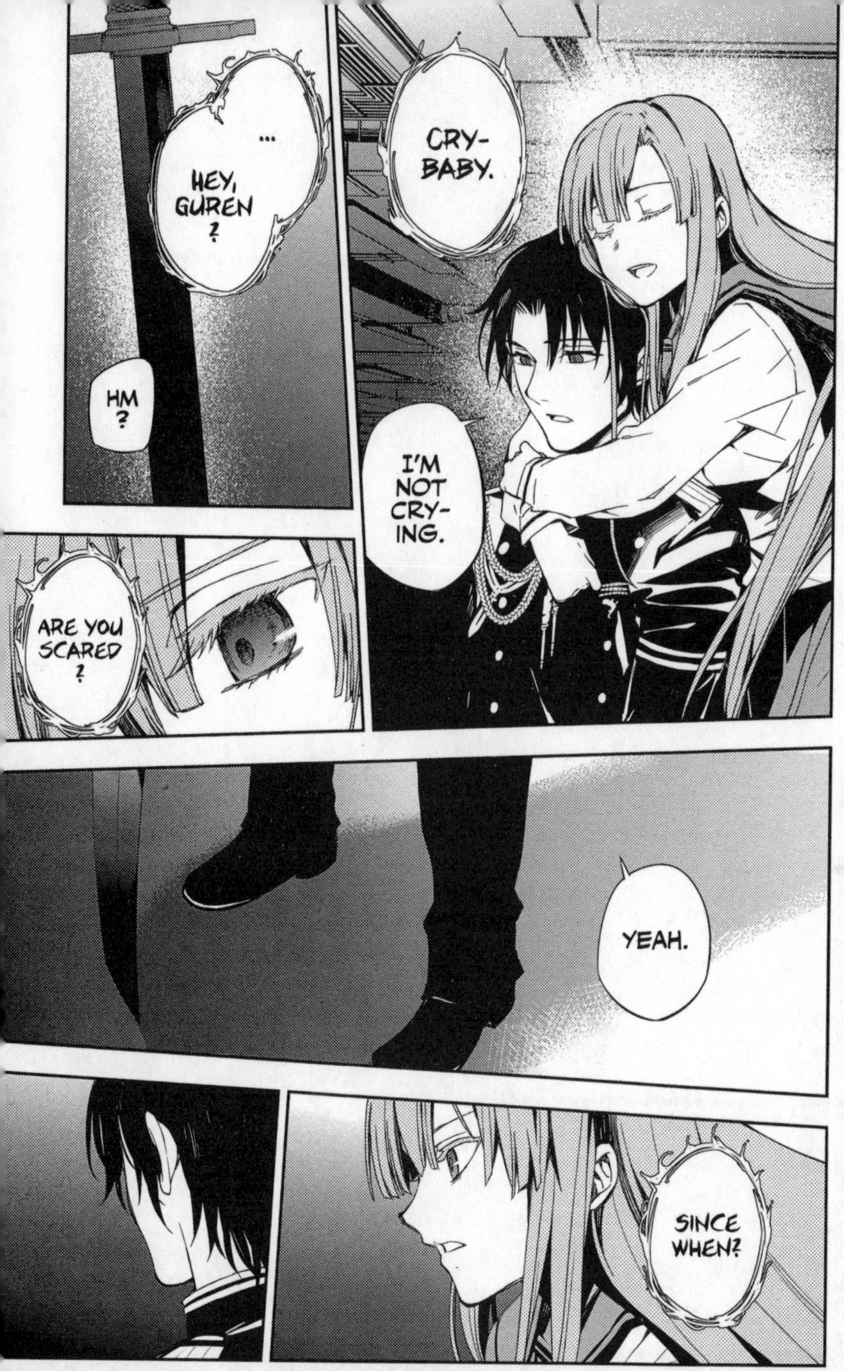
CRY-BABY.
I'M NOT CRY-ING.
... HEY, GUREN?
HM?
ARE YOU SCARED?
YEAH.
SINCE WHEN?

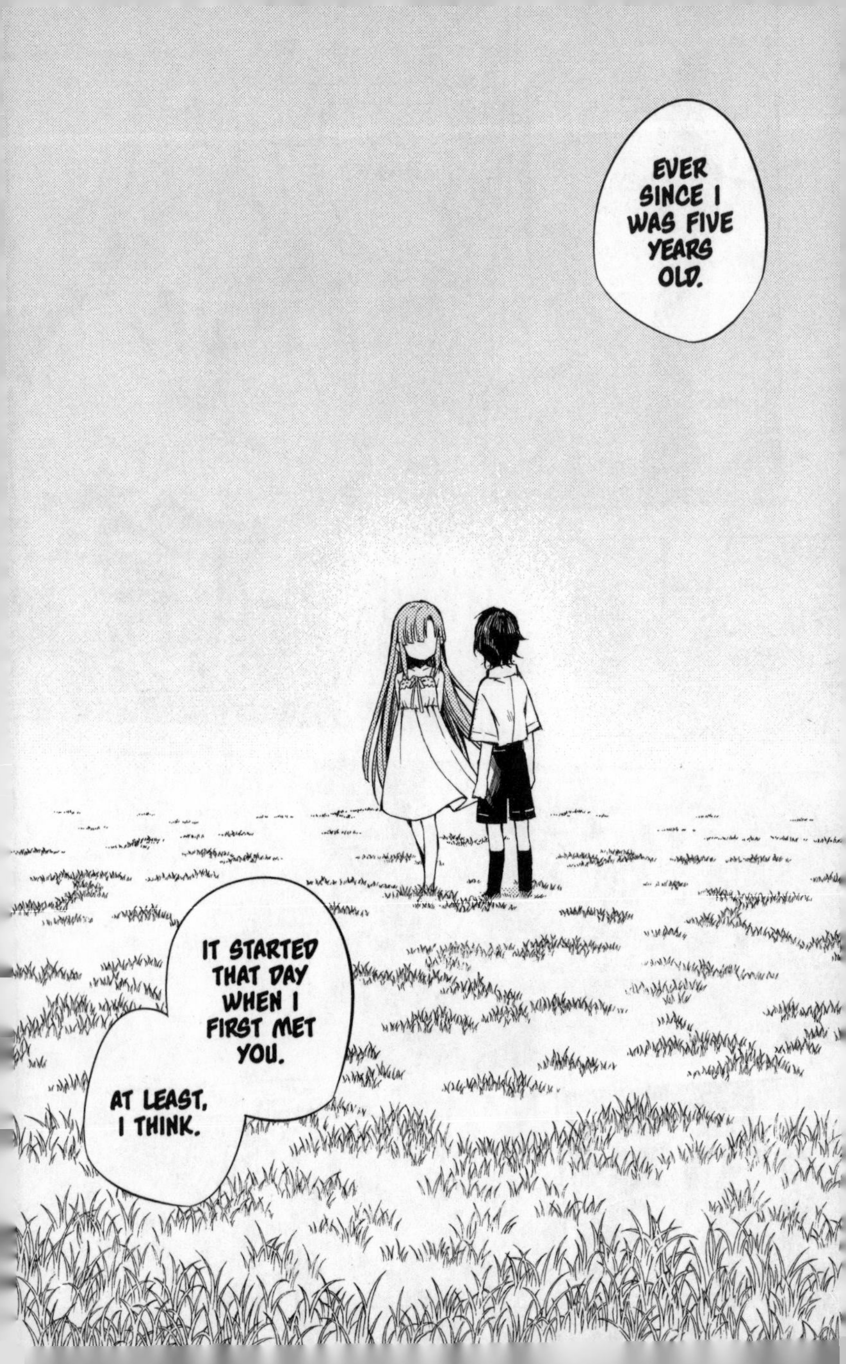
EVER SINCE I WAS FIVE YEARS OLD.
IT STARTED THAT DAY WHEN I FIRST MET YOU.
AT LEAST, I THINK.

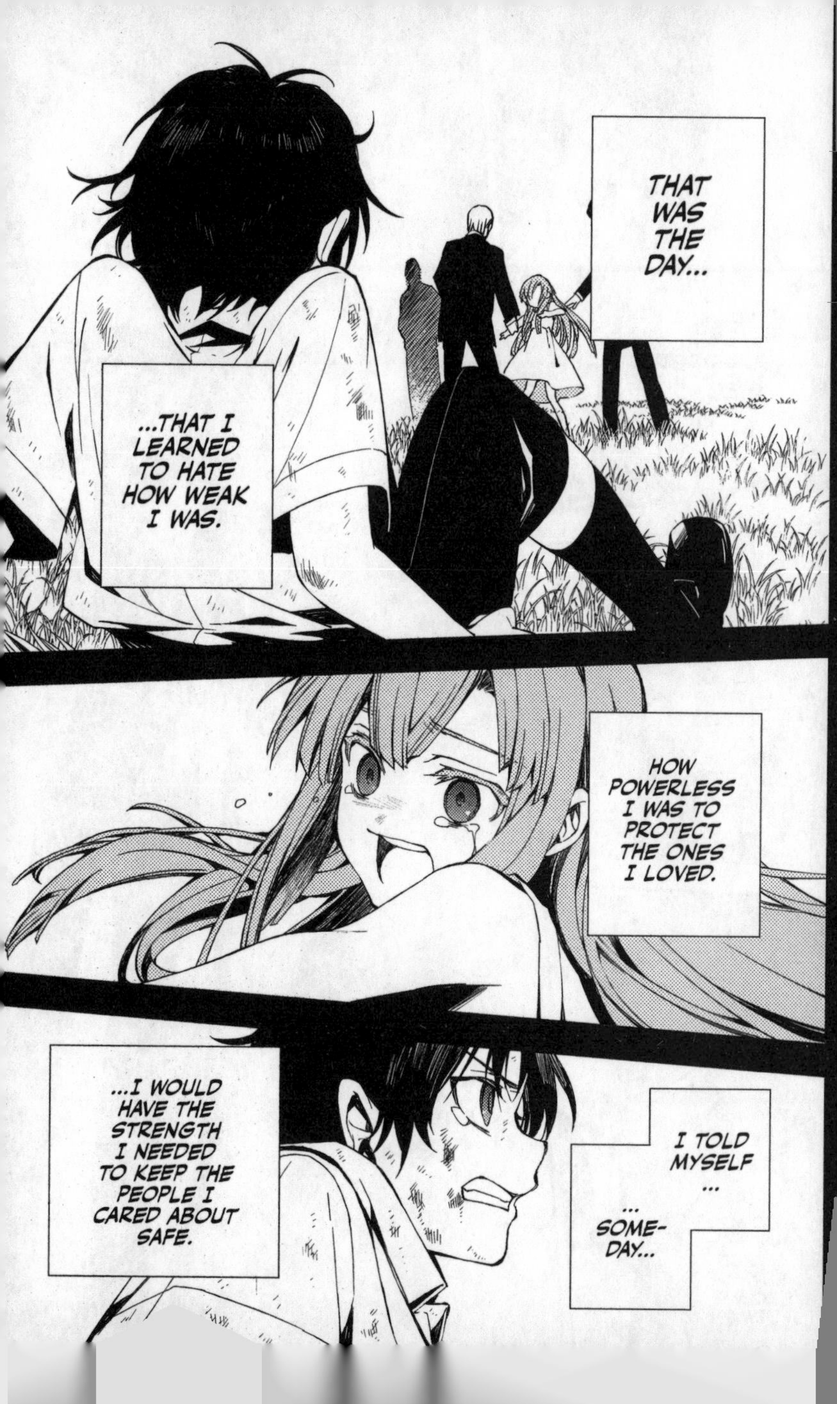
THAT WAS THE DAY...
...THAT I LEARNED TO HATE HOW WEAK I WAS.
HOW POWERLESS I WAS TO PROTECT THE ONES I LOVED.
I TOLD MYSELF ... ... SOME-DAY...
...I WOULD HAVE THE STRENGTH I NEEDED TO KEEP THE PEOPLE I CARED ABOUT SAFE.

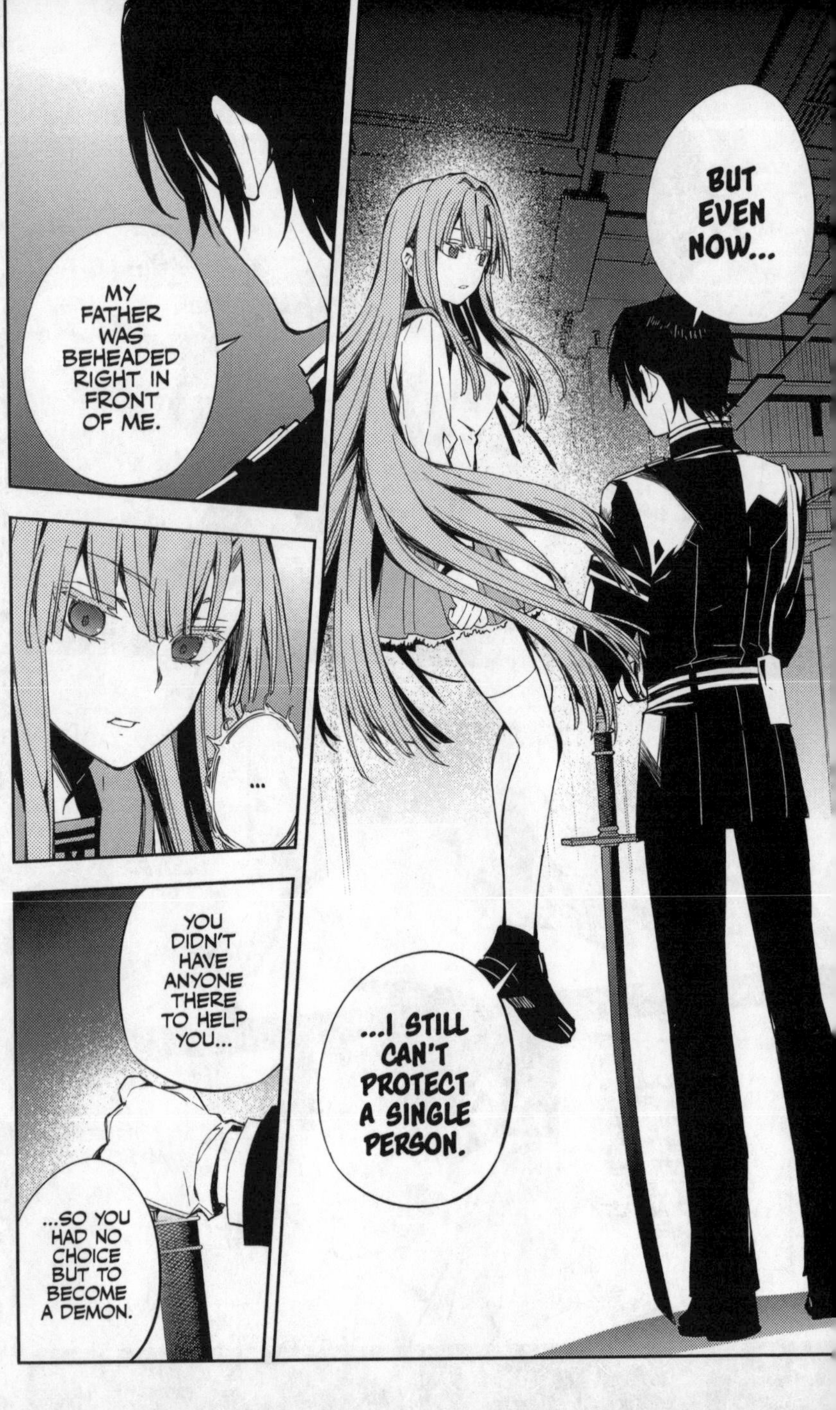
BUT EVEN NOW...
...I STILL CAN'T PROTECT A SINGLE PERSON.
MY FATHER WAS BEHEADED RIGHT IN FRONT OF ME.
...
YOU DIDN'T HAVE ANYONE THERE TO HELP YOU...
...SO YOU HAD NO CHOICE BUT TO BECOME A DEMON.

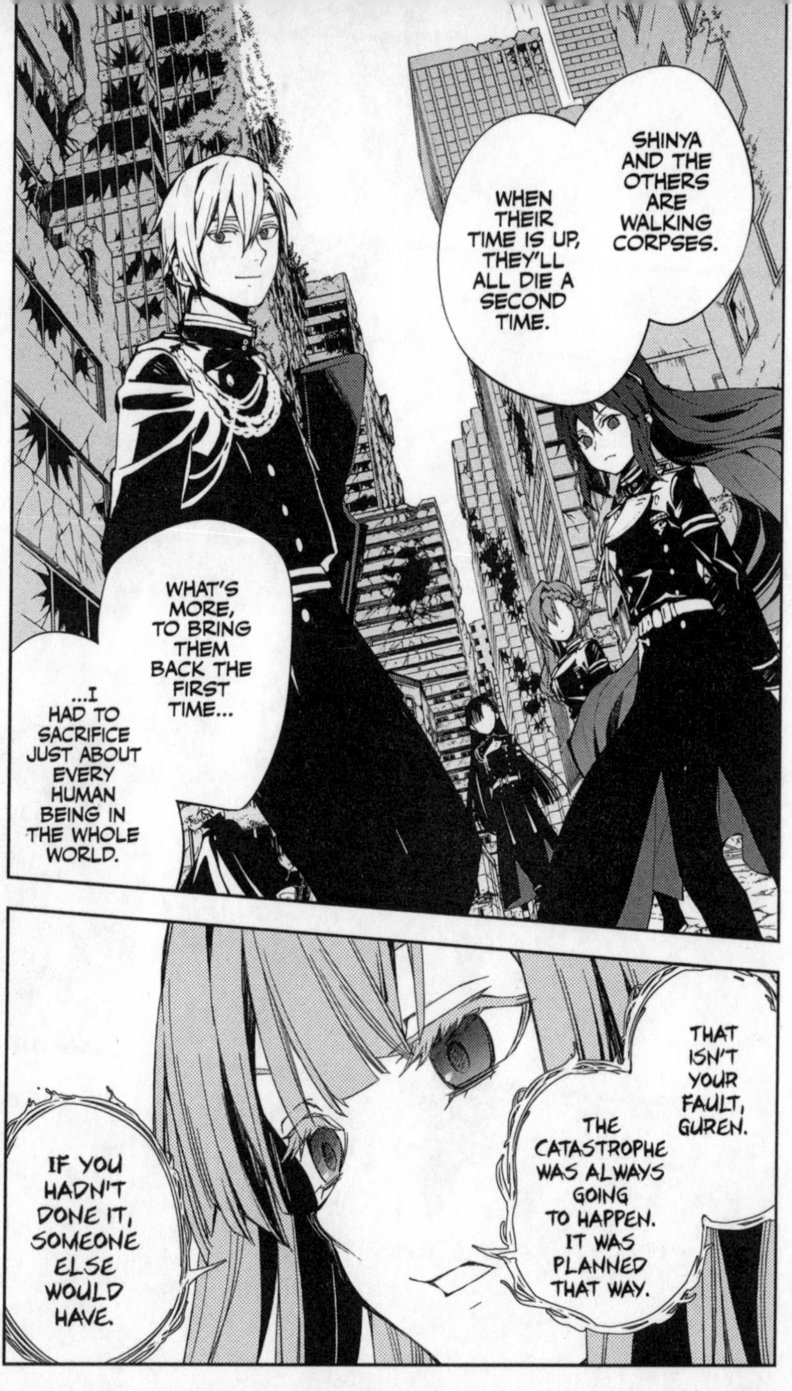
SHINYA AND THE OTHERS ARE WALKING CORPSES.
WHEN THEIR TIME IS UP, THEY'LL ALL DIE A SECOND TIME.
WHAT'S MORE, TO BRING THEM BACK THE FIRST TIME...
...I HAD TO SACRIFICE JUST ABOUT EVERY HUMAN BEING IN THE WHOLE WORLD.
THAT ISN'T YOUR FAULT, GUREN.
THE CATASTROPHE WAS ALWAYS GOING TO HAPPEN. IT WAS PLANNED THAT WAY.
IF YOU HADN'T DONE IT, SOMEONE ELSE WOULD HAVE.

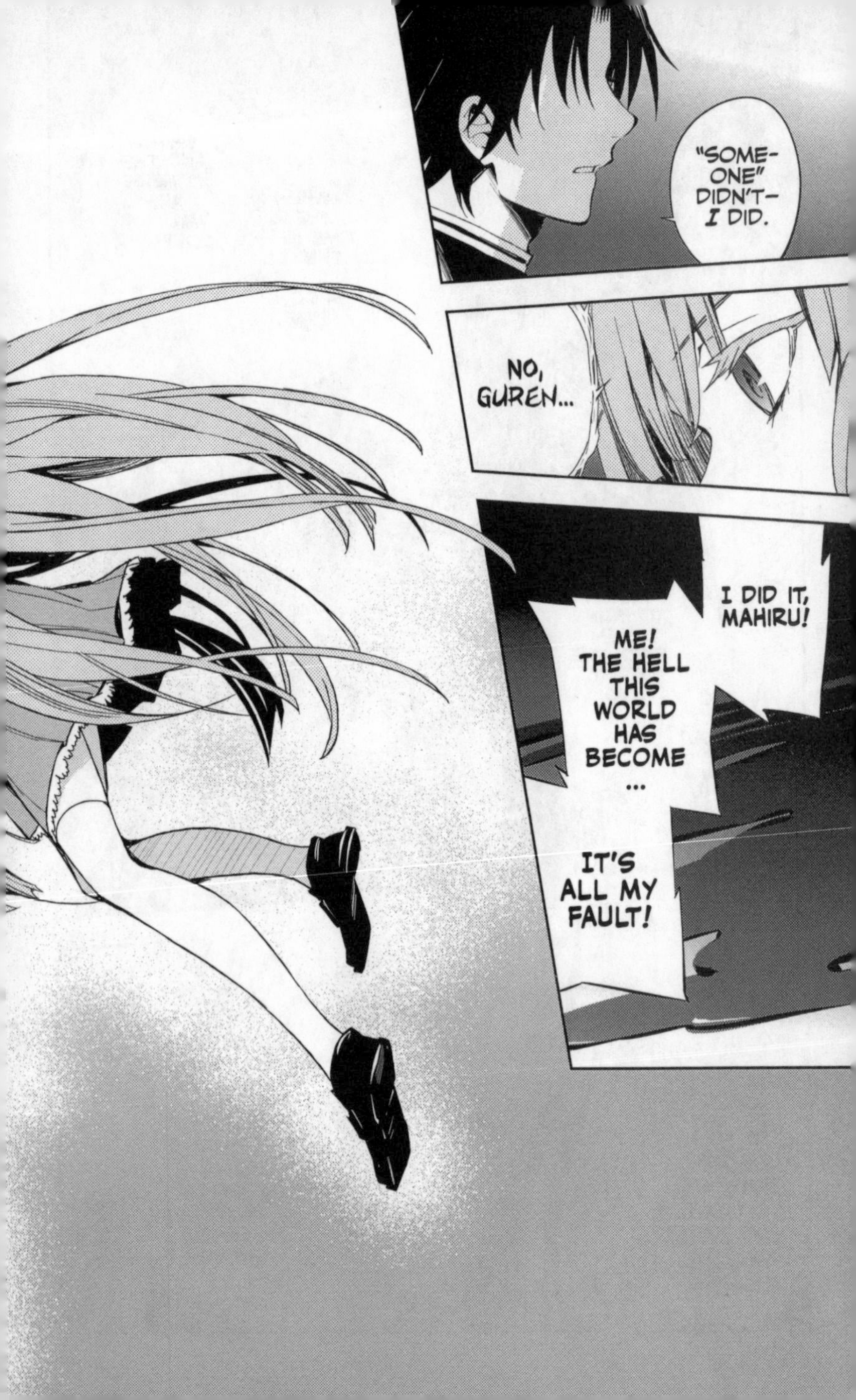
"SOME-ONE" DIDN'T—I DID.
NO, GUREN...
I DID IT, MAHIRU!
ME! THE HELL THIS WORLD HAS BECOME...
IT'S ALL MY FAULT!

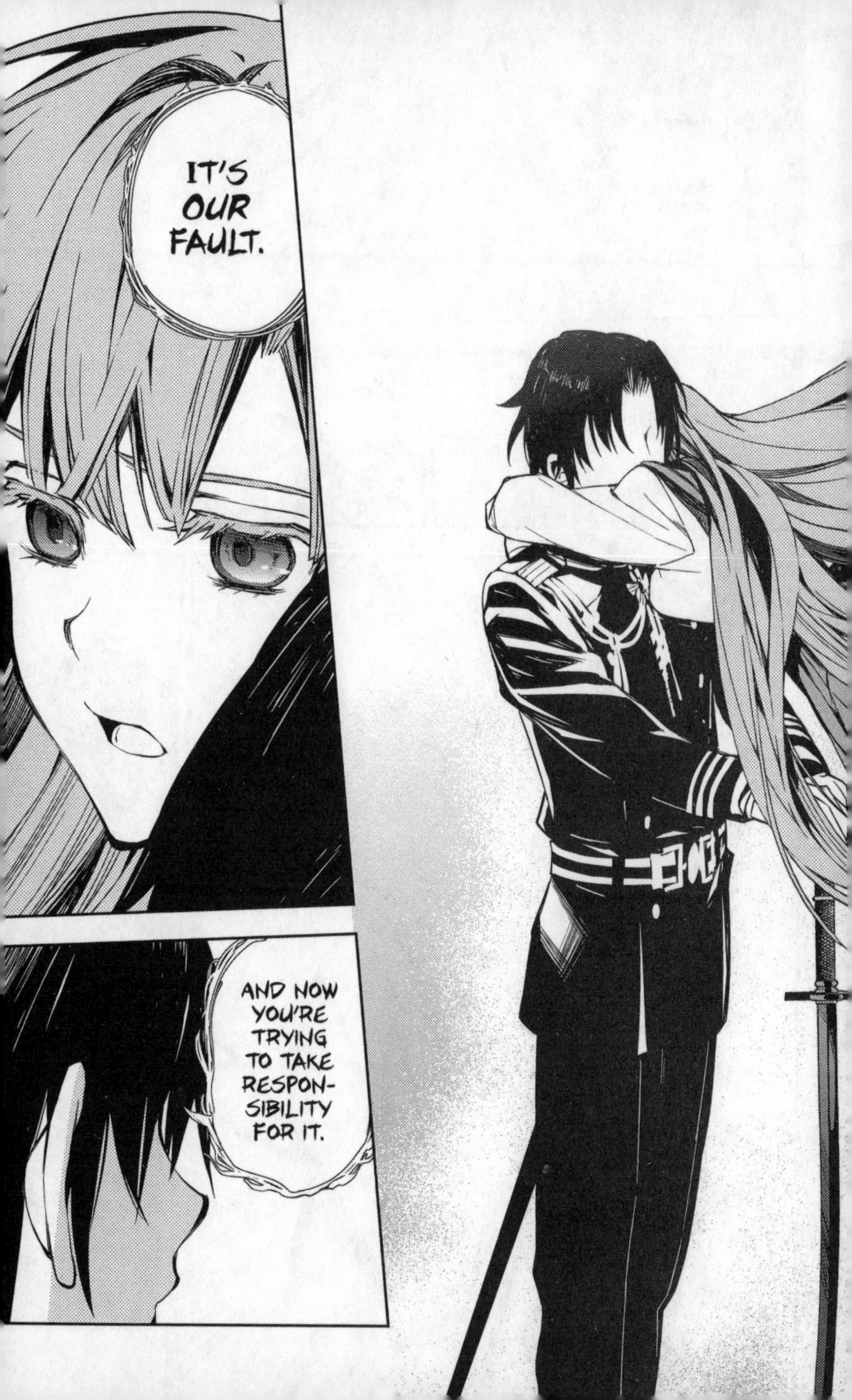
IT'S OUR FAULT.
AND NOW YOU'RE TRYING TO TAKE RESPONSIBILITY FOR IT.

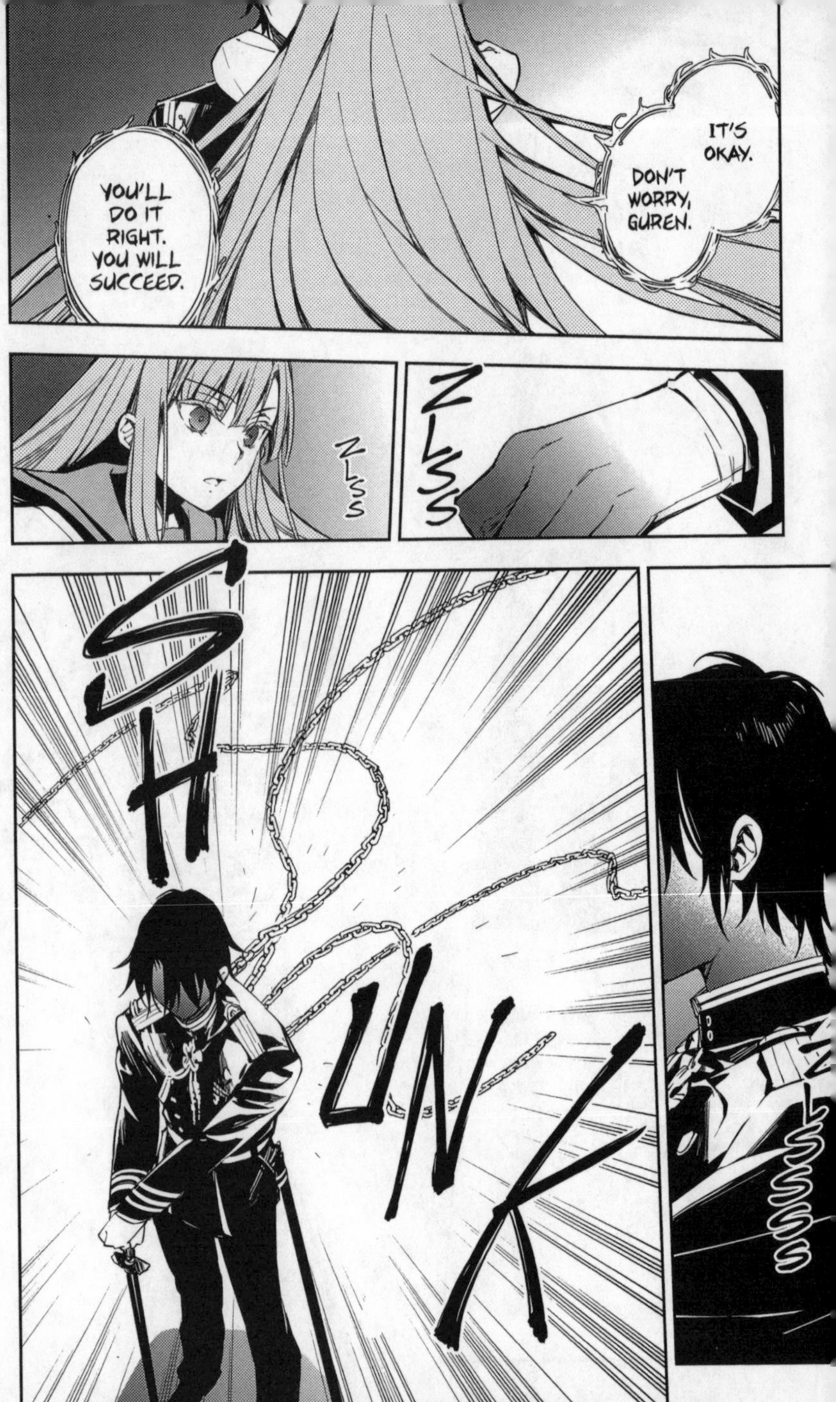
IT'S OKAY.
DON'T WORRY, GUREN.
YOU'LL DO IT RIGHT. YOU WILL SUCCEED.
ZLSS
ZLSS
ZLSSSSS
SHUNK

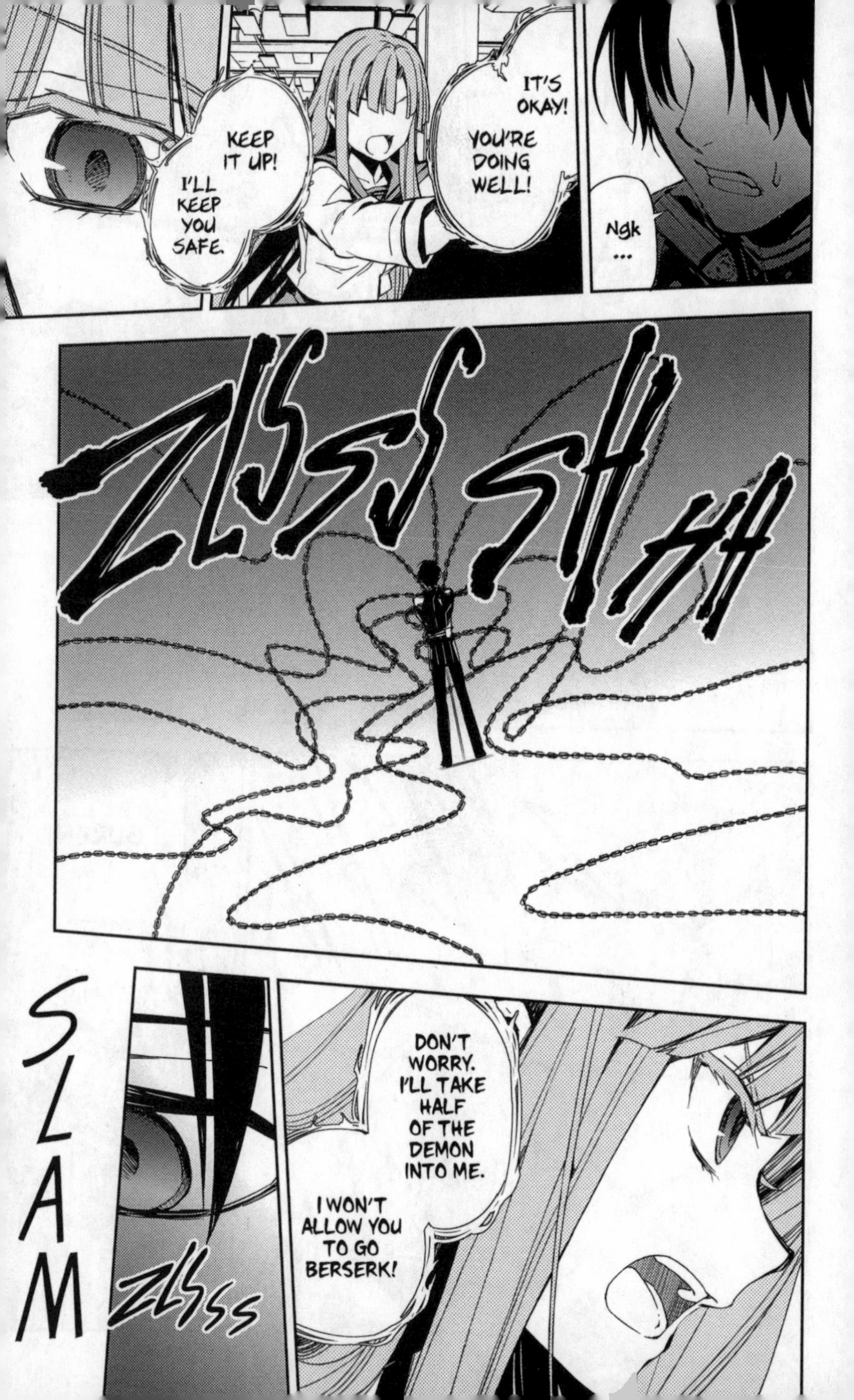
Ngk ...
IT'S OKAY! YOU'RE DOING WELL!
KEEP IT UP! I'LL KEEP YOU SAFE.
ZISSSHH
DON'T WORRY. I'LL TAKE HALF OF THE DEMON INTO ME.
I WON'T ALLOW YOU TO GO BERSERK!
SLAM
ZISSSS

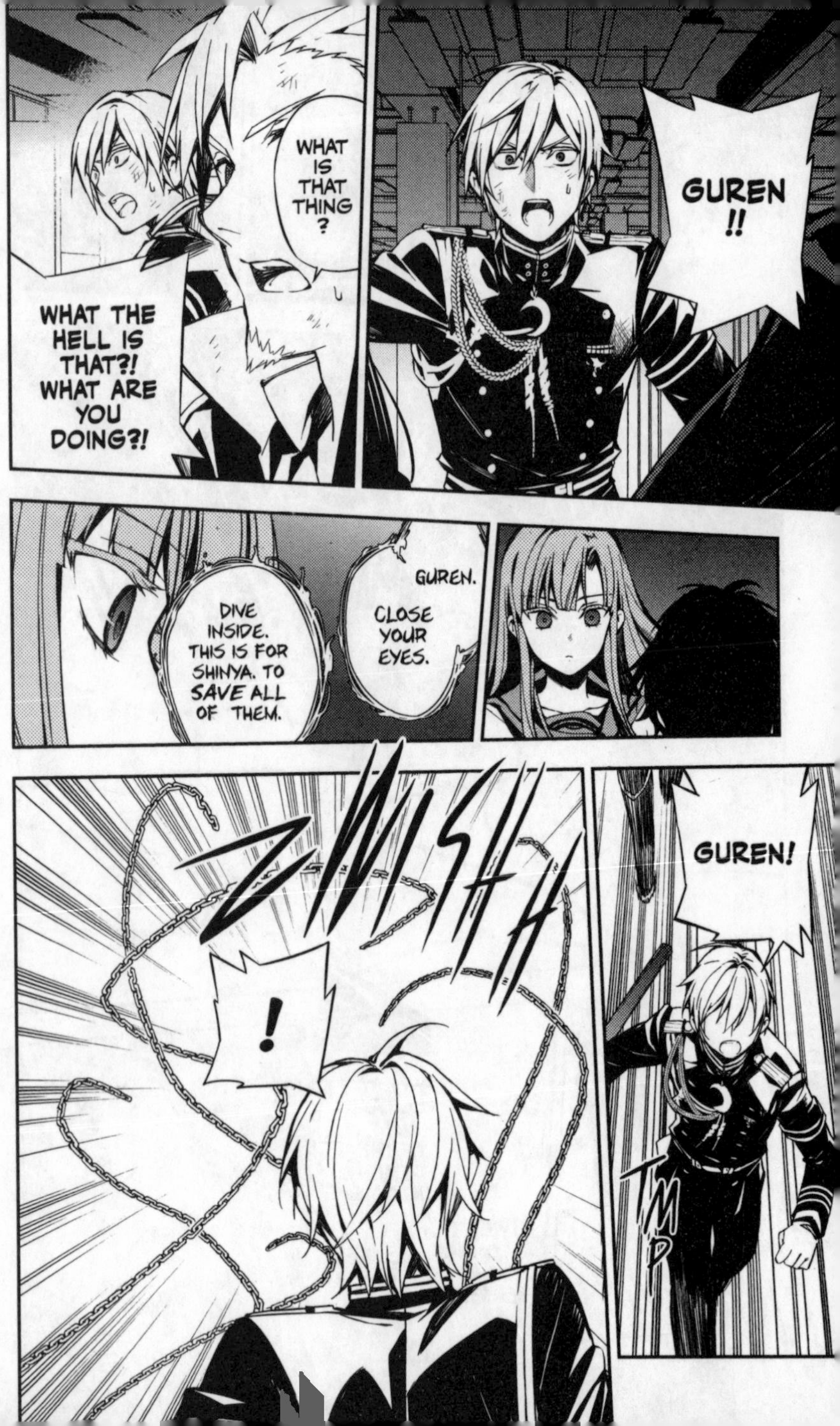
GUREN !!
WHAT IS THAT THING?
WHAT THE HELL IS THAT?! WHAT ARE YOU DOING?!
GUREN.
CLOSE YOUR EYES.
DIVE INSIDE. THIS IS FOR SHINYA. TO SAVE ALL OF THEM.
GUREN!
TMP
ZWISHH
!

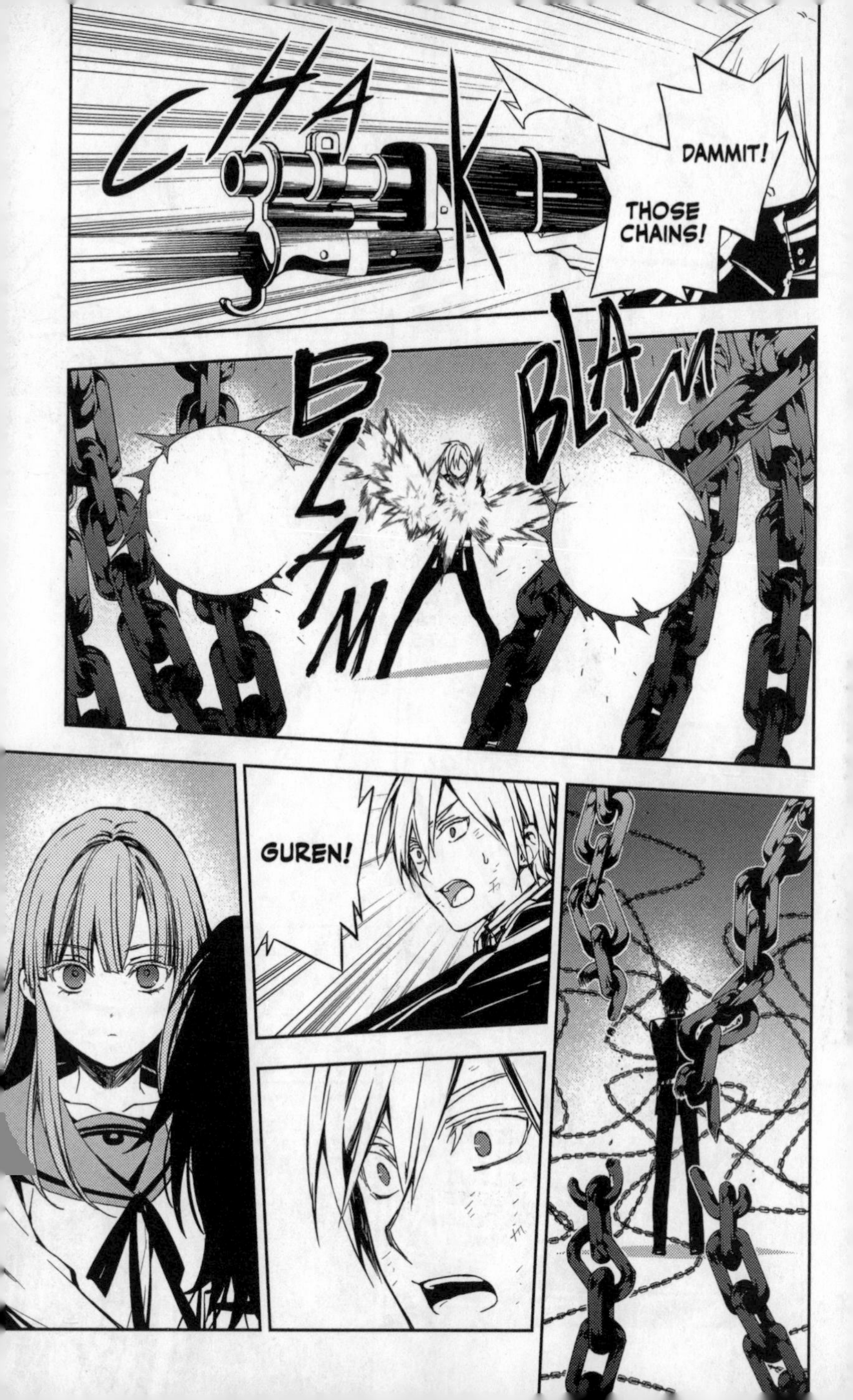
DAMMIT!
THOSE CHAINS!
CHAKK
BLAM
BLAM
GUREN!

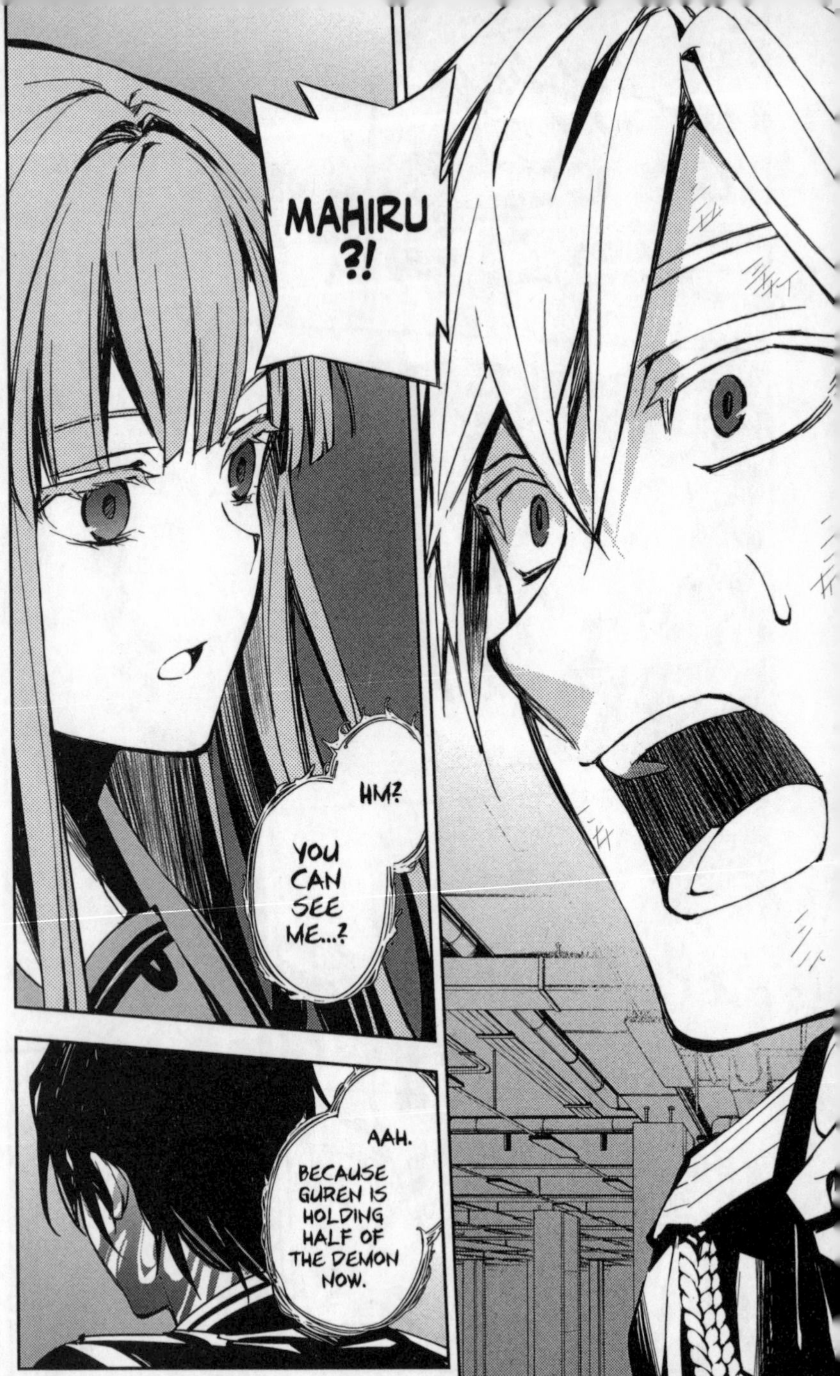
MAHIRU ?!
HM? YOU CAN SEE ME...?
AAH. BECAUSE GUREN IS HOLDING HALF OF THE DEMON NOW.

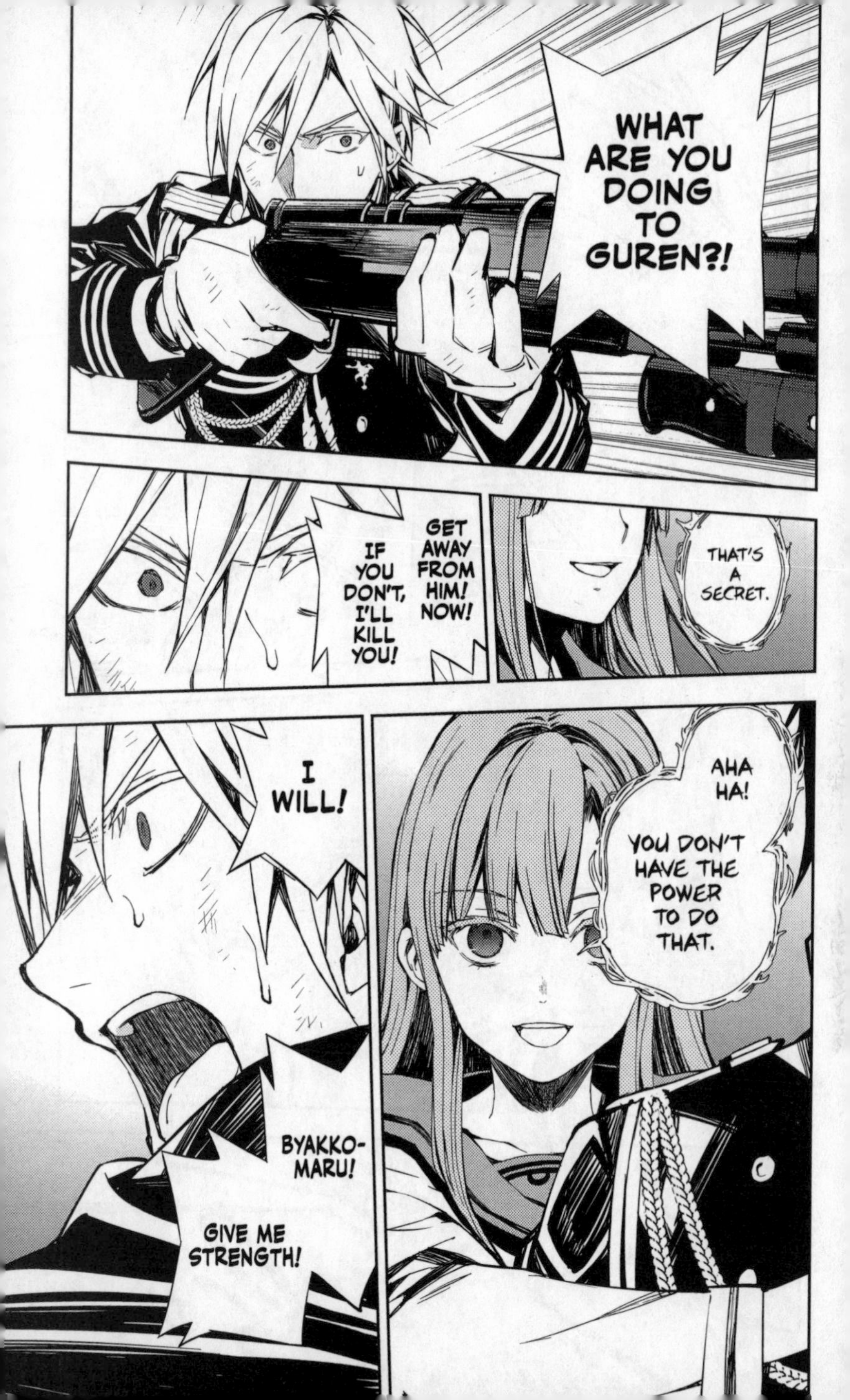
WHAT ARE YOU DOING TO GUREN?!
THAT'S A SECRET.
GET AWAY FROM HIM! NOW!
IF YOU DON'T, I'LL KILL YOU!
AHA HA!
YOU DON'T HAVE THE POWER TO DO THAT.
I WILL!
BYAKKO-MARU!
GIVE ME STRENGTH!

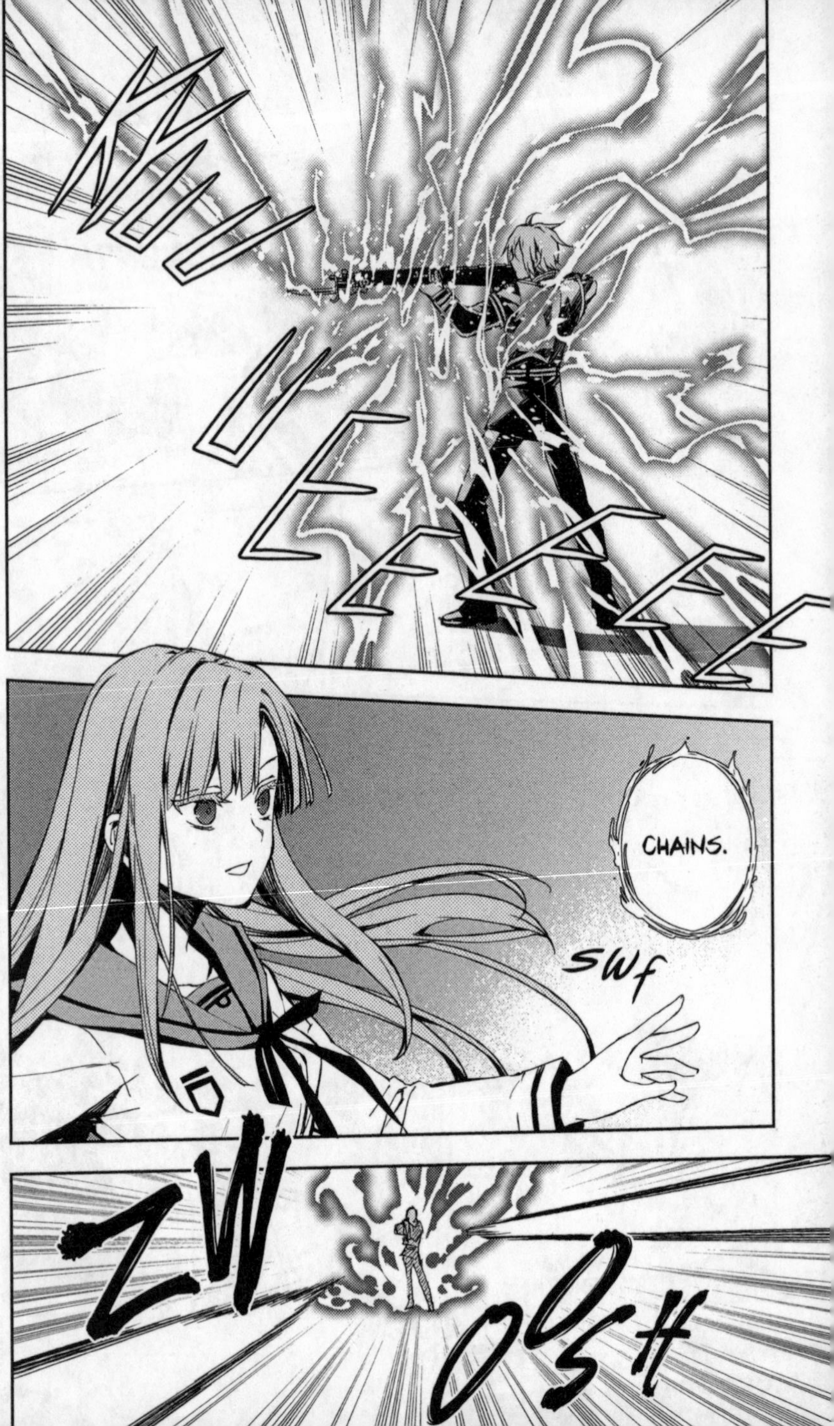
KRZZ
CHAINS.
SWF
ZWOOSH

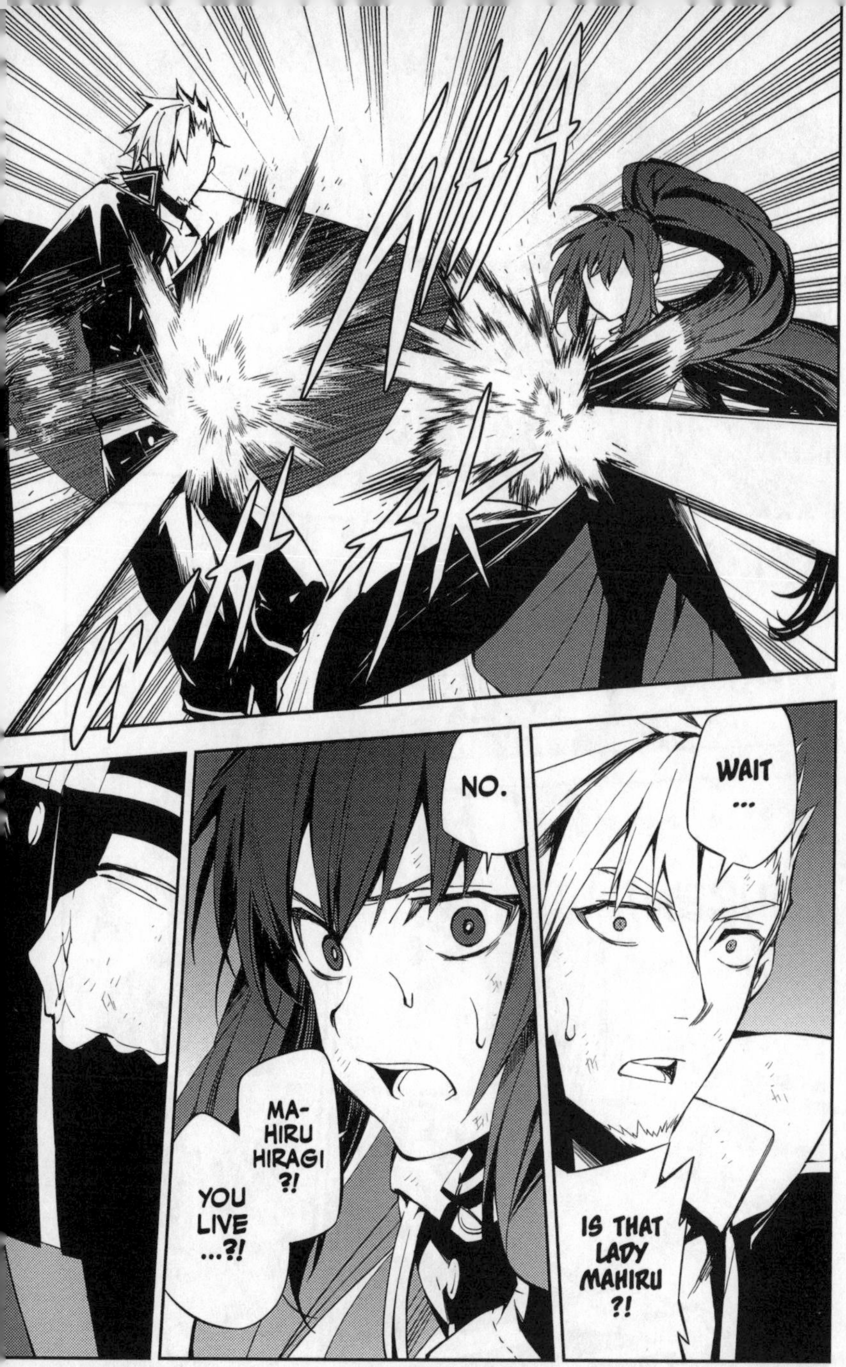
WHAK
WAIT ...
IS THAT LADY MAHIRU ?!
NO.
MA-HIRU HIRAGI ?!
YOU LIVE ...?!

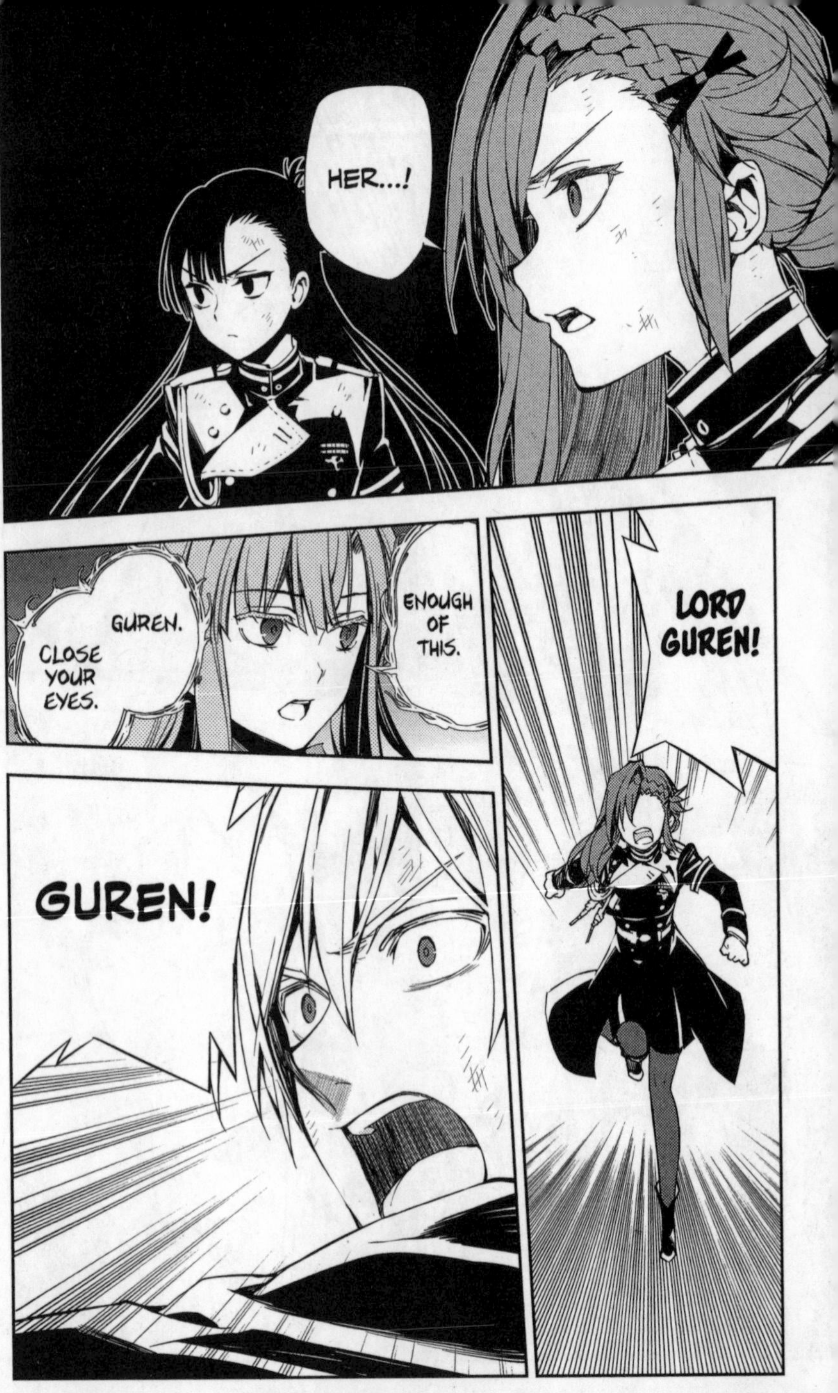
HER...!
LORD GUREN!
ENOUGH OF THIS.
GUREN.
CLOSE YOUR EYES.
GUREN!

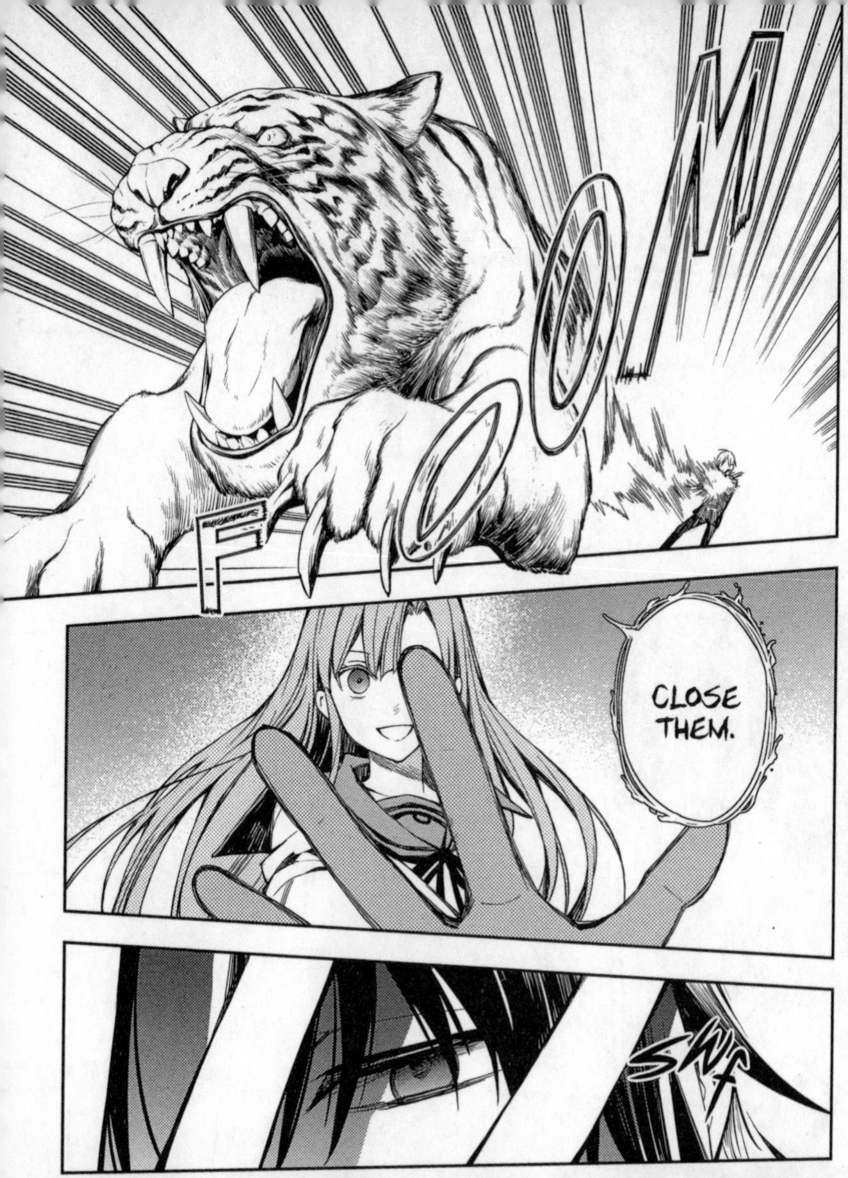
FOOOOM
CLOSE THEM.
SWF

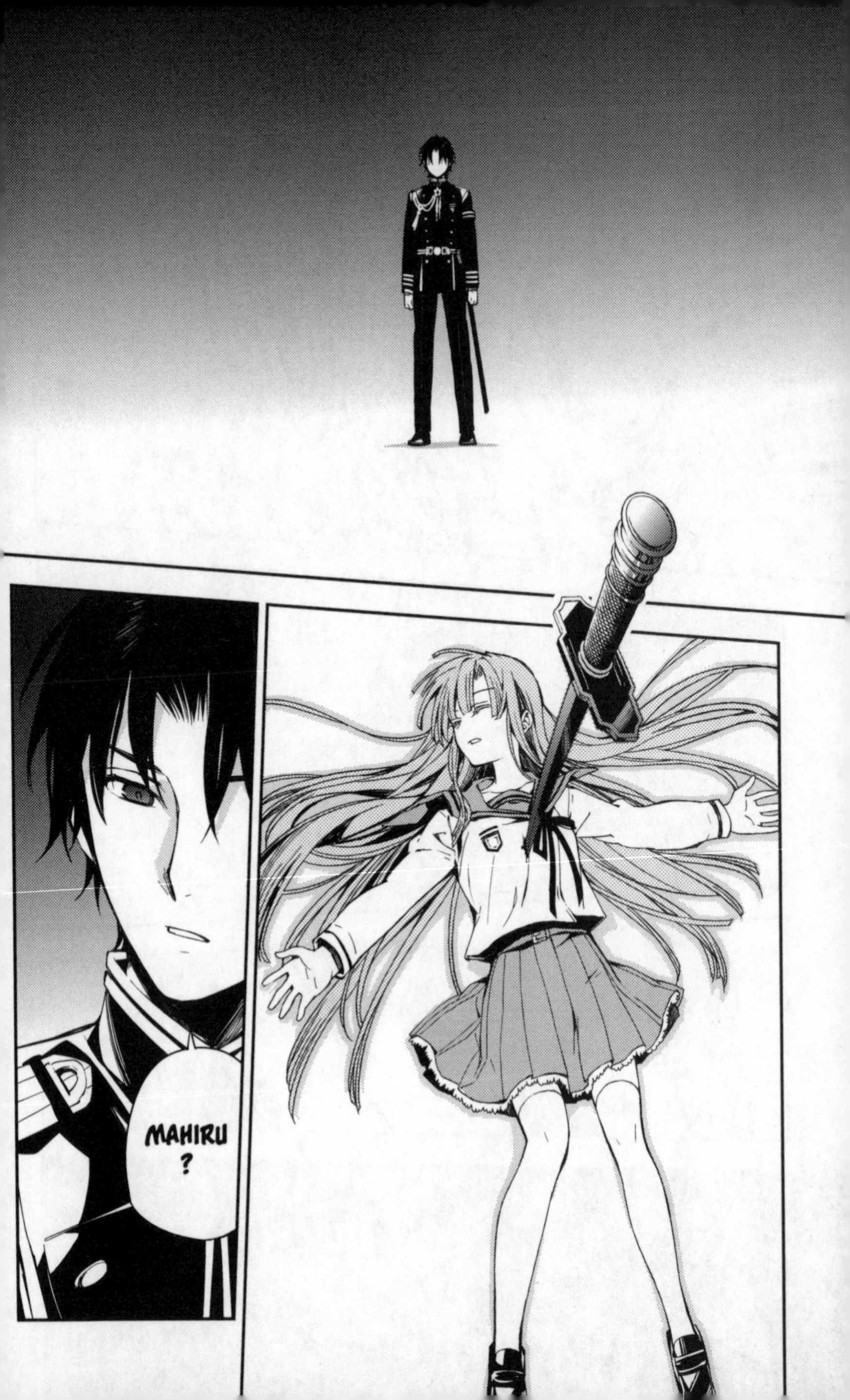
MAHIRU
?

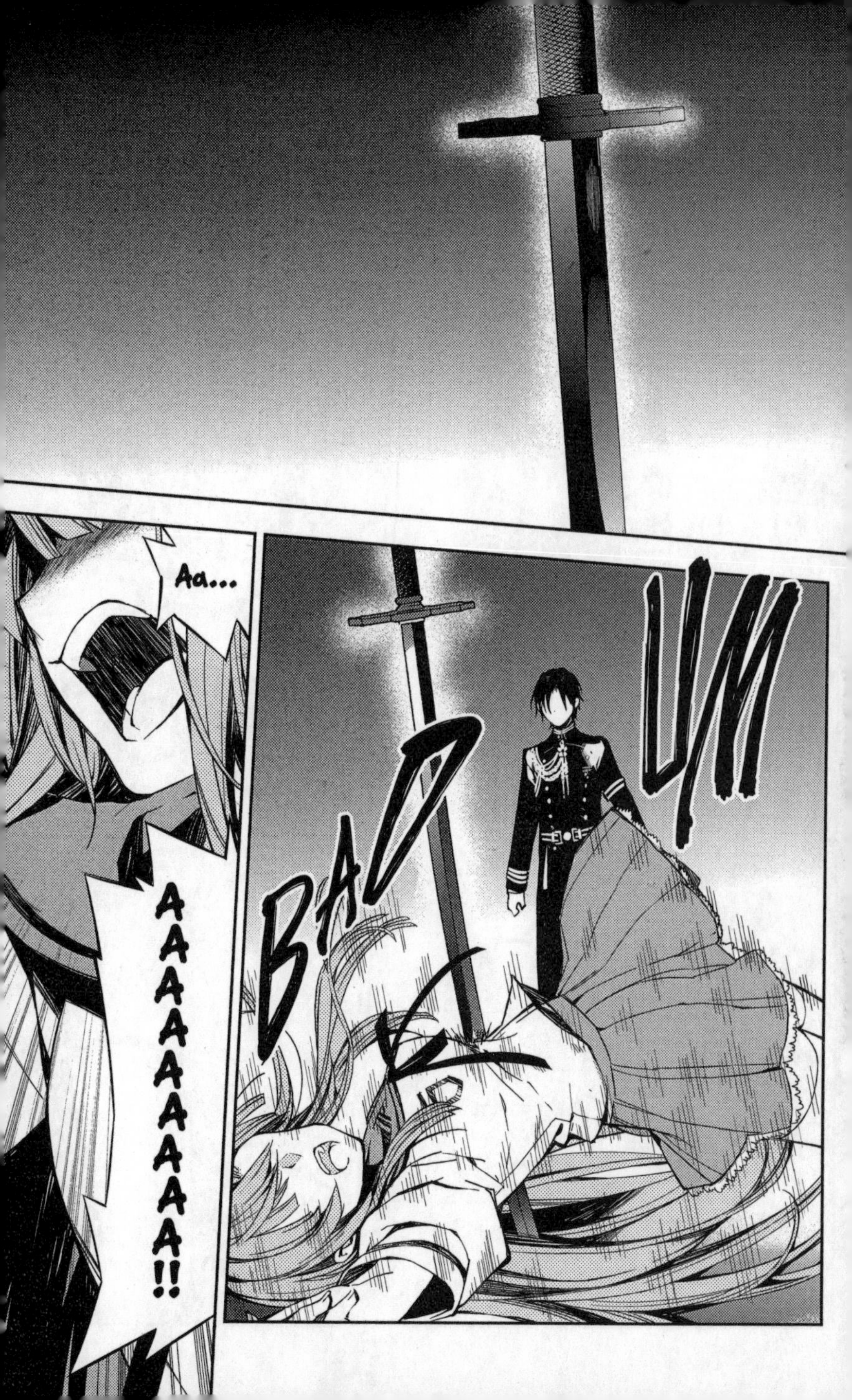
BADUM
Aa...
AAAAAAAAA!!

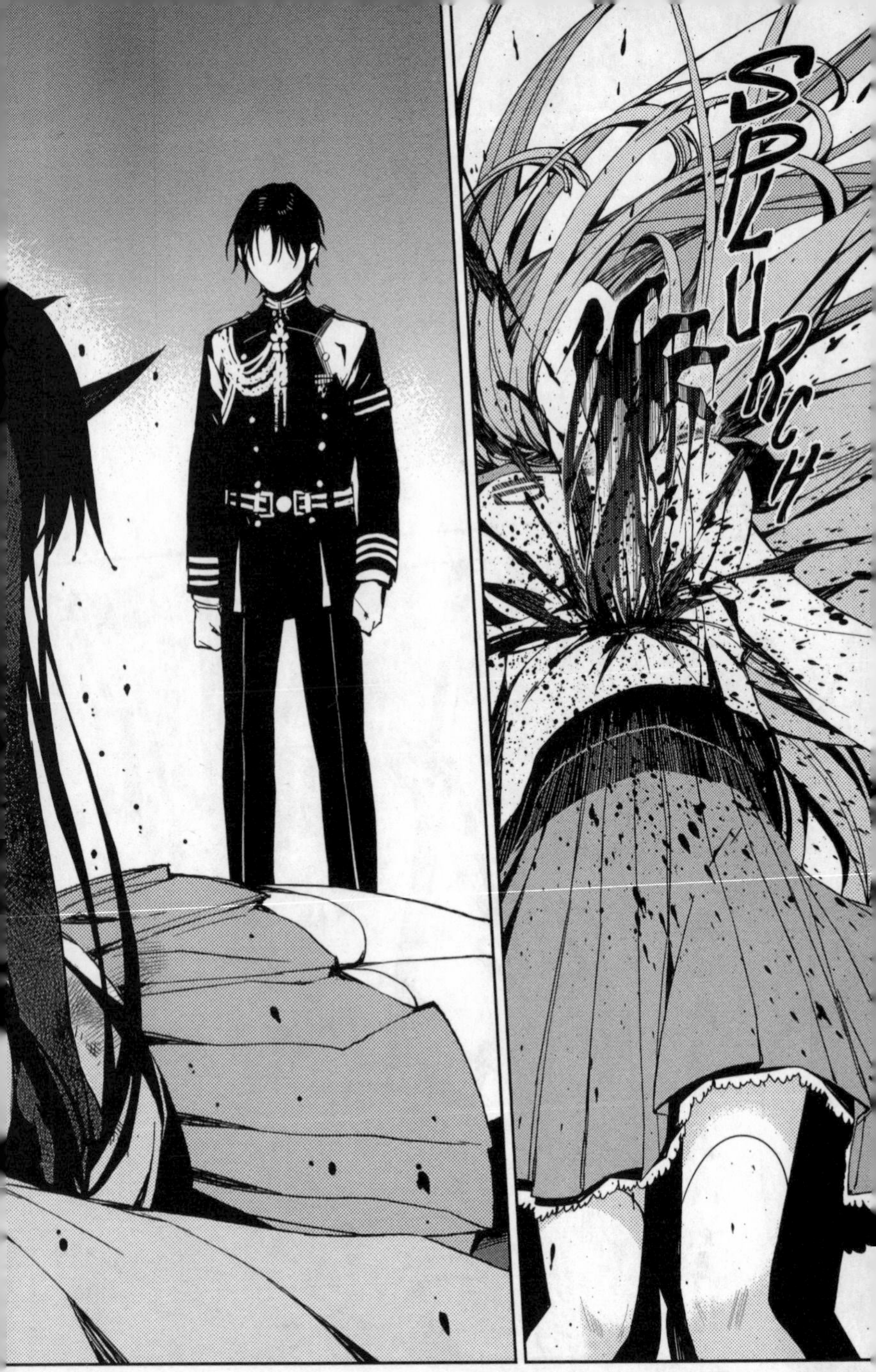
SPLURCH

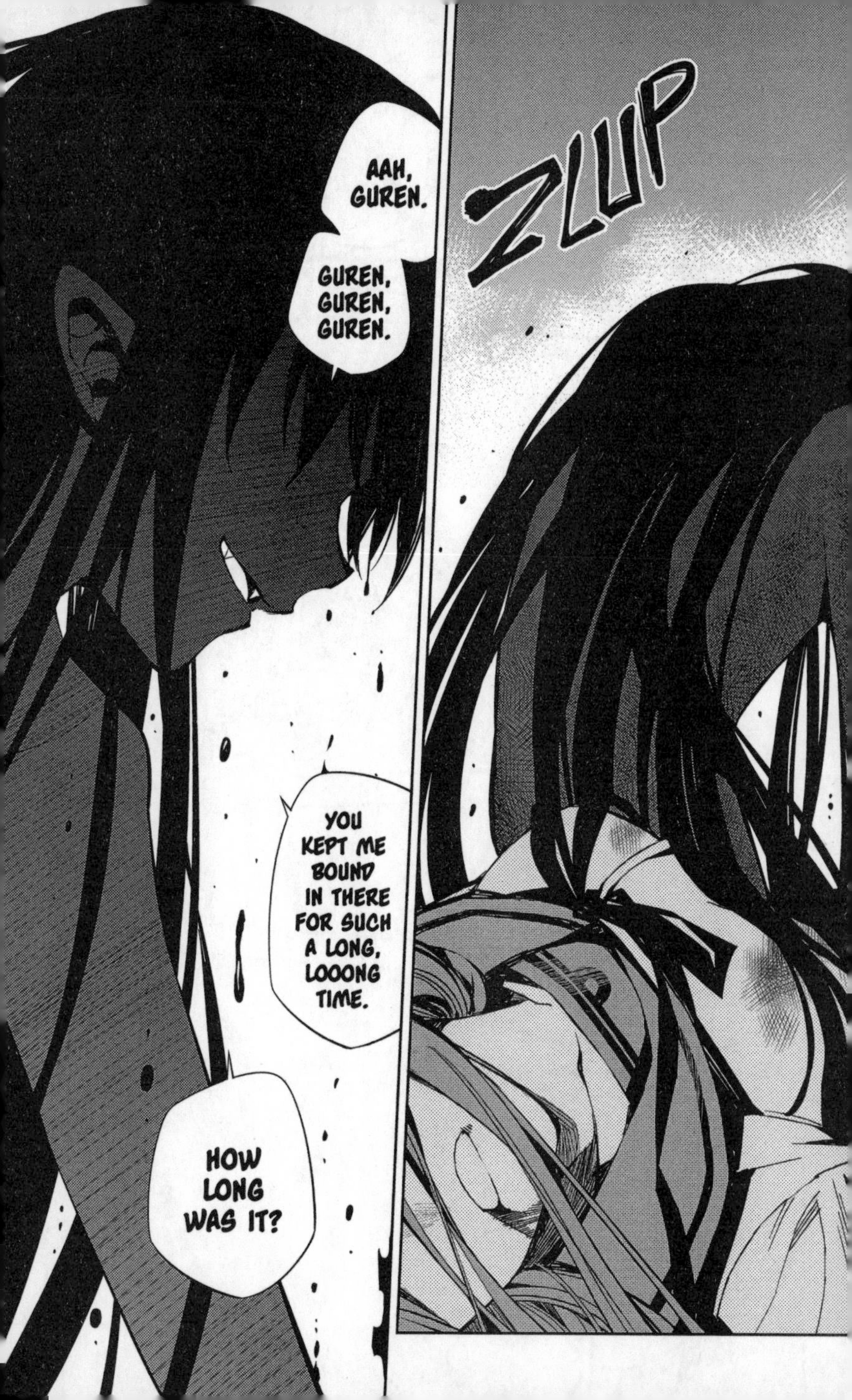
ZLUP
AAH, GUREN.
GUREN, GUREN, GUREN.
YOU KEPT ME BOUND IN THERE FOR SUCH A LONG, LOOONG TIME.
HOW LONG WAS IT?

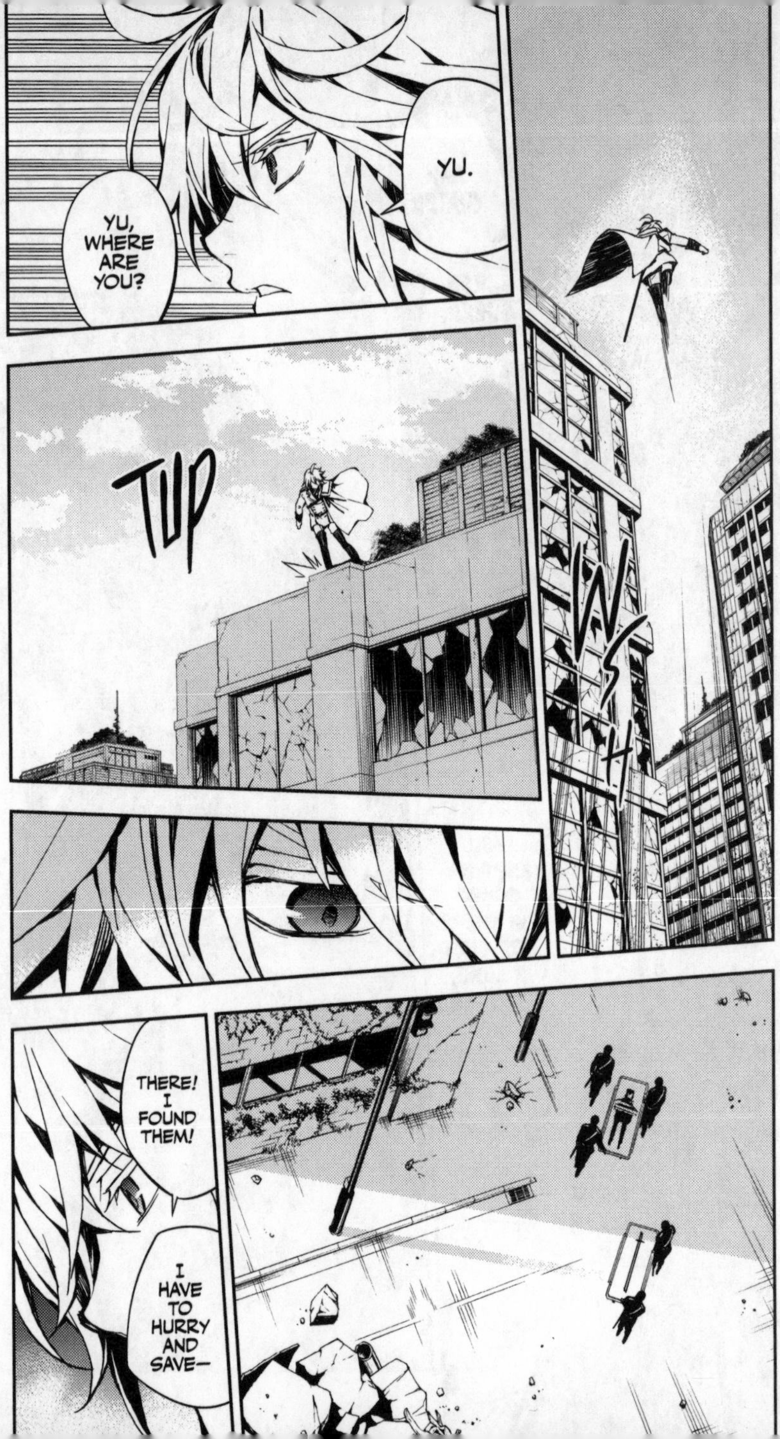
WSH
YU.
YU, WHERE ARE YOU?
TUP
THERE! I FOUND THEM!
I HAVE TO HURRY AND SAVE—

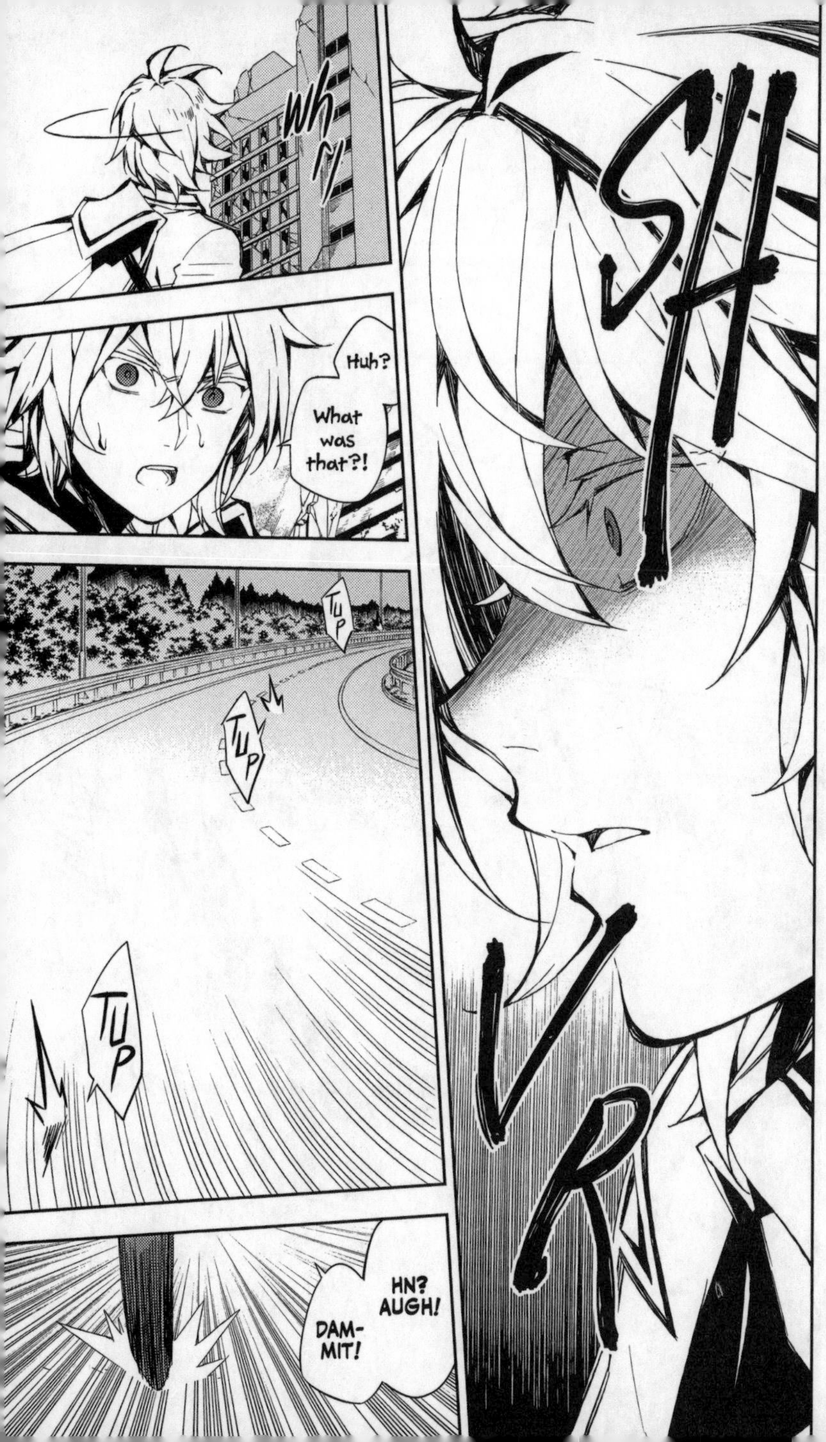
SHVR
wh~
Huh?
What was that?!
TUP
TUP
TUP
HN? AUGH!
DAM-MIT!

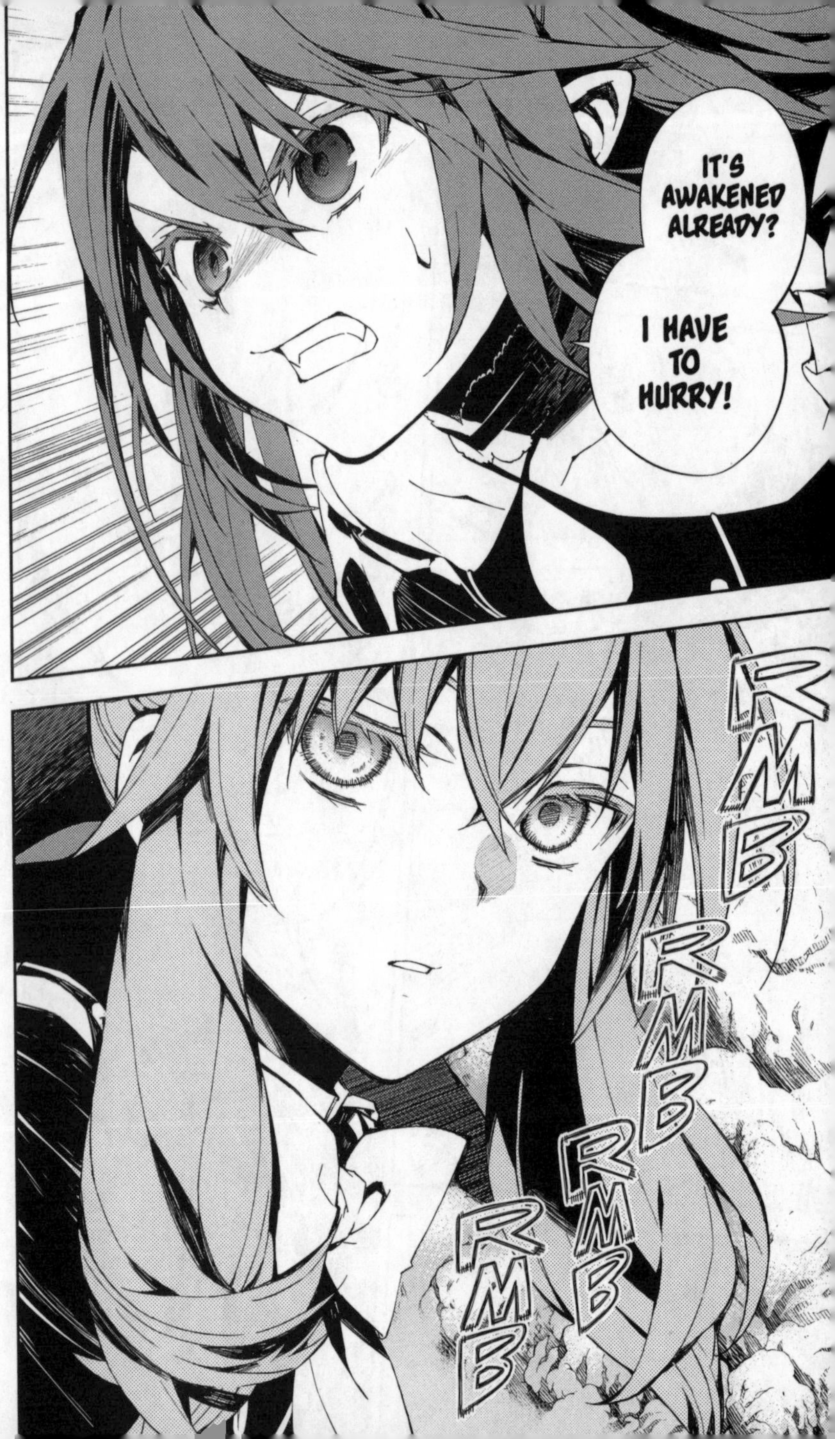
IT'S AWAKENED ALREADY?
I HAVE TO HURRY!
RMB RMB RMB RMB

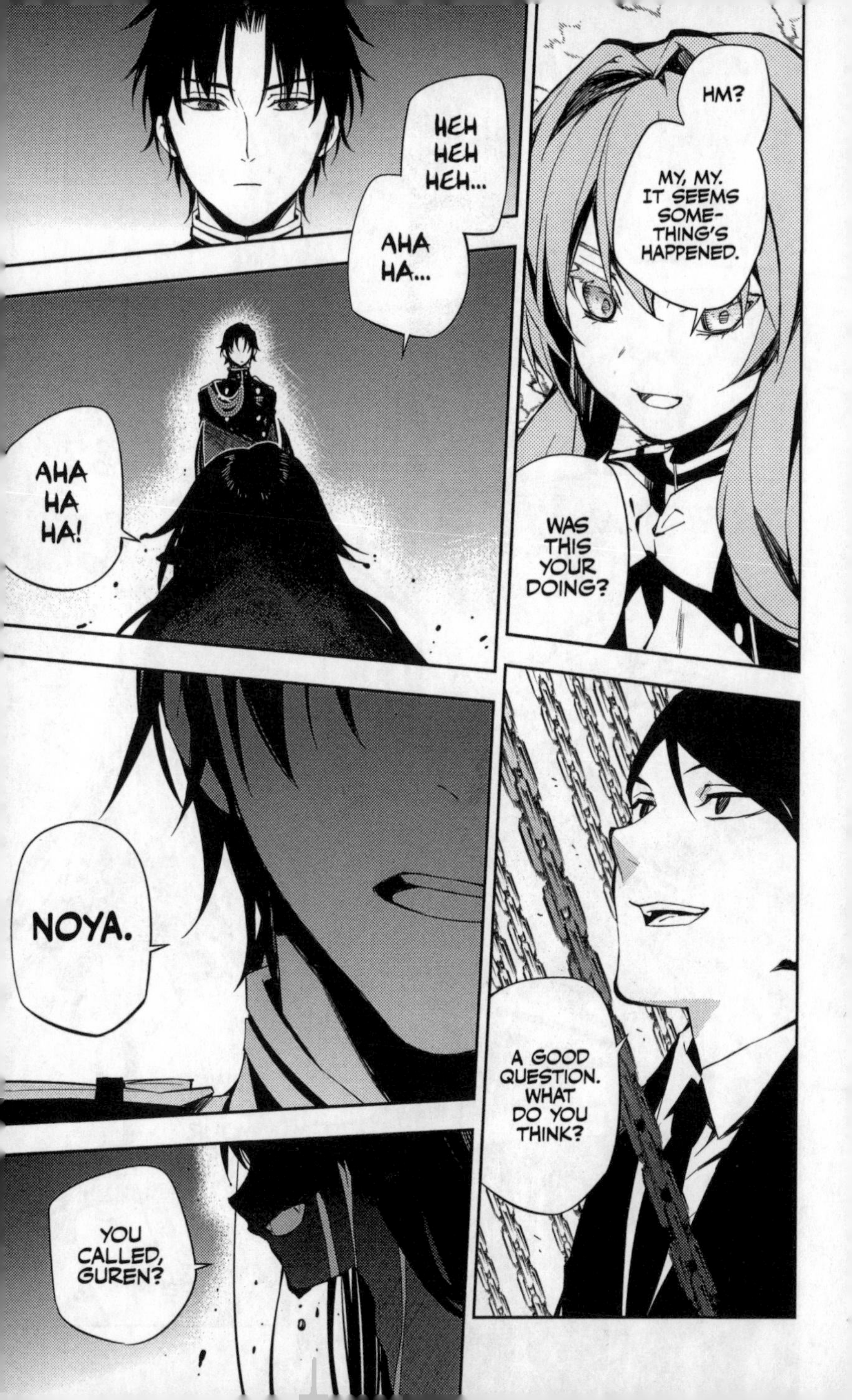
HM?
MY, MY. IT SEEMS SOME-THING'S HAPPENED.
WAS THIS YOUR DOING?
HEH HEH HEH...
AHA HA...
AHA HA HA!
A GOOD QUESTION. WHAT DO YOU THINK?
NOYA.
YOU CALLED, GUREN?

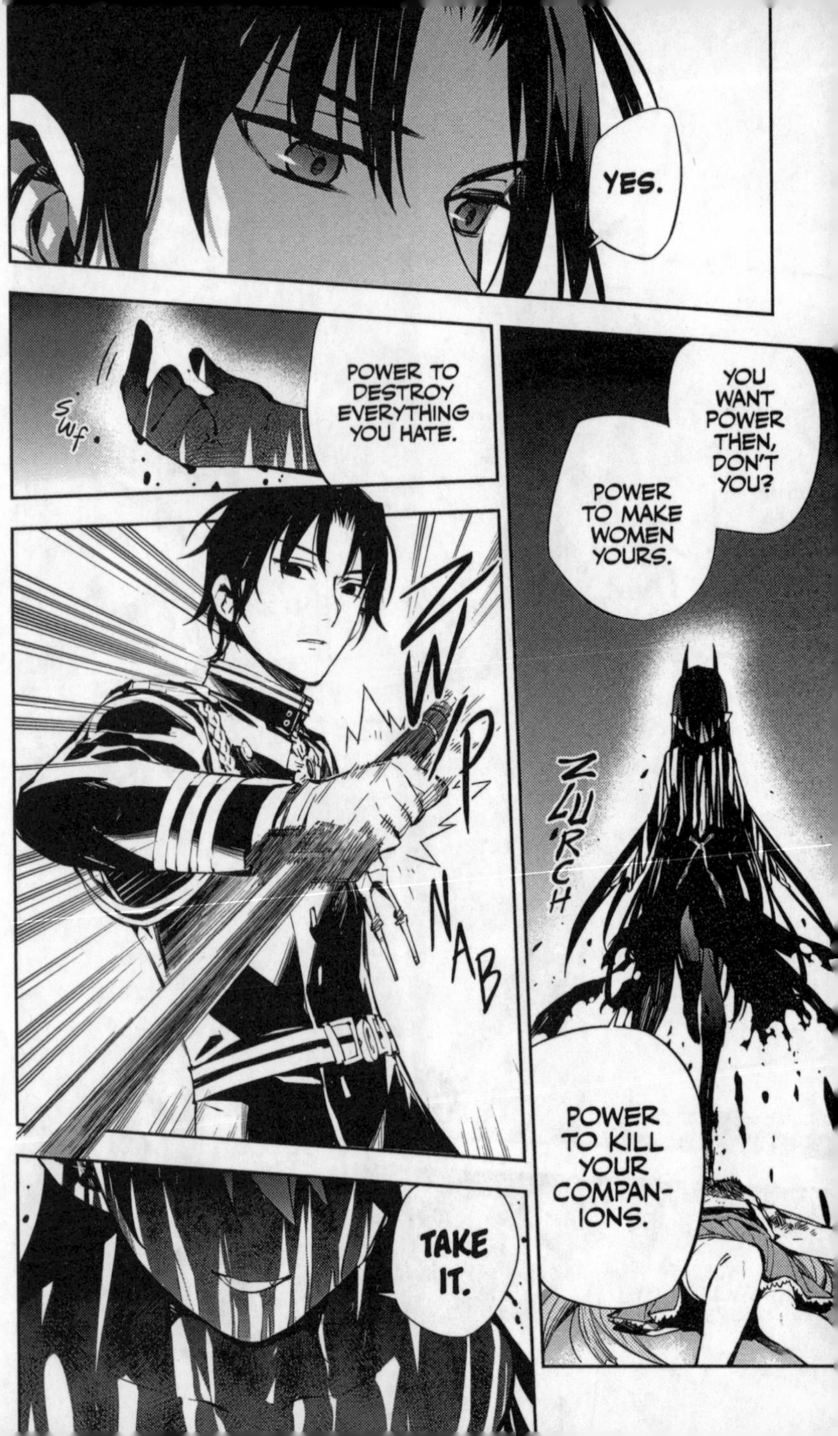
YES.
YOU WANT POWER THEN, DON'T YOU?
POWER TO MAKE WOMEN YOURS.
ZLURCH
POWER TO KILL YOUR COMPANIONS.
SWF
POWER TO DESTROY EVERYTHING YOU HATE.
ZWIP
NAB
TAKE IT.

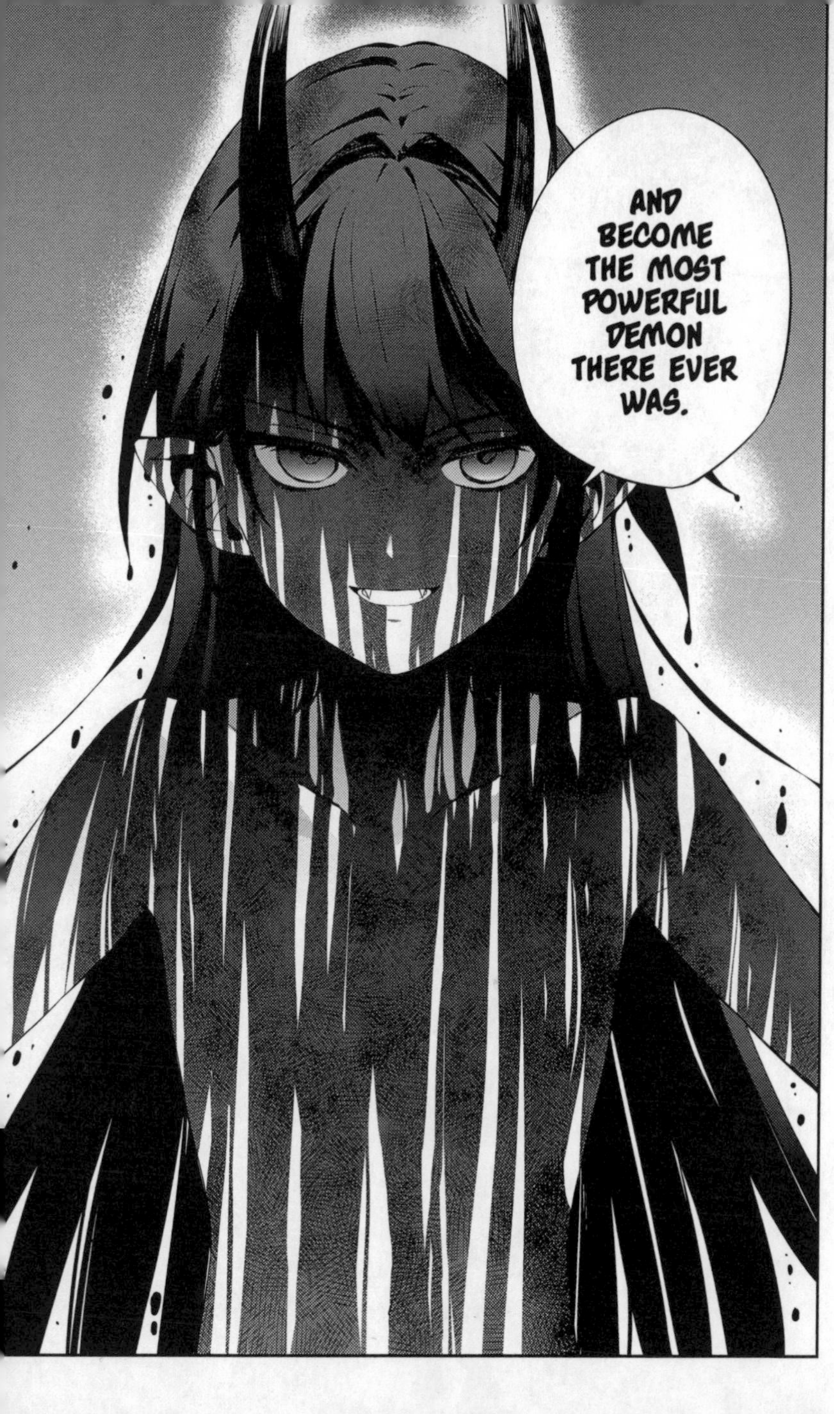
AND BECOME THE MOST POWERFUL DEMON THERE EVER WAS.

Seraph of the End
VAMPIRE REIGN

Chapter 83
Two Demons

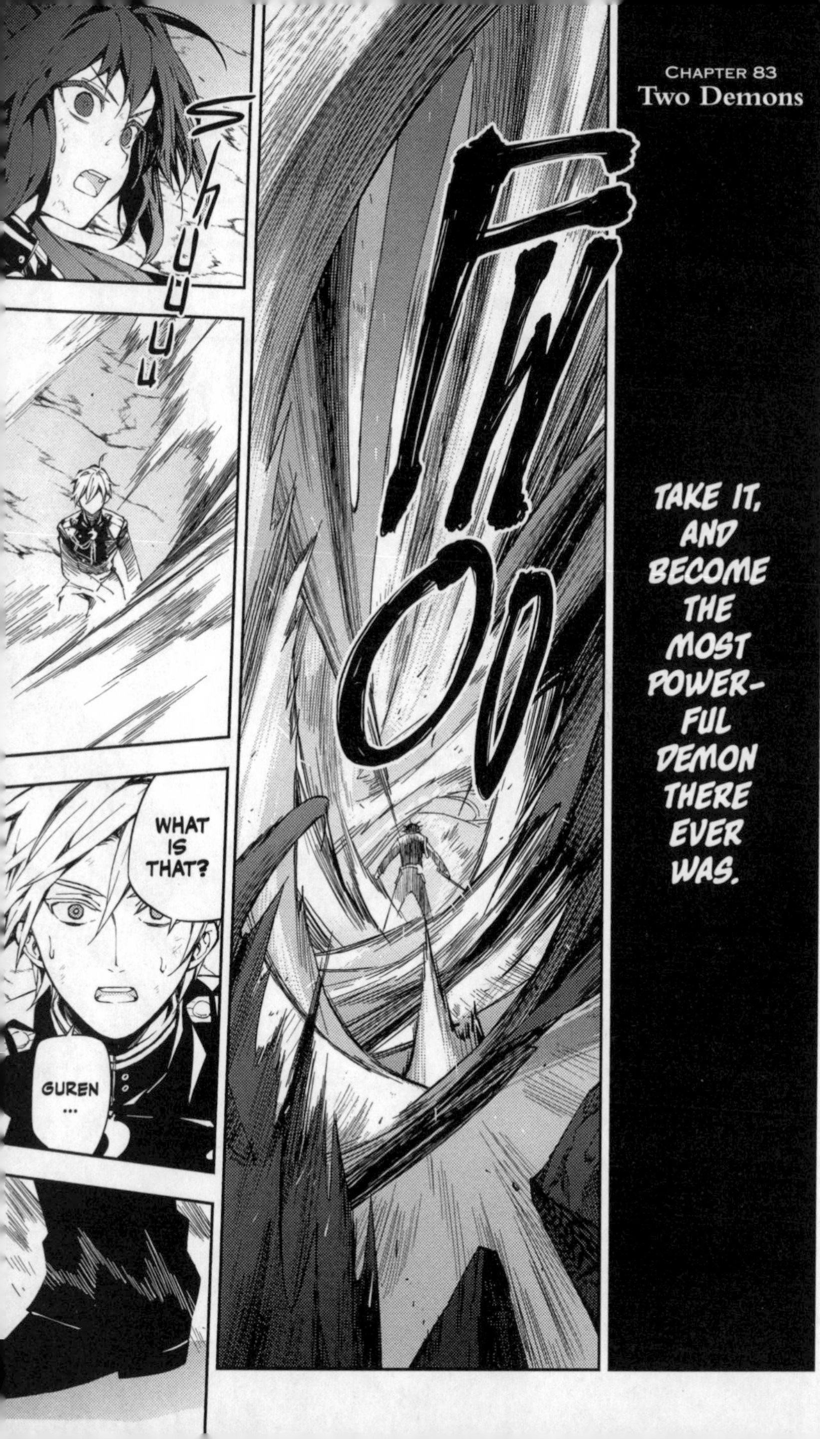
TAKE IT, AND BECOME THE MOST POWER-FUL DEMON THERE EVER WAS.
FWOO
SHUUUUU
WHAT IS THAT?
GUREN...

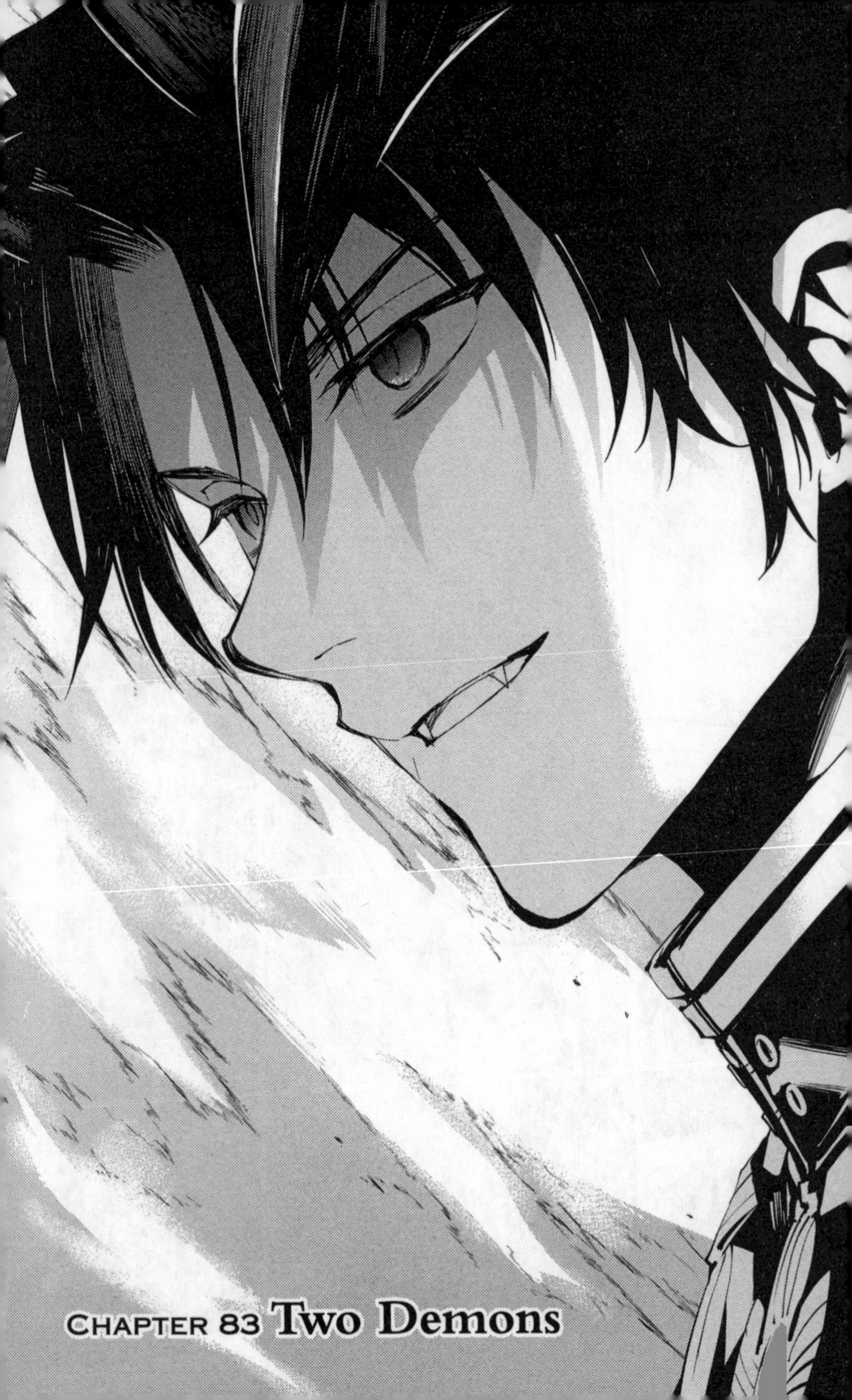
CHAPTER 83 Two Demons

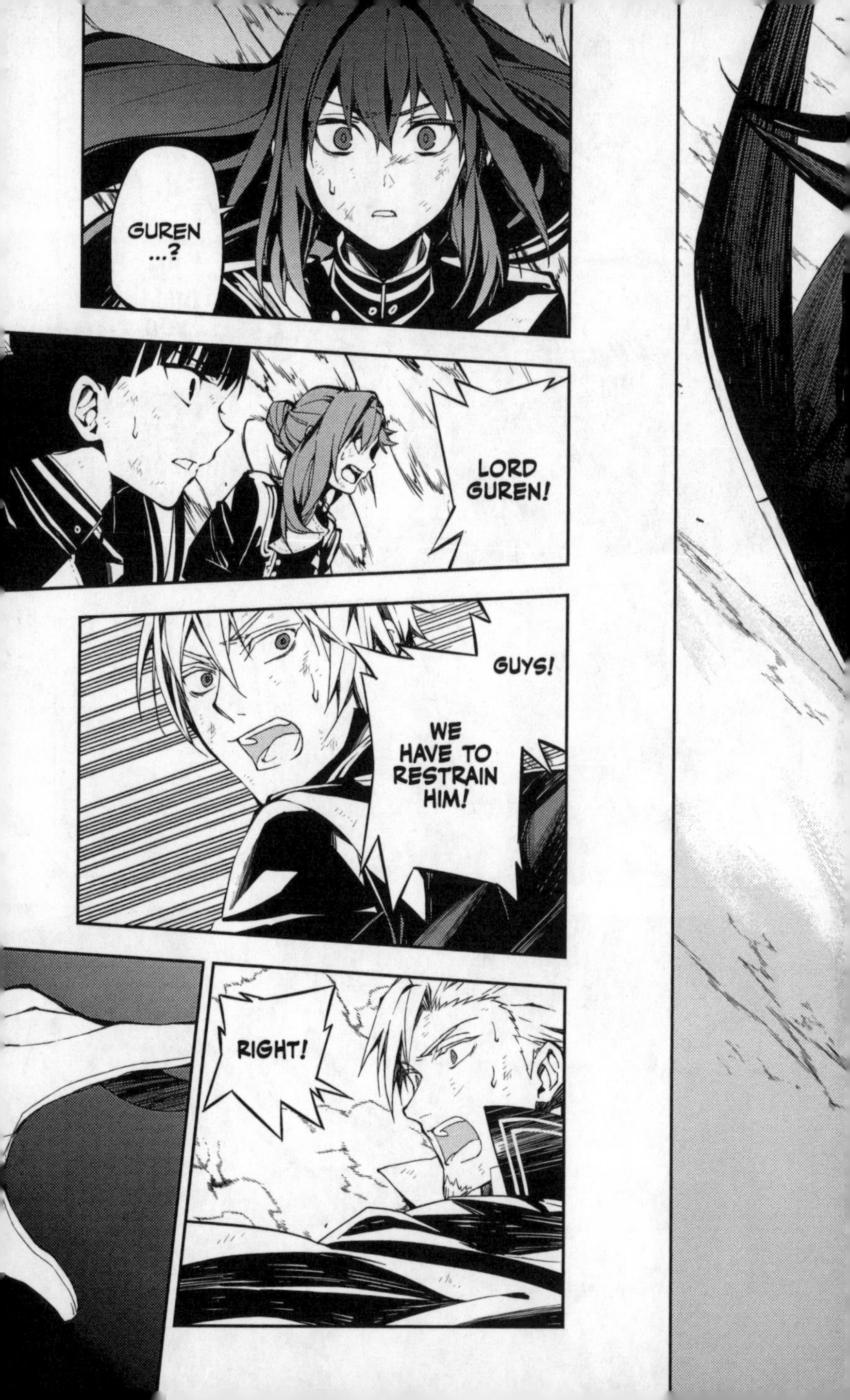
GUREN ...?
LORD GUREN!
GUYS!
WE HAVE TO RESTRAIN HIM!
RIGHT!

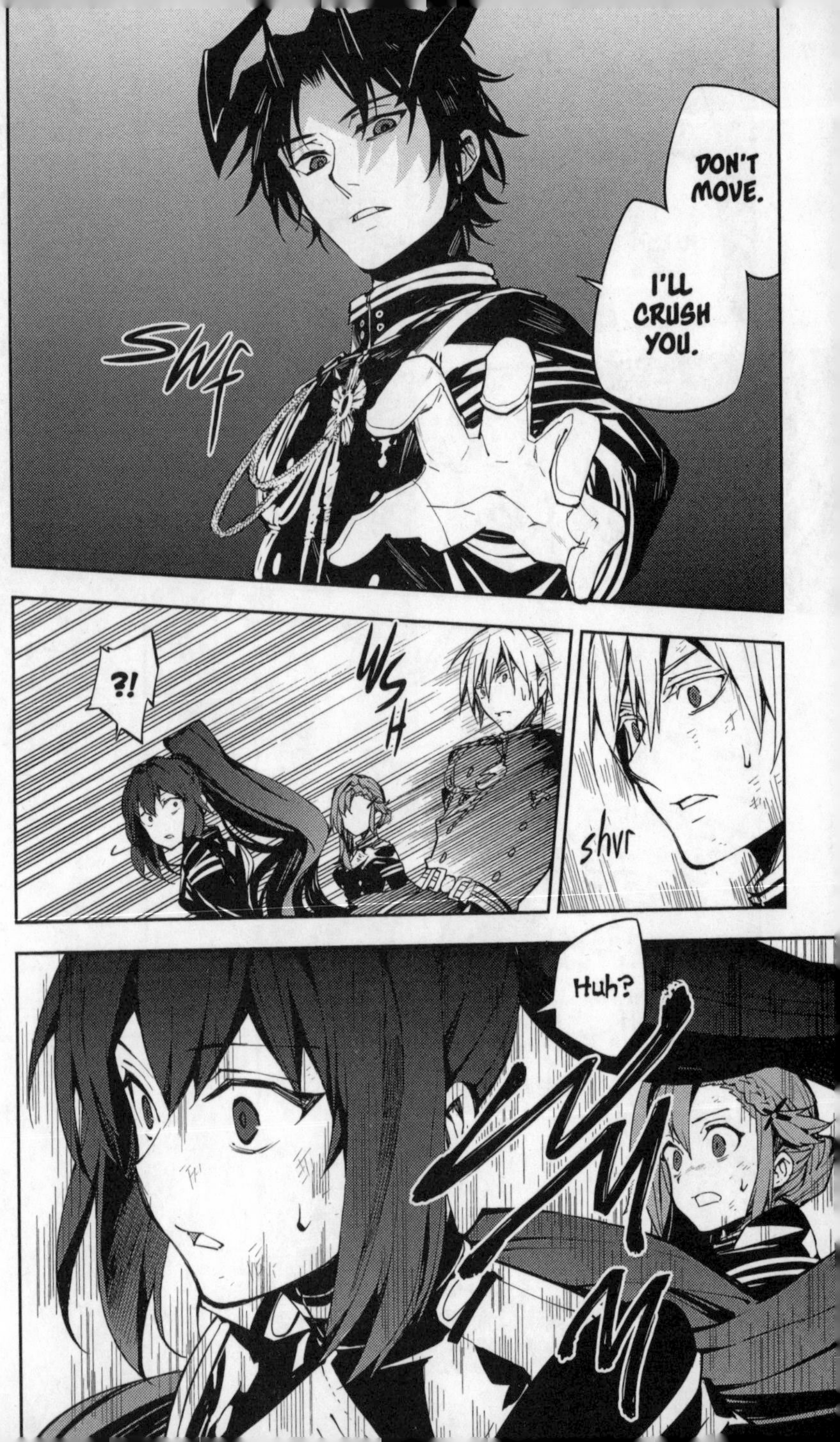
DON'T MOVE.
I'LL CRUSH YOU.
SWF
shvr
WSH
?!
Huh?
VMM

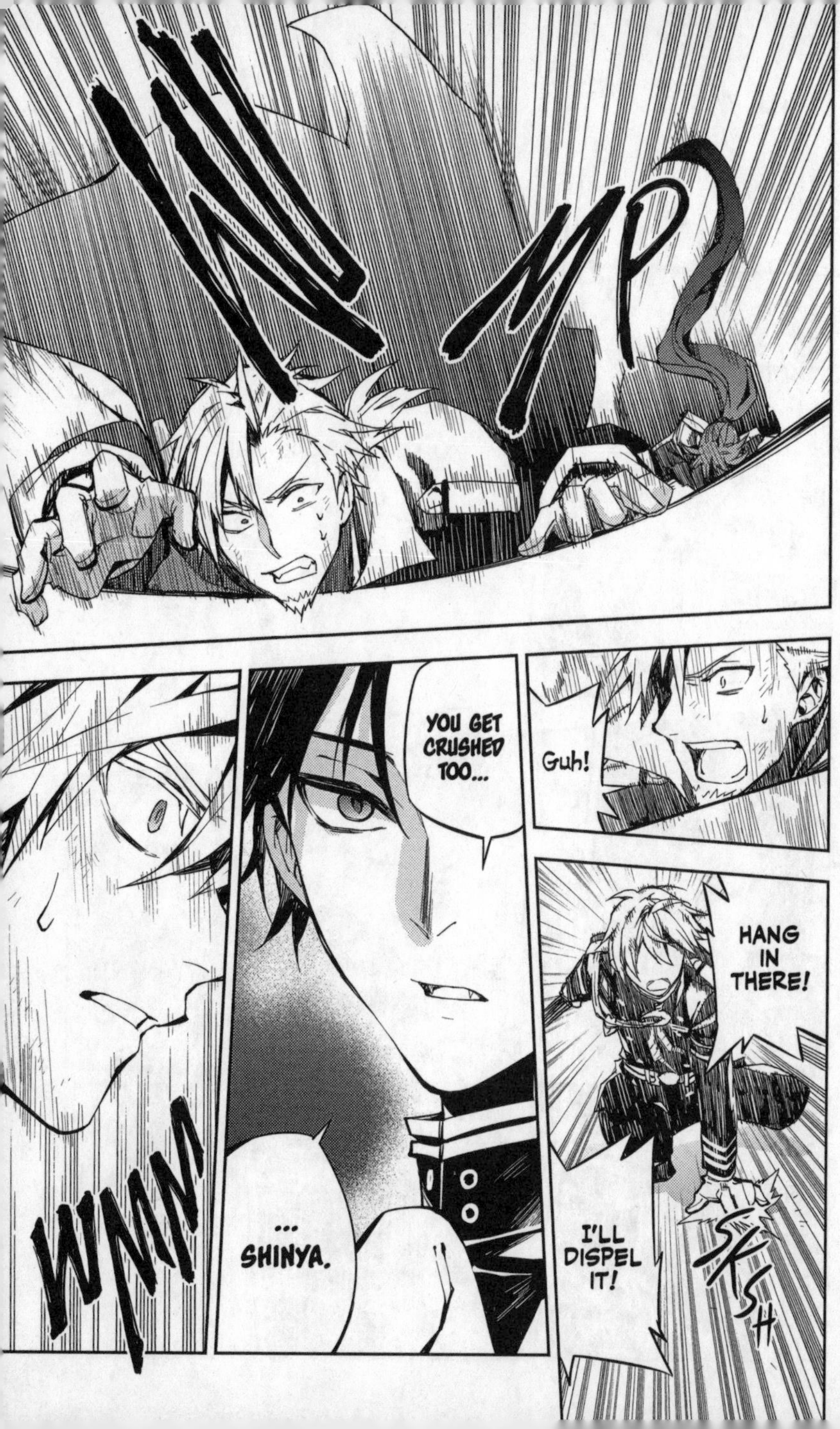
Guh!
HANG IN THERE!
I'LL DISPEL IT!
SKSH
YOU GET CRUSHED TOO...
...SHINYA.

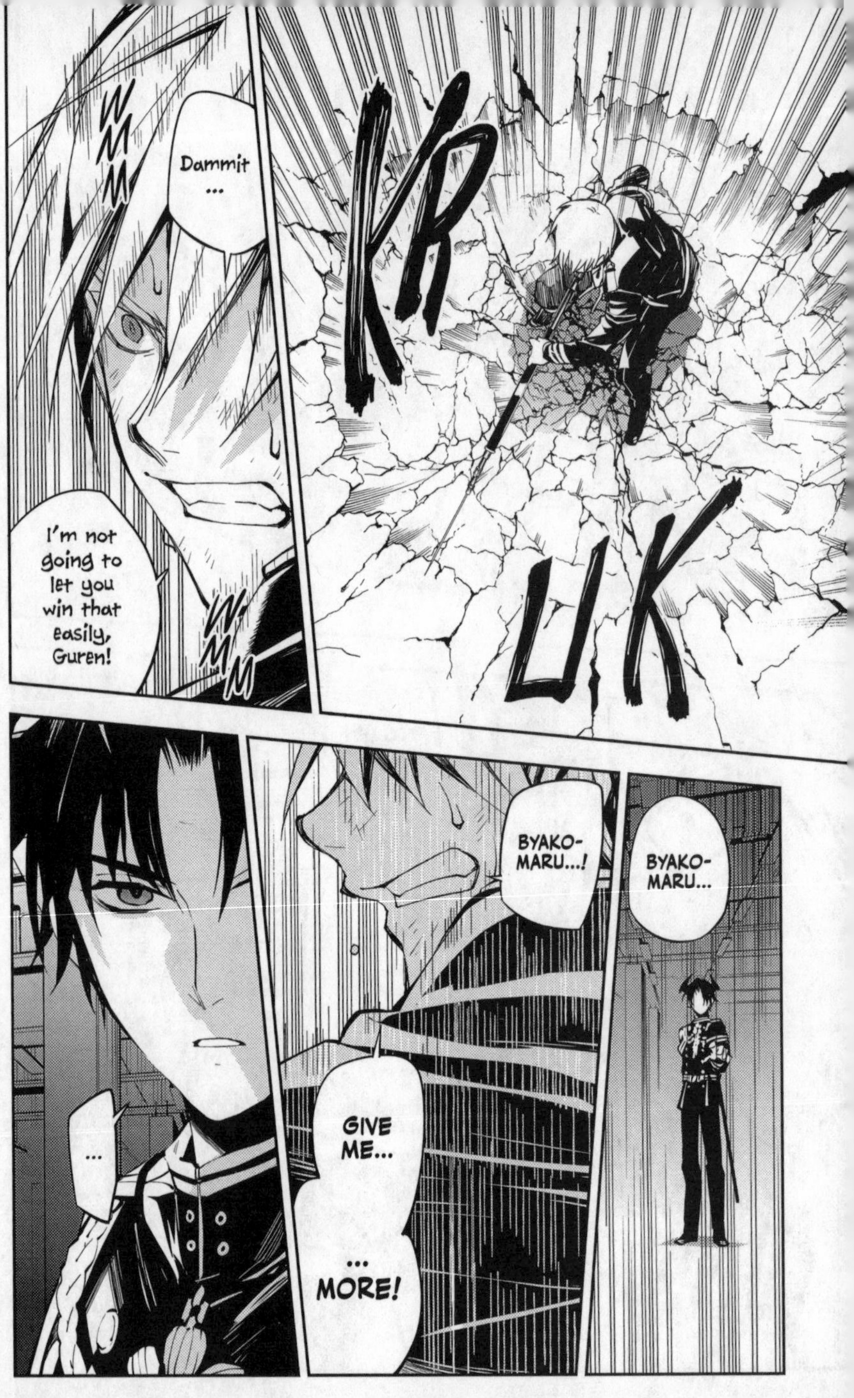
KRUK
Dammit ...
I'm not going to let you win that easily, Guren!
BYAKO-MARU...
BYAKO-MARU...!
GIVE ME...
... MORE!
...

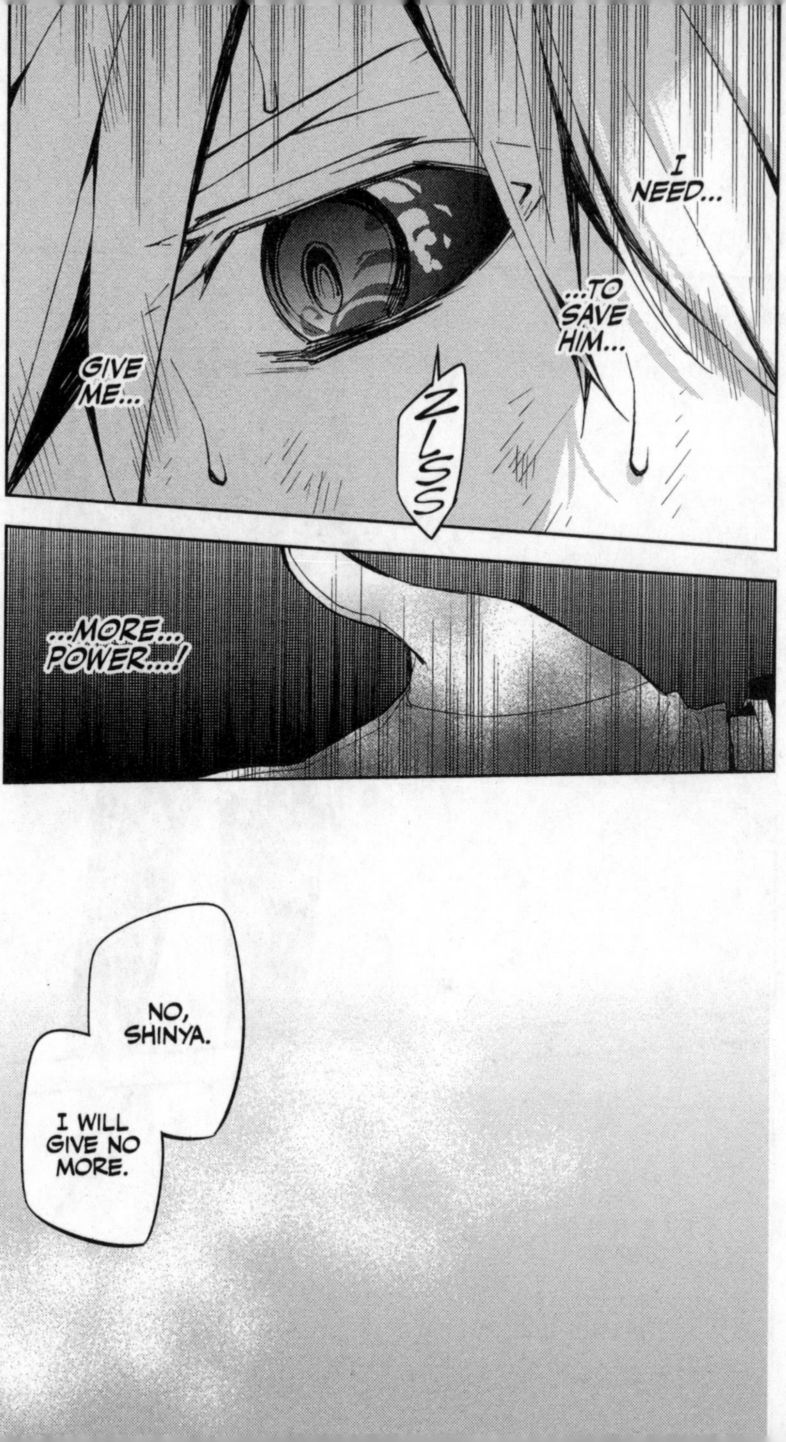
I NEED...
...TO SAVE HIM...
ZLSS
GIVE ME...
...MORE... POWER...!
NO, SHINYA.
I WILL GIVE NO MORE.

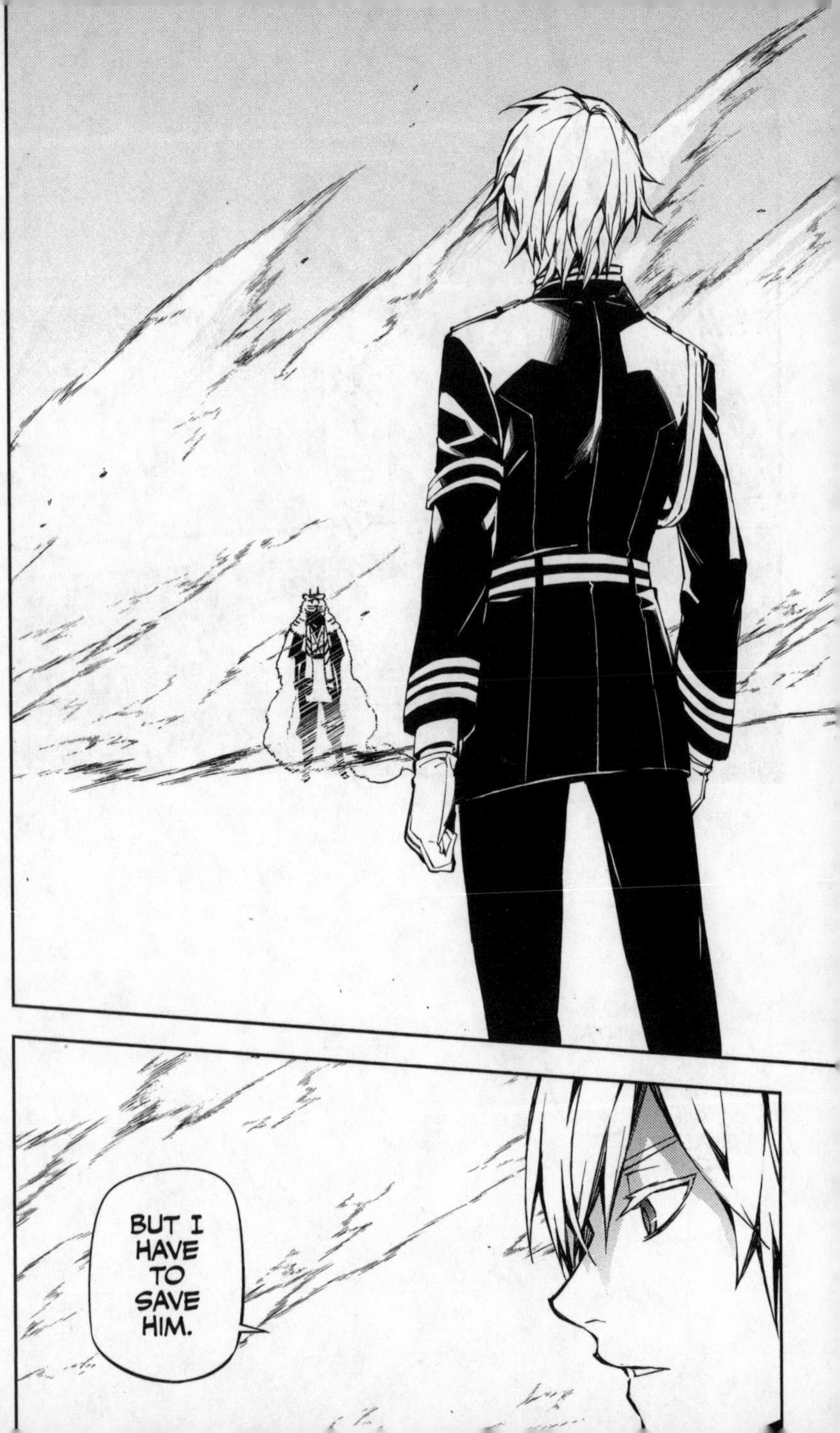
BUT I HAVE TO SAVE HIM.

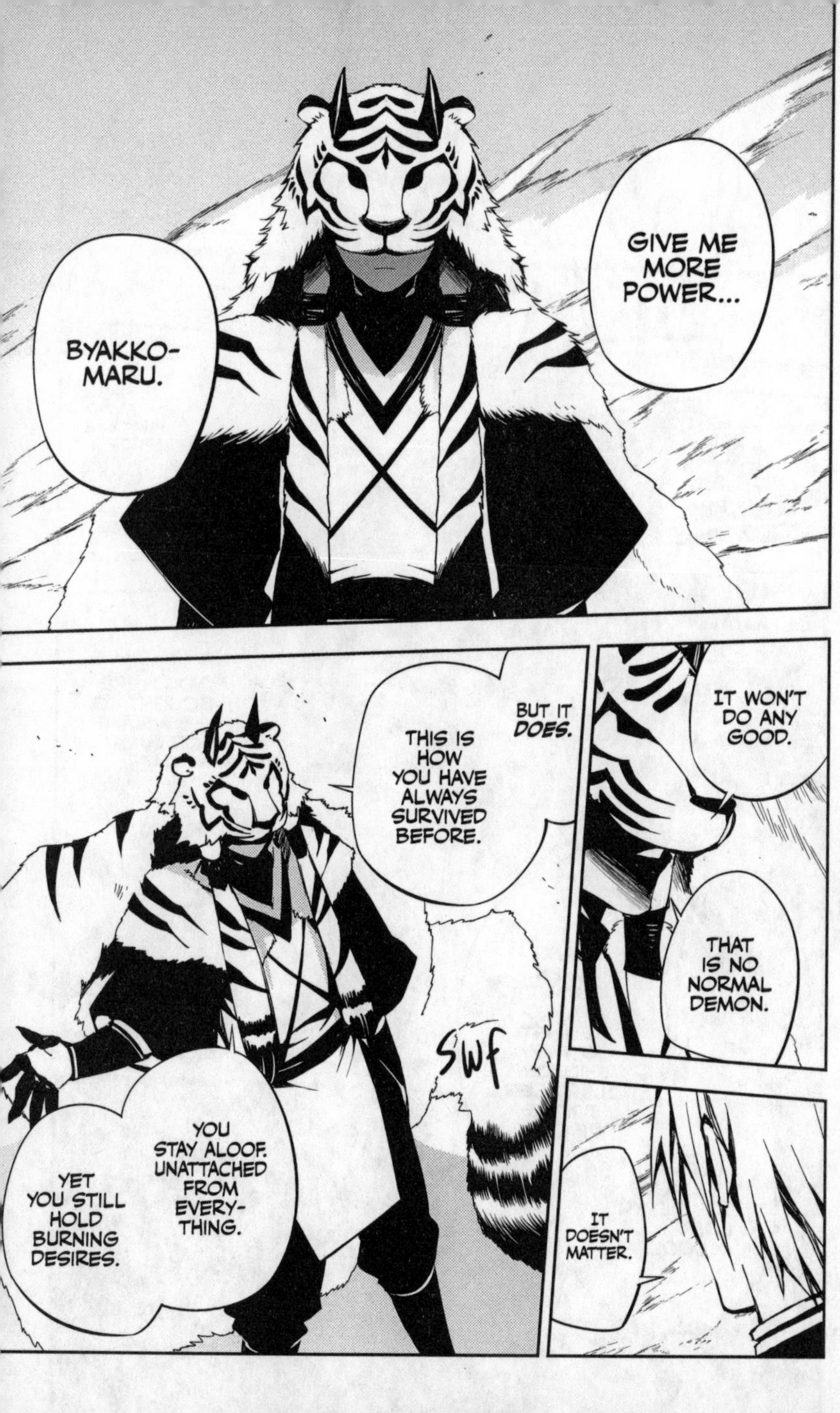
GIVE ME MORE POWER...
BYAKKO-MARU.
IT WON'T DO ANY GOOD.
THAT IS NO NORMAL DEMON.
IT DOESN'T MATTER.
BUT IT DOES.
THIS IS HOW YOU HAVE ALWAYS SURVIVED BEFORE.
SWF
YOU STAY ALOOF. UNATTACHED FROM EVERY-THING.
YET YOU STILL HOLD BURNING DESIRES.

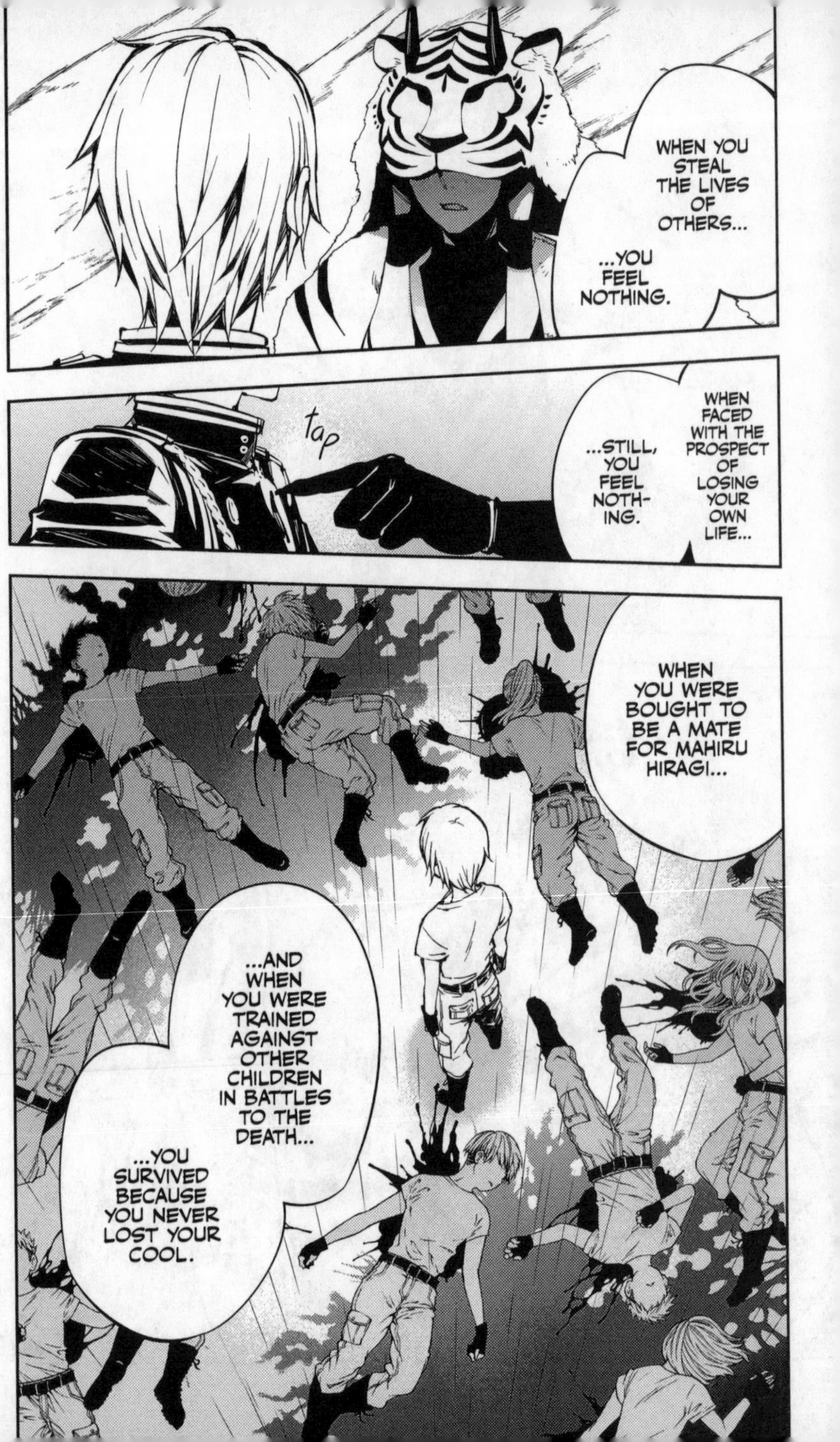
WHEN YOU STEAL THE LIVES OF OTHERS...
...YOU FEEL NOTHING.
WHEN FACED WITH THE PROSPECT OF LOSING YOUR OWN LIFE...
...STILL, YOU FEEL NOTH-ING.
tap
WHEN YOU WERE BOUGHT TO BE A MATE FOR MAHIRU HIRAGI...
...AND WHEN YOU WERE TRAINED AGAINST OTHER CHILDREN IN BATTLES TO THE DEATH...
...YOU SURVIVED BECAUSE YOU NEVER LOST YOUR COOL.

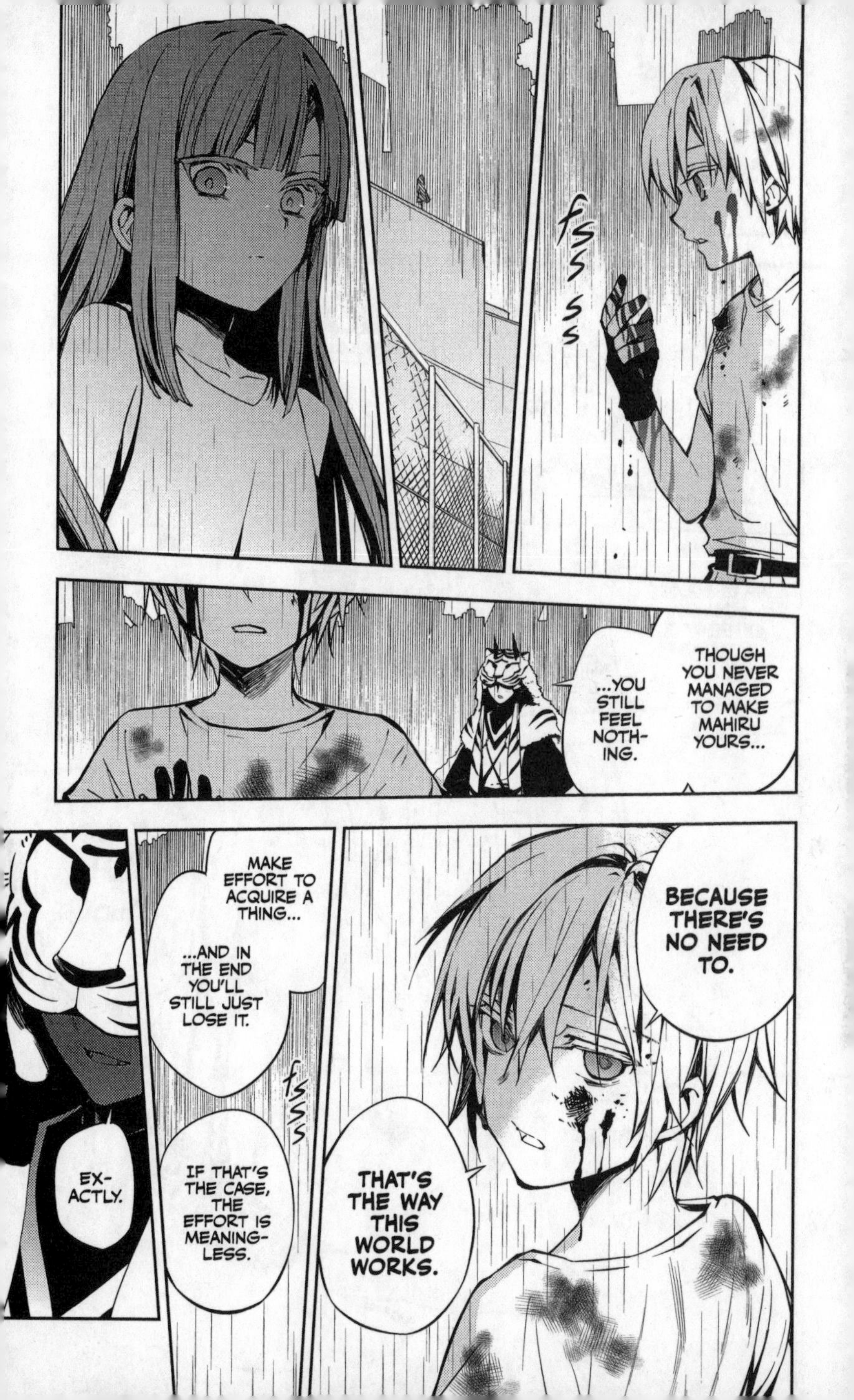
FSSS SS
THOUGH YOU NEVER MANAGED TO MAKE MAHIRU YOURS...
...YOU STILL FEEL NOTHING.
BECAUSE THERE'S NO NEED TO.
THAT'S THE WAY THIS WORLD WORKS.
FSSS
MAKE EFFORT TO ACQUIRE A THING...
...AND IN THE END YOU'LL STILL JUST LOSE IT.
IF THAT'S THE CASE, THE EFFORT IS MEANINGLESS.
EXACTLY.

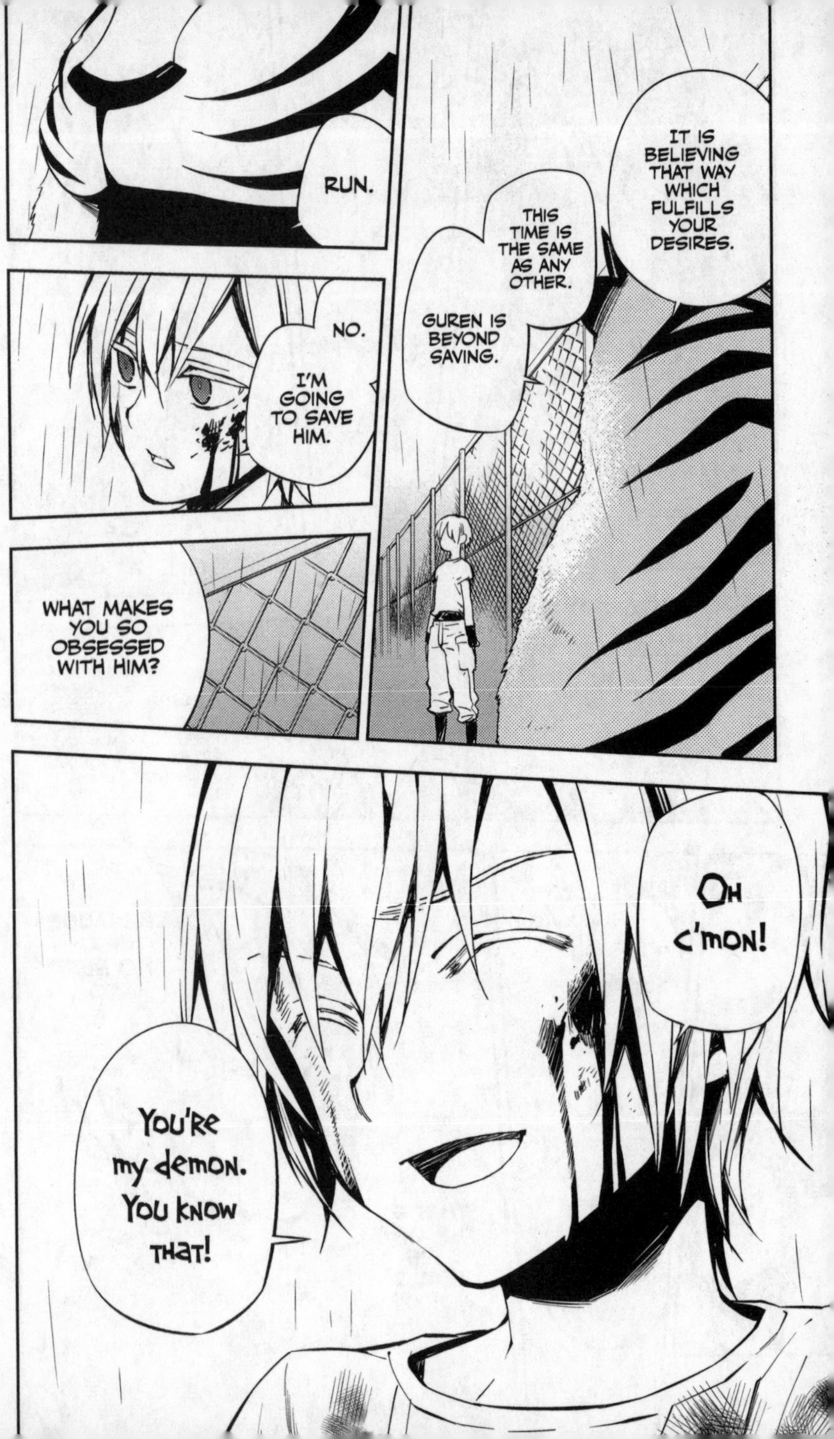
IT IS BELIEVING THAT WAY WHICH FULFILLS YOUR DESIRES.
THIS TIME IS THE SAME AS ANY OTHER.
GUREN IS BEYOND SAVING.
RUN.
NO.
I'M GOING TO SAVE HIM.
WHAT MAKES YOU SO OBSESSED WITH HIM?
OH C'MON!
YOU'RE MY DEMON. YOU KNOW THAT!

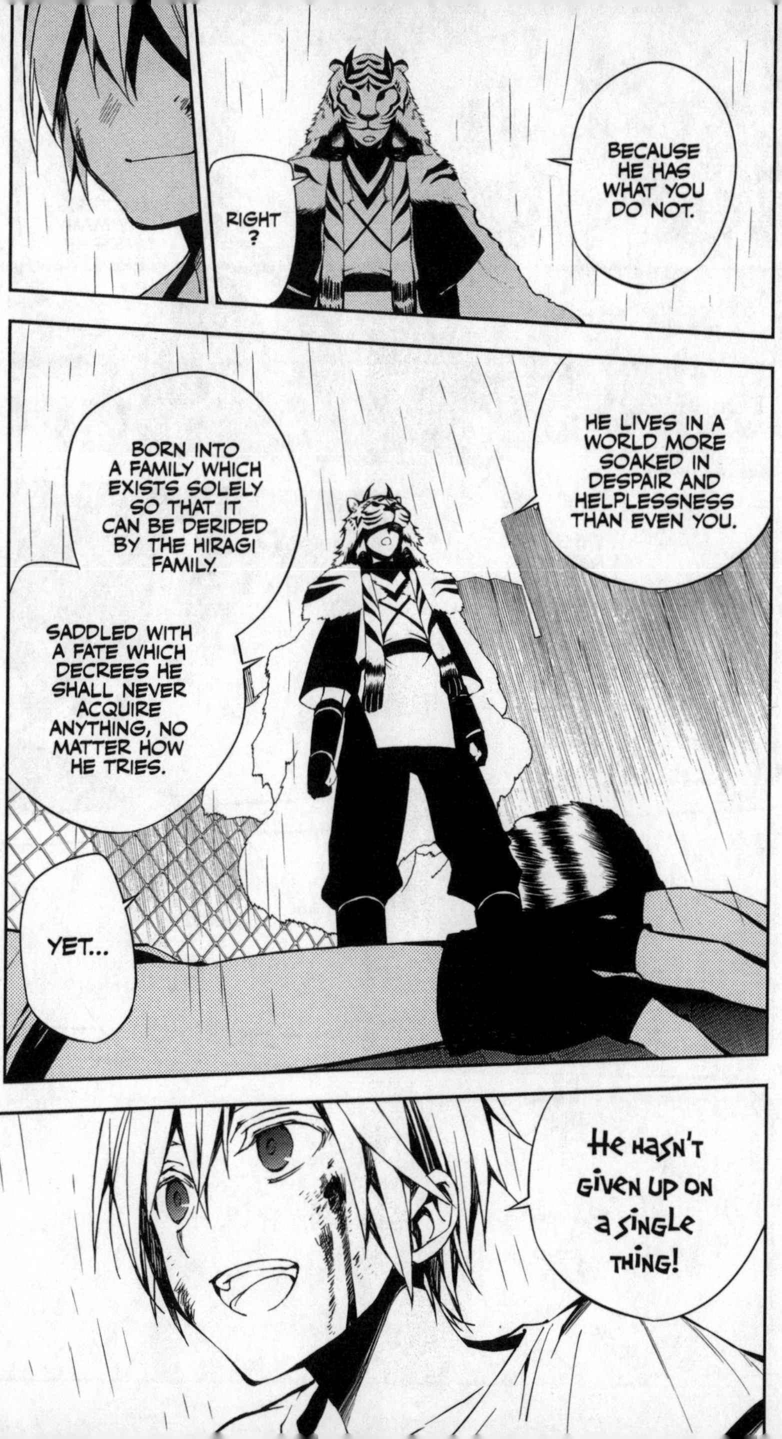
BECAUSE HE HAS WHAT YOU DO NOT.
RIGHT?
HE LIVES IN A WORLD MORE SOAKED IN DESPAIR AND HELPLESSNESS THAN EVEN YOU.
BORN INTO A FAMILY WHICH EXISTS SOLELY SO THAT IT CAN BE DERIDED BY THE HIRAGI FAMILY.
SADDLED WITH A FATE WHICH DECREES HE SHALL NEVER ACQUIRE ANYTHING, NO MATTER HOW HE TRIES.
YET...
He hasn't given up on a single thing!

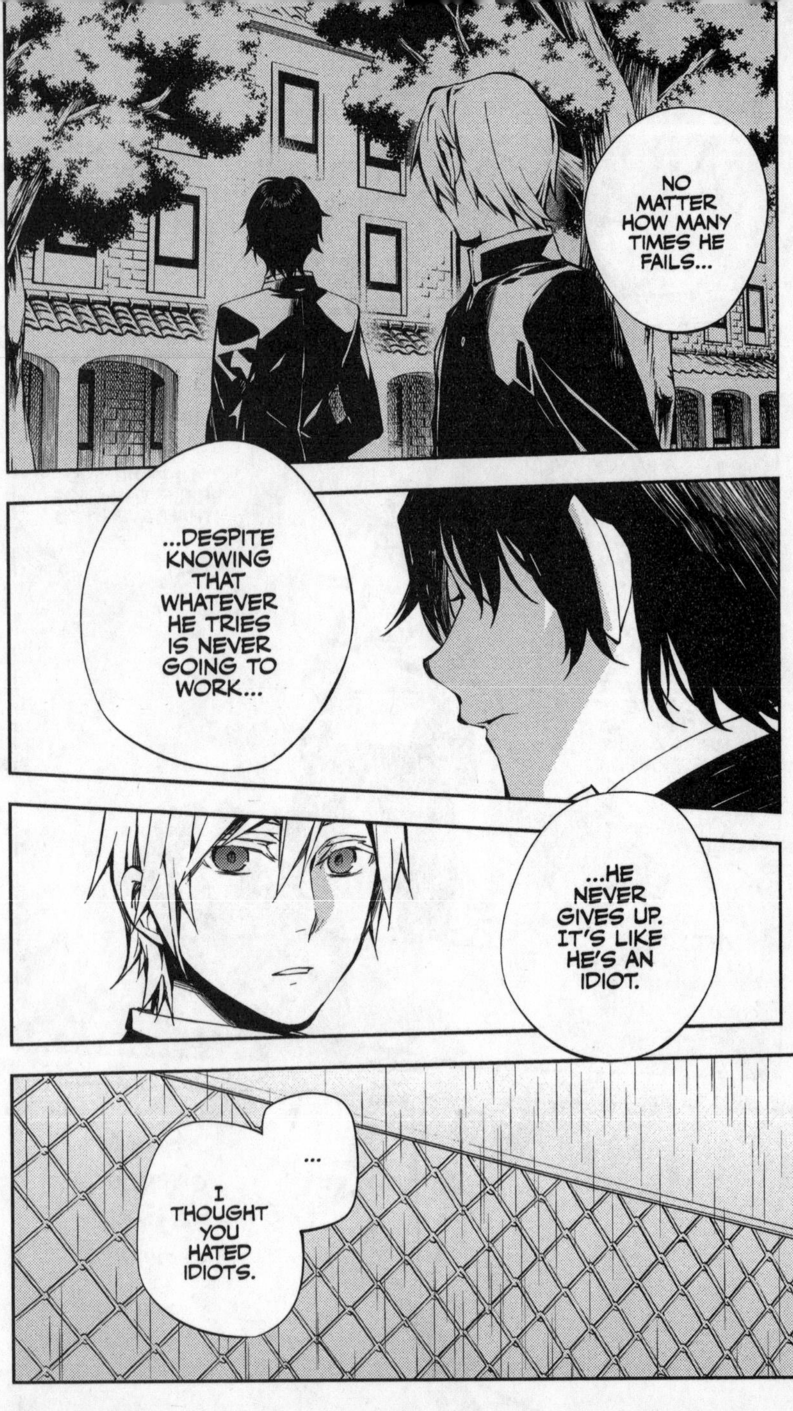
NO MATTER HOW MANY TIMES HE FAILS...
...DESPITE KNOWING THAT WHATEVER HE TRIES IS NEVER GOING TO WORK...
...HE NEVER GIVES UP. IT'S LIKE HE'S AN IDIOT.
...
I THOUGHT YOU HATED IDIOTS.

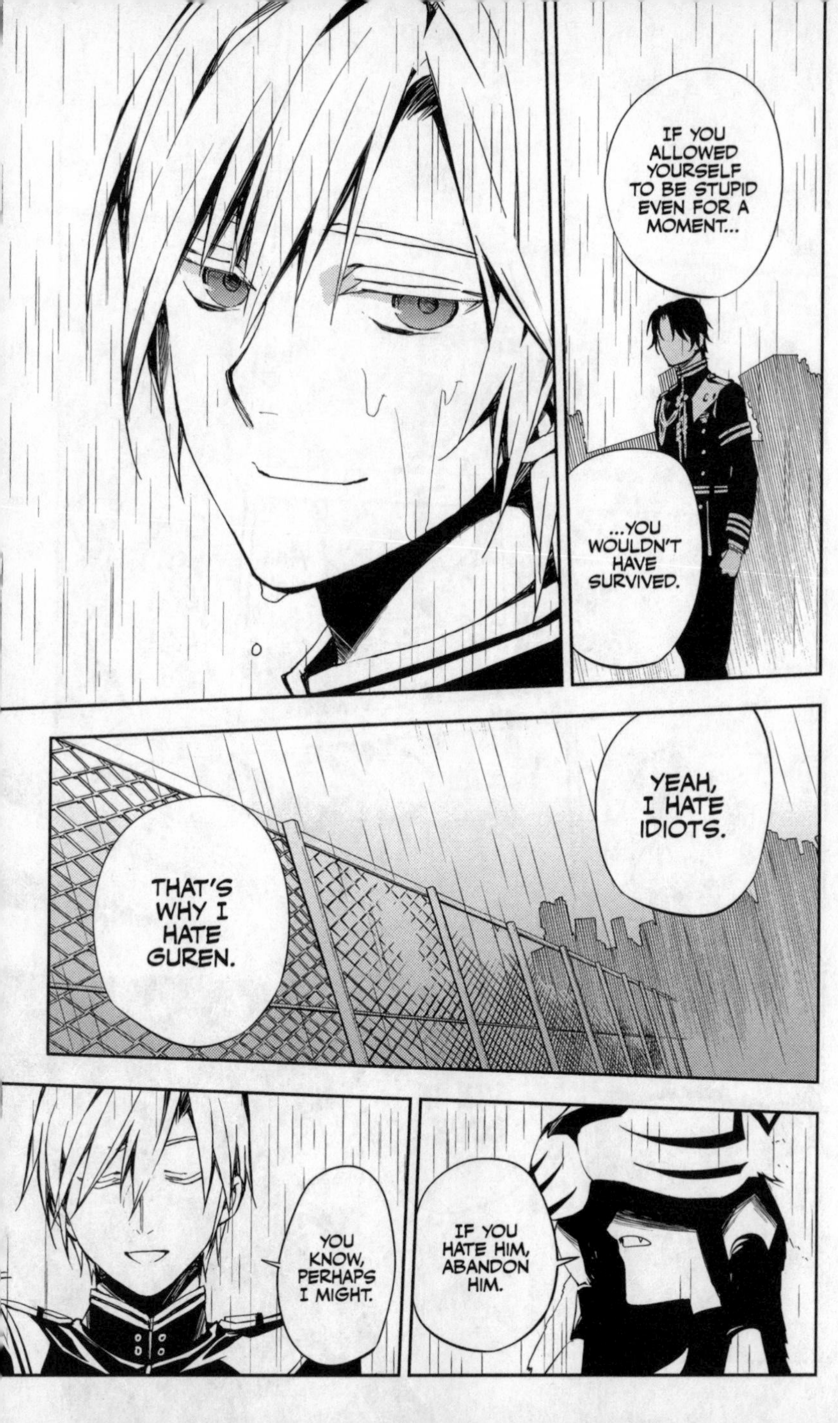
IF YOU ALLOWED YOURSELF TO BE STUPID EVEN FOR A MOMENT...
...YOU WOULDN'T HAVE SURVIVED.
YEAH, I HATE IDIOTS.
THAT'S WHY I HATE GUREN.
IF YOU HATE HIM, ABANDON HIM.
YOU KNOW, PERHAPS I MIGHT.

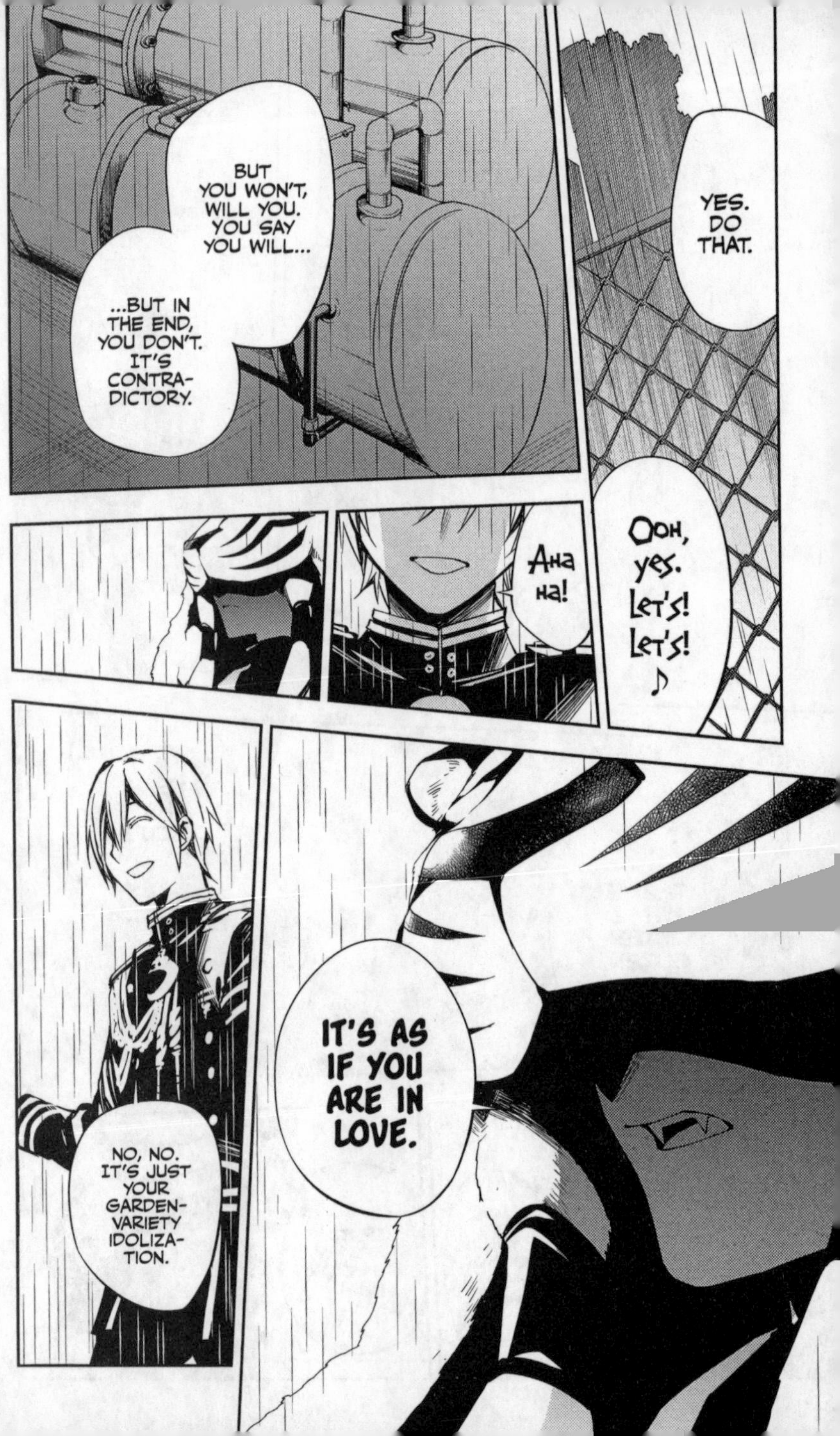
YES. DO THAT.
OOH, YES. LET'S! LET'S! ♪
BUT YOU WON'T, WILL YOU. YOU SAY YOU WILL...
...BUT IN THE END, YOU DON'T. IT'S CONTRA-DICTORY.
AHA HA!
IT'S AS IF YOU ARE IN LOVE.
NO, NO. IT'S JUST YOUR GARDEN-VARIETY IDOLIZA-TION.

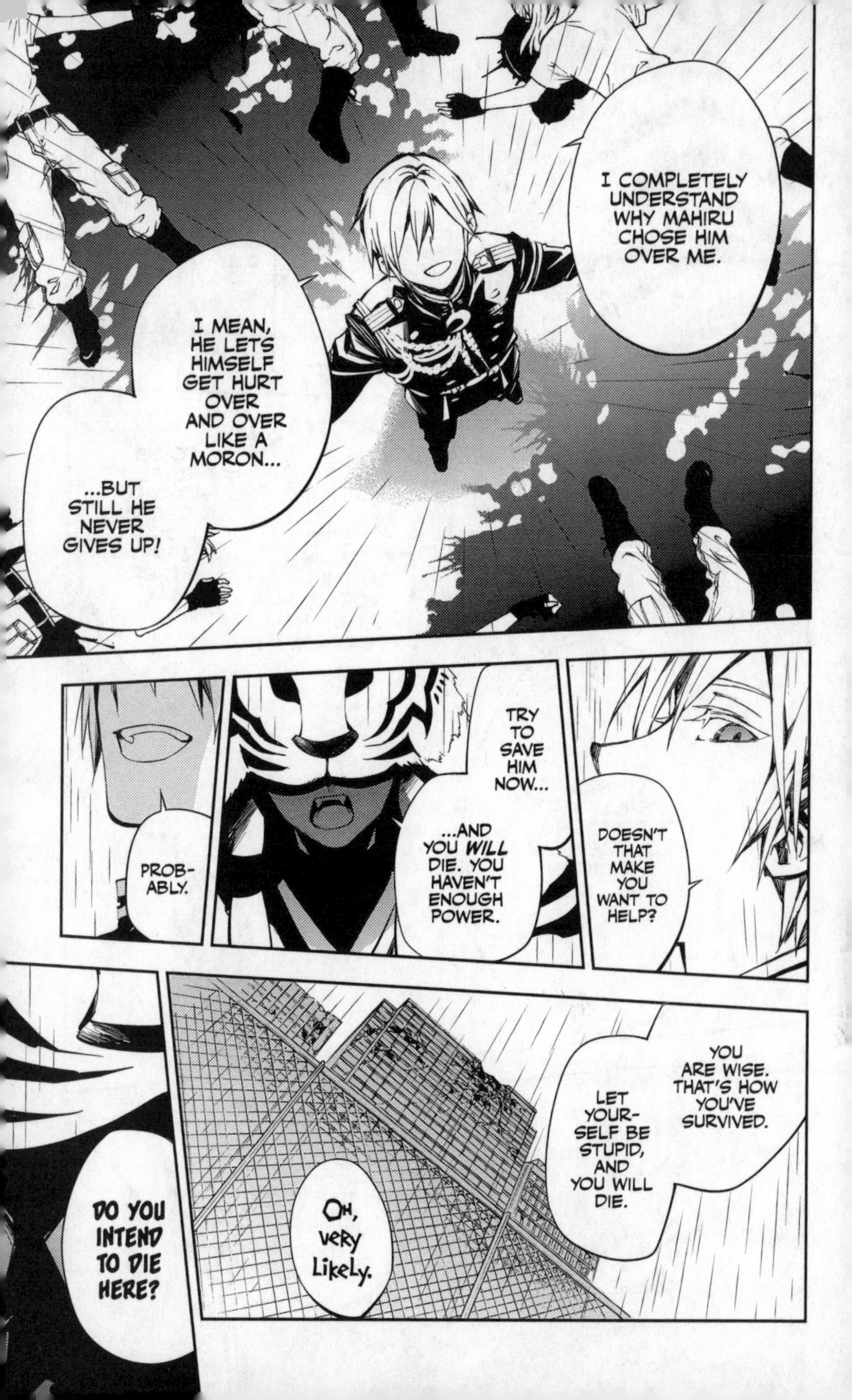

I COMPLETELY UNDERSTAND WHY MAHIRU CHOSE HIM OVER ME.
I MEAN, HE LETS HIMSELF GET HURT OVER AND OVER LIKE A MORON...
...BUT STILL HE NEVER GIVES UP!
DOESN'T THAT MAKE YOU WANT TO HELP?
TRY TO SAVE HIM NOW...
...AND YOU *WILL* DIE. YOU HAVEN'T ENOUGH POWER.
PROB-ABLY.
YOU ARE WISE. THAT'S HOW YOU'VE SURVIVED.
LET YOUR-SELF BE STUPID, AND YOU WILL DIE.
Oh, very Likely.
DO YOU INTEND TO DIE HERE?

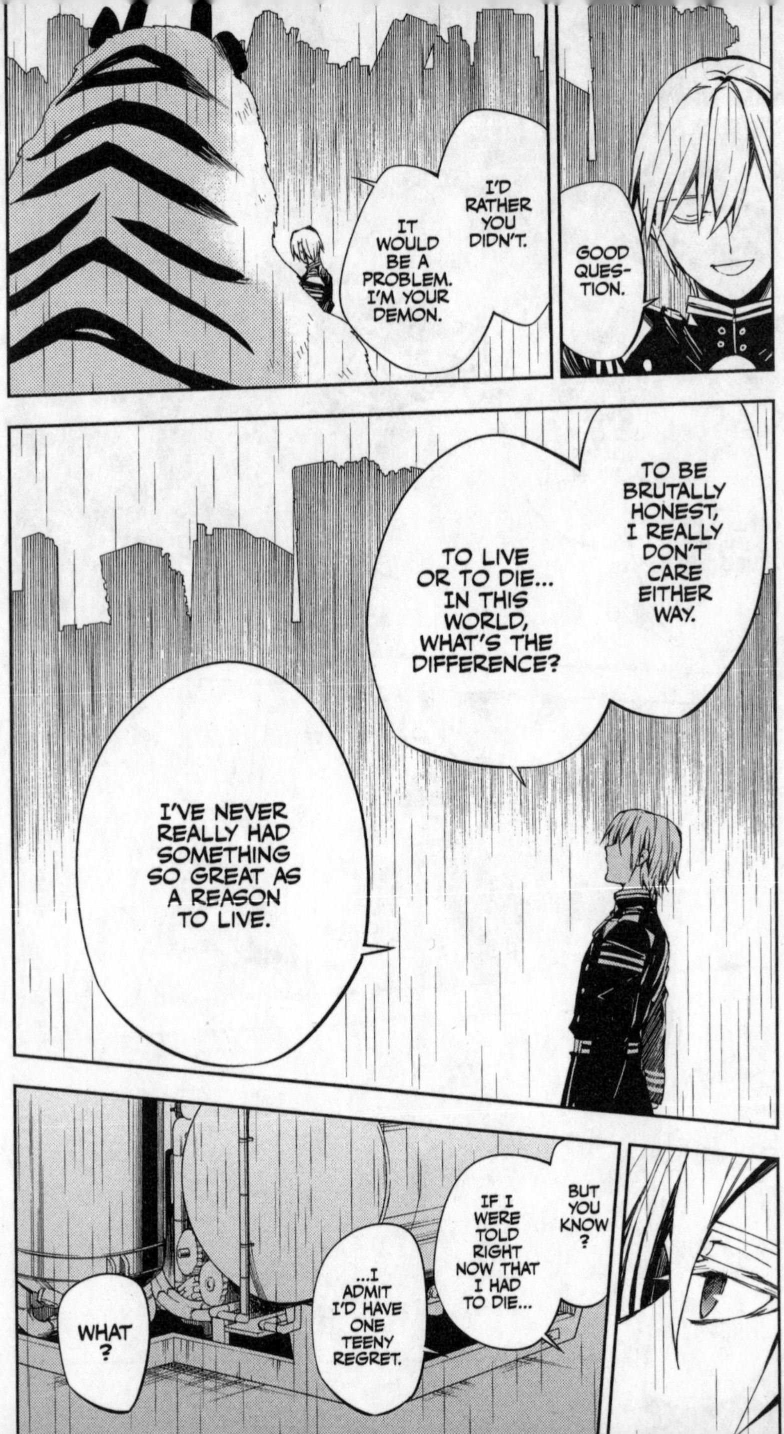
GOOD QUESTION.
I'D RATHER YOU DIDN'T.
IT WOULD BE A PROBLEM. I'M YOUR DEMON.
TO BE BRUTALLY HONEST, I REALLY DON'T CARE EITHER WAY.
TO LIVE OR TO DIE... IN THIS WORLD, WHAT'S THE DIFFERENCE?
I'VE NEVER REALLY HAD SOMETHING SO GREAT AS A REASON TO LIVE.
BUT YOU KNOW?
IF I WERE TOLD RIGHT NOW THAT I HAD TO DIE...
...I ADMIT I'D HAVE ONE TEENY REGRET.
WHAT?

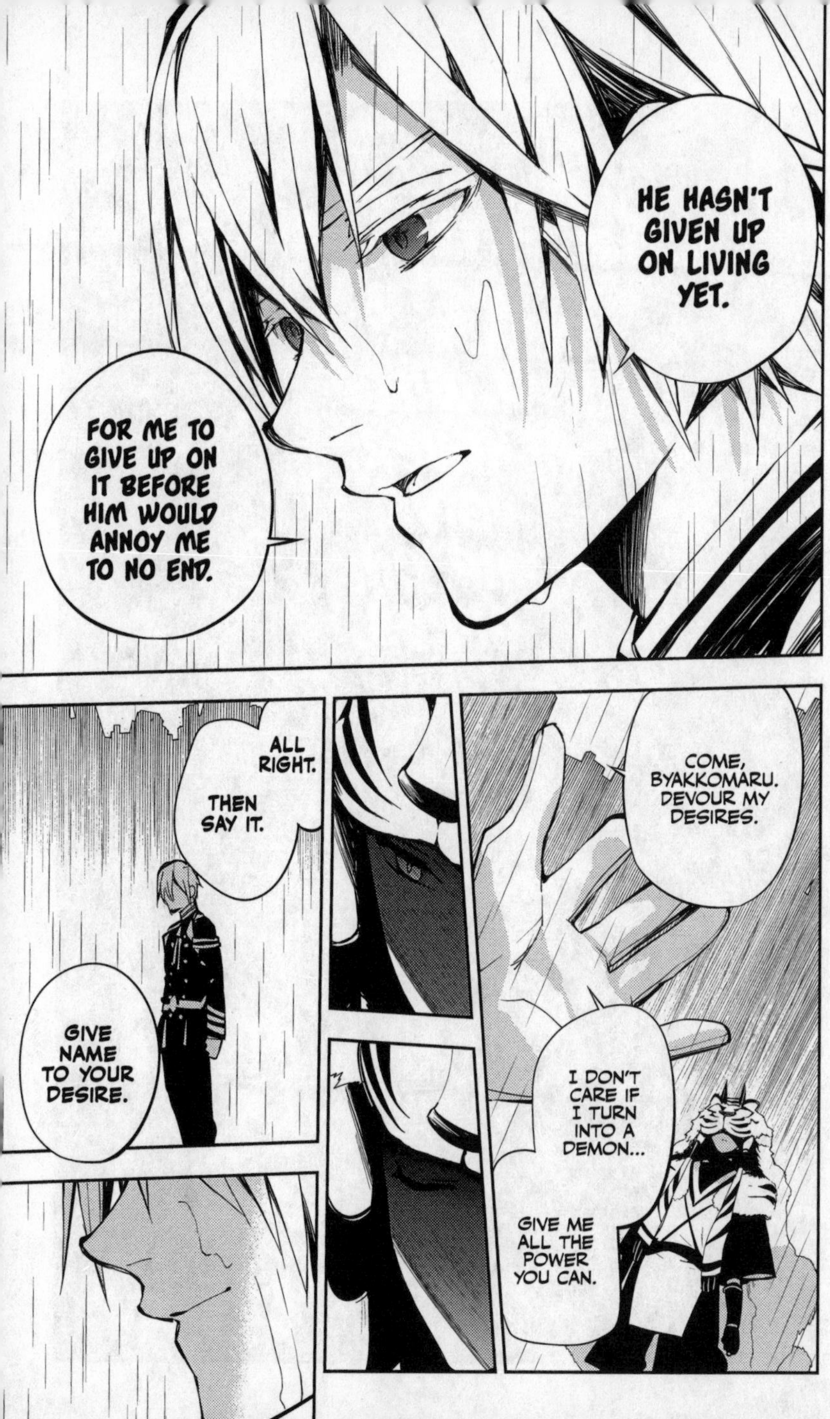
HE HASN'T GIVEN UP ON LIVING YET.
FOR ME TO GIVE UP ON IT BEFORE HIM WOULD ANNOY ME TO NO END.
COME, BYAKKOMARU. DEVOUR MY DESIRES.
I DON'T CARE IF I TURN INTO A DEMON...
GIVE ME ALL THE POWER YOU CAN.
ALL RIGHT.
THEN SAY IT.
GIVE NAME TO YOUR DESIRE.

I WILL
NEVER
GIVE
UP ON
GUREN.

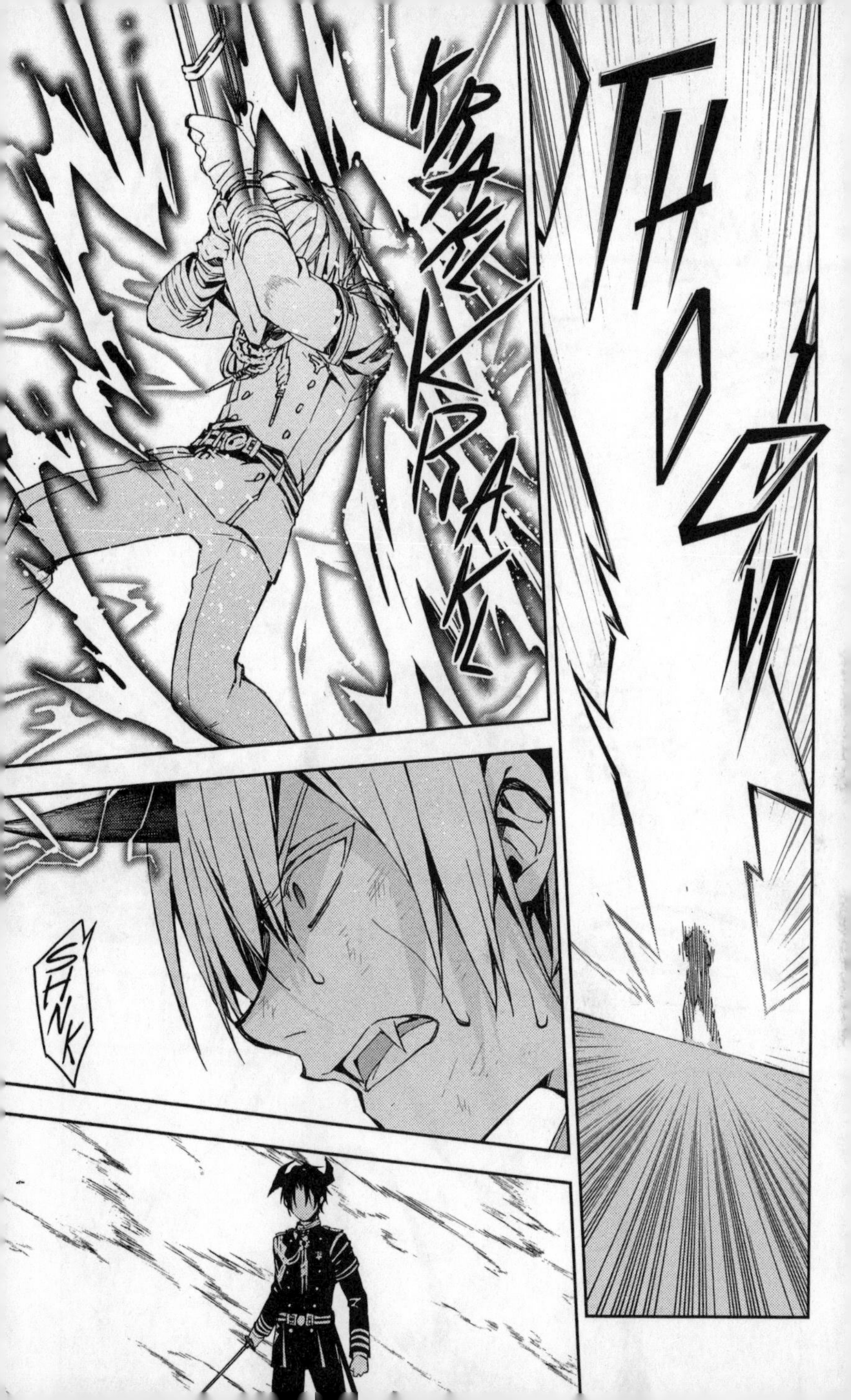
THOOOM
KRAKL KRAKL
SHNK

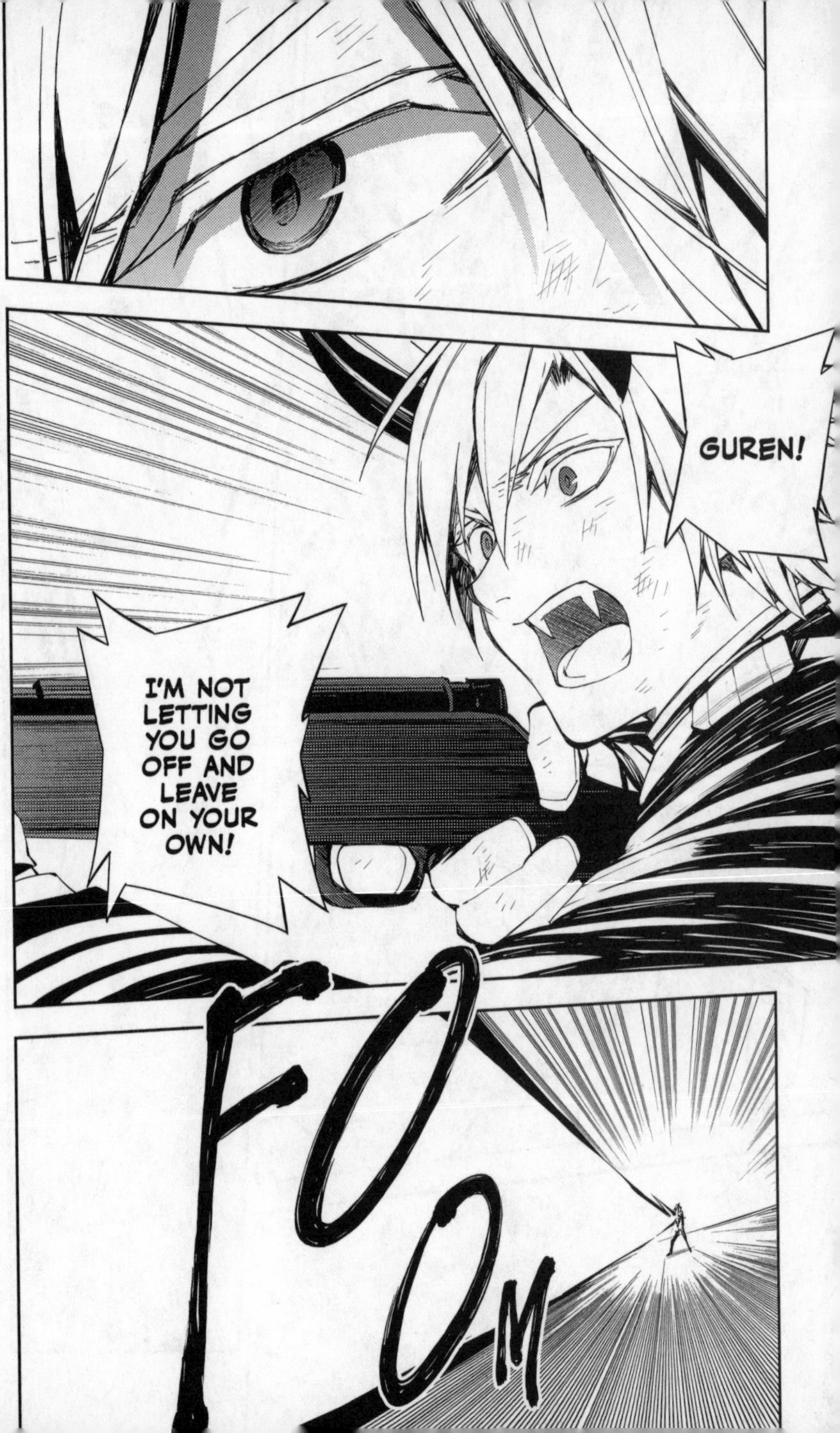
GUREN!
I'M NOT LETTING YOU GO OFF AND LEAVE ON YOUR OWN!
FOOM

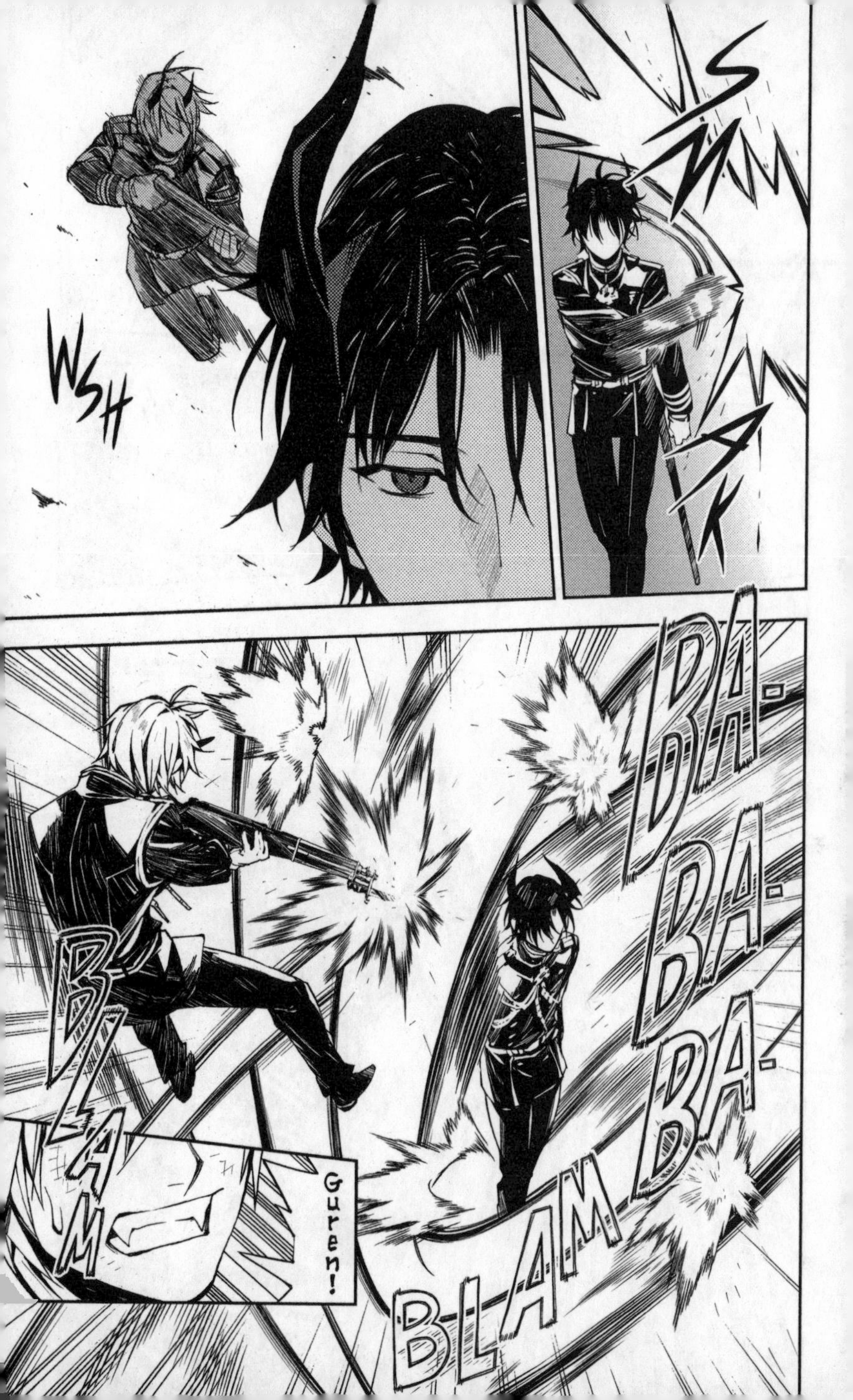
SWAK
SWAK
WSH
BA-BA-BA-BA-
BLAM
BLAM-BLAM
Guren!

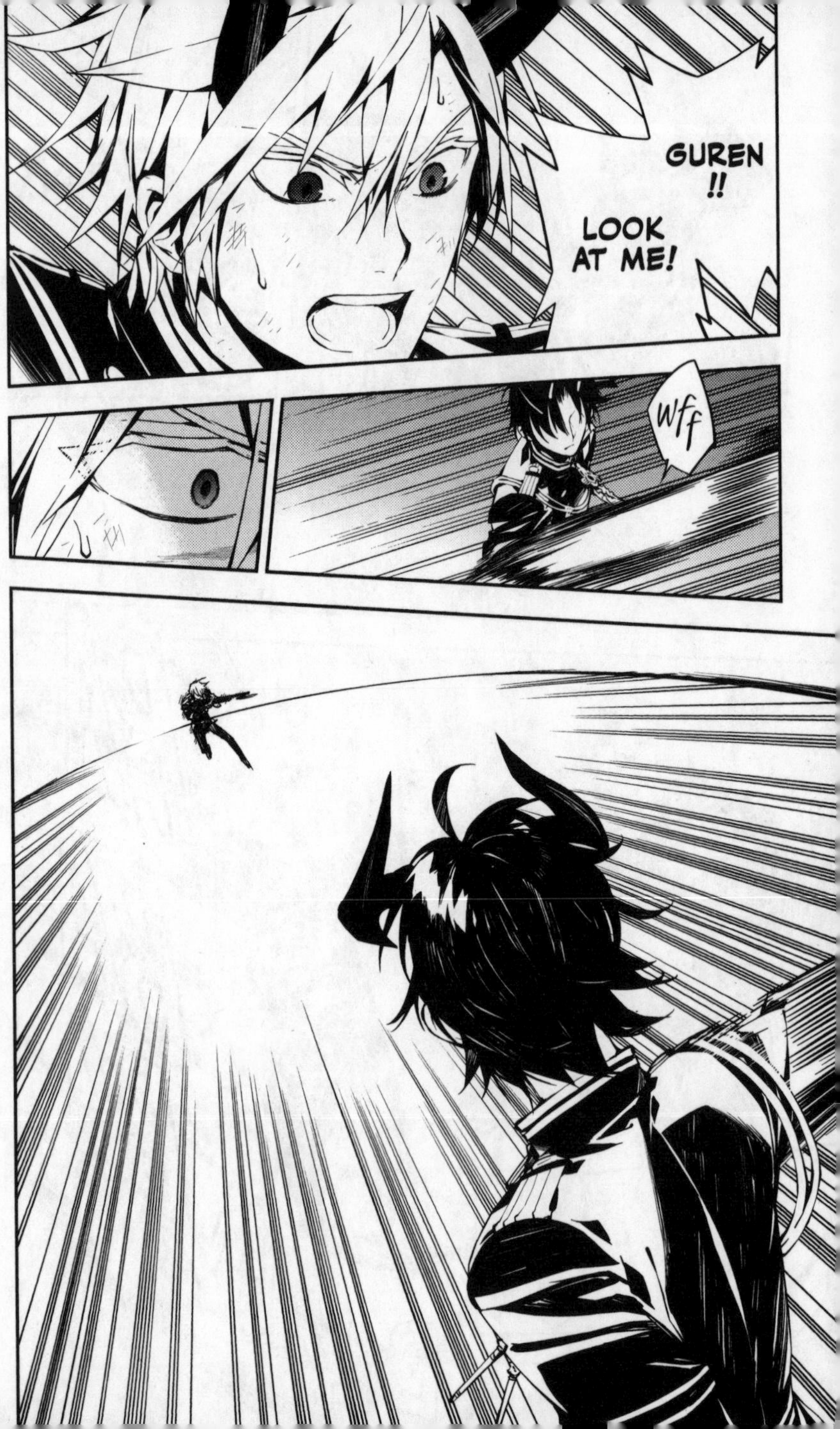
GUREN !!
LOOK AT ME!
wff

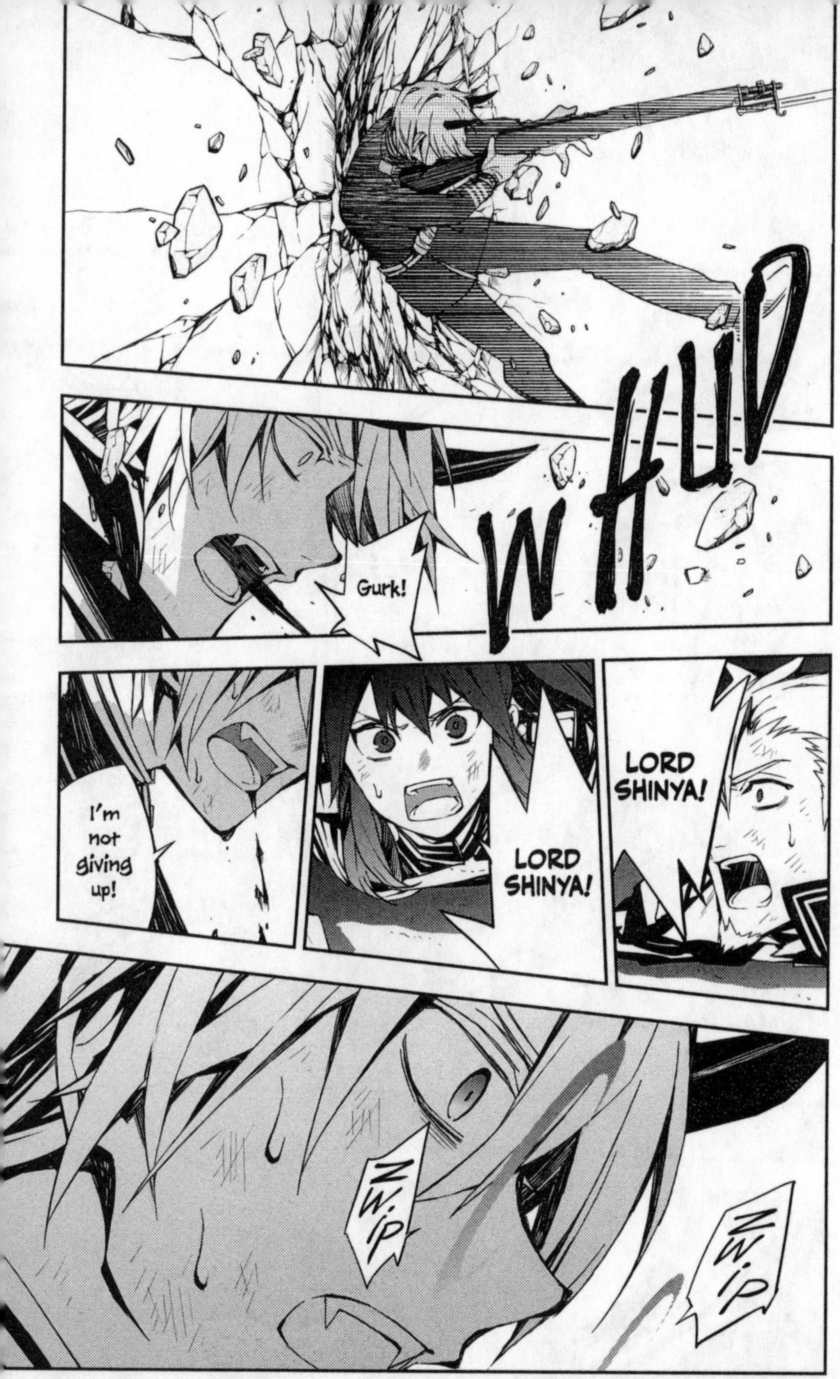
WHUD
Gurk!
LORD SHINYA!
LORD SHINYA!
I'm not giving up!
ZWIP
ZWIP

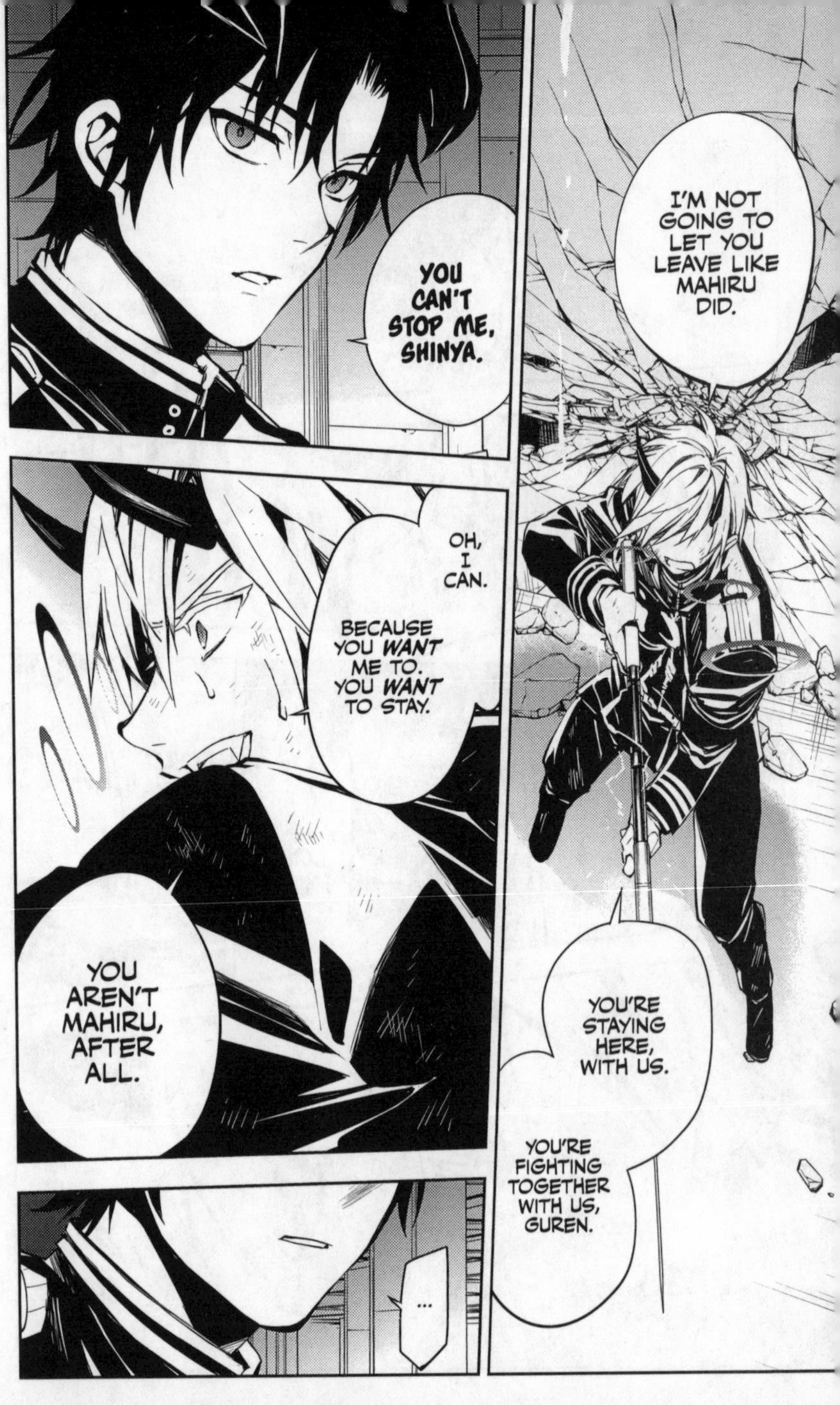
I'M NOT GOING TO LET YOU LEAVE LIKE MAHIRU DID.
YOU'RE STAYING HERE, WITH US.
YOU'RE FIGHTING TOGETHER WITH US, GUREN.
YOU CAN'T STOP ME, SHINYA.
OH, I CAN.
BECAUSE YOU *WANT* ME TO. YOU *WANT* TO STAY.
YOU AREN'T MAHIRU, AFTER ALL.
...

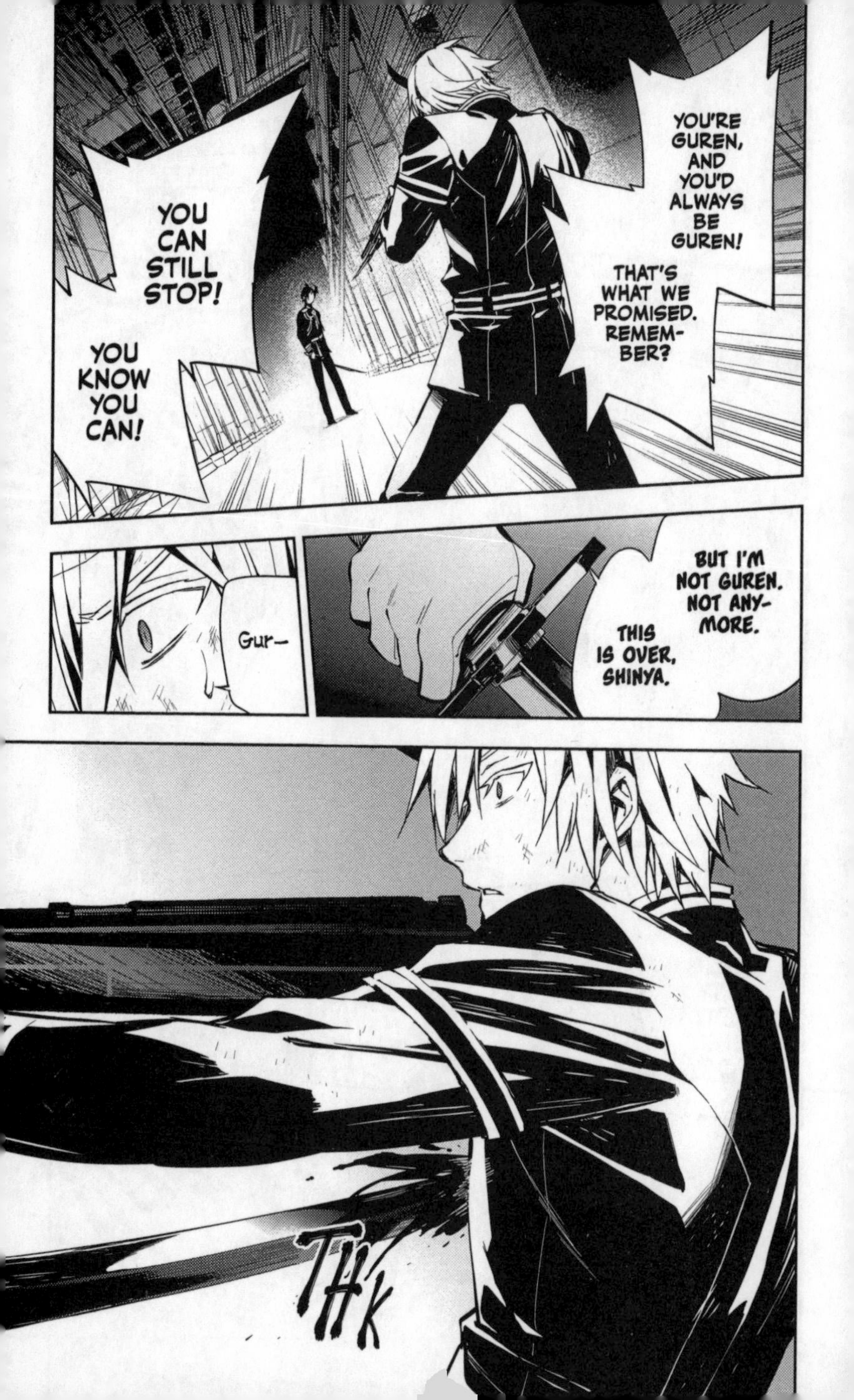
YOU'RE GUREN, AND YOU'D ALWAYS BE GUREN!
THAT'S WHAT WE PROMISED. REMEMBER?
YOU CAN STILL STOP!
YOU KNOW YOU CAN!
BUT I'M NOT GUREN. NOT ANYMORE.
THIS IS OVER, SHINYA.
Gur–
THK

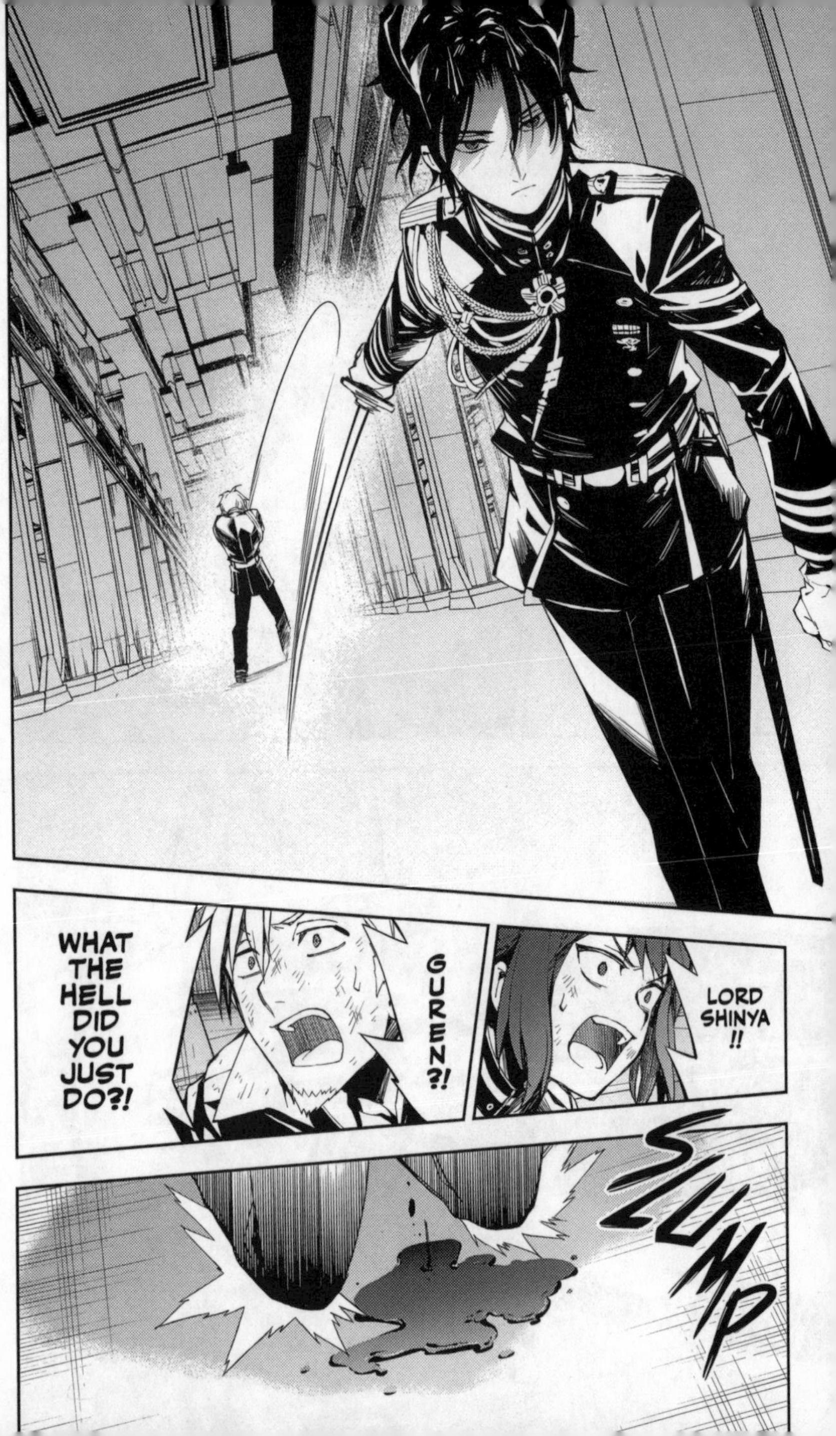
LORD SHINYA!!
GUREN?!
WHAT THE HELL DID YOU JUST DO?!
SLUMP

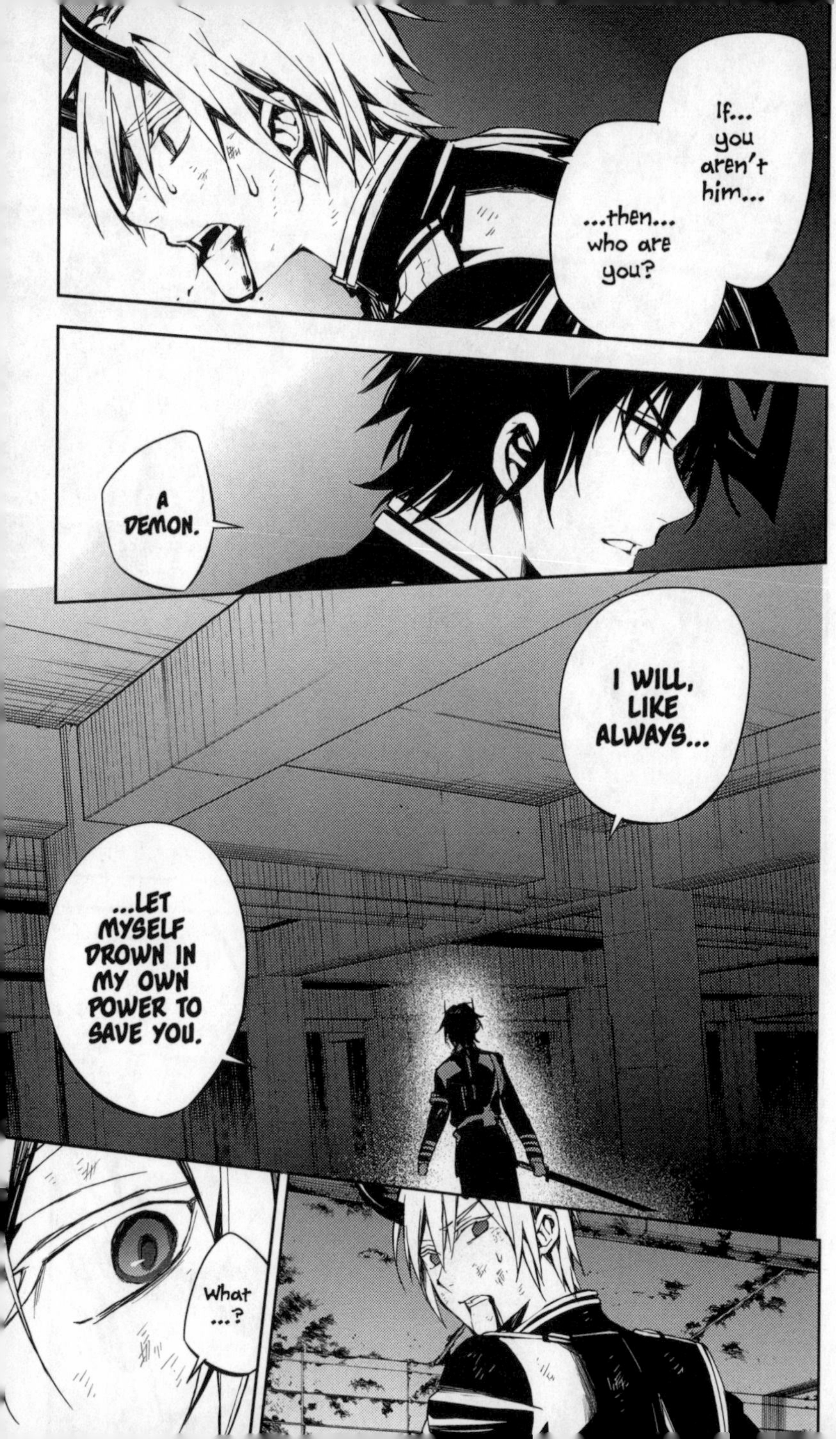
If... you aren't him...
...then... who are you?
A DEMON.
I WILL, LIKE ALWAYS...
...LET MYSELF DROWN IN MY OWN POWER TO SAVE YOU.
What ...?

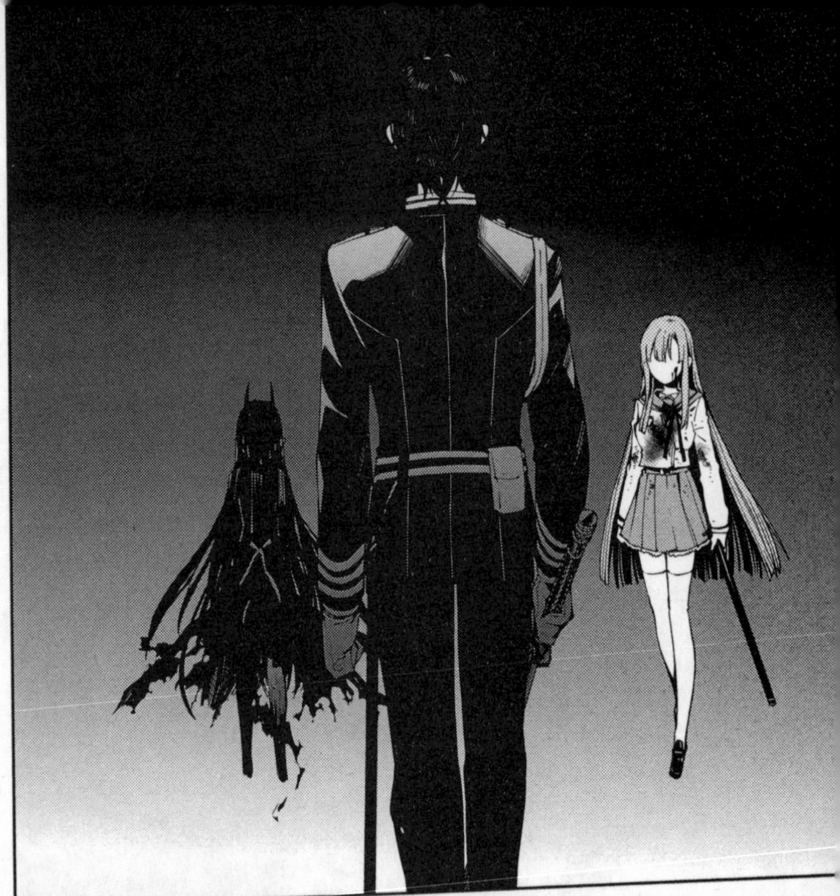

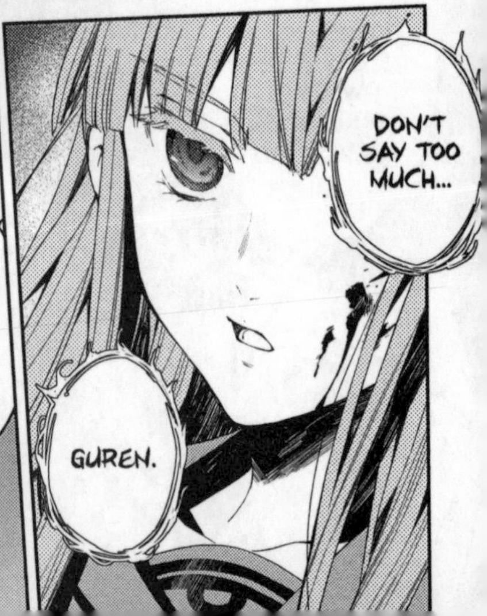
DON'T SAY TOO MUCH...
GUREN.

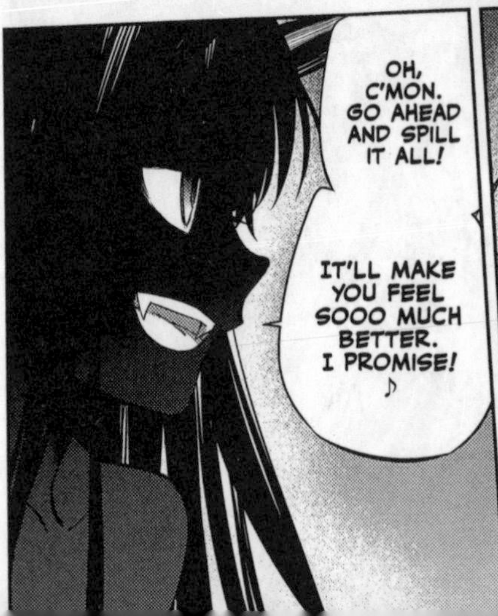
OH, C'MON. GO AHEAD AND SPILL IT ALL!
IT'LL MAKE YOU FEEL SOOO MUCH BETTER. I PROMISE! ♪

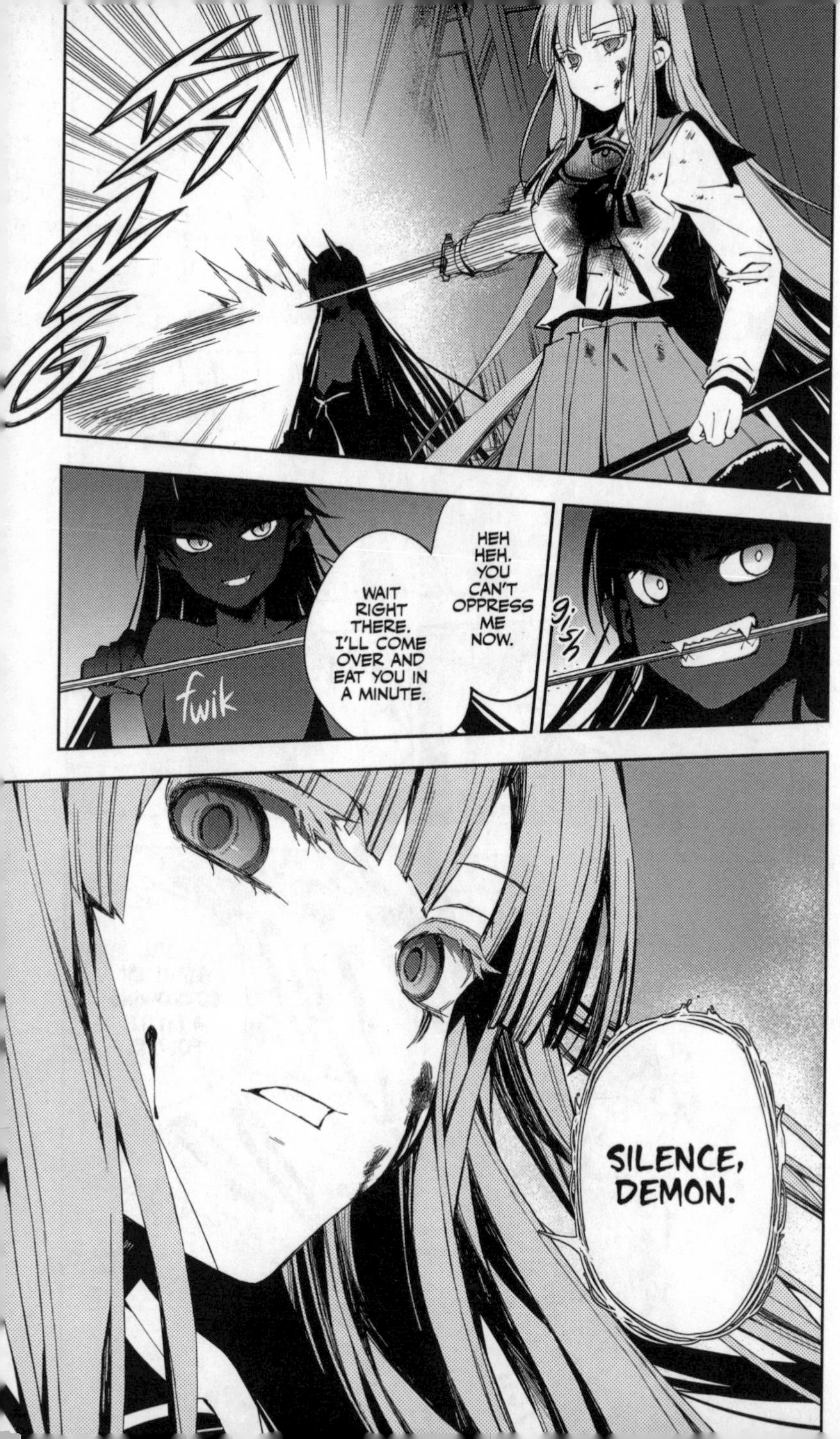
KANG
gish
HEH HEH. YOU CAN'T OPPRESS ME NOW.
WAIT RIGHT THERE. I'LL COME OVER AND EAT YOU IN A MINUTE.
fwik
SILENCE, DEMON.

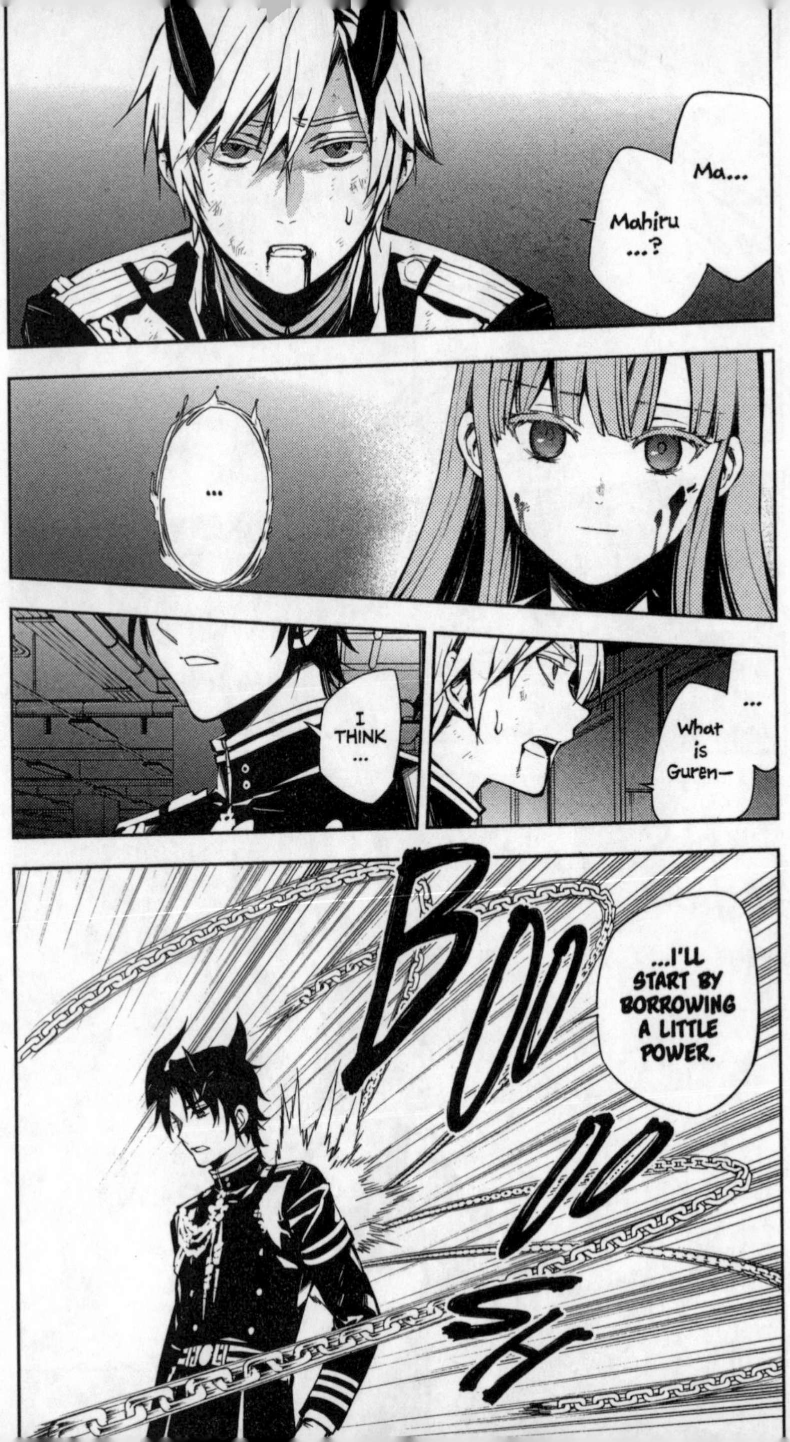
Ma... Mahiru ...?
...
... What is Guren—
I THINK ...
...I'LL START BY BORROWING A LITTLE POWER.
BOOOOSH

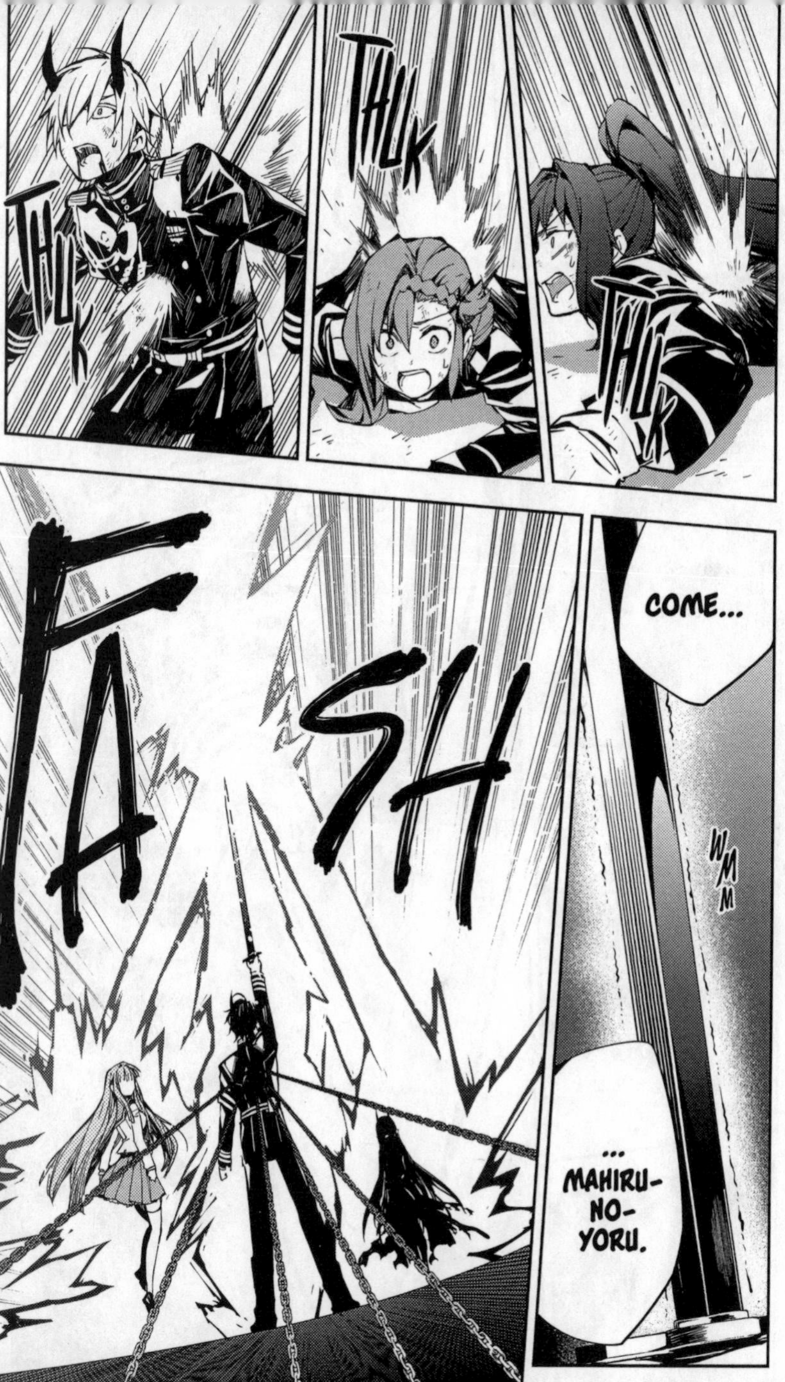
THUK
THUK
THUK
COME...
WMM
...MAHIRU-NO-YORU.
FASH

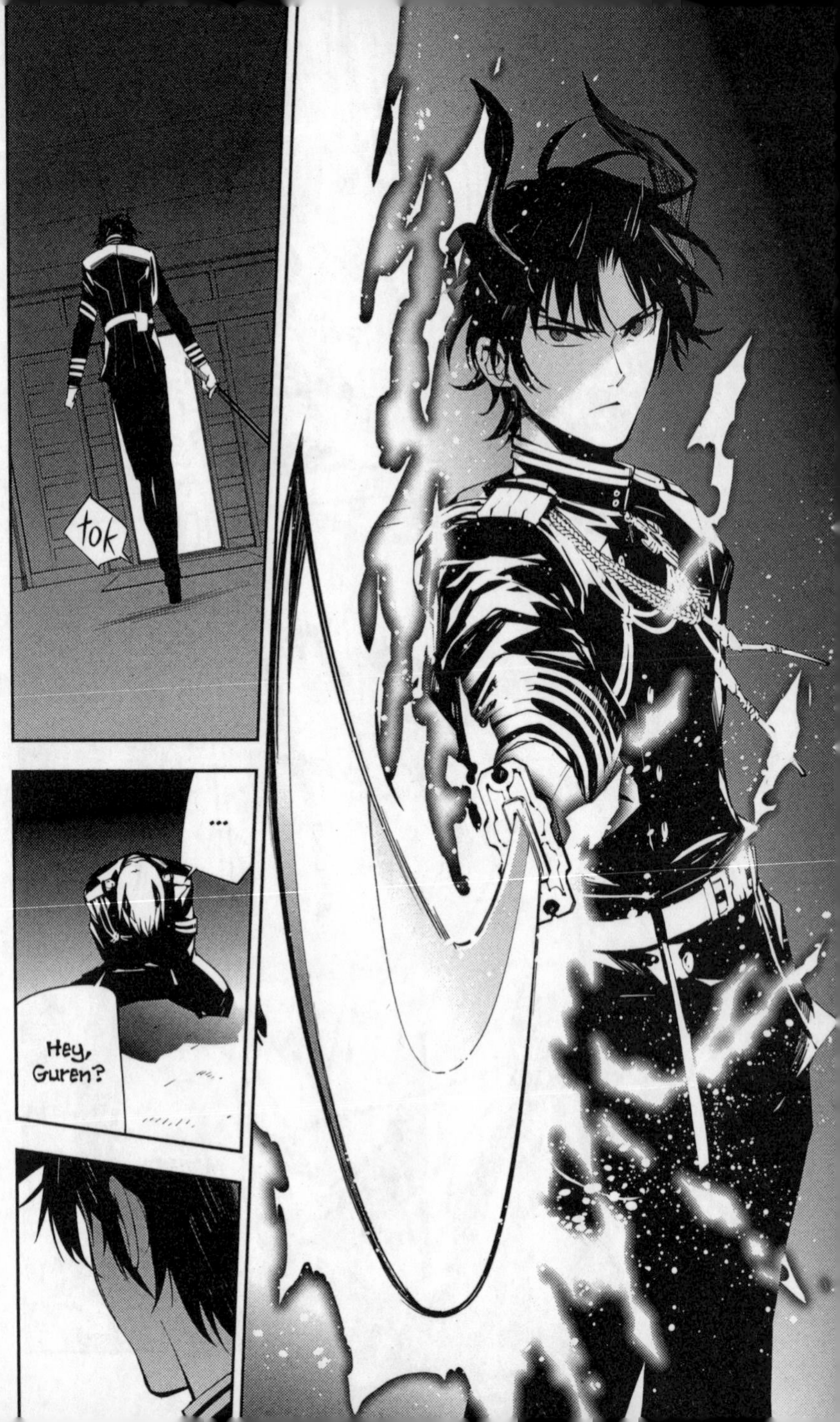
tok
...
Hey, Guren?

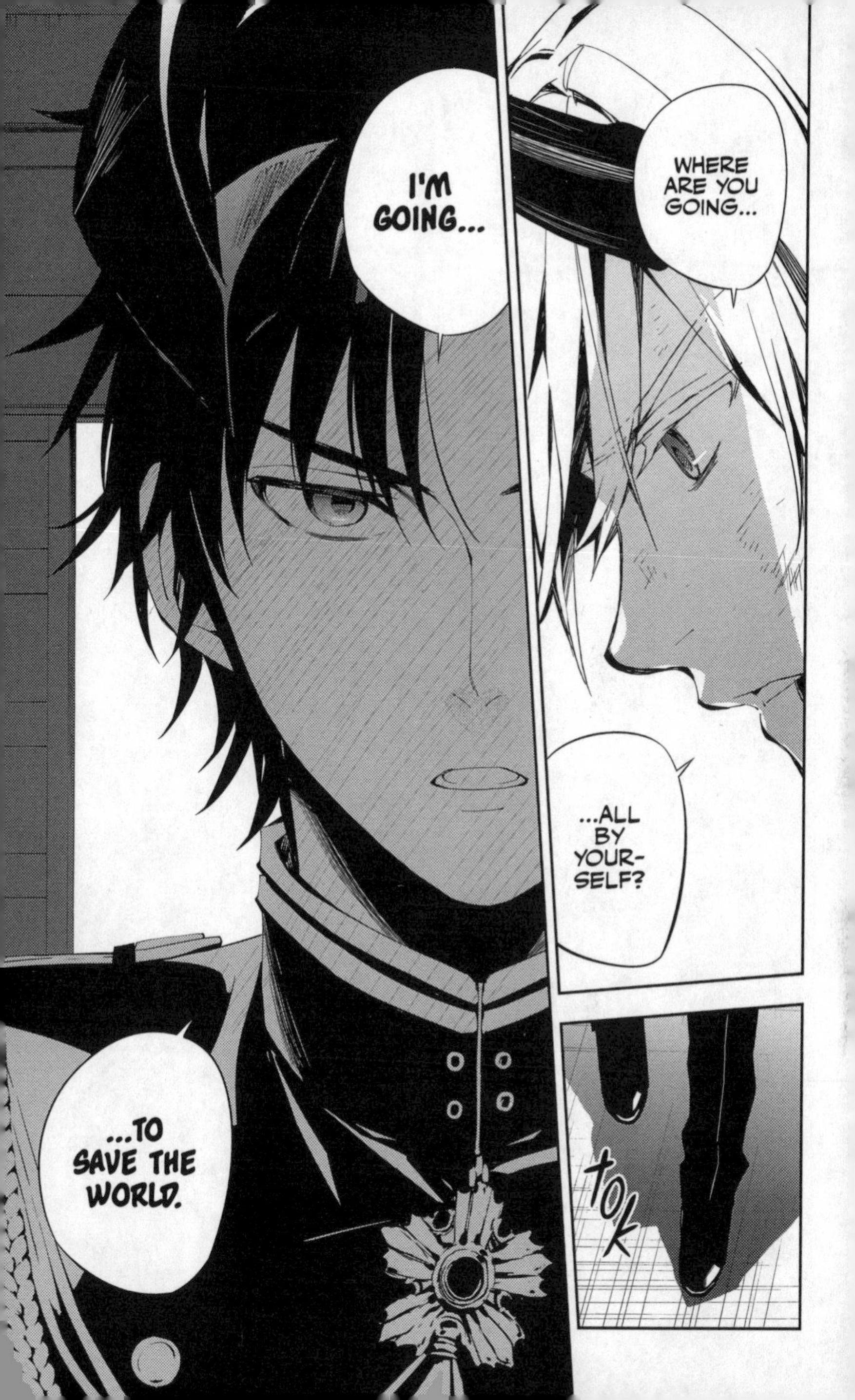
WHERE ARE YOU GOING...
...ALL BY YOUR-SELF?
TOK
I'M GOING...
...TO SAVE THE WORLD.

Seraph of the End
—VAMPIRE REIGN—

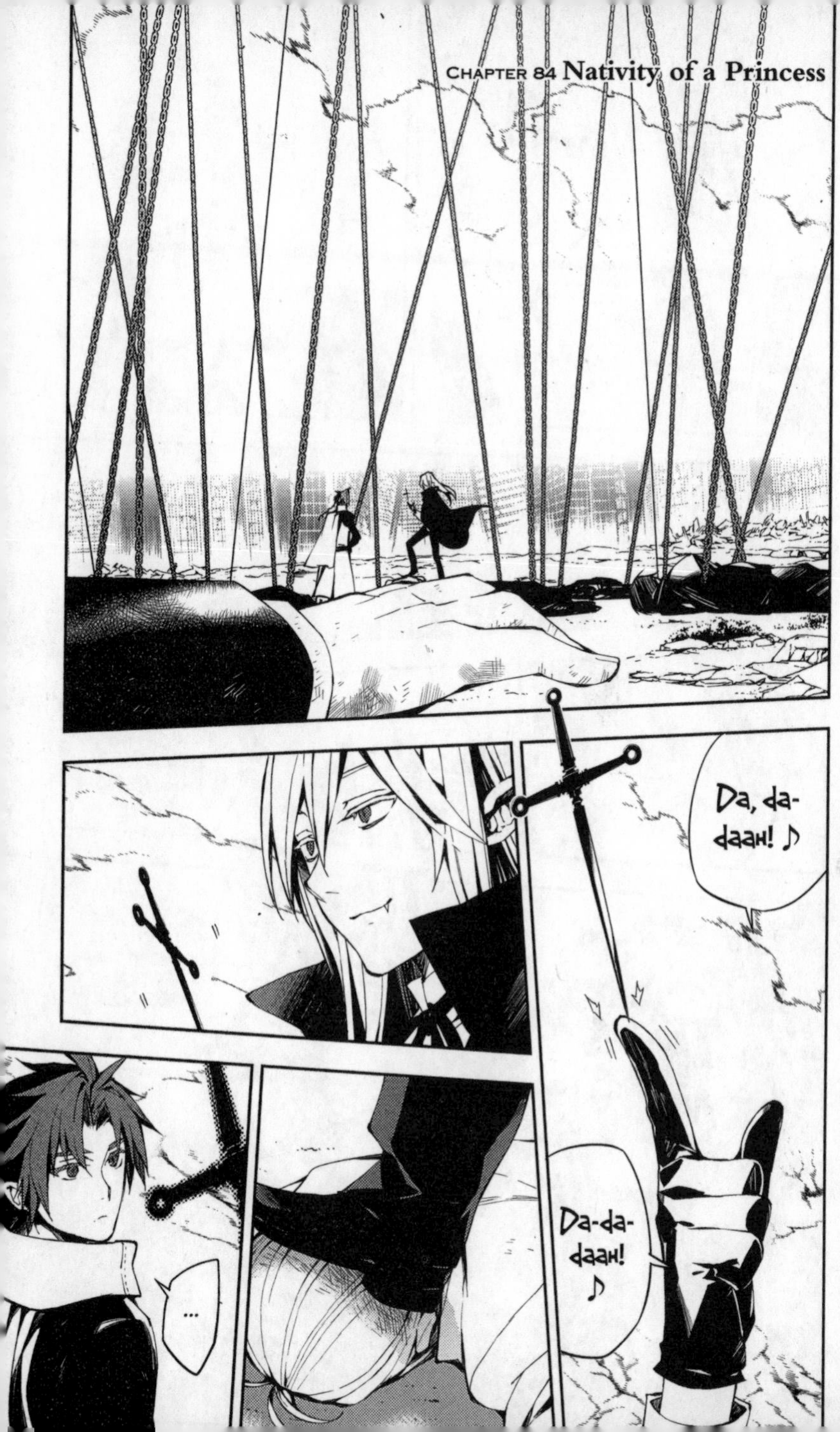
Chapter 84 Nativity of a Princess
Da, da-daaah! ♪
Da-da-daaah! ♪
...

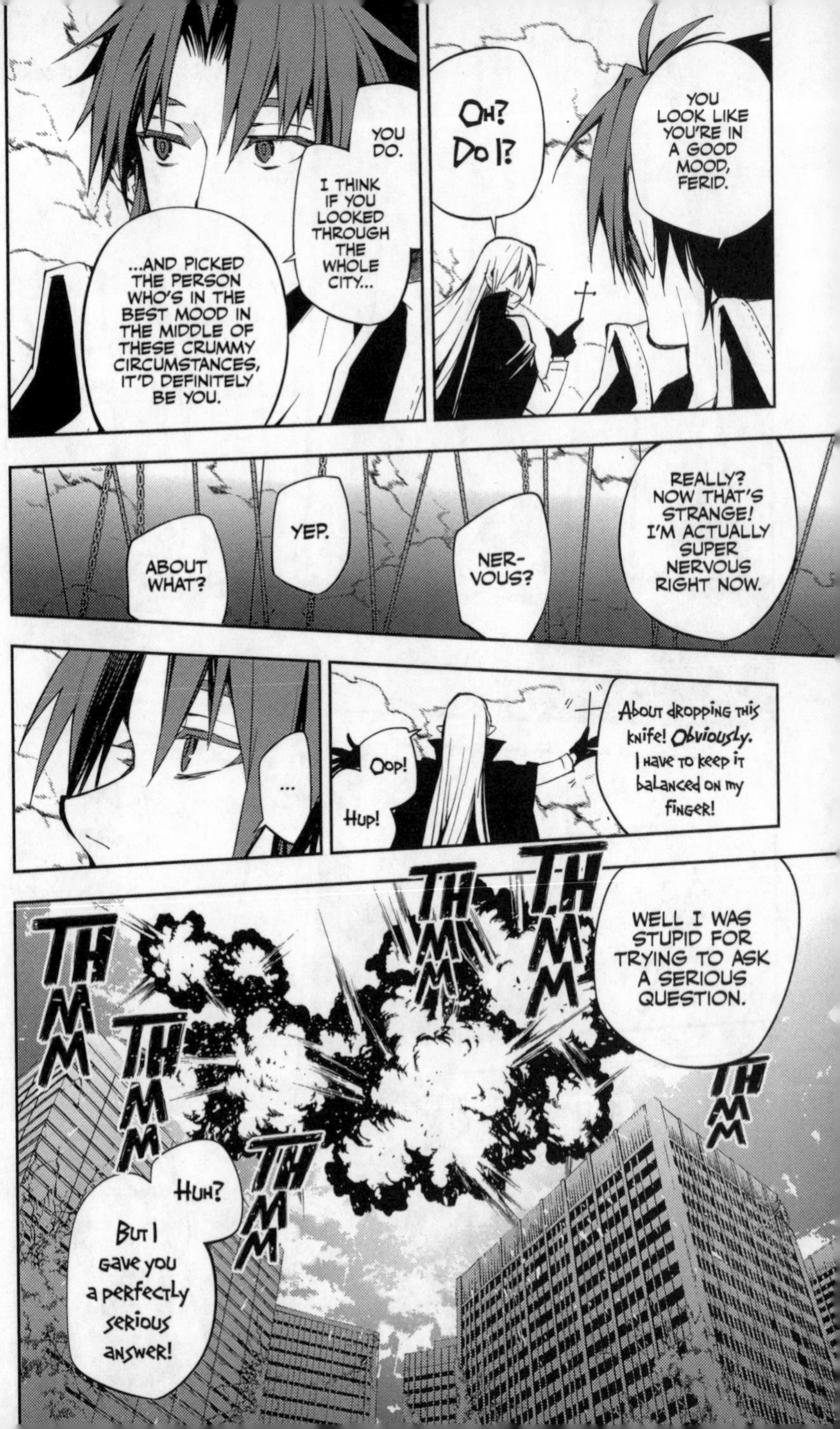
YOU LOOK LIKE YOU'RE IN A GOOD MOOD, FERID.
OH? DO I?
YOU DO.
I THINK IF YOU LOOKED THROUGH THE WHOLE CITY...
...AND PICKED THE PERSON WHO'S IN THE BEST MOOD IN THE MIDDLE OF THESE CRUMMY CIRCUMSTANCES, IT'D DEFINITELY BE YOU.
REALLY? NOW THAT'S STRANGE! I'M ACTUALLY SUPER NERVOUS RIGHT NOW.
NER-VOUS?
YEP.
ABOUT WHAT?
About dropping this knife! Obviously. I have to keep it balanced on my finger!
Oop!
Hup!
...
WELL I WAS STUPID FOR TRYING TO ASK A SERIOUS QUESTION.
THMM
THMM
THMM
THMM
THMM
THMM
Huh?
But I gave you a perfectly serious answer!

CHAPTER 84
Nativity of a Princess

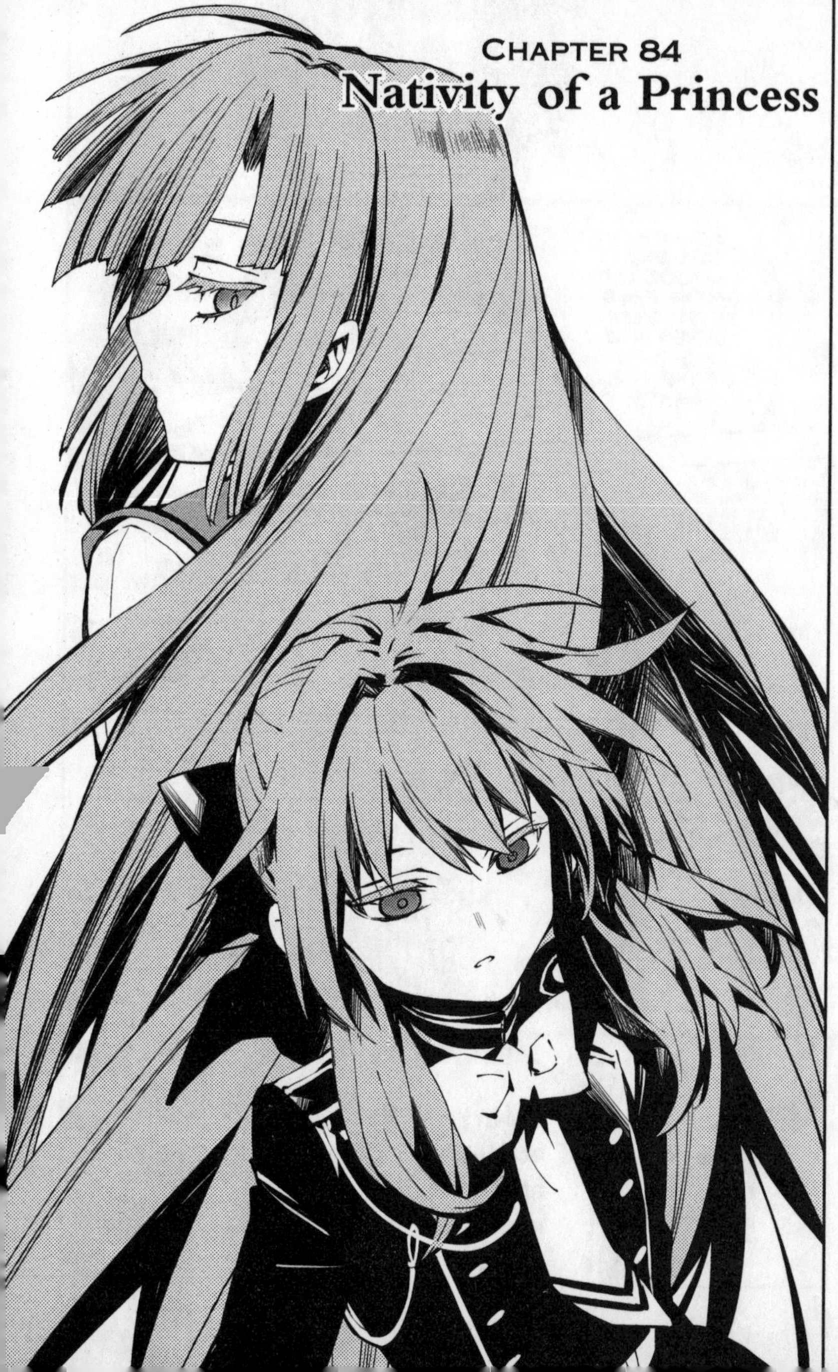

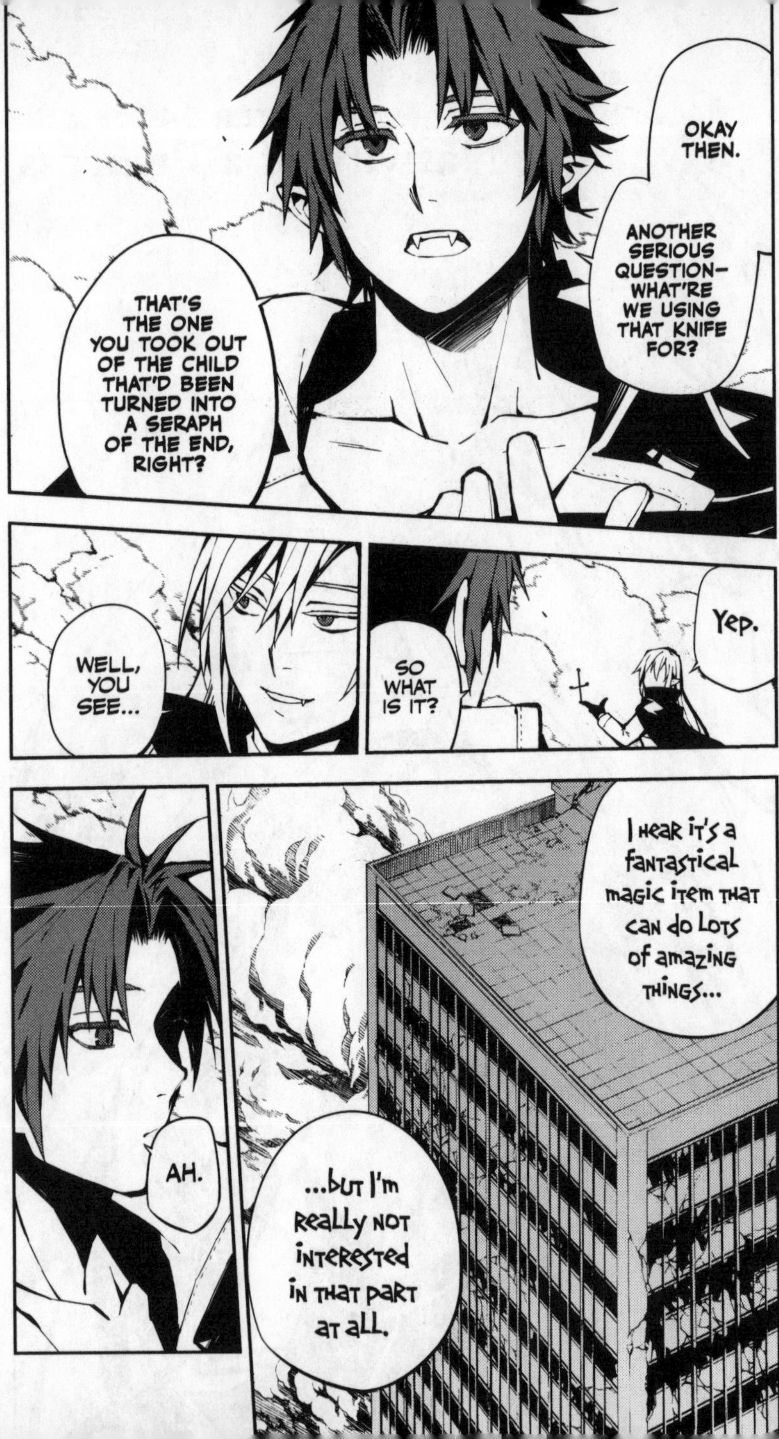
OKAY THEN.
ANOTHER SERIOUS QUESTION—WHAT'RE WE USING THAT KNIFE FOR?
THAT'S THE ONE YOU TOOK OUT OF THE CHILD THAT'D BEEN TURNED INTO A SERAPH OF THE END, RIGHT?
Yep.
SO WHAT IS IT?
WELL, YOU SEE...
I hear it's a fantastical magic item that can do lots of amazing things...
...but I'm really not interested in that part at all.
AH.

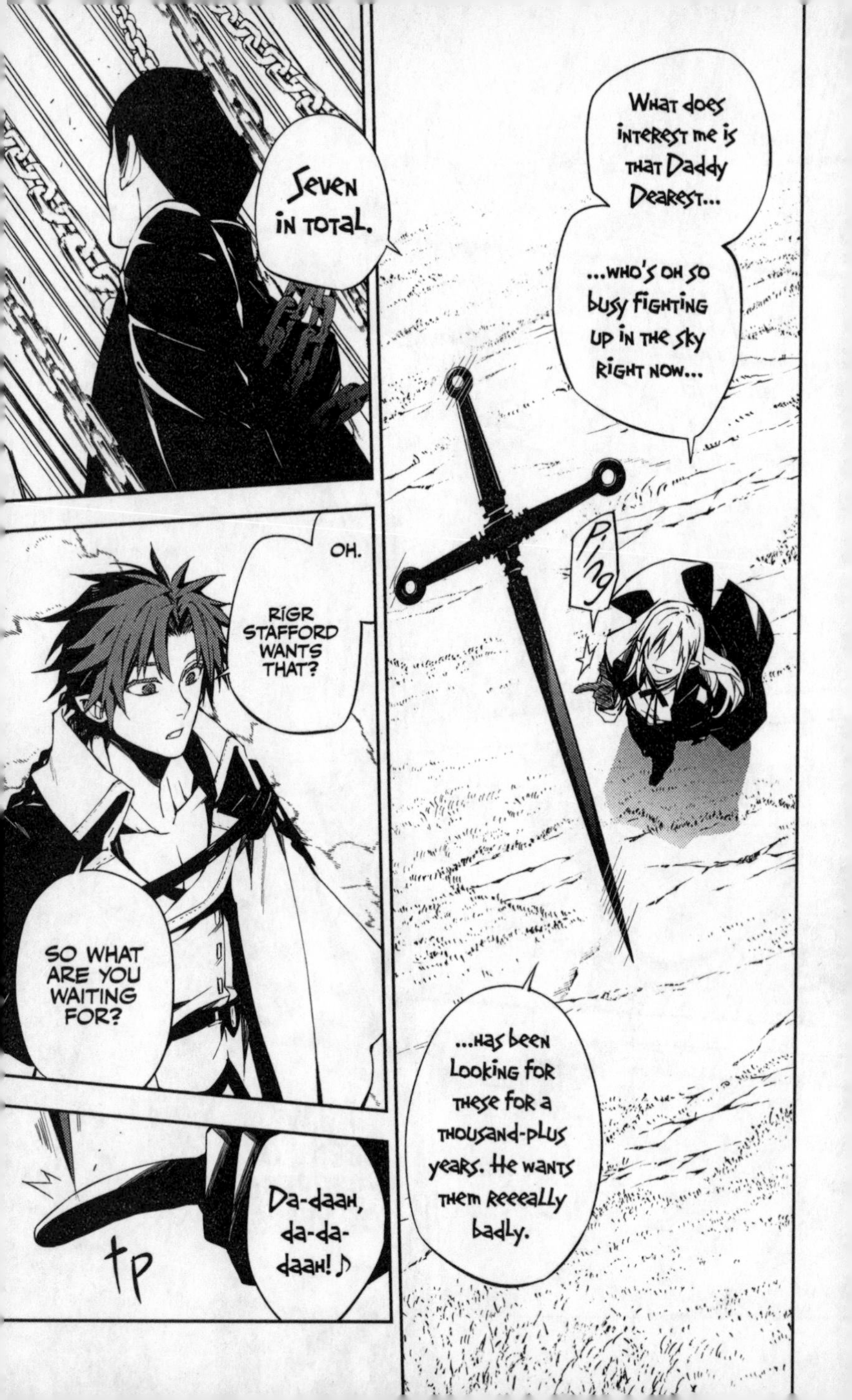
What does interest me is that Daddy Dearest...
...who's oh so busy fighting up in the sky right now...
Ping
...has been looking for these for a thousand-plus years. He wants them reeeally badly.
Seven in total.
Oh.
Rigr Stafford wants that?
So what are you waiting for?
tp
Da-daah, da-da-daah! ♪

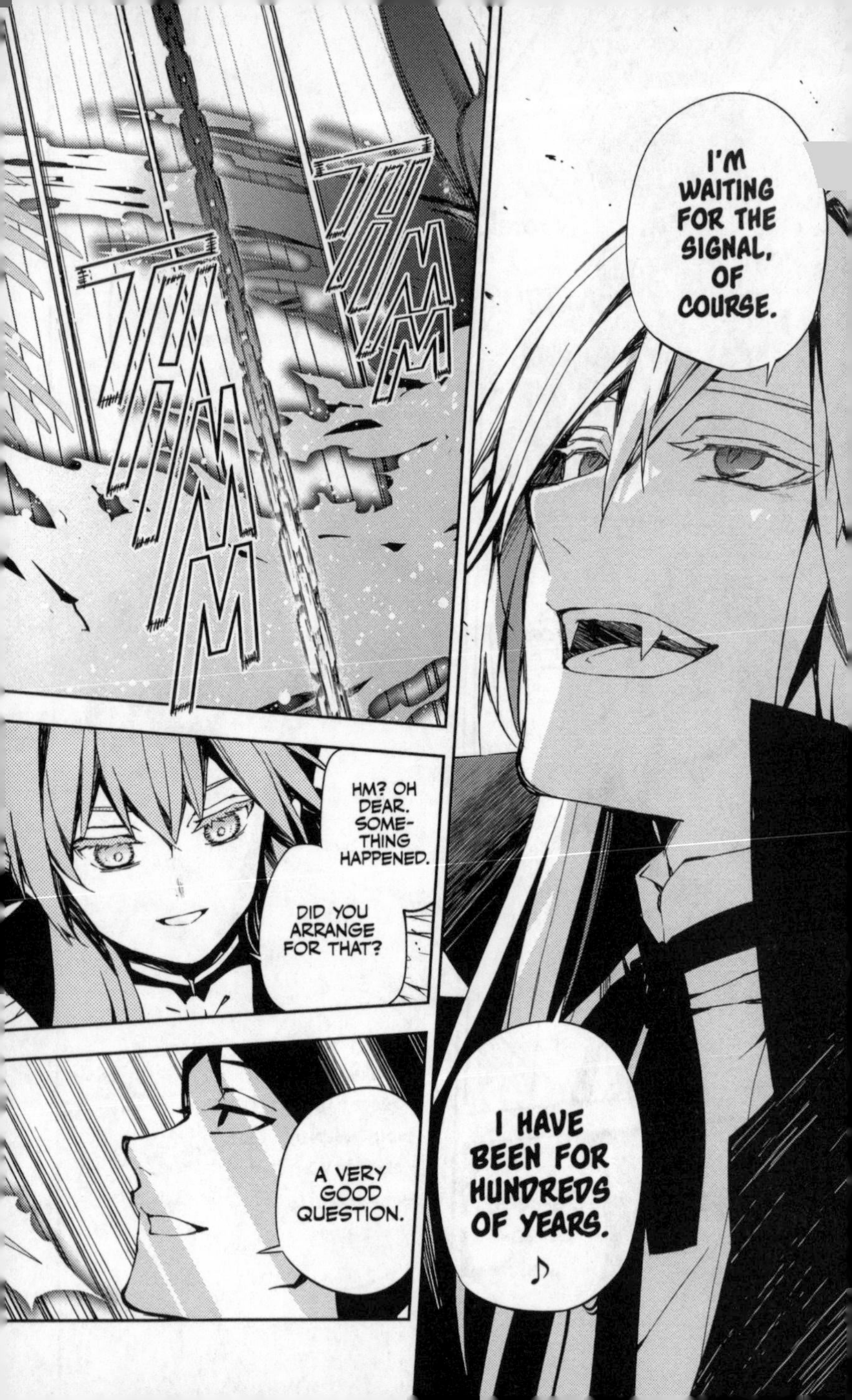
I'M WAITING FOR THE SIGNAL, OF COURSE.
I HAVE BEEN FOR HUNDREDS OF YEARS. ♪
THMM
THMMM
HM? OH DEAR. SOME-THING HAPPENED.
DID YOU ARRANGE FOR THAT?
A VERY GOOD QUESTION.

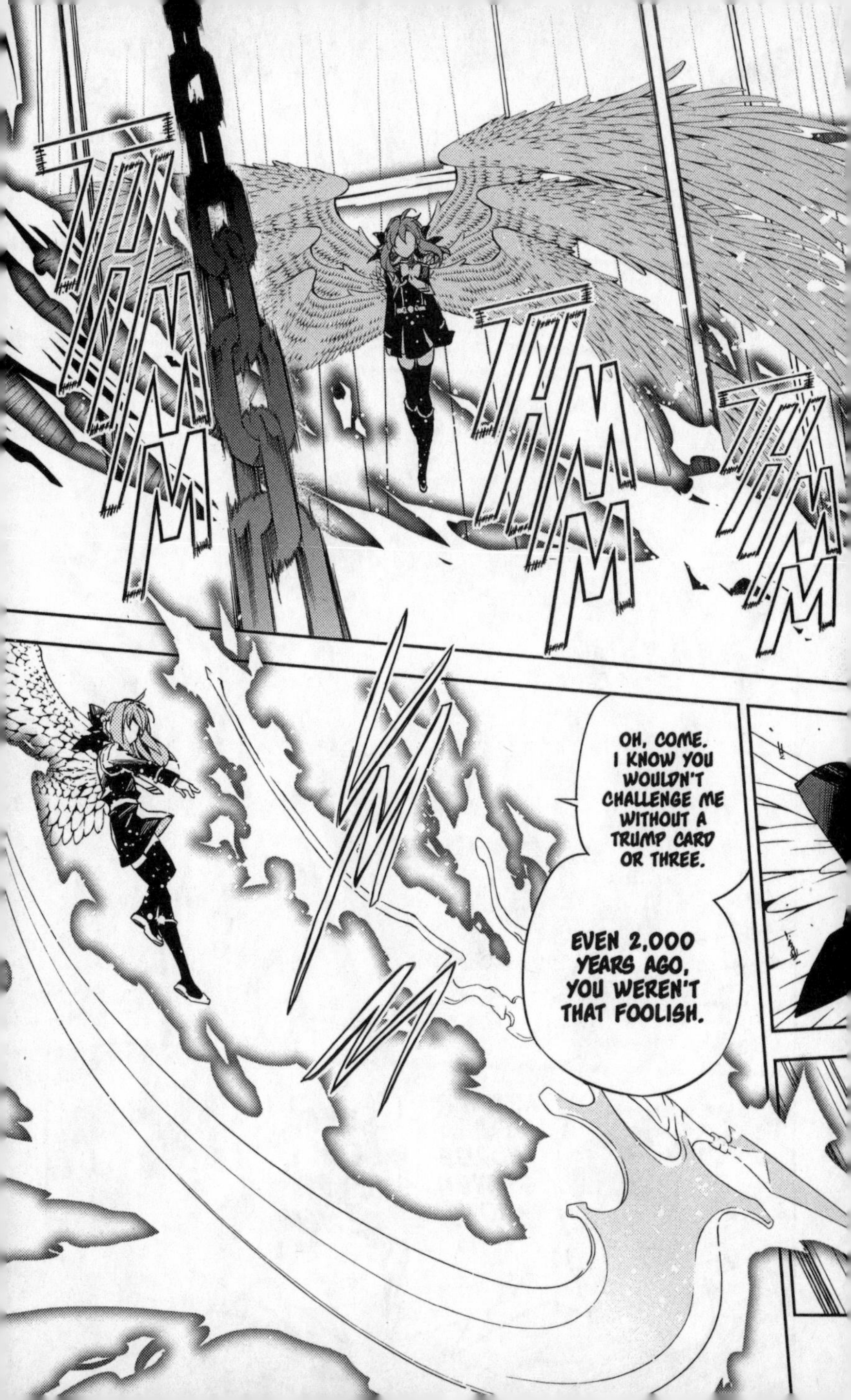
THMMM
THMMM
THMMM
OH, COME. I KNOW YOU WOULDN'T CHALLENGE ME WITHOUT A TRUMP CARD OR THREE.
EVEN 2,000 YEARS AGO, YOU WEREN'T THAT FOOLISH.
VWM

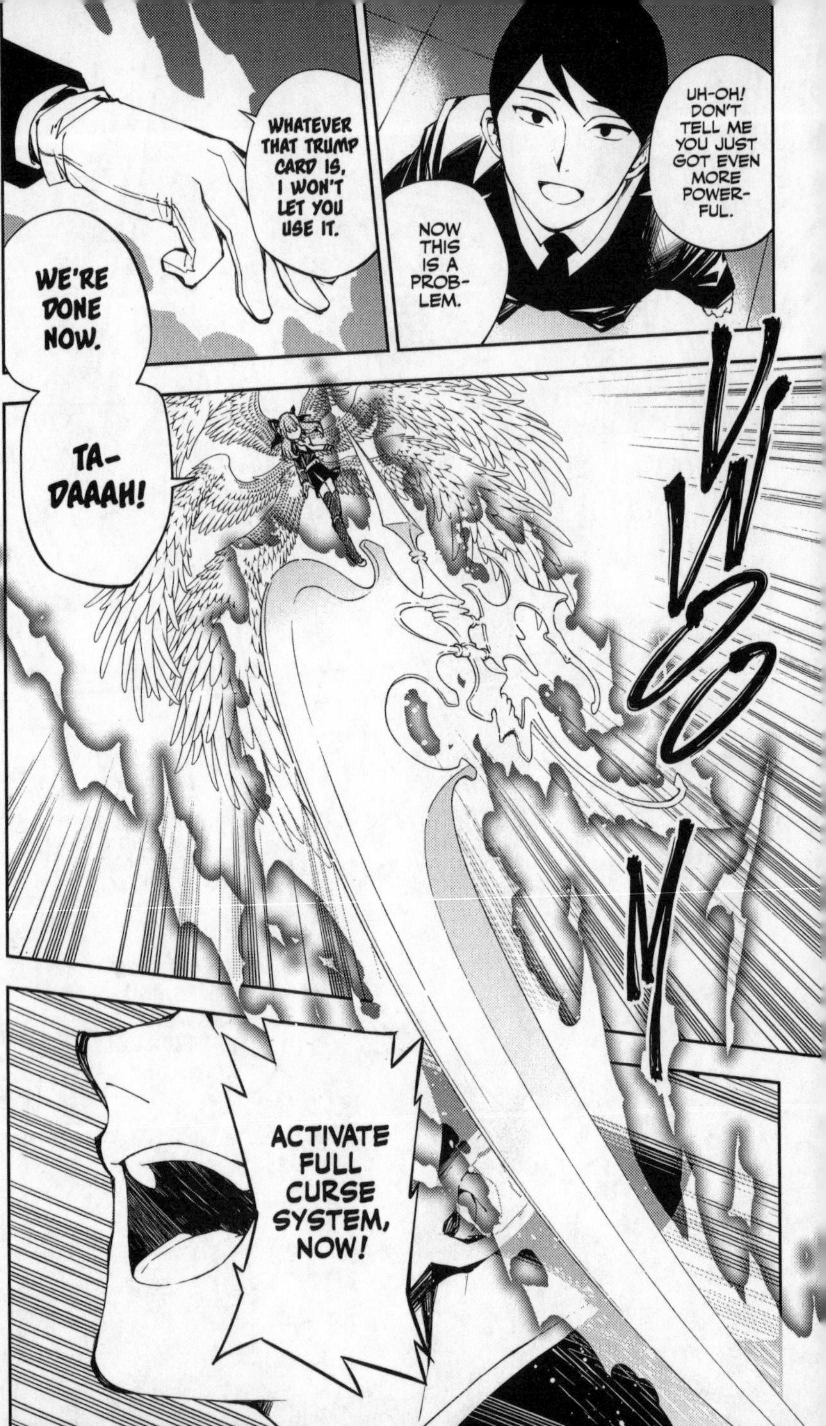
UH-OH! DON'T TELL ME YOU JUST GOT EVEN MORE POWER-FUL.
NOW THIS IS A PROB-LEM.
WHATEVER THAT TRUMP CARD IS, I WON'T LET YOU USE IT.
WE'RE DONE NOW.
TA-DAAAH!
VWOOOM
ACTIVATE FULL CURSE SYSTEM, NOW!

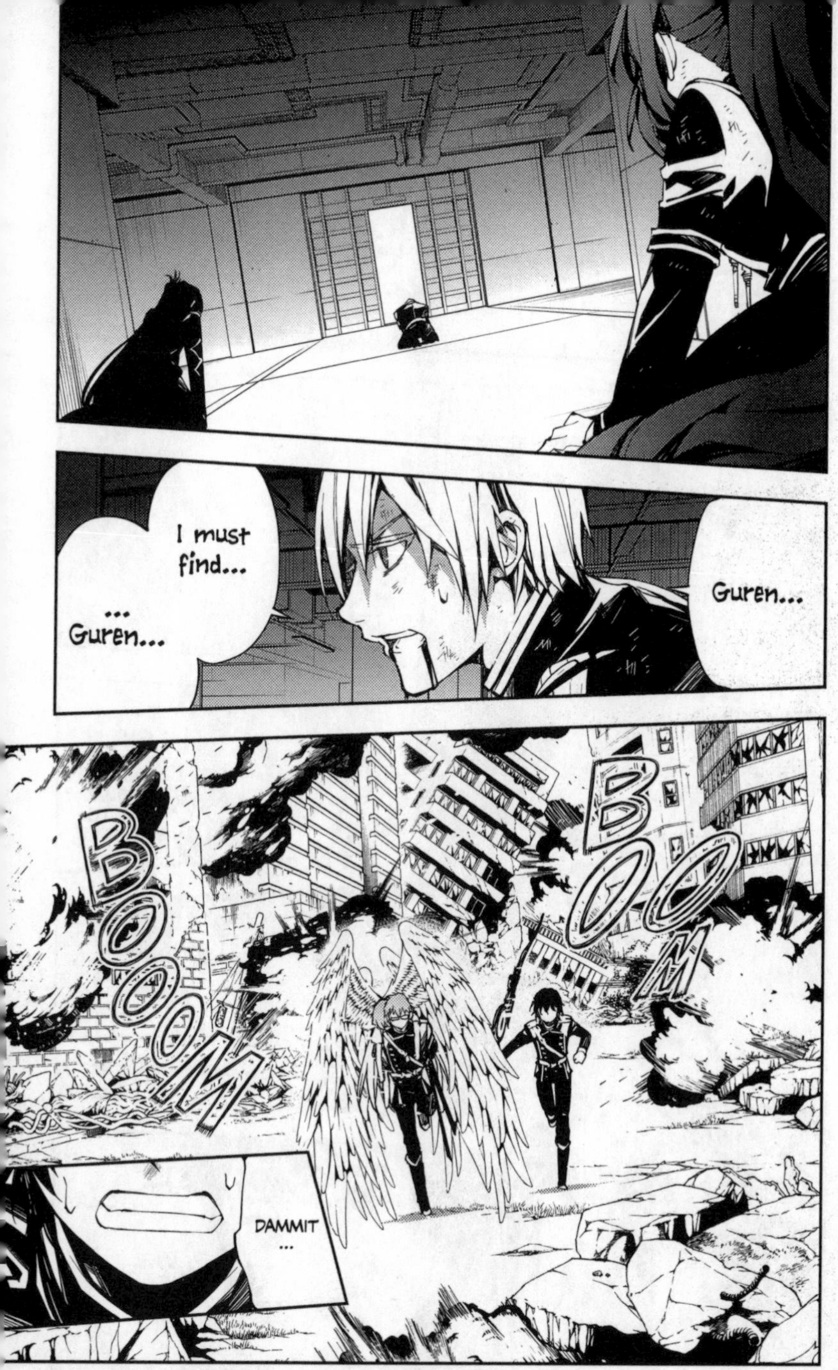
Guren...
I must find... ...Guren...
BOOM
BOOOOM
DAMMIT...

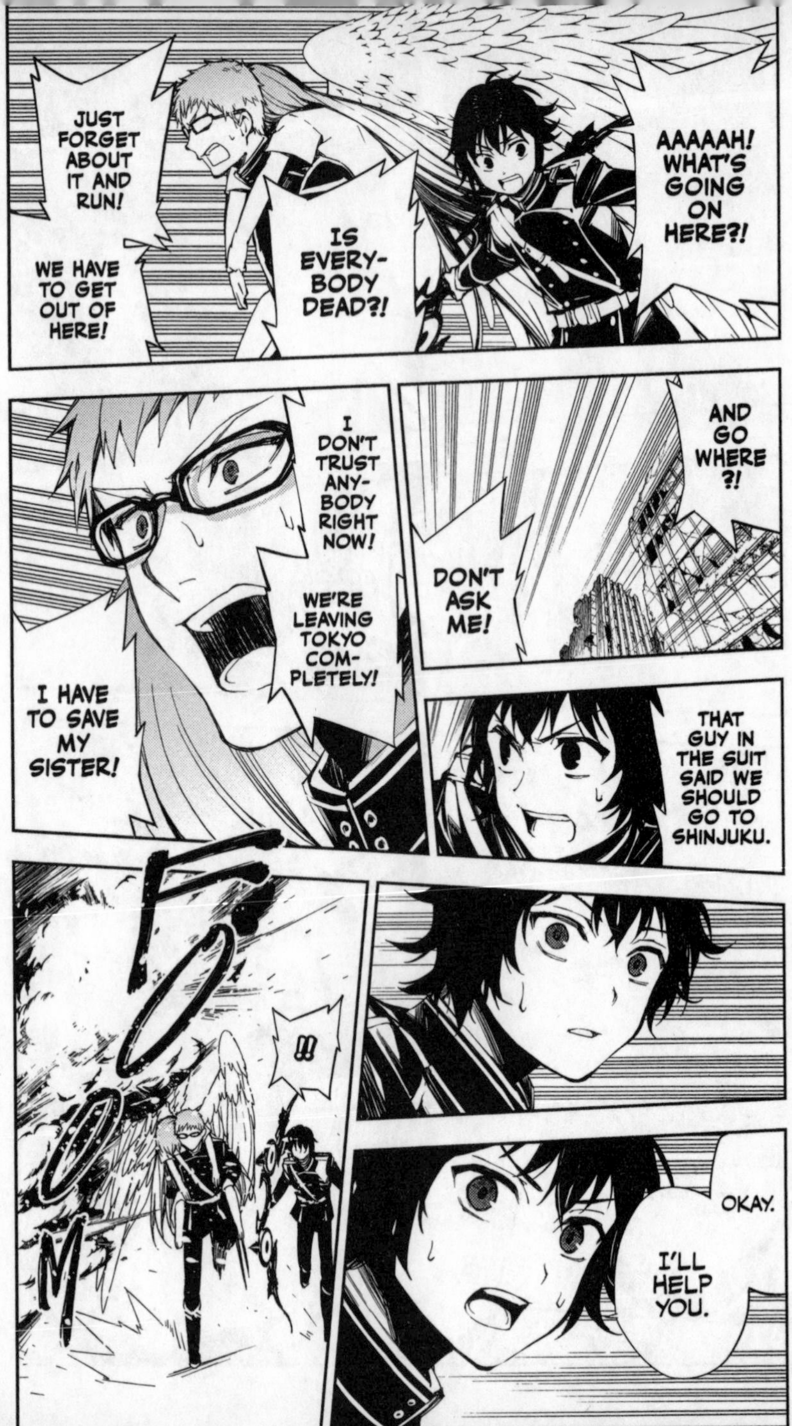
AAAAAH! WHAT'S GOING ON HERE?!
IS EVERY-BODY DEAD?!
JUST FORGET ABOUT IT AND RUN!
WE HAVE TO GET OUT OF HERE!
AND GO WHERE ?!
DON'T ASK ME!
I DON'T TRUST ANY-BODY RIGHT NOW!
WE'RE LEAVING TOKYO COM-PLETELY!
I HAVE TO SAVE MY SISTER!
THAT GUY IN THE SUIT SAID WE SHOULD GO TO SHINJUKU.
OKAY.
I'LL HELP YOU.
!!

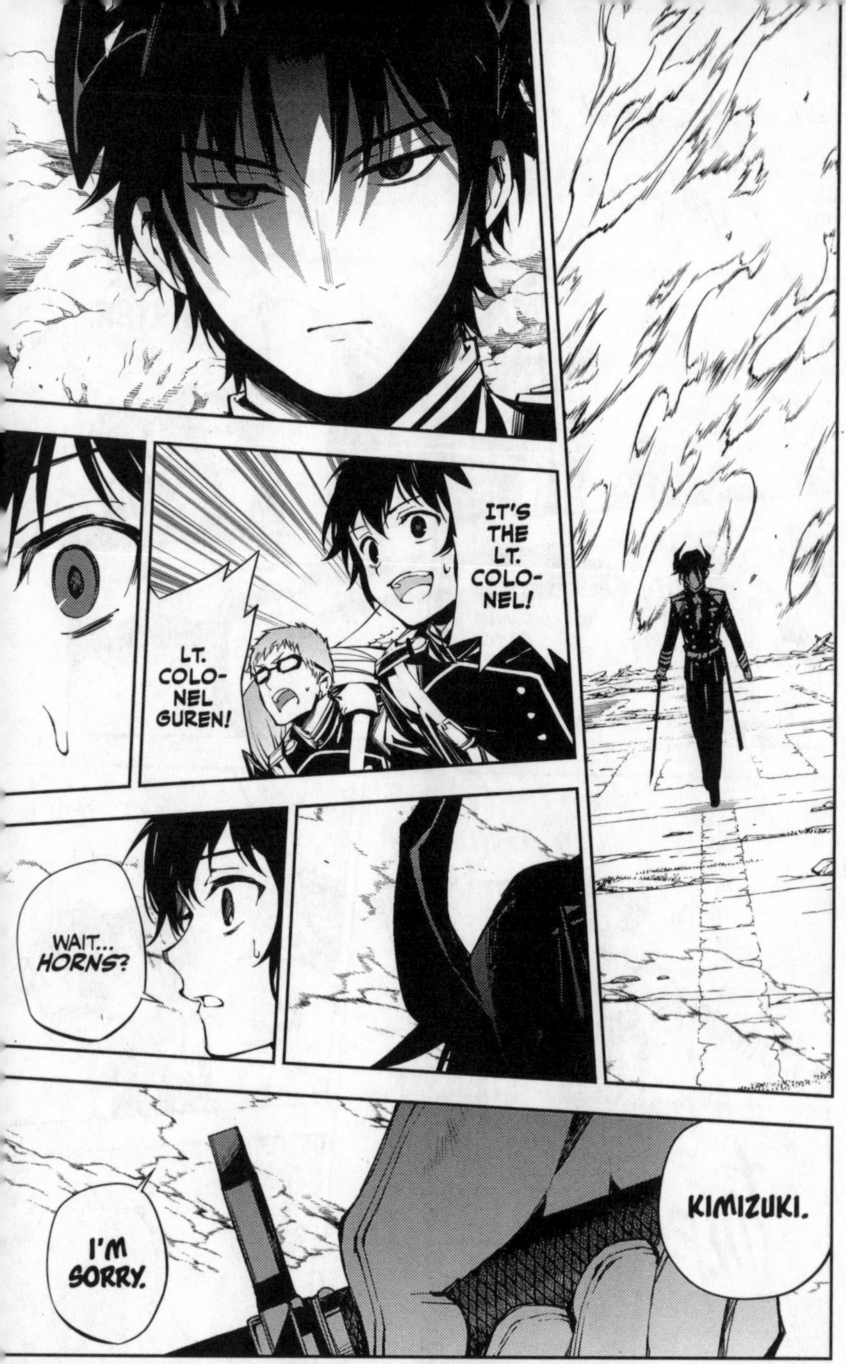
IT'S THE LT. COLONEL!
LT. COLONEL GUREN!
WAIT... HORNS?
KIMIZUKI.
I'M SORRY.

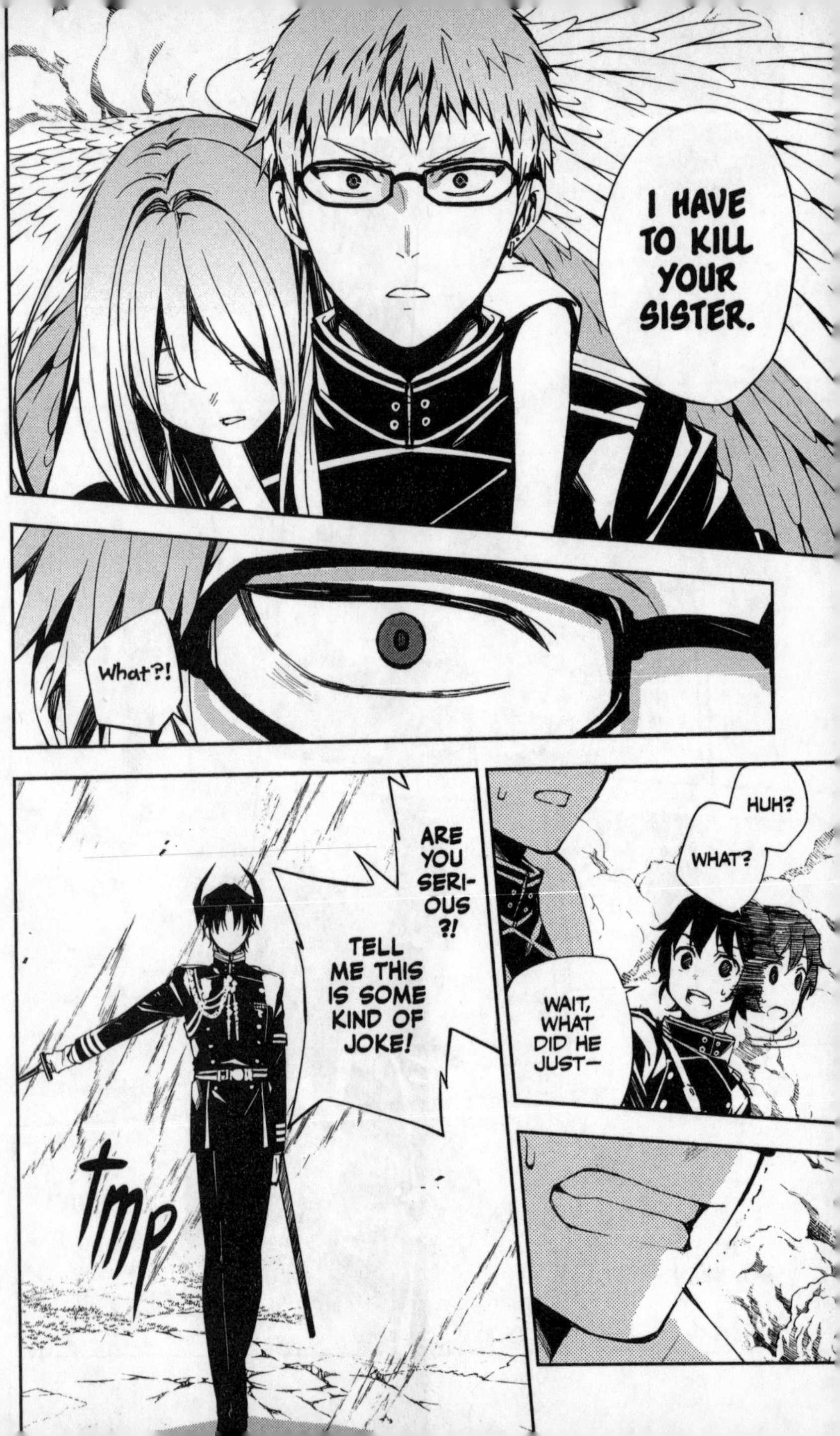
I HAVE TO KILL YOUR SISTER.
What?!
HUH?
WHAT?
WAIT, WHAT DID HE JUST—
ARE YOU SERI-OUS?!
TELL ME THIS IS SOME KIND OF JOKE!
tmp

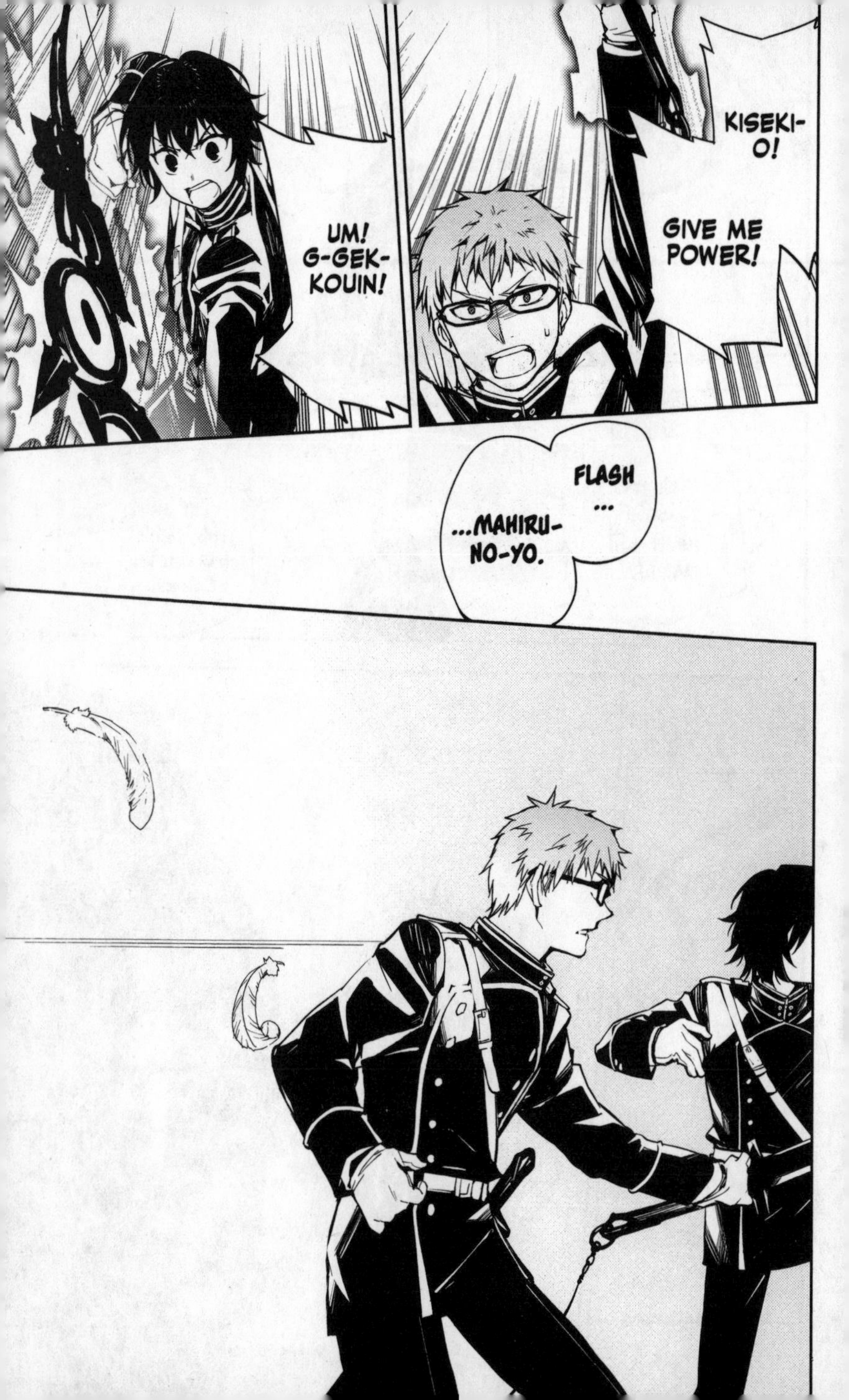
KISEKI-O!
GIVE ME POWER!
UM! G-GEK-KOUIN!
FLASH ...
...MAHIRU-NO-YO.

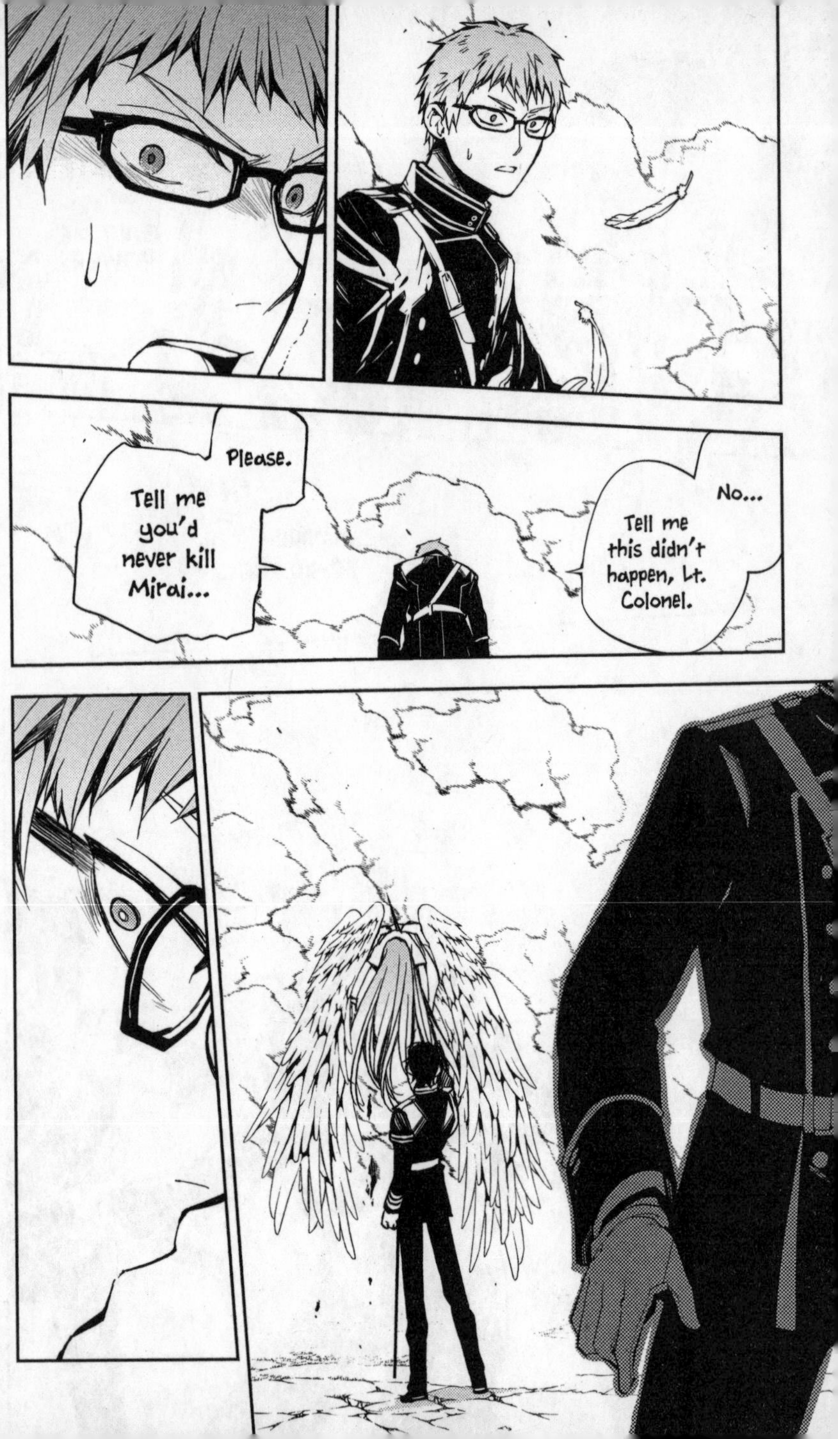
No...
Tell me this didn't happen, Lt. Colonel.
Please.
Tell me you'd never kill Mirai...

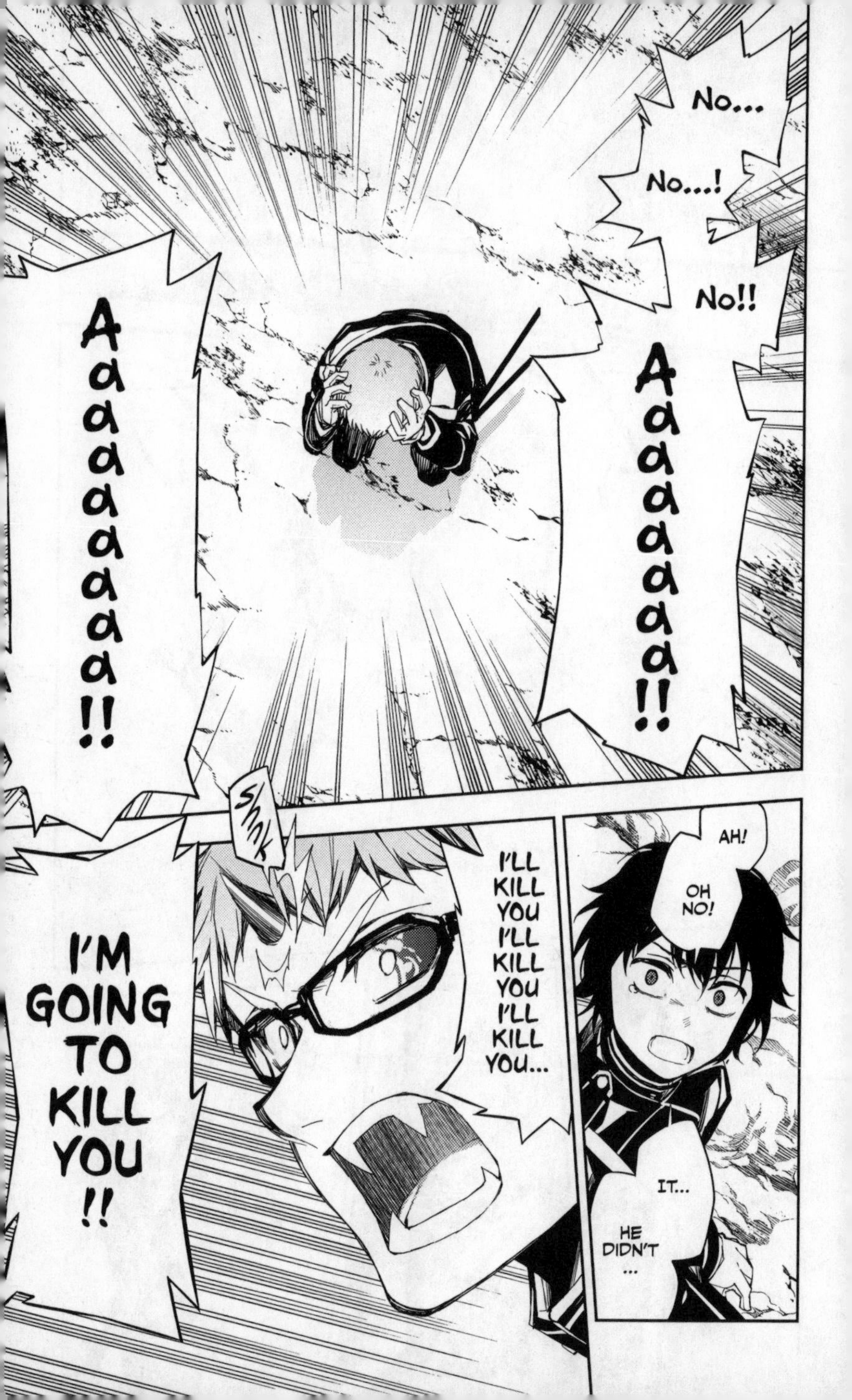

No... No...! No!!
Aaaaaaaaa!!
Aaaaaaaaa!!
AH!
OH NO!
IT...
HE DIDN'T ...
SHINK
I'LL KILL YOU I'LL KILL YOU I'LL KILL YOU...
I'M GOING TO KILL YOU!!

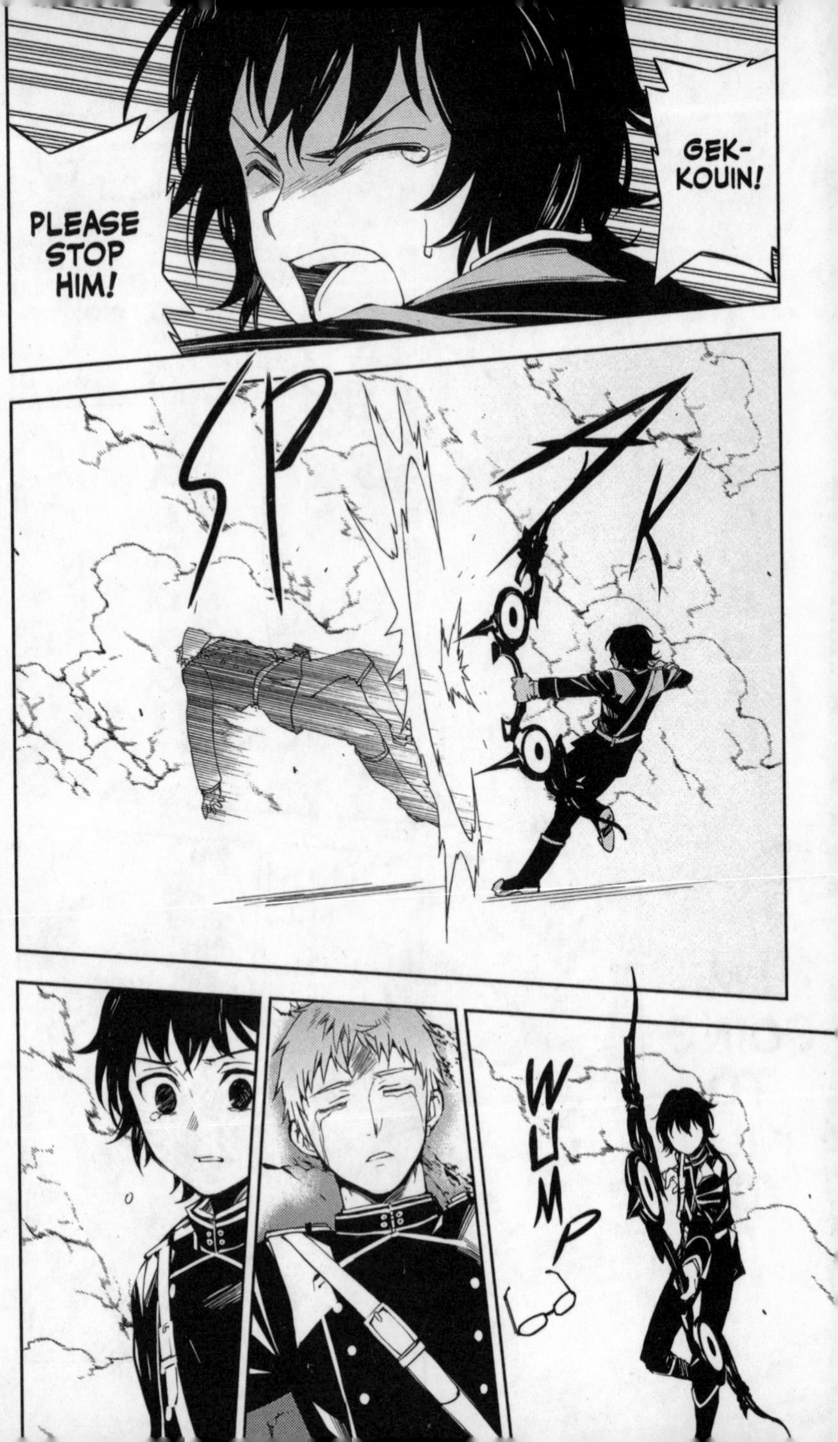
GEK-
KOUIN!
PLEASE
STOP
HIM!
SPAK
WUMP

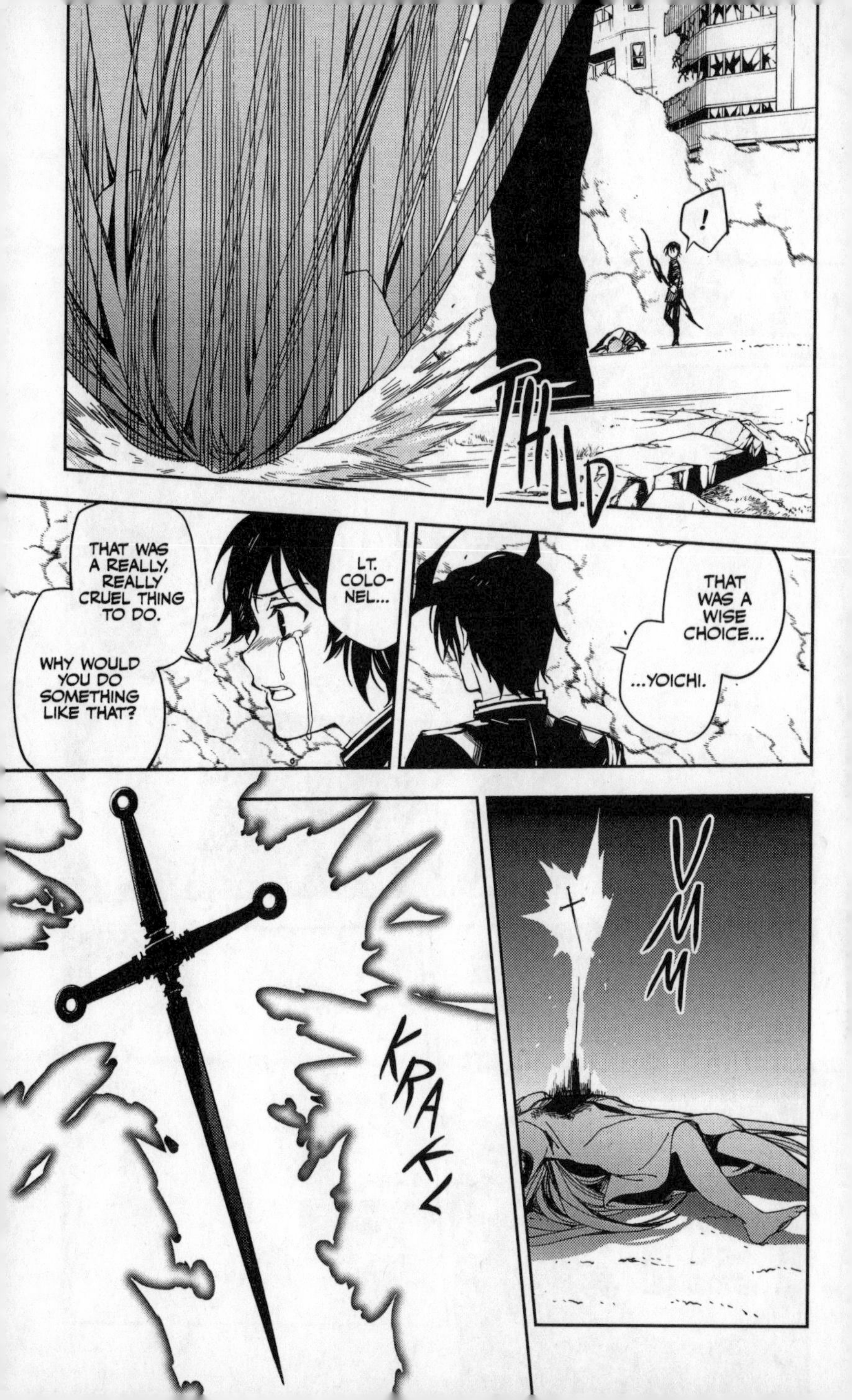
!
THUD
THAT WAS A WISE CHOICE...
...YOICHI.
LT. COLONEL...
THAT WAS A REALLY, REALLY CRUEL THING TO DO.
WHY WOULD YOU DO SOMETHING LIKE THAT?
VMMM
KRAKL

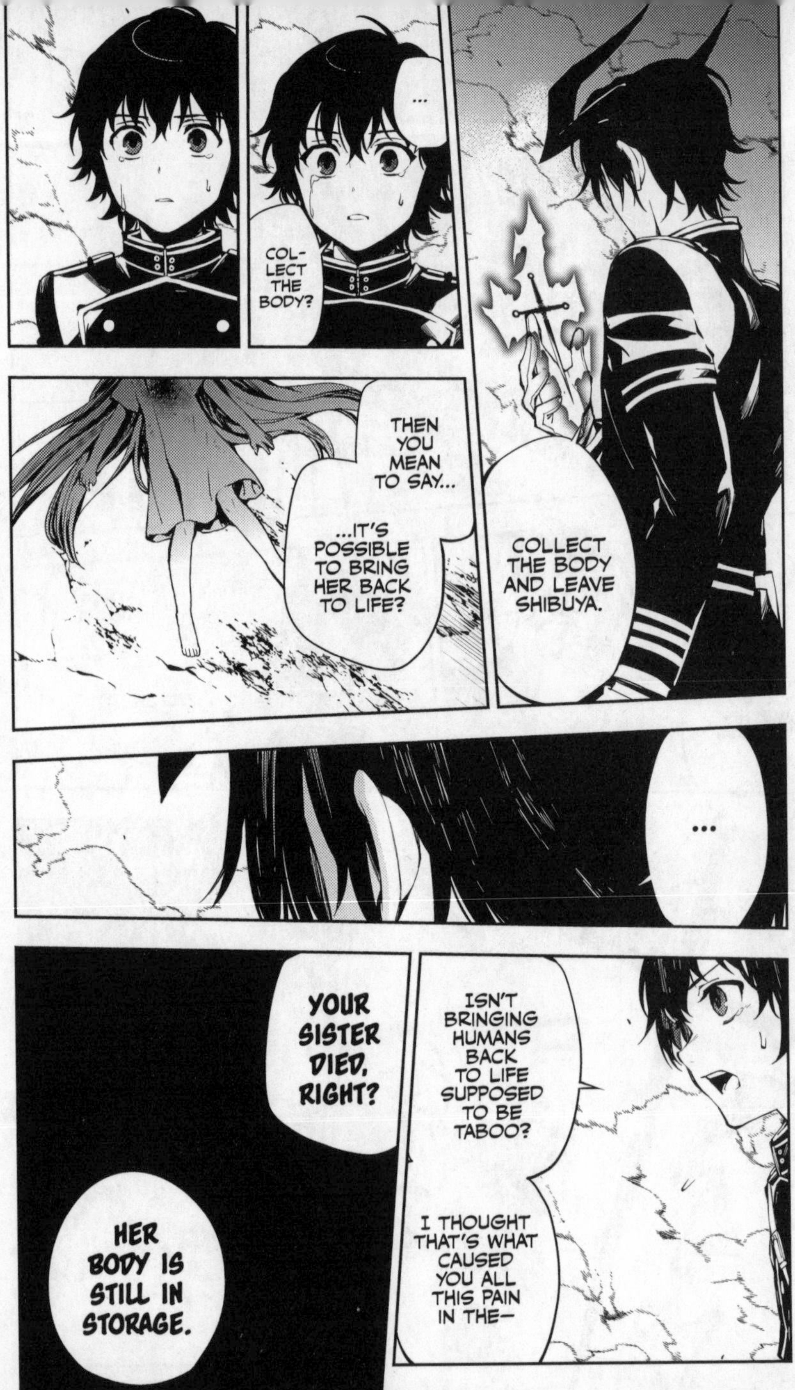
COLLECT THE BODY AND LEAVE SHIBUYA.
...
COL-LECT THE BODY?
THEN YOU MEAN TO SAY...
...IT'S POSSIBLE TO BRING HER BACK TO LIFE?
...
ISN'T BRINGING HUMANS BACK TO LIFE SUPPOSED TO BE TABOO?
I THOUGHT THAT'S WHAT CAUSED YOU ALL THIS PAIN IN THE—
YOUR SISTER DIED, RIGHT?
HER BODY IS STILL IN STORAGE.

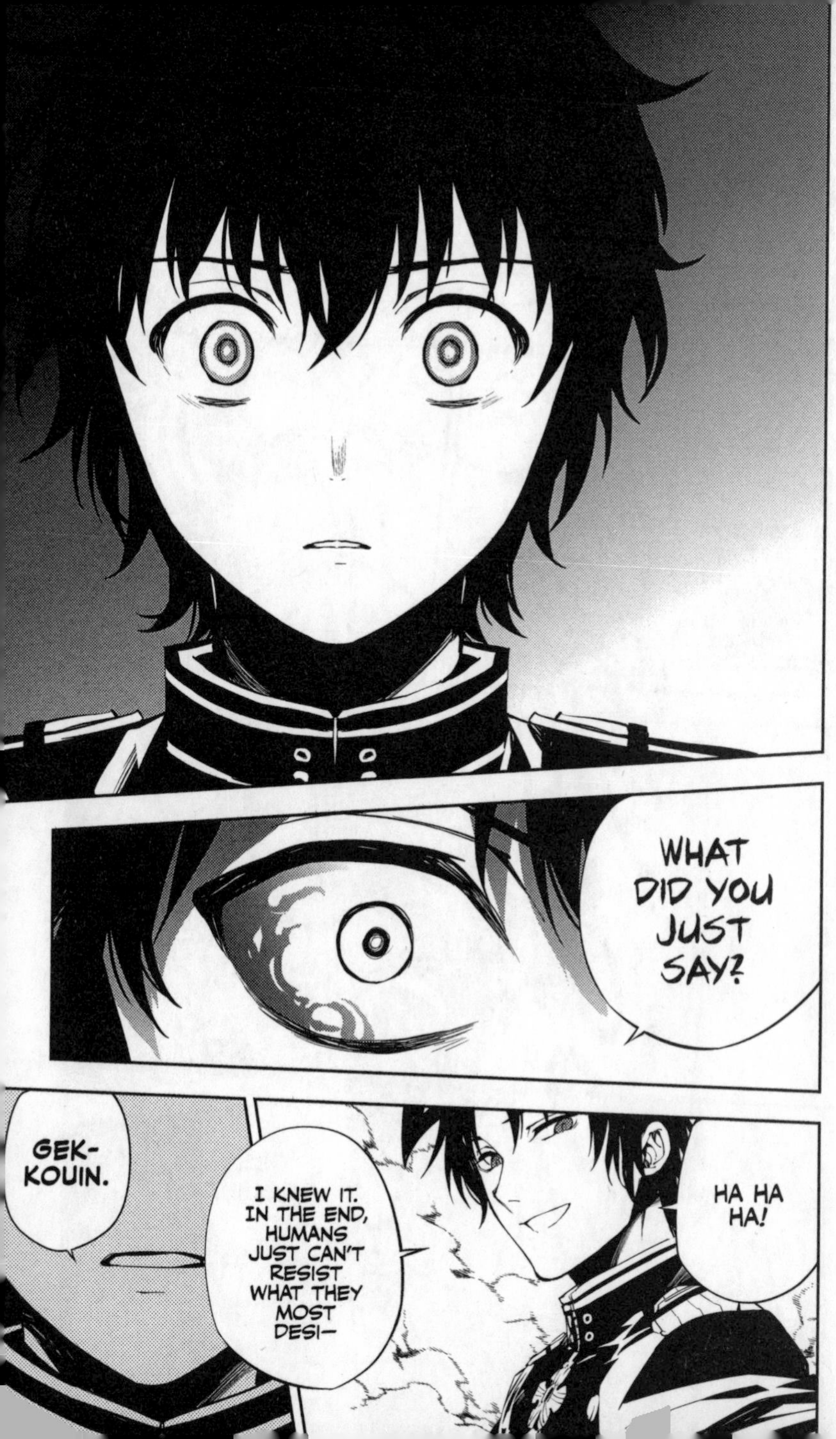
WHAT DID YOU JUST SAY?
HA HA HA!
I KNEW IT. IN THE END, HUMANS JUST CAN'T RESIST WHAT THEY MOST DESI—
GEK-KOUIN.

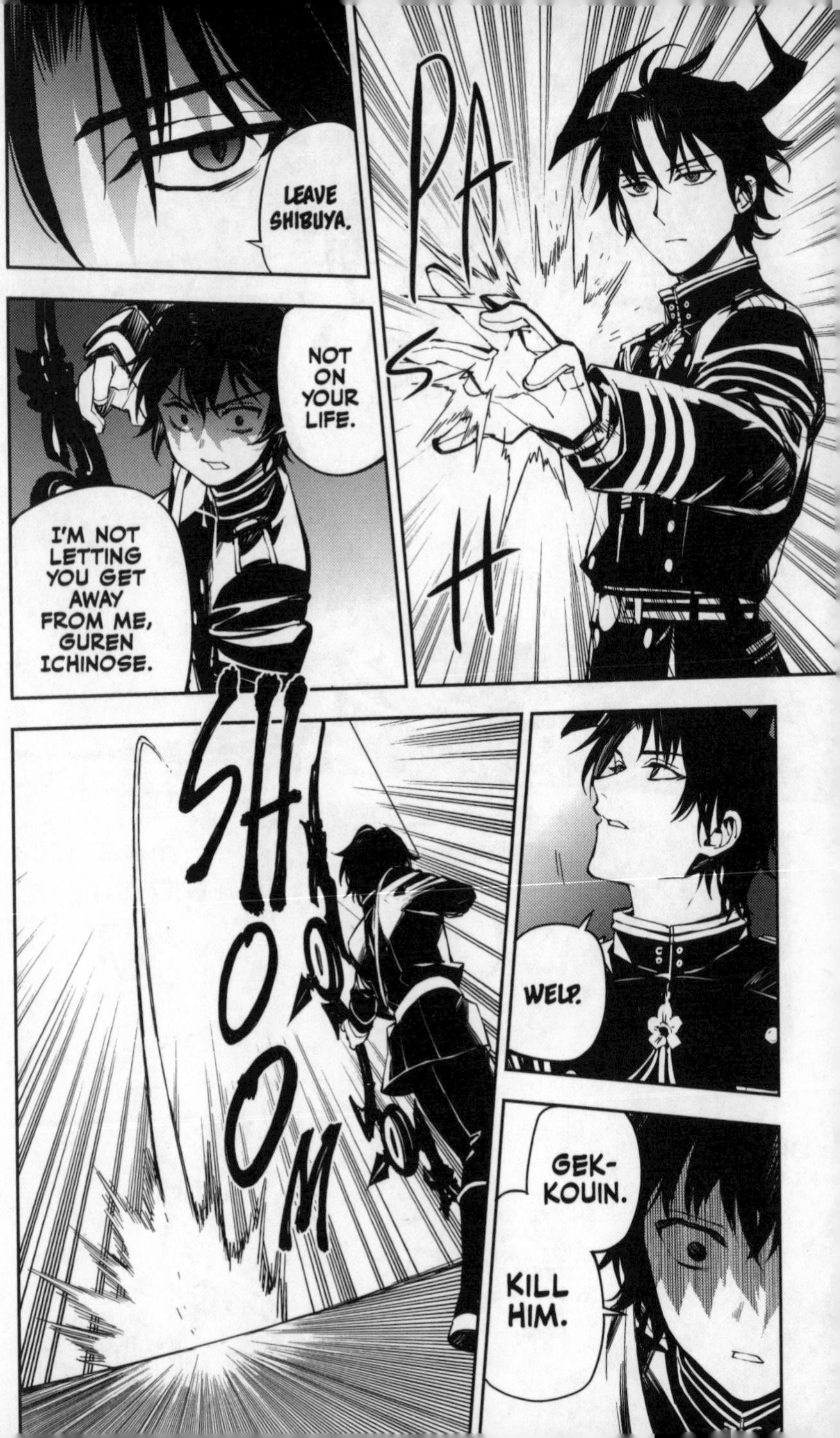
PASH
LEAVE SHIBUYA.
NOT ON YOUR LIFE.
I'M NOT LETTING YOU GET AWAY FROM ME, GUREN ICHINOSE.
WELP.
GEK-KOUIN.
KILL HIM.
SHOOM

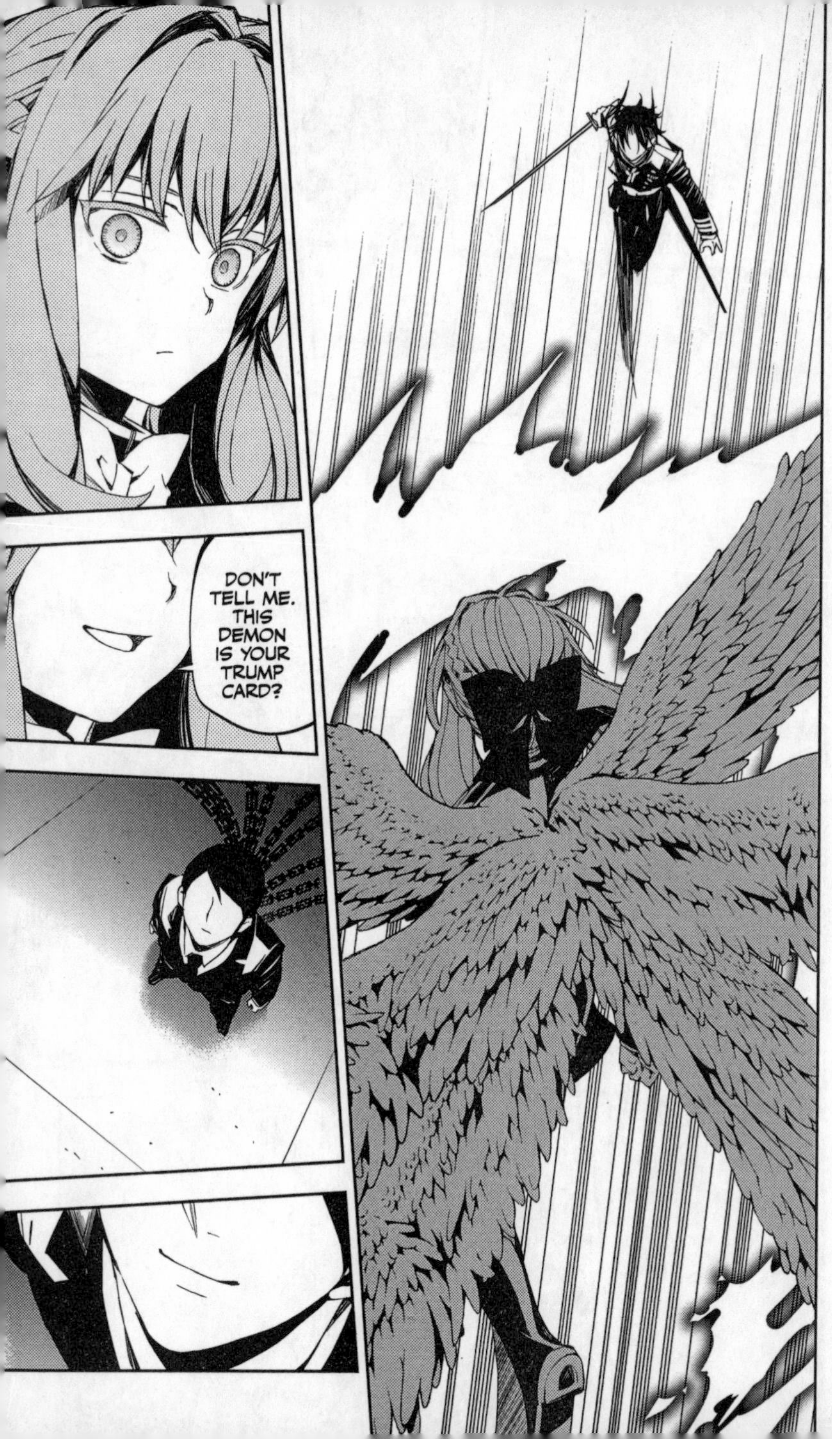
DON'T TELL ME. THIS DEMON IS YOUR TRUMP CARD?

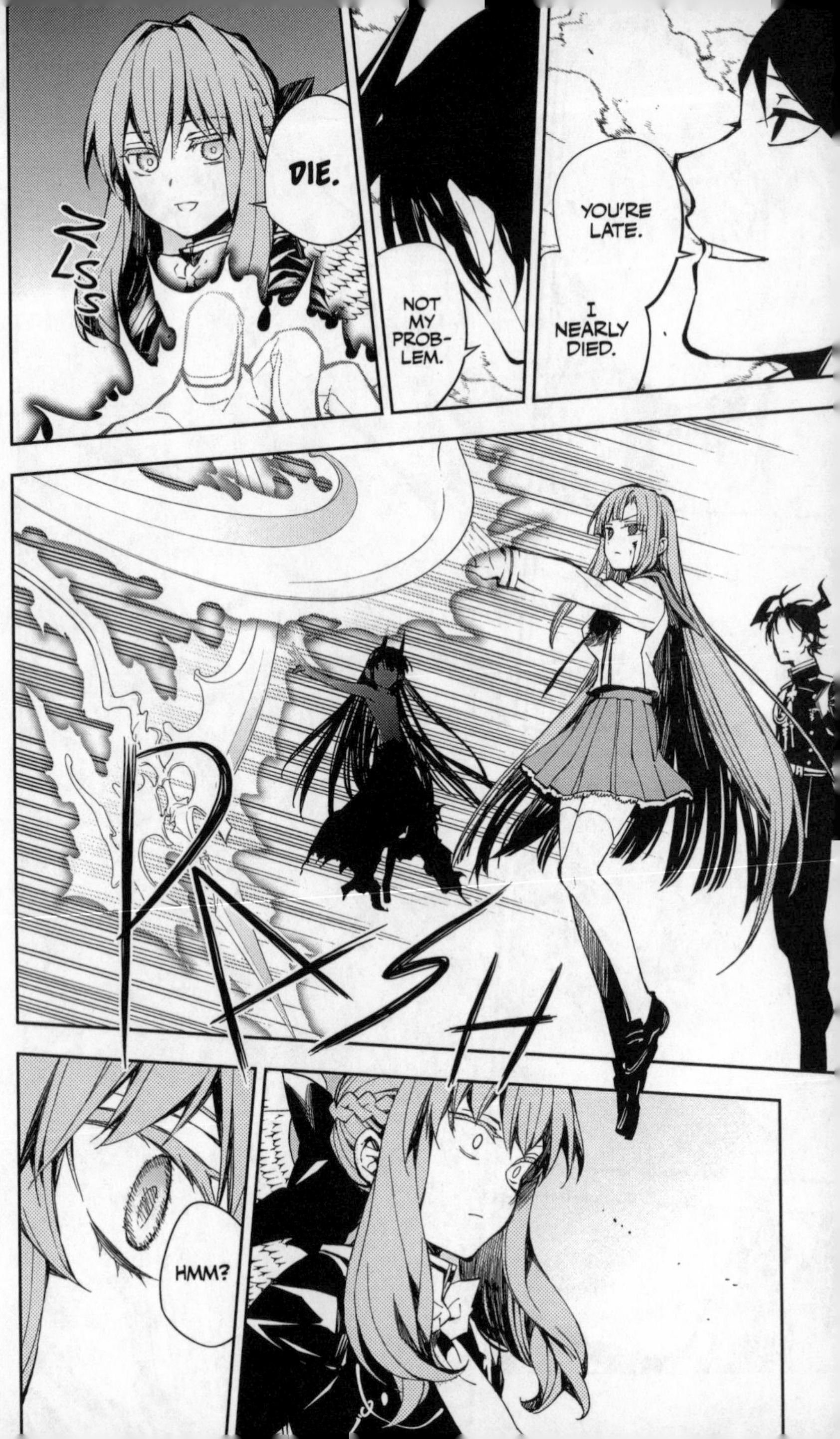
YOU'RE LATE.
I NEARLY DIED.
NOT MY PROB-LEM.
DIE.
PASH
HMM?

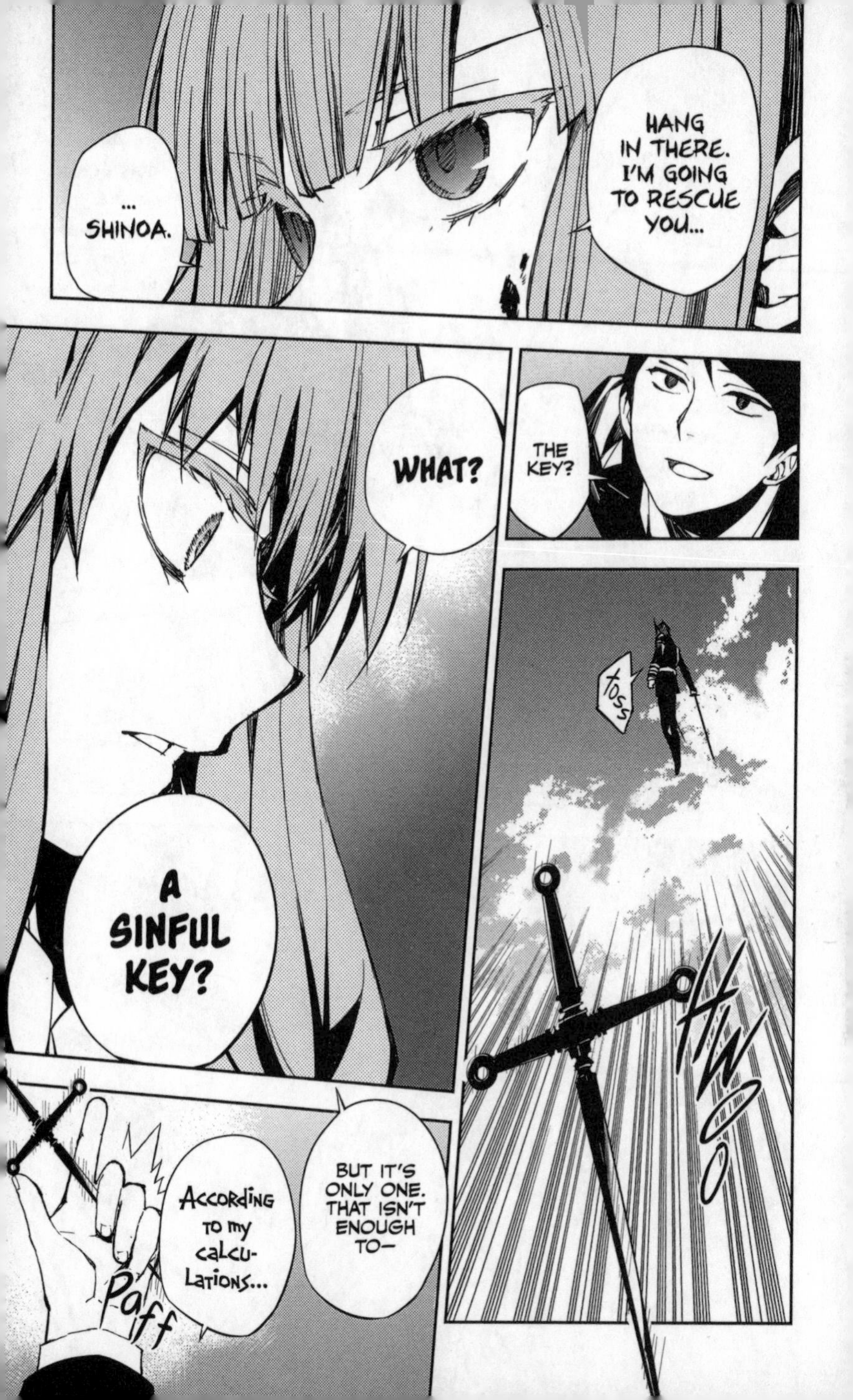

HANG IN THERE. I'M GOING TO RESCUE YOU...
...SHINOA.
THE KEY?
TOSS
HWOO
WHAT?
A SINFUL KEY?
BUT IT'S ONLY ONE. THAT ISN'T ENOUGH TO—
According to my calcu-lations...
Paff

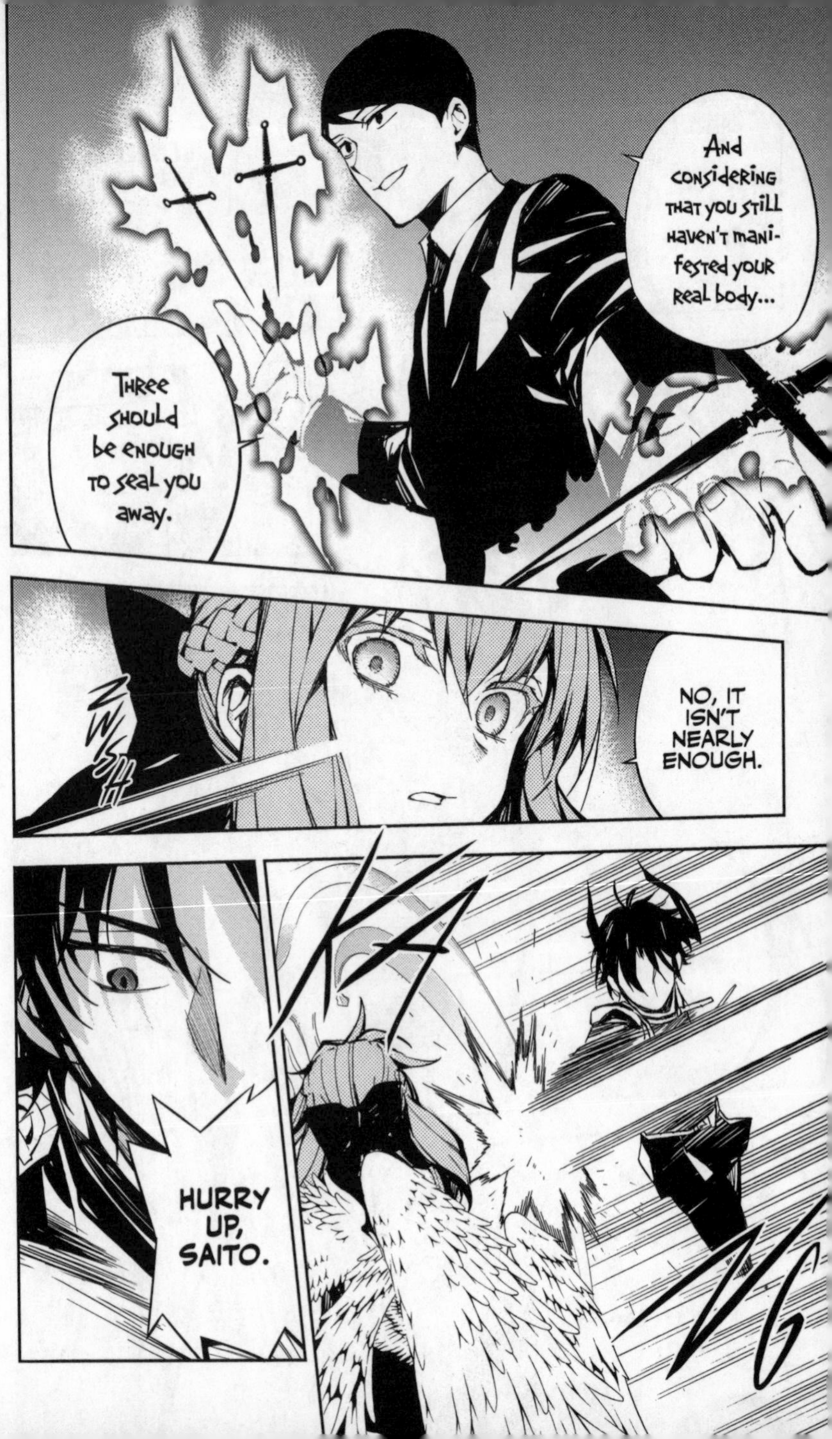
And considering that you still haven't manifested your real body...
Three should be enough to seal you away.
NO, IT ISN'T NEARLY ENOUGH.
KA
HURRY UP, SAITO.

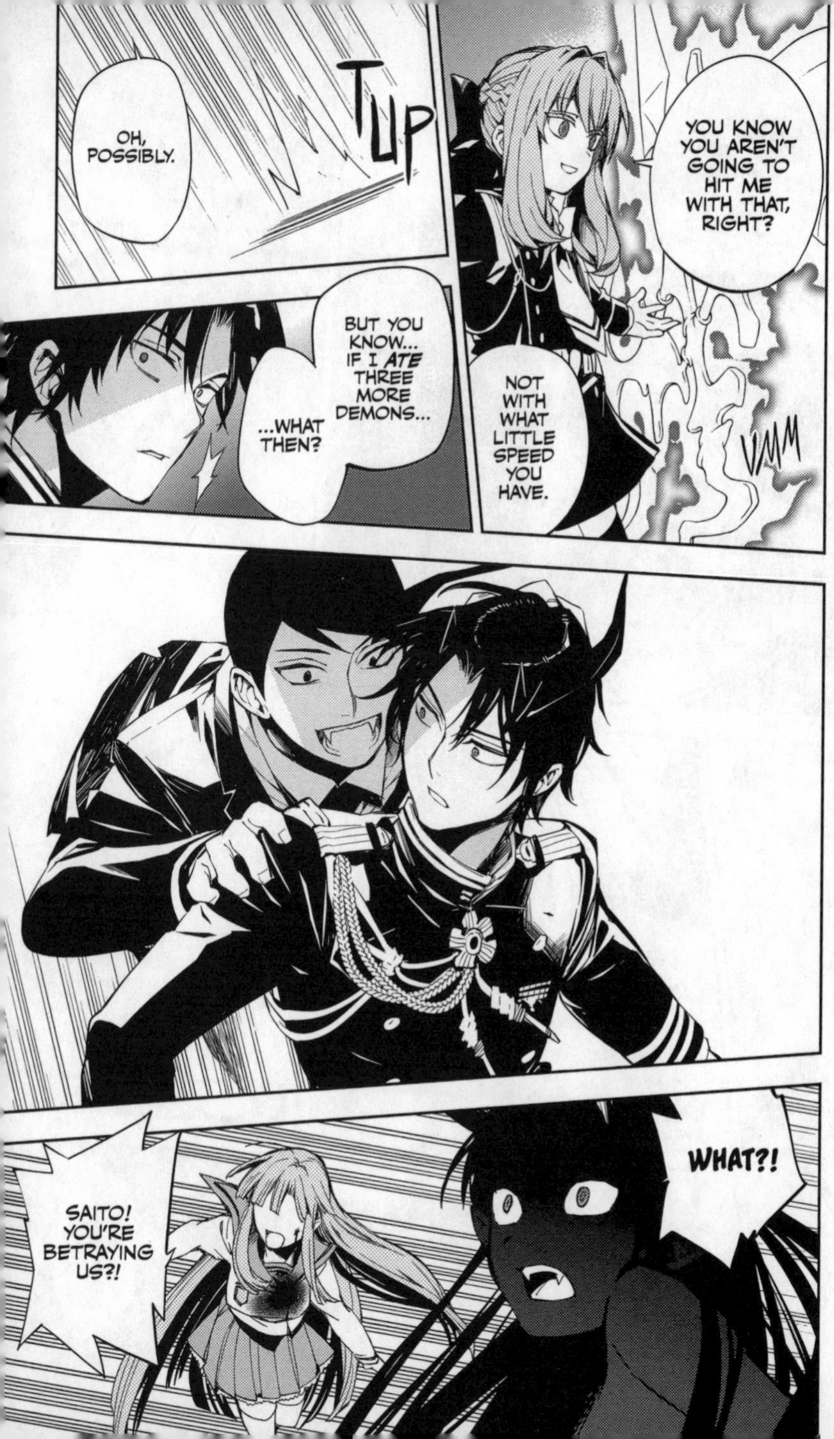
YOU KNOW YOU AREN'T GOING TO HIT ME WITH THAT, RIGHT?
VMM
NOT WITH WHAT LITTLE SPEED YOU HAVE.
TUP
OH, POSSIBLY.
BUT YOU KNOW... IF I *ATE* THREE MORE DEMONS...
...WHAT THEN?
WHAT?!
SAITO! YOU'RE BETRAYING US?!

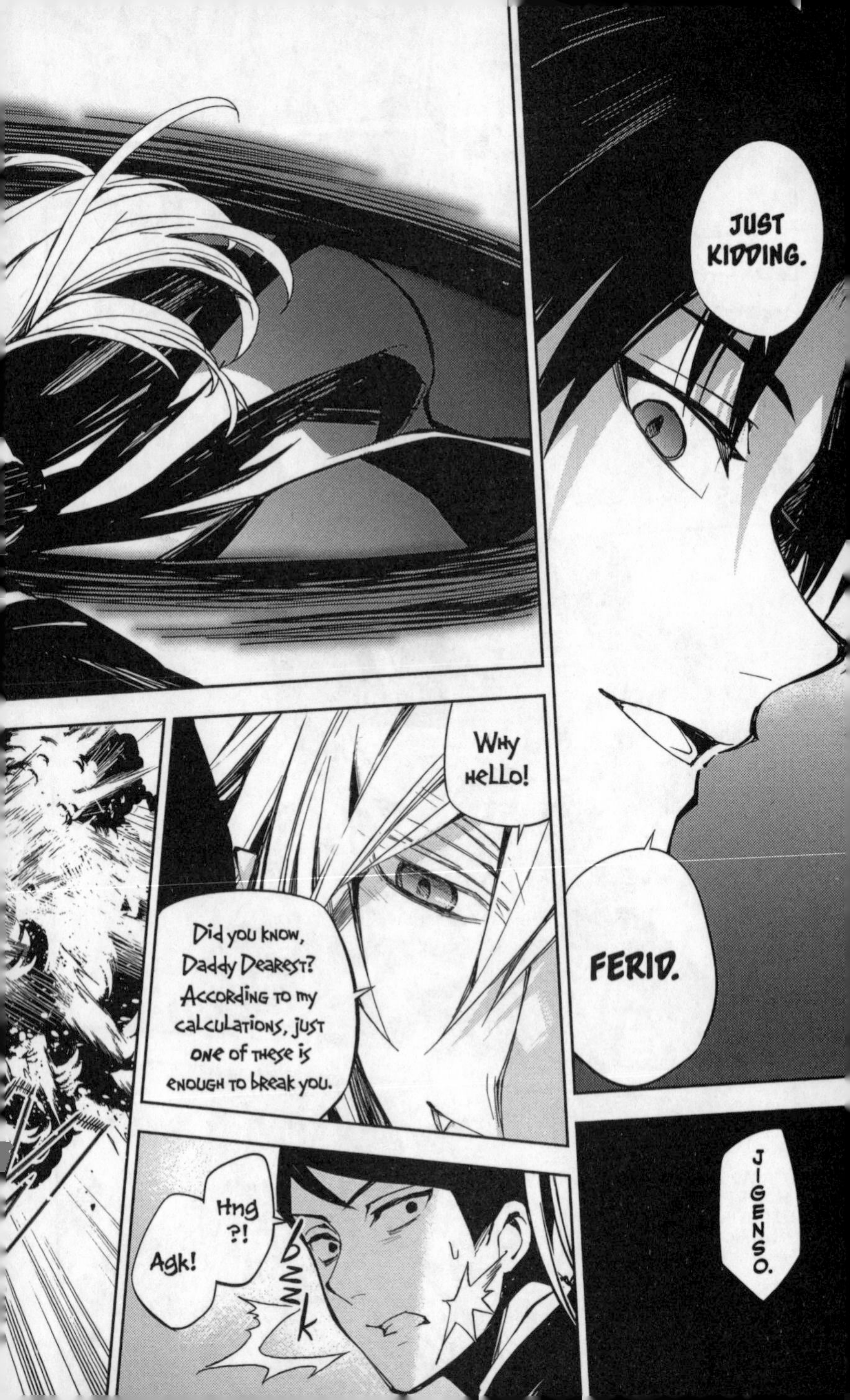
JUST KIDDING.
FERID.
JIGENSO.
Why hello!
Did you know, Daddy Dearest? According to my calculations, just one of these is enough to break you.
Hng ?!
Agk!
BONK

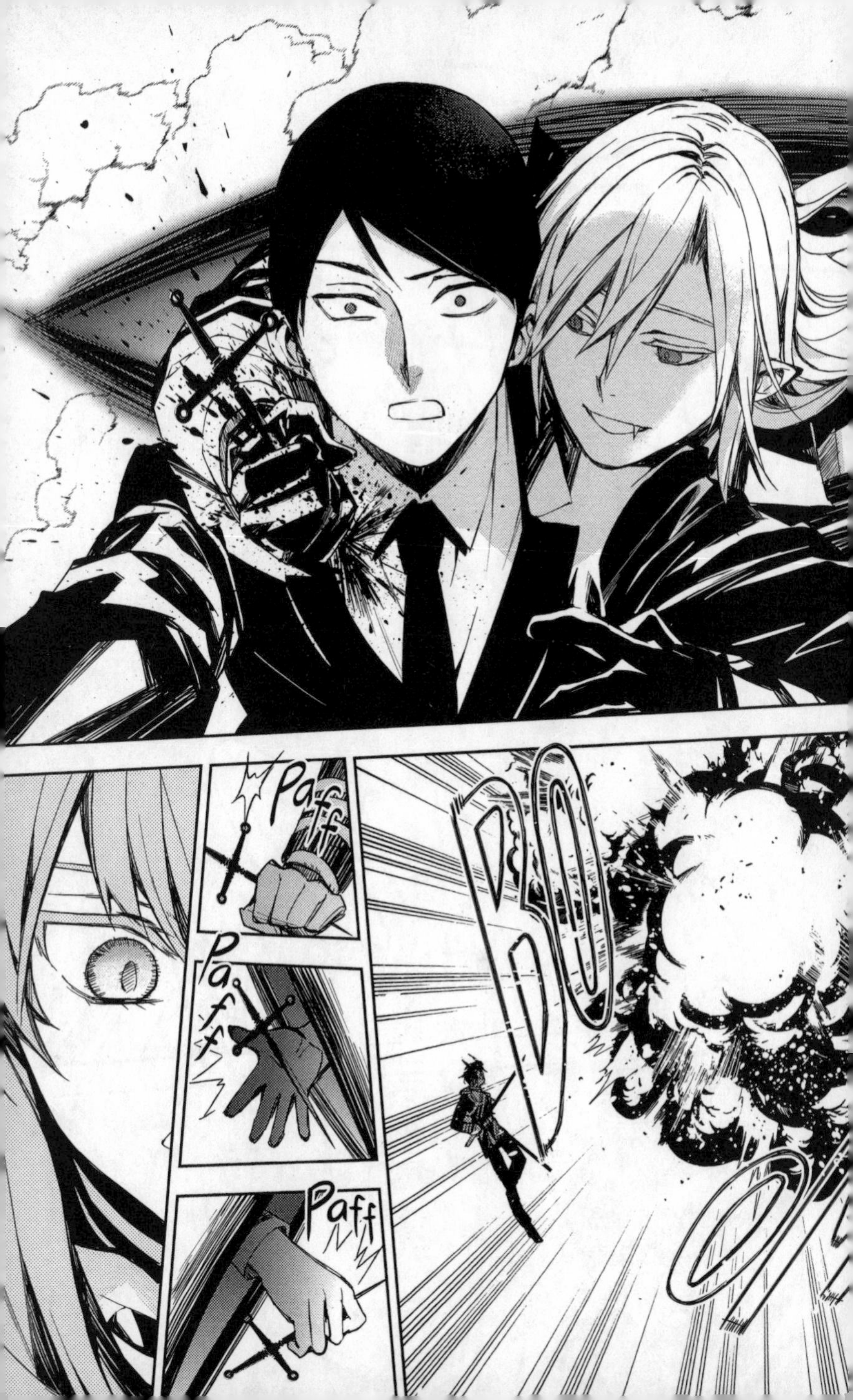
Paff
Paff
Paff

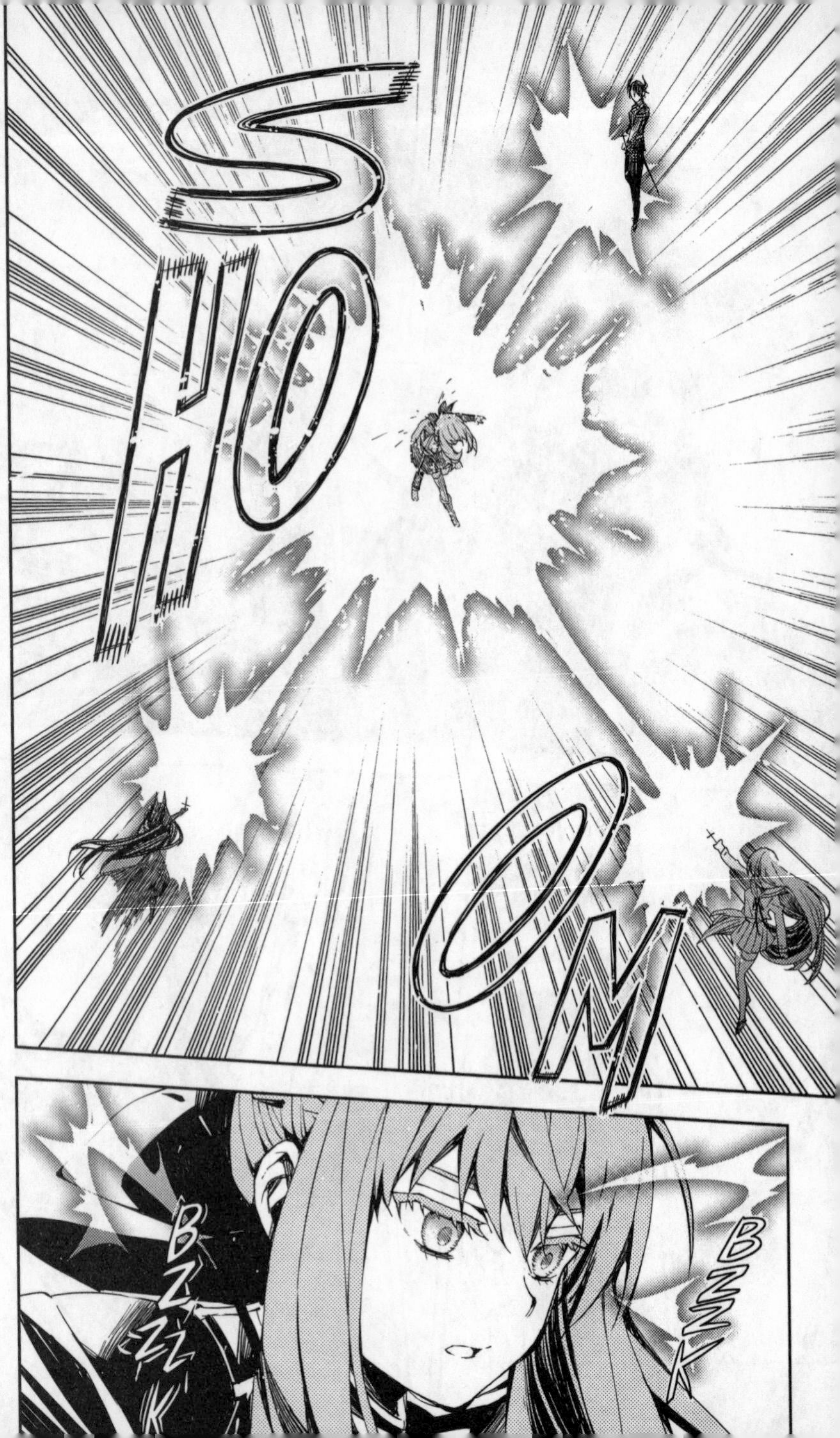
SHOOM
BZZZK
BZZZK

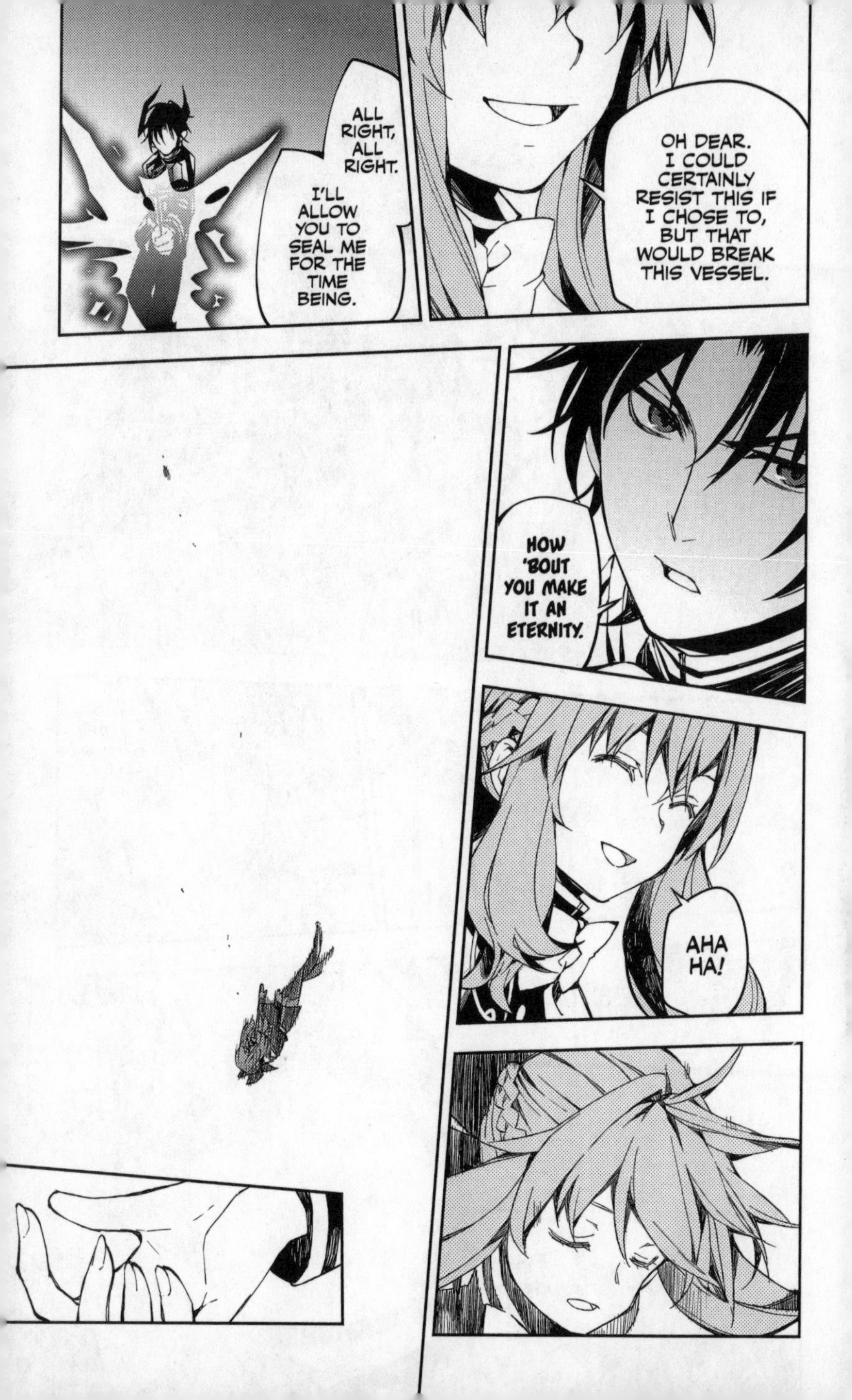
OH DEAR. I COULD CERTAINLY RESIST THIS IF I CHOSE TO, BUT THAT WOULD BREAK THIS VESSEL.
ALL RIGHT, ALL RIGHT.
I'LL ALLOW YOU TO SEAL ME FOR THE TIME BEING.
HOW 'BOUT YOU MAKE IT AN ETERNITY.
AHA HA!

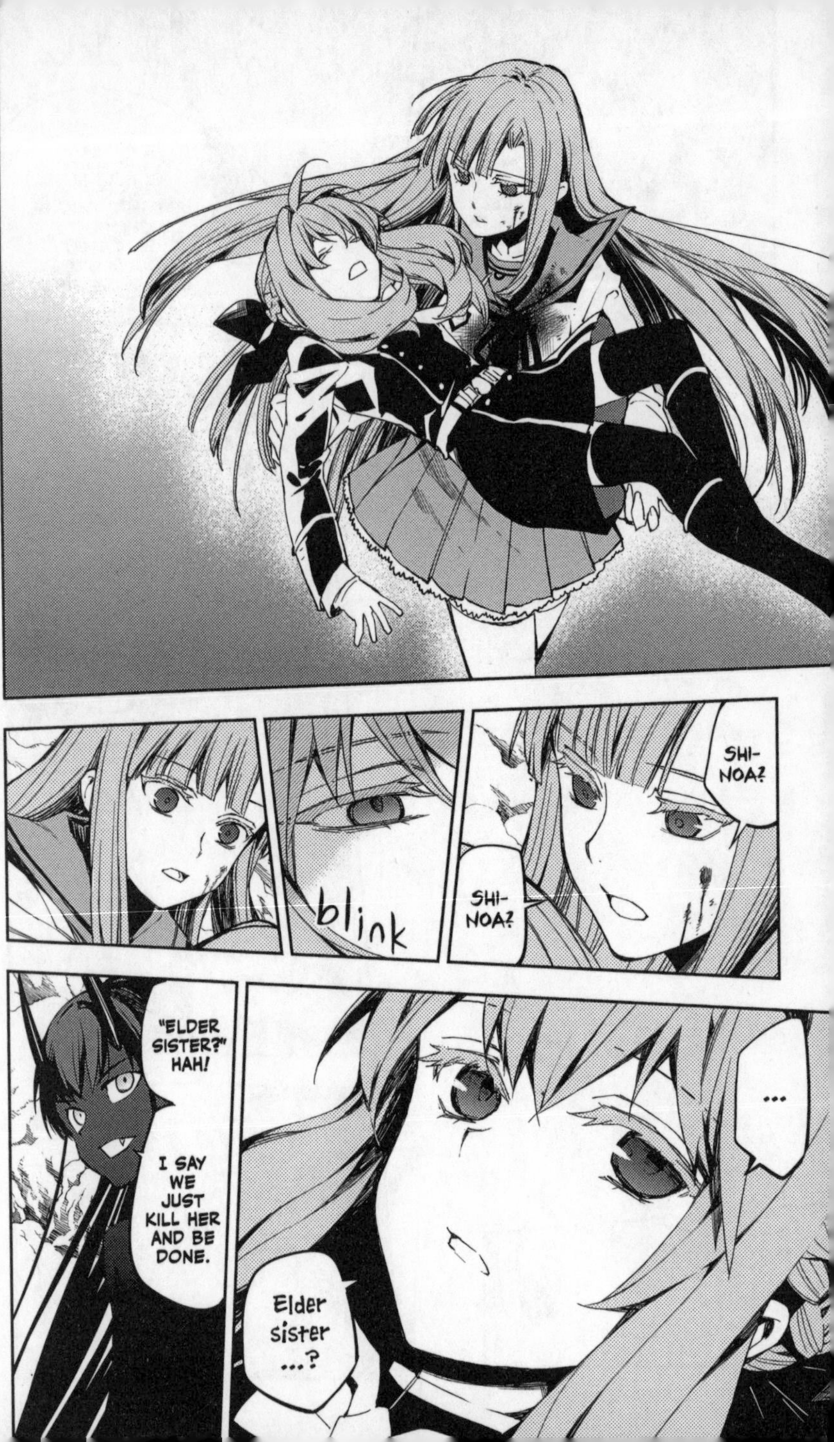
SHI-
NOA?
SHI-
NOA?
blink
...
Elder sister ...?
"ELDER SISTER?" HAH!
I SAY WE JUST KILL HER AND BE DONE.

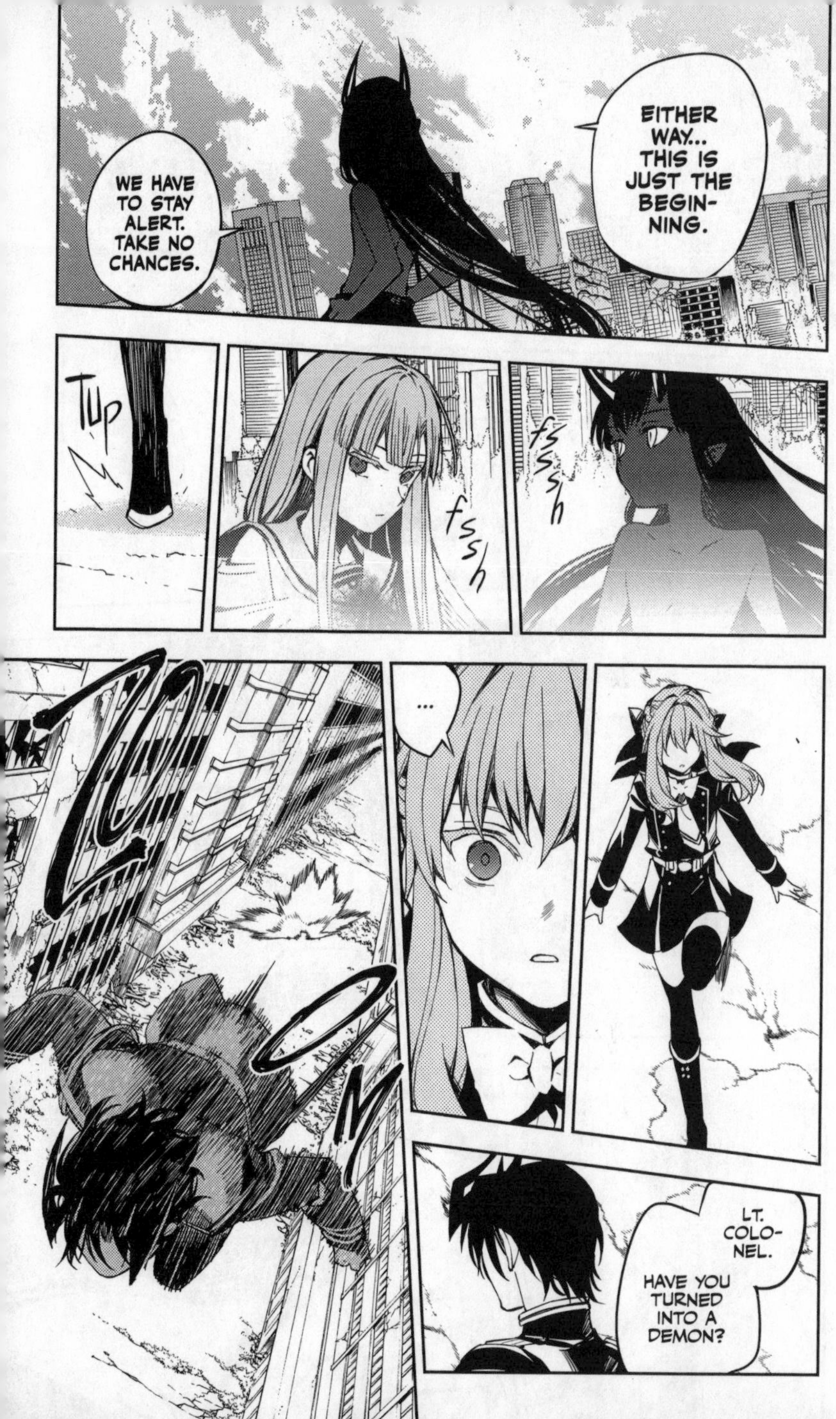
EITHER WAY... THIS IS JUST THE BEGIN-NING.
WE HAVE TO STAY ALERT. TAKE NO CHANCES.
fssh
fssh
TUP
...
LT. COLO-NEL.
HAVE YOU TURNED INTO A DEMON?
ZOOM

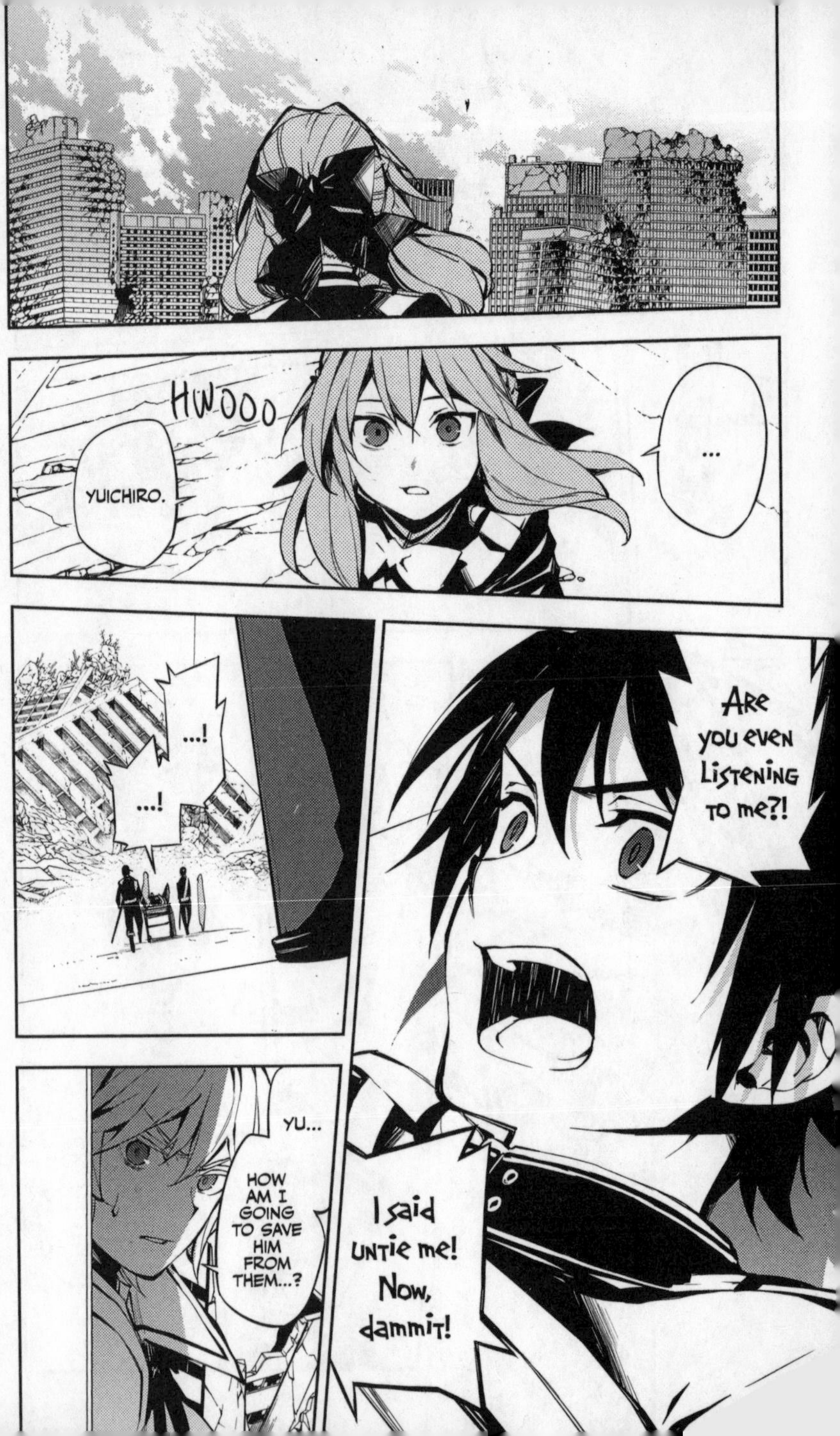
...
HWOOO
YUICHIRO.
Are you even listening to me?!
I said untie me! Now, dammit!
...!
...!
YU...
HOW AM I GOING TO SAVE HIM FROM THEM...?

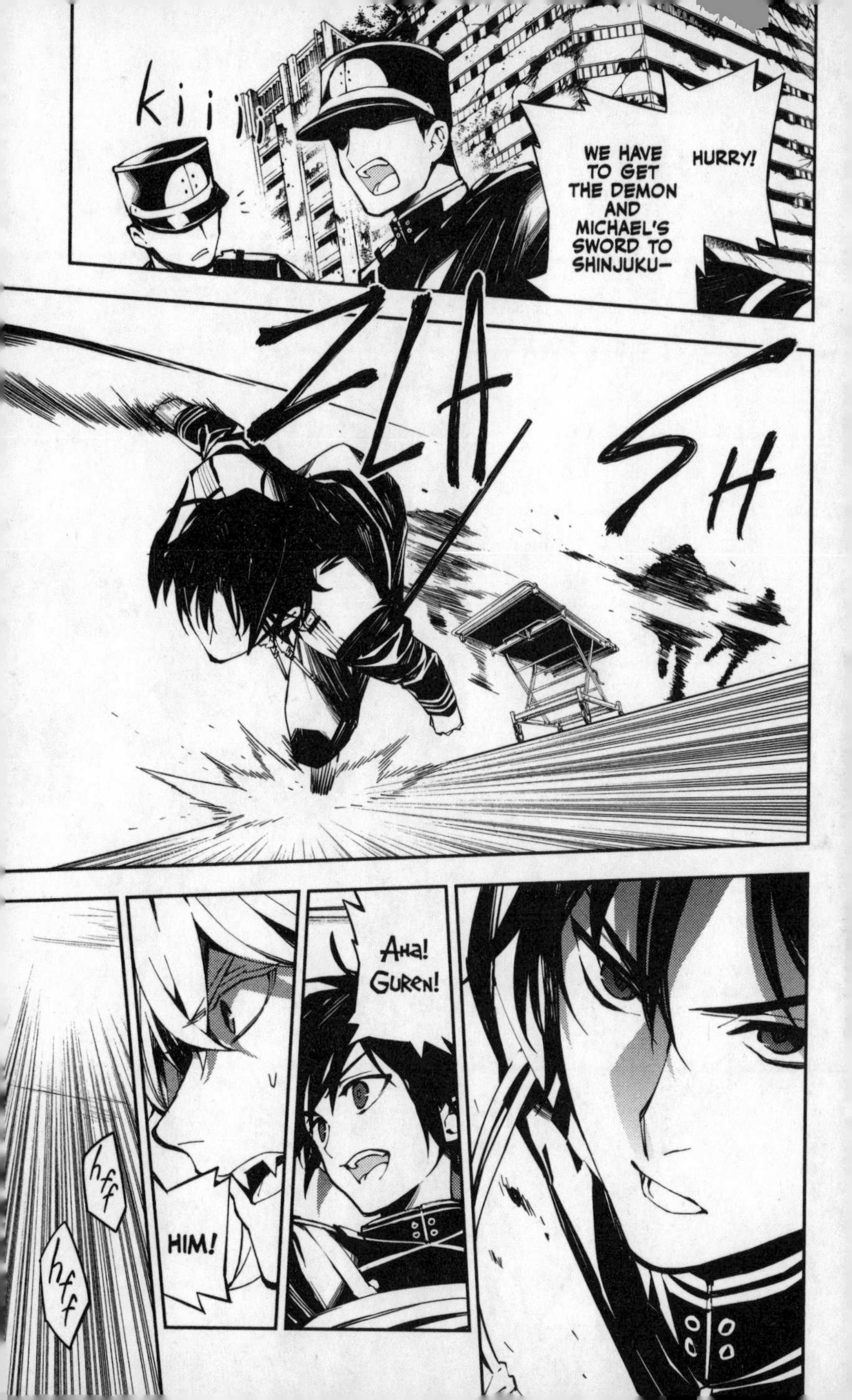
HURRY!
WE HAVE TO GET THE DEMON AND MICHAEL'S SWORD TO SHINJUKU—
kiii
ZLASH
AHA! GUREN!
HIM!
hff
hff

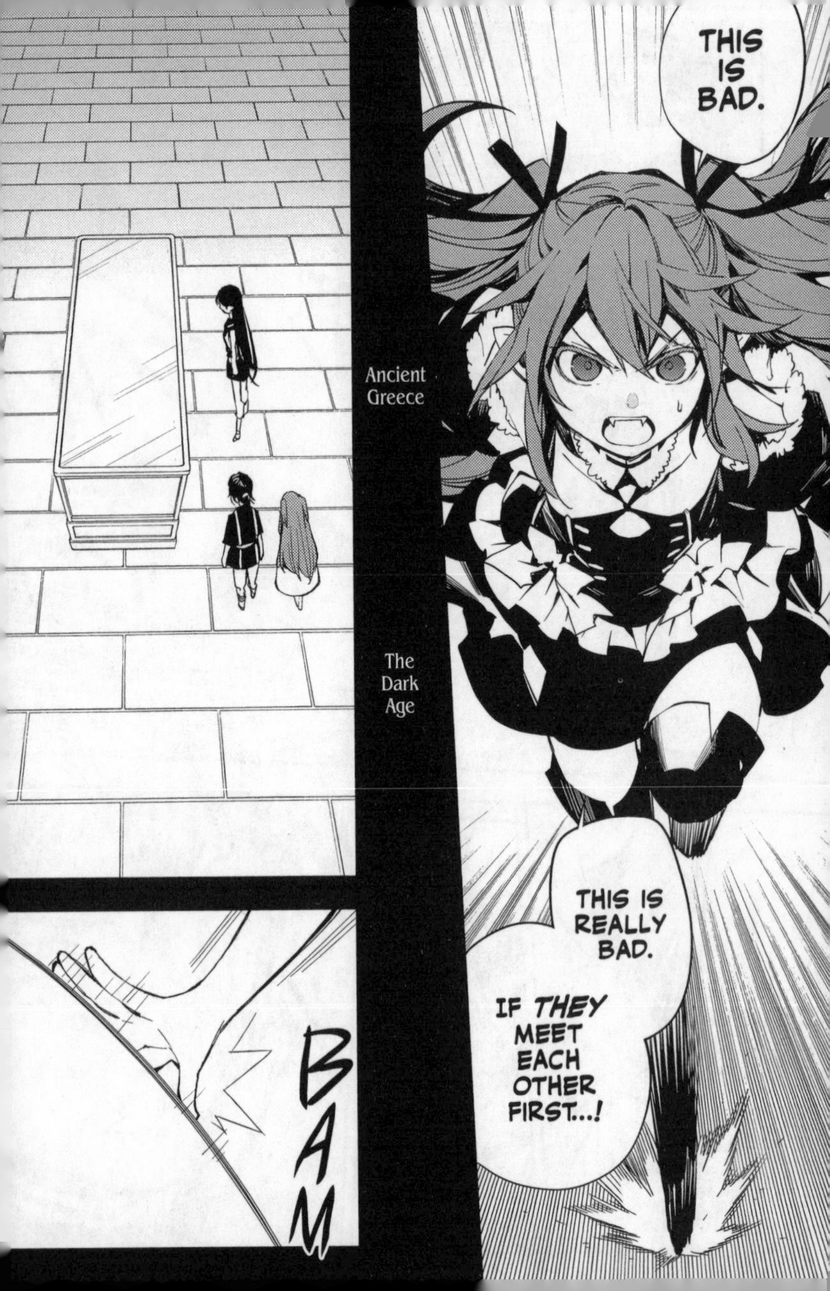
THIS IS BAD.
THIS IS REALLY BAD.
IF THEY MEET EACH OTHER FIRST...!
Ancient Greece
The Dark Age
BAM

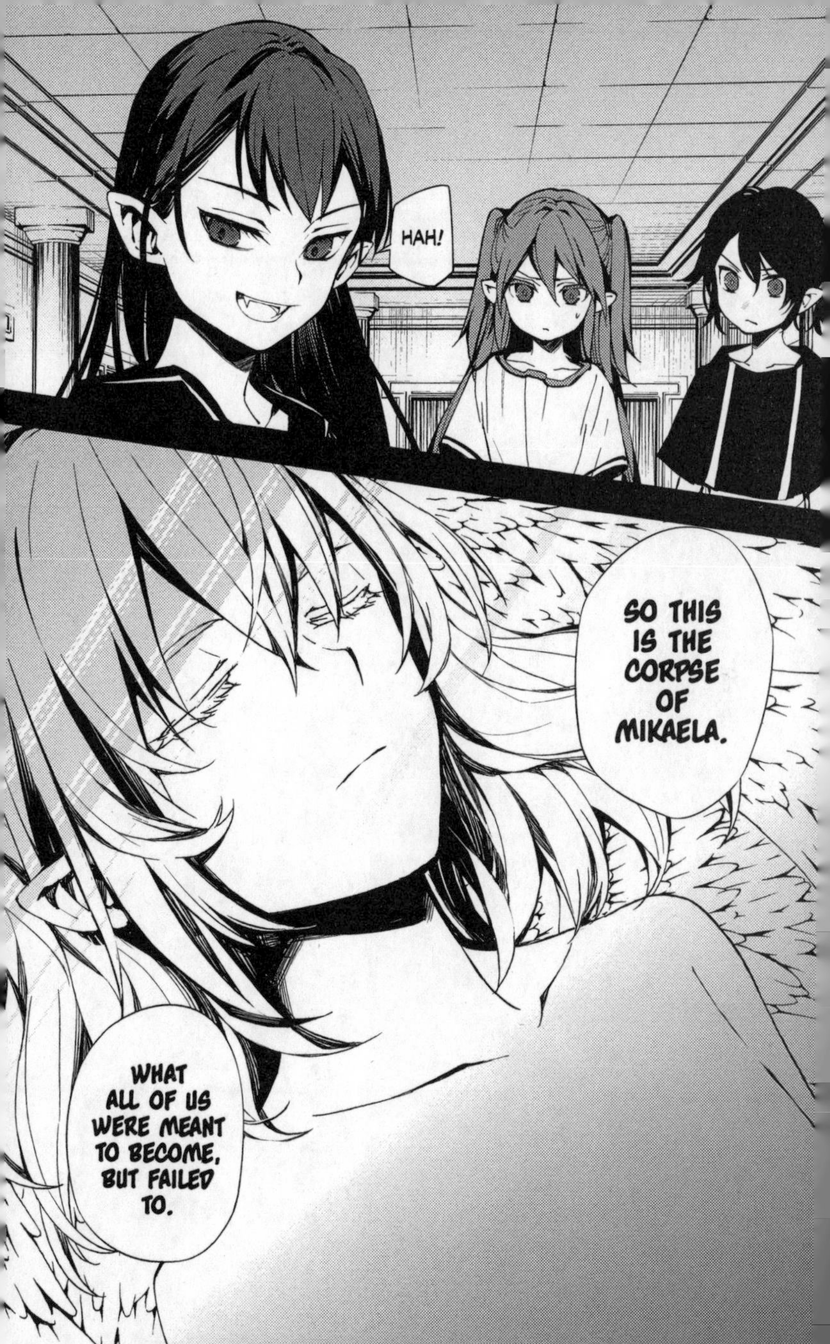
HAH!
SO THIS IS THE CORPSE OF MIKAELA.
WHAT ALL OF US WERE MEANT TO BECOME, BUT FAILED TO.

Seraph of the End: Vampire Reign 20 / END

Seraph of the End
VAMPIRE REIGN

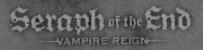

Series Total 10 Million Copies In Print

Seraph of the End Whole Series

ALL CHARACTERS POPULARITY POLL RESULTS!!!

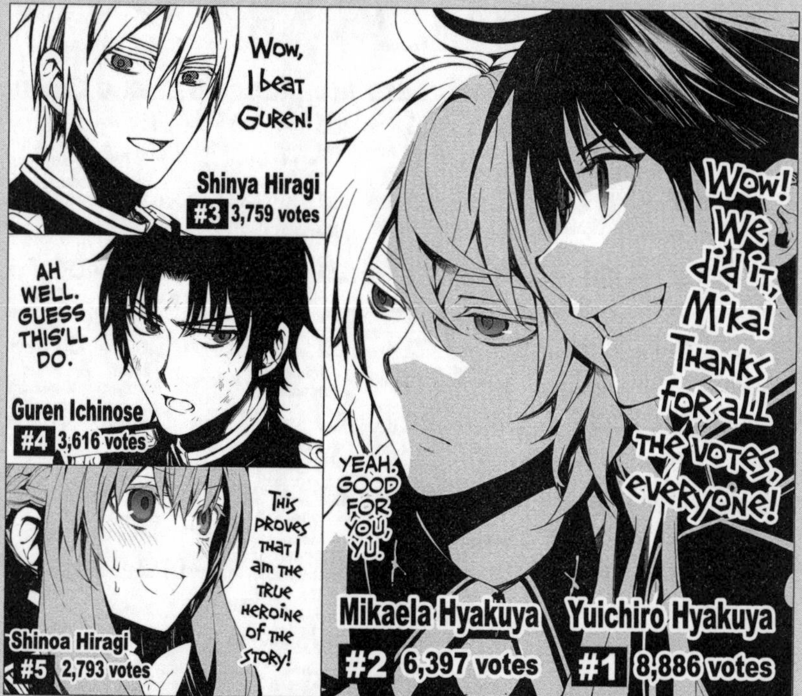

Wow! We did it, Mika! Thanks for all the votes, everyone!
Yuichiro Hyakuya
#1 8,886 votes
YEAH, GOOD FOR YOU, YU.
Mikaela Hyakuya
#2 6,397 votes
Wow, I beat Guren!
Shinya Hiragi
#3 3,759 votes
AH WELL. GUESS THIS'LL DO.
Guren Ichinose
#4 3,616 votes
This proves that I am the true heroine of the story!
Shinoa Hiragi
#5 2,793 votes

Total Votes Cast 46,285

THESE ARE THE TOP characters across the WHOLE series!!

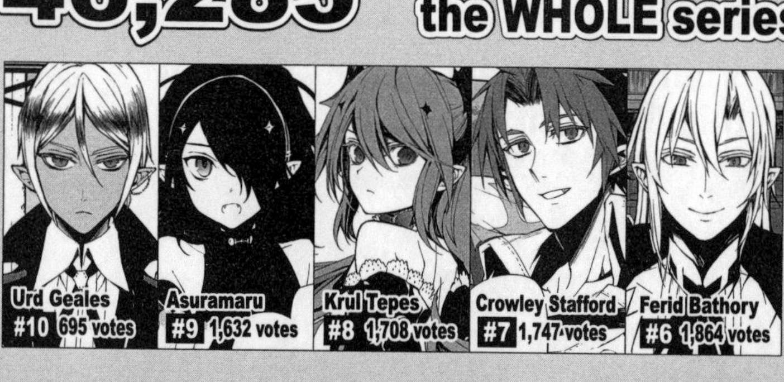

Ferid Bathory
#6 1,864 votes
Crowley Stafford
#7 1,747 votes
Krul Tepes
#8 1,708 votes
Asuramaru
#9 1,632 votes
Urd Geales
#10 695 votes

Vampires & Demons control the #6~10 spots!!

OOH! OOH! CROWLEY, REMEMBER WHEN YOU SAID THIS...?

THE "THIRTEENTH PROGENITOR" THING IS ALL JUST A FRONT.
IN REALITY, MY STRENGTH IS A LOT GREATER THAN THAT.
I'M CLOSER TO A SEVENTH PROGENITOR.

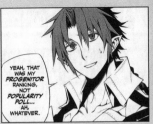

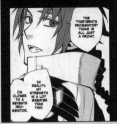

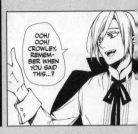

YEAH, THAT WAS MY PROGENITOR RANKING, NOT POPULARITY POLL... AH, WHATEVER.

And here are places #11 and down!

Rank	Votes	Name
#11	678 votes	Mahiru Hiragi
#12	520 votes	Kureto Hiragi
#13	474 votes	Yoichi Saotome
#14	374 votes	Shiho Kimizumi
#15	332 votes	Ky Luc
#16	316 votes	Lacus Welt
#17	312 votes	Mitsuba Sangu
#18	300 votes	Rígr Stafford Saito / Makoto Kishima
#19	277 votes	Keigo Atobe
#20	240 votes	Makoto Narumi
#21	231 votes	Lest Karr
#21	231 votes	Shikama Doji (Shika Madu)
#23	203 votes	Mito Jujo
#24	170 votes	Sayuri Hanayori
#25	161 votes	Rene Simm
#26	155 votes	Shusaku Iwasaki
#27	146 votes	Lucal Wesker
#28	145 votes	Aiko Aihara
#29	113 votes	Akane Iida
#30	98 votes	Arcane
#31	94 votes	Norito Goshi
#32	91 votes	Shigure Yukimi
#33	89 votes	Byakko-maru
#34	78 votes	Aoi Sangu
#35	77 votes	Aoyama's Dad
#36	76 votes	Gekkouin
#37	76 votes	Kiseki-oh
#38	72 votes	Noya
#39	63 votes	Ches Bell
#40	62 votes	Bastaya Irclu
#41	55 votes	Saia Aiuchi (Class 1-9 teacher)
#42	49 votes	Raimeiki
#43	44 votes	Daigo Aoyama
#44	33 votes	Sakae Ichinose
#45	31 votes	Mirai Kimizuki (Fifth Trumpet/ Abaddon)
#46	28 votes	Rika Inoue
#47	22 votes	Horn Skuld
#48	21 votes	Caek Sanorium
#49	19 votes	Mizuba Aoyama
#50	18 votes	Jose
#51	17 votes	Seishiro Hiragi
#52	16 votes	Yayoi Endo
#52	16 votes	Tanaka
#54	15 votes	Yumiko
#55	14 votes	The Angel (Sixth Trumpet)
#55	14 votes	Hina
#55	14 votes	Jigento
#55	14 votes	Shibuya 2nd High Teacher
#59	13 votes	Mikaela's Mom
#59	13 votes	Victor
#61	12 votes	Eita Kusunoki
#62	11 votes	Sakuma
#63	10 votes	Tohito Jujo
#63	10 votes	Metomoe Saotome (Yoichi's Sister)
#65	9 votes	Esther Lee
#65	9 votes	The Director
#65	9 votes	Mitsuba's Old Squad Leader
#65	9 votes	Tenri Hiragi
#69	8 votes	Gustavo
#69	8 votes	Hinue
#69	8 votes	Mitsuki Iori
#69	8 votes	Yuichiro's Dad
#73	7 votes	Alfred
#73	7 votes	Taro Kagiyama
#73	7 votes	Lou
#76	6 votes	Chimera
#76	6 votes	Ella
#76	6 votes	Kuro Kuki
#76	6 votes	Nix Parthe
#76	6 votes	Siren
#81	5 votes	Gilbert Chartres
#81	5 votes	Marun
#81	5 votes	Rosso
#81	5 votes	Yuji
#81	5 votes	Yumi
#86	4 votes	Fuola Honte
#86	4 votes	Minowa
#86	4 votes	Shiro
#86	4 votes	Satoshi Yamanaka
#90	3 votes	Joseph von Esterhazy
#90	3 votes	Dai
#90	3 votes	Mikaela's Dad
#90	3 votes	Rugi
#90	3 votes	Tohru
#95	2 votes	Roy Lurand
#95	2 votes	Masanori Hanayori
#95	2 votes	Mel Stefano
#95	2 votes	Nardo Wein
#95	2 votes	Midori Sugiyama
#95	2 votes	Yuichiro's Mom
#95	2 votes	Samidare Yukimi

← **Visit the official website to view this list with character pictures!!**

Celebrating the Character Poll!

A Bonus Skit from Takaya Kagami!

It's a special ONE-SHOT STORY!

STARTS NEXT PAGE!!

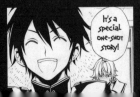

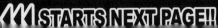

CHARACTER RANKINGS

Author: Takaya Kagami

Seraph of the End Character Popularity Poll Bonus Skit

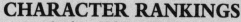

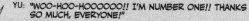

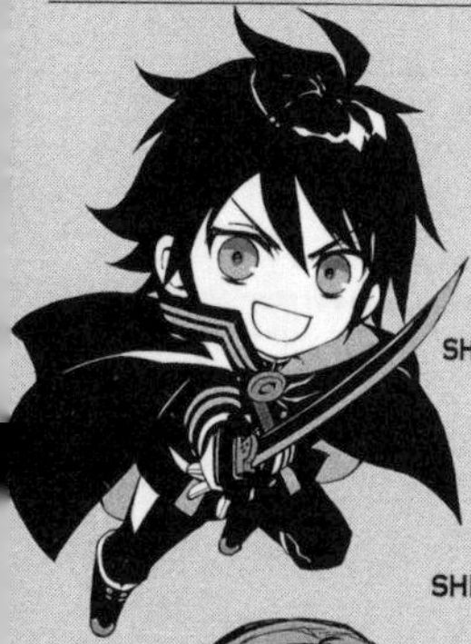

YU: "WOO-HOO-HOOOOOO!! I'M NUMBER ONE!! THANKS SO MUCH, EVERYONE!"

SHINOA: "WHOA NOW. HOLD ON. BACK UP. WHAT DO YOU MEAN THE ULTIMATE SUPERHEROINE—MOI—DID NOT GET VOTED NUMBER ONE? THAT CAN'T BE RIGHT. THERE IS SOMETHING FISHY GOING ON HERE. I CALL SHENANIGANS!"

YU: "WHAT PLACE DID YOU GET?"

SHINOA: "HM? WHY, NUMBER ONE, OF COURSE."

YU: "HUH? UH, WAIT A SEC. I'M NUMBER ONE."

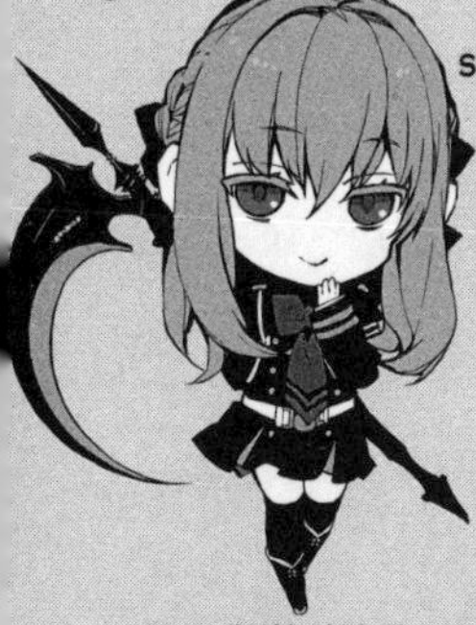

SHINOA: "OH? ARE YOU CERTAIN YOU WEREN'T SEEING THINGS? I'M VERY SURE *I* WAS NUMBER ONE."

YU: "NO WAY. YOU CAN'T BE. I LOOKED AT THE LIST JUST A MINUTE AGO, AND I WAS NUMBER ONE. HEY MIKA?"

MIKA: "HM? WHAT IS IT, YU?"

YU: "I'M NUMBER ONE ON THE POLL. RIGHT?"

MIKA: "HUH? NO. I WAS."

YU: "WHAAA?! OH C'MON. NOT YOU, TOO! HECK, YOU LOOKED AT THE LIST WITH ME JUST A MINUTE AGO!"

MIKA: "YEP. AND I WAS NUMBER ONE."

YU: "WHOA, WHOA. YOU WEREN'T AND YOU KNOW IT."

MIKA: "AHA HA! I'M KIDDING, I'M KIDDING. HOW ABOUT WE LOOK AT IT THIS WAY—I'M THE NUMBER ONE VAMPIRE ON THE POLL."

SHINOA: "OOH, AND THEN I WOULD BE NUMBER ONE ON THE HYPER POWERFUL BEAUTIFUL ANGEL SHINOA POLL."

SHINYA: "BOY, THERE SURE ARE A LOT OF NUMBER ONES RUNNING AROUND."

YU: "HUH? HOLD ON... WHAT KIND OF POLL WAS THIS AGAIN?"

GUREN: "HN? THE SHORTEST CHARACTER POLL, OF COURSE."

YU: "HEY!!"

SHINOA: "WHAT?! MY WORD! THEN I'M DEFINITELY AT THE VERY BOTTOM OF THAT POLL."

GUREN: "WHAT ARE YOU TALKING ABOUT? YOU'RE CLEARLY NUMBER ONE."

SHINOA: "NO, NO. I COULDN'T POSSIBLY. I'M OVER SIX FEET TALL, YOU KNOW."

YU: "WELL THEN I'M OVER NINE FEET TALL!"

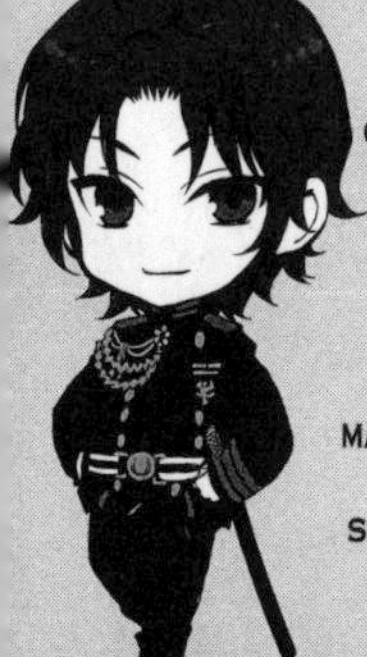

GUREN: "OH? IS THAT SO. WELL THEN, AT A MERE 5'11", I GUESS THAT MAKES ME NUMBER ONE. THANK YOU, EVERYONE. I'M HONORED TO BE FIRST PLACE. I HOPE YOU WILL CONTINUE TO SUPPORT ME IN THE FUTURE."

MAHIRU: "EEE! GUREN, YOU'RE SOOO COOOL."

SHINYA: "EEE! GUREN, YOU'RE SOOO COOOL! EVEN THOUGH I BEAT YOU IN REAL RANKINGS."

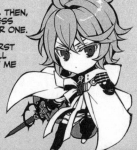

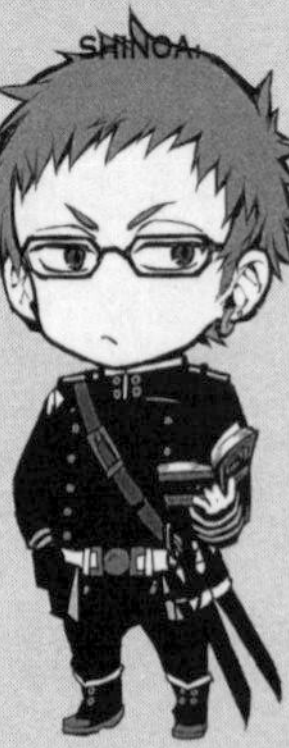
SHINOA

GUREN: "PSHH. YOU HAD A NOT-TOO-BAD PERSONAL SCENE RIGHT AROUND THE TIME OF VOTING. THAT INFLUENCED THINGS."

SHINYA: "YOU KNOW WHAT? YOU'RE ABSOLUTELY RIGHT. YOU ARE THE TRUE NUMBER ONE. EEE! GUREN, YOU'RE SOOO COOOL."

MAHIRU: "EEE! GUREN, YOU'RE SOOO COOOL."

GUREN: "YOU TWO ARE MOCKING ME, AREN'T YOU."

SHINYA & MAHIRU: "AHA HA!"

FERID: "SO! SINCE THIS SADLY WAS NOT 'THE PEOPLE MOST IN FAVOR OF WORLD PEACE' POLL, I WAS NOT ABLE TO REACH THE NUMBER ONE RANK. BUT! I'M POSITIVE THE NEXT POLL WILL BE THE 'PEOPLE MOST AGAINST GLOBAL WARMING' POLL, IN WHICH I WILL CLEARLY BE NUMBER ONE. I LOOK FORWARD TO EVERYONE'S SUPPORT."

YU: "WHAT'S GLOBAL WARMING?"

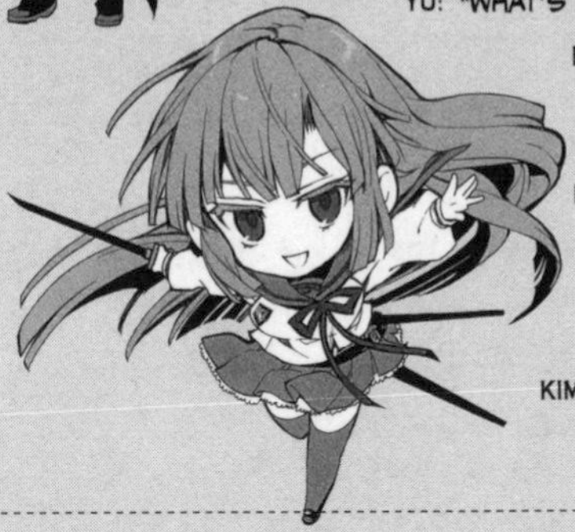

FERID: "IT'S A TERM FOR HOW EVERYONE LOVES HAWAII."

YU: "WHAT'S HAWAII?"

FERID: "YOU KNOW WHAT? I THINK YOU CAN BE NUMBER ONE."

YU: "WOO-HOOOOO! I'M NUMBER ONE! EVERYONE, THANKS FOR ALL YOUR SUPPORT!"

KIMIZUKI: "YOU KNOW THAT'S THE 'BIGGEST IDIOT' POLL, RIGHT?"

YU: ""WHAAA?!"

AFTERWORD

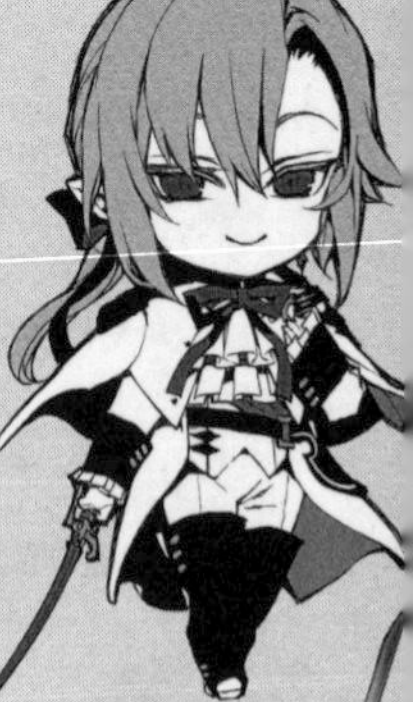

WE DID IT! WE FINALLY CROSSED THE 20 THRESH-OLD. AND AT THE SAME TIME, WE HELD A SERIES-WIDE CHARACTER POPULARITY POLL. THE POLL WAS ANNOUNCED AT THE SAME TIME AS THE BIG CELEBRATION OF REACHING TEN MILLION UNITS SOLD, WHICH GOT BIG SPLASH PAGES ON THE COVERS OF BOTH *JUMP SQUARE* AND *MONTHLY SHONEN MAGAZINE*. ACCORDING TO WHAT I'VE HEARD FROM PEOPLE IN THE INDUSTRY, PLANNING SUCH A BIG EVENT BETWEEN BOTH SHUEISHA AND KODANSHA WAS APPARENTLY UNHEARD OF. I'M HONORED THAT WE GOT TO BE ONE OF THE FIRST TO DO SO WITH *SERAPH OF THE END*. WE NEVER WOULD'VE MADE IT TO THAT POINT WITHOUT SUPPORT FROM READERS LIKE YOU. THANK YOU VERY MUCH. THE STORY IS GOING TO KEEP RAMPING UP EVEN FURTHER FROM HERE, SO I HOPE THAT ALL OF YOU WILL STICK ALONG FOR THE RIDE.

—TAKAYA KAGAMI

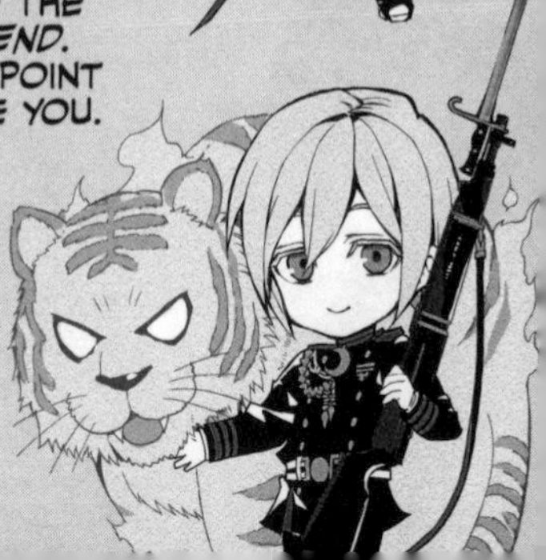

A brilliant sketch of Yuichiro by the author!

TAKAYA KAGAMI is a prolific light novelist whose works include the action and fantasy series *The Legend of the Legendary Heroes*, which has been adapted into manga, anime and a video game. His previous series, *A Dark Rabbit Has Seven Lives*, also spawned a manga and anime series.

66 I picked up an Apple Watch to help me manage my time and boy am I already seeing results. Was I really wasting so much time before? 99

YAMATO YAMAMOTO, born 1983, is an artist and illustrator whose works include the *Kure-nai* manga and the light novels *Kure-nai*, *9S -Nine S-* and *Denpa Teki na Kanojo*. Both *Denpa Teki na Kanojo* and *Kure-nai* have been adapted into anime.

66 The battle between the Demon Army and the Hyakuya Sect. The clash between the First and Saito. Guren and Mahiru's suspicious behavior. There're a lot of things to watch in volume 20! 99

DAISUKE FURUYA previously assisted Yamato Yamamoto with storyboards for *Kure-nai*.

Seraph of the End
—VAMPIRE REIGN—

VOLUME 20
SHONEN JUMP MANGA EDITION

STORY BY **TAKAYA KAGAMI**
ART BY **YAMATO YAMAMOTO**
STORYBOARDS BY **DAISUKE FURUYA**

TRANSLATION **Adrienne Beck**
TOUCH-UP ART & LETTERING **Sabrina Heep**
DESIGN **Shawn Carrico**
EDITOR **Marlene First**

OWARI NO SERAPH © 2012 by Takaya Kagami,
Yamato Yamamoto, Daisuke Furuya
All rights reserved. First published in Japan in 2012 by SHUEISHA Inc., Tokyo.
English translation rights arranged by SHUEISHA Inc.

Printed in the U.S.A.

Published by VIZ Media, LLC
P.O. Box 77010
San Francisco, CA 94107

10 9 8 7 6 5 4 3 2 1
First printing, February 2021

viz.com

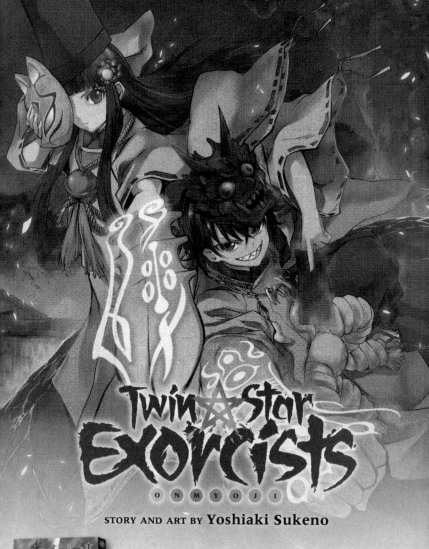

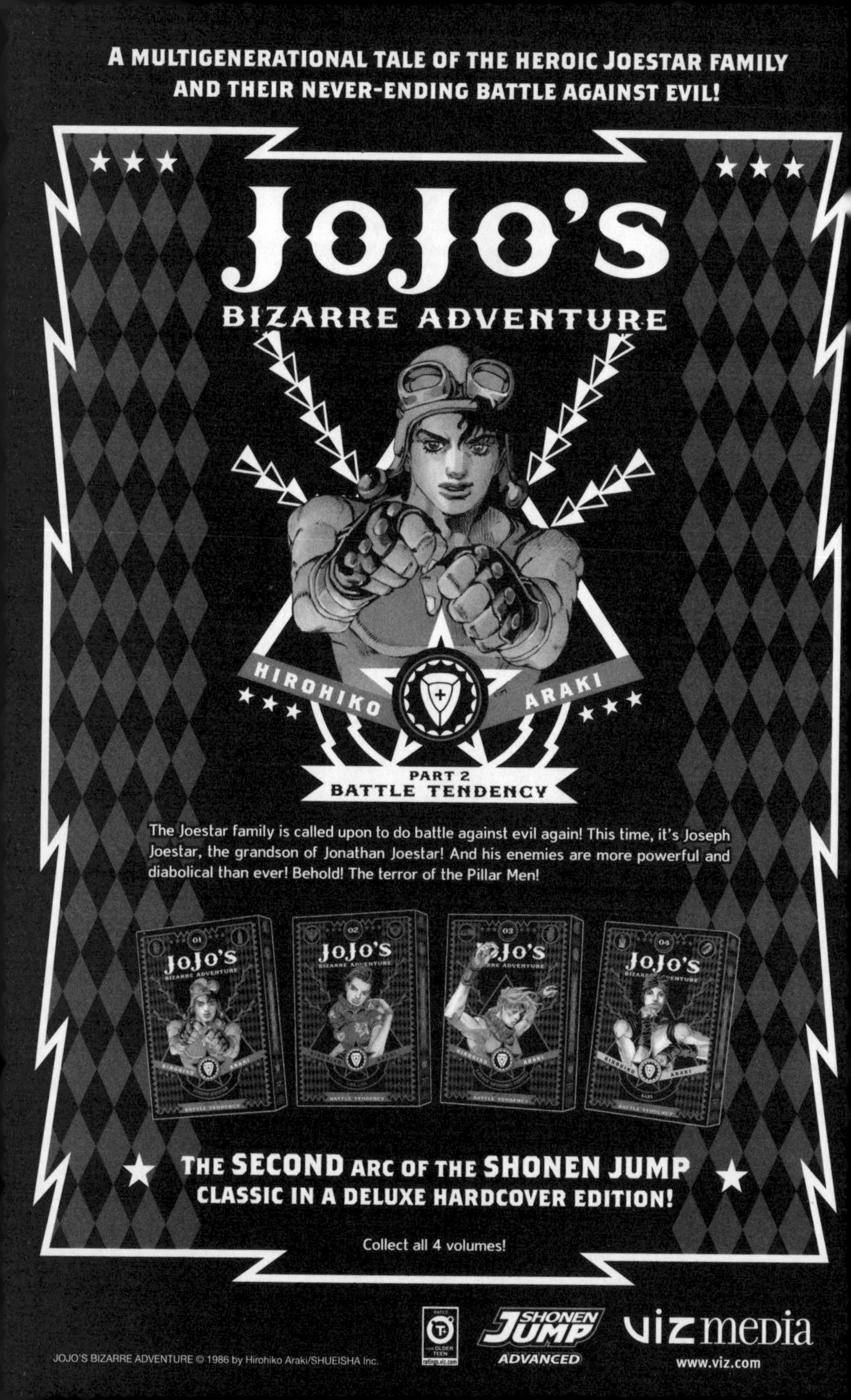
A MULTIGENERATIONAL TALE OF THE HEROIC JOESTAR FAMILY AND THEIR NEVER-ENDING BATTLE AGAINST EVIL!
JoJo's
BIZARRE ADVENTURE
HIROHIKO ARAKI
PART 2
BATTLE TENDENCY
The Joestar family is called upon to do battle against evil again! This time, it's Joseph Joestar, the grandson of Jonathan Joestar! And his enemies are more powerful and diabolical than ever! Behold! The terror of the Pillar Men!
THE SECOND ARC OF THE SHONEN JUMP CLASSIC IN A DELUXE HARDCOVER EDITION!
Collect all 4 volumes!
JOJO'S BIZARRE ADVENTURE © 1986 by Hirohiko Araki/SHUEISHA Inc.
RATED T+ FOR OLDER TEEN ratings.viz.com
SHONEN JUMP ADVANCED
viz media
www.viz.com

Black ✦ Clover

STORY & ART BY YŪKI TABATA

Asta is a young boy who dreams of becoming the greatest mage in the kingdom. Only one problem—he can't use any magic! Luckily for Asta, he receives the incredibly rare five-leaf clover grimoire that gives him the power of anti-magic. Can someone who can't use magic really become the Wizard King? One thing's for sure—Asta will never give up!

SHONEN JUMP   VIZ media
www.viz.com

YOU'RE READING THE

WRONG WAY!

SERAPH OF THE END reads from right to left, starting in the upper-right corner. Japanese is read from right to left, meaning that action, sound effects, and word-balloon order are completely reversed from English order.

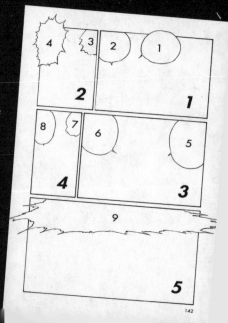